GRAMMAR

Parts of Speech	Nouns 366	Pronouns 366	Verbs 367	Adjectives 367	Adverbs 367	Prepositions 367	Conjunctions 368	Interjections 368		Glossary of Usage, Mechanics, Common Errors 459
Syntax	TheSentence: Three Forms 369	Agreement: Subject-Verb 372	Agreement: Pronouns 373	Pronouns: Subject-Object 385	Reference 391	Tense 377	Mood 380	Possessive Pronouns, Gerunds 390	Misplaced Modifiers 395	The English Language 339

MECHANICS

Format	General Physical Format 31	Indentation 56	Quotations 57	Letter Writing 488	Abbreviations 459	Numbers 494	Italics 434	Capitals 454	Spelling 445
Punctuation	The Period 406	The Comma: Between Clauses 410	The Comma: Introductory Phrases 415	The Comma: Restrictive, Nonrestrictive 419	Semicolon 424 Colon 427	Quotation Marks 432	Dash 430 Ellipses 436	Parentheses 430 Brackets 431	It's 440 Apostrophe-s 438 Hyphen 441

WRITING ABOUT LITERATURE

Approaches	Finding a Thesis 254	Present Tense 291	Explication 254	Evaluation 289	Paraphrase 261	Summary 262	Parody 262	Criticism: Four Questions 289		
Point of View	The Written Voice 271	Omniscient Narrator 272	First-Person Observer 272	First-Person Participant 272		Narrative			Character-ization 276	Narration and Scene
Poetic Figures	Metaphor 185	Allusion 269	Symbol 270	Meter 264		The Drama	Setting 273	Plot Plotting Structure 275	Stage Directions 280	
							Now 280	Exposition 280		

RESEARCH

The Research Paper	Choice of Subject 299	The Job of Research 302	Note Taking 302	Plagiarism 298	The First Draft 304	The Final Draft 306	Footnotes 306	Bibliography 315	The Full Research Paper 320
The Library	Encyclopedias, Almanacs 533, 536	The Card Catalog 358	Cataloging Systems 540	Indexes to Periodicals, Newspapers 544	Literary Bibliographies 548				

* The page numbers in the boxes refer to the beginning discussion of each topic.

The Complete Stylist and Handbook

The Complete Stylist and Handbook

SHERIDAN BAKER

The University of Michigan

Thomas Y. Crowell Company
New York   Established 1834

Library of Congress Cataloging in Publication Data

Baker, Sheridan Warner
  The complete stylist and handbook.
  Previous editions published in 1966 and 1972
under title: The complete stylist.
  Includes index.
  1. English language—Rhetoric.   I. Title.
PE1408.B283   1976   808′ .042   75-29332
ISBN 0-690-00801-5

Thomas Y. Crowell Company
666 Fifth Avenue
New York, New York 10019

Typography and cover design by Robert Carola

Manufactured in the United States of America

Preface

Teachers and students who have tested my short rhetoric, THE PRACTICAL STYLIST, and its larger version, THE COMPLETE STYLIST, have made many suggestions that, together with my own classroom experience, have prompted me to this new synthesis, arrangement, and expansion, THE COMPLETE STYLIST AND HANDBOOK. I have divided the book into THE RHETORIC, which treats the essentials of writing and the practical problems confronting the beginning writer, and THE HANDBOOK, which offers a thorough-going reference and guide to grammar, mechanics, troublesome points of usage, and the English language itself.

The Approach

My approach to writing stresses rhetoric, which I see as the art of communication and persuasion, the styling of language to attract, edify, and convince the reader. Further, I emphasize argument as the quickest and clearest teacher of rhetorical principles; I begin at the big end of the compositional problem with the whole essay's two most essential rhetorical principles, inner idea and outer form—thesis and structure. Having suggested the communicative and clarifying powers in thesis and structure, I deal with the progressively smaller and more powerful units—paragraphs, sentences, words. Then I proceed to the very practical activities of testing one's arguments with the elements of logic, of testing and improving the structure of one's writing with outlining. And I include what I intend as a high point or coalescence, an essay on writing about literature, which suggests numerous applications of rhetorical principles, and I conclude THE RHETORIC with a discussion of research, offering a full paper by one of my students to exemplify the process. To meet the widely varying needs of students, I quote and analyze the work of recognized writers, and students' papers, providing marginal glosses to amplify the texts with greater detail.

The sections of THE HANDBOOK, especially those covering grammar, spelling, punctuation, and usage, reinforce the chapters of THE RHETORIC, and may be integrated with assignments as needed, or assigned as separate readings and exercises.

Instructors will find plenty of leeway for their own courses, and for their own kinds of classes. Many teachers prefer to begin with sentences and paragraphs before launching into the big ideas of composition; others begin with the basic tools, as presented in THE HANDBOOK. Any tack that will get students to the essences and wonders of language is fine.

Exercises

The chapters of THE RHETORIC and most sections of THE HANDBOOK contain new exercises to bring the discussions home to students.* I include probably more than enough exercises for any one group. The exercises, placed at appropriate intervals within the chapters and sections, range from short-sentence revisions to short

---

* A considerable number of the exercises are adaptations from *Problems in Exposition: Supplementary Exercises for The Complete Stylist and The Practical Stylist;* my very special thanks go to Dwight W. Stevenson, who, as my coauthor of *Problems in Exposition,* has made a significant contribution to the exercises in both THE RHETORIC and THE HANDBOOK.

essays, offering students the fullest possible chance to remedy their weaknesses and improve their strengths. Throughout, I have tried to encourage students' sense of the play and wonder of language, the pleasure in mastering the ordinary by trying the extraordinary in sentence and vocabulary, and the creative discoveries of revision.

What's New

Those familiar with THE COMPLETE STYLIST (now in its second edition), which most closely resembles this book, will at once notice here a number of changes — which I hope are improvements. I move much more quickly into the very stuff of writing, subject and thesis, which now is the subject of the first chapter rather than the second; I introduce the paragraph before dealing with the middle (the "orders") of the essay; the chapter on outlines now more properly follows the full introduction to rhetoric and, usefully I think, immediately precedes the considerations of writing about literature and research. (I have dropped the "Four Excursions" from THE COMPLETE STYLIST, keeping only the "terrible essay" here as an entertaining and enlightening exercise.) To strengthen THE HANDBOOK as a reference, I have moved the chapter on punctuation, with discussions of spelling and capitalization, into a new section immediately following "A Writer's Grammar." I have divided the research chapter in THE COMPLETE STYLIST into three: one chapter directly on research, another containing a full research paper with supporting notes and full glosses, and, in THE HANDBOOK, a guide to the most useful library references for students at the outset of their college careers. Entirely new are the chapter introducing the analysis of literature in THE RHETORIC and the essay on the English language, which begins THE HANDBOOK.

I have freshened the examples throughout THE RHETORIC and THE HANDBOOK, and clarified many points queried by instructors and students. As compared with the other STYLISTS, this book greatly expands the exercises, and places them strategically, affording the teacher many more opportunities to reinforce the concepts and to devise stimulating writing assignments for classes of very differing accomplishments.

In Summary

In THE RHETORIC, Chapter 1 confronts the prime problem, what to write about. Chapter 2 moves quickly into rhetoric—argument—the underlying theme of the whole book, emphasizing the student's own "written voice" and one's attitude toward subject and reader. Chapter 3 introduces the essay's basic structure; Chapter 4, its basic unit—the paragraph.

Chapter 5 rounds out the basic principles of inner idea and outer form. On completing this chapter, students will have learned to discover a thesis, to qualify it, and to give it the argumentative thrust that organizes the whole essay from within. Around this the concept of structure emerges: first, the basic Beginning, Middle, and End; then the basic paragraph reflecting this structure; then the several orders that range from the temporal and spatial to the inductive and deductive—the leading in and the leading out.

Chapter 6 moves on to descriptive, narrative, and expository paragraphs, exploring the full dimensions of prose. Chapter 7 presents the sentence with advice on structural clarity—coordination and subordination, modifying and paralleling—and with some encouragement of variety, a number of exercises to invite students to try out various patterns and extend their rhetorical range. Chapter 8 concentrates on correcting wordy and jargonish sentences; again, there are copious exercises. Section C in THE HANDBOOK reinforces Chapters 7 and 8 by considering the meaning of punctuation.

Chapter 9 deals with words—abstract and concrete, metaphor, allusion, diction—building and using a vocabulary. It distinguishes between meaningful words and wordiness, and shows how diction can get out of hand. Advice on spelling and capitalization in Section C gives added support.

Chapter 10, "Straight and Crooked Thinking," refines the logic that runs through the book—that writing is itself a discovery of reasons and reason, that writing both clarifies and creates thought, of which it is the palpable substance. This chapter introduces the logical fallacies, those daily pitfalls of persuasion, and the syllogism.

Chapter 11 considers outlines, supporting the general structural lessons of Chapters 1 through 6, and showing how a sentence-outline can help us to grasp what we read, as well as to test our own writing.

Chapter 12 shows how analyzing a poem, a novel, a play, can help us as both writers and readers. There is more than enough description and example to offer teachers a selection and students a base for the serious study of literature.

Chapter 13 lays out the elements of research, which students can supplement with Section F, "The Uses of the Library." Chapter 14 closes THE RHETORIC with a student's research paper, glossed to sum up the essentials of writing taught in the text, and the technicalities discussed in Chapter 13.

The Reinforcement

THE HANDBOOK both reinforces THE RHETORIC and offers a useful general reference to the mechanics and customs that characterize the best American writing. Section A contains a history of the English language, with material on the American idiom and Black English. Grammar, punctuation, capitalization, and spelling — the basics — I examine in the next two sections (B and C). The glossary (Section D) presents (1) customary usage, with many examples, and (2) further grammatical discussions together with abbreviations, hyphenations, letter writing, and similar matters not often found so handily. I have cross-referenced entries to expanded textual discussions. In Section E, I include a glossary of classically useful rhetorical devices. Students sometimes inquire about them, and they are nowhere else to be found, all in one place. They also offer additional opportunities, for students so inclined, for studying those linguistic patterns — psychological, really — that have endured for two thousand years and more. Finally, I close the book with a guide to using the library (Section F), one complete enough to carry students well into their later college years.

The Instructor's Manual

I have written an Instructor's Manual, the first time I have done so, to accompany THE COMPLETE STYLIST AND HANDBOOK. In working out solutions to exercises and suggestions for teaching, I have deepened my awareness — since writing is discovery — of the myriad problems confronting today's English instructors. This led to a number of late but important changes in the text itself, better to adapt it to a wide spectrum of pedagogical approaches and to make it enlightening to students without concealing the existence of standards.

In THE COMPLETE STYLIST AND HANDBOOK, I have striven to get at the essential powers of the essay, as they dwell in this language of ours, the writing of which is our only steady means of getting our thinking straight and clear. Throughout, I urge students to see that style is both personal and public, a matter of finding one's self in language—one's own personality written into reason and looking its best.

SHERIDAN BAKER

Contents

THE RHETORIC

CONTENTS

CONTENTS

CONTENTS

THE HANDBOOK

THE
RHETORIC

One
Subject
and
Thesis

THE STYLISTIC APPROACH

Style in writing is something like style in a car, a gown, or a Greek temple—the ordinary materials of this world so poised and perfected as to stand out from the landscape and compel a second look, something that hangs in the reader's mind, like a vision. It is your own voice, with the hems and haws chipped out, speaking the common language uncommonly well. It calls for a craftsman who has discovered the knots and potentials in his material, one who has learned to like words as some people like polished wood or stones, one who has learned to enjoy phrasing and syntax, and the very punctuation that keeps them straight. It is a labor of love, and like love it can bring pleasure and satisfaction.

Style is not for the gifted only. Quite the contrary. Everyone, indeed, already has a style, and a personality, and can develop both. The stylistic side of writing is, in fact, the only side that can be analyzed and learned. The stylistic approach is the practical approach: you learn some things to do and not to do, as you would learn strokes in tennis. Your ultimate game is up to you, but you can at least begin in good form. Naturally, it takes practice. You have to keep at it. Like the doctor and the lawyer and the golfer and the tennis player, you just keep practicing — even to write a practically perfect letter. But if you like the game, you can probably learn to play it well. You will at least be able to write a respectable sentence, and to express your thoughts clearly, without puffing and flailing.

In the essay, as in business, trying to get started and getting off on the wrong foot account for most of our lost motion. So you will start by learning how to find a thesis, which will virtually organize your essay for you. Next you will study the relatively simple structure of the essay, and the structure of the paragraph — the architecture of spatial styling. Then, for exercise, you will experiment with various styles of sentence, playing with length and complexity. And finally you will get down to words themselves. Here is where writing tells; and here, as in ancient times, you will be in touch with the mystery. But again, there are things to do and things not to do, and these can be learned. So, to begin.

WHAT SHALL I WRITE?

First you need a subject, and then you need a thesis. Yes, but *what shall I write?* That is the question, persisting from the first Christmas thank-you letter down to this very night. Here you are, an assignment due and the paper as blank as your mind. The Christmas letter may give us a clue. Your mother probably told you, as mine did, to write about what you had been doing. Almost anything would do — Cub Scouts, Brownies, the birthday party, skating — so long as you had been doing it. As you wrote, it grew interesting all over again. Finding a mature subject is no different: look for something you have experienced, or thought about. The more it matters to you, the more you can make it matter to your readers. It might be skiing. It might be dress. It might be roommates, the Peloponnesian War, a political protest, a personal discovery of racial tensions, an experience as a nurse's aide. But do not tackle a big philosophical abstraction, like Freedom, or a big subject, like the

Supreme Court. They are too vast, your time and space and knowledge all too small. You would probably manage no more than a collection of platitudes. Start rather with something specific, like baby-sitting, and let the ideas of freedom and justice arise from there. An abstract idea is a poor beginning. To be sure, as you move ahead through your course in writing, you will work more directly with ideas, with problems posed by literature, with questions in the great civilizing debate about what we are doing in this strange world and universe. But again, look for something within your concern. The best subjects lie nearest at hand, and nearest the heart.

Suppose we start simply with "The Teen-Ager." That, in the recent past, is certainly close enough. Moreover, it will illustrate admirably how to generalize from your own experience, and how to cut your subject down to manageable size. Your first impulse might be to describe the temptations of theft, or drugs, or first cars, and the realities of breaking the law. Were you to write this in the first person, it might be amusing, especially to your acquaintances and friends. But it would remain merely personal; it would still lack an important ingredient of adulthood. You would still be working in that bright, self-centered spotlight of consciousness in which we live before we really begin to grow up, in which the child assumes that all his experiences are unique. If you shift from "me" to "the teen-ager," however, you will be stepping into maturity: acknowledging that others have gone through exactly the same thing, that your particular experiences have illustrated once again the general dynamics of youth and the group. So you will write not "I was afraid to say anything" but "The teen-ager fears going against the group more than death itself. When the speedometer hits 100, silence is the rule, though the heart is screaming in every throat." You simply assume you are normal and fairly representative, and you then generalize with confidence, transposing your particular experiences, your particular thoughts and reactions, into statements about the general ways of the world. You might want to sharpen your statement a little more, as you turn your subject into a thesis, asserting something like: "The thrilling high-speed ride, if survived, will probably open the teen-ager's eyes to the dynamics of the group." Put your proposition into one sentence. This will get you focused. And now you are ready to begin.

WHERE ESSAYS FAIL

You can usually blame a bad essay on a bad beginning. If your essay falls apart, it probably has no primary idea to hold it together. "What's the big idea?" we used to ask. The phrase will serve as a reminder that you must find the "big idea" behind your several smaller thoughts and musings before you start to write. In the beginning was the *logos,* says the Bible — the idea, the plan, caught in a flash as if in a single word. Find your *logos,* and you are ready to round out your essay and set it spinning.

The big idea behind our ride in the speeding car was that in adolescence, especially, the group can have a very deadly influence on the individual. If you had not focused your big idea in a thesis, you might have begun by picking up thoughts at random, something like this:

> **Everyone thinks he is a good driver. There are more accidents caused by young drivers than any other group. Driver education is a good beginning, but further practice is very necessary. People who object to driver education do not realize that modern society, with its suburban pattern of growth, is built around the automobile. The car becomes a way of life and a status symbol. When teen-agers go too fast they are probably only copying their own parents.**

A little reconsideration, aimed at a good thesis-sentence, could turn this into a reasonably good beginning:

> **Modern society is built on the automobile. Children play with tiny cars; teen-agers long to take out the car alone. Soon they are testing their skills at higher and higher speeds, especially with a group of friends along. One final test at extreme speeds usually suffices. It is usually a sobering experience, if survived, and can open one's eyes to the deadly dynamics of the group.**

Thus the central idea, or thesis, is your essay's life and spirit. If your thesis is sufficiently firm and clear, it may tell you immediately how to organize your supporting material and so obviate elaborate planning. If you do not find a thesis, your essay will be a tour through the miscellaneous. An essay replete with scaffolds and catwalks—"We have just seen this; now let us turn to this"—is an essay in which the inherent idea is weak or nonexistent. A purely expository and descriptive essay, one simply about "Cats," for instance, will have to rely on outer scaffolding alone (some orderly progression from Persia to Siam) since it really has no idea at all. It is all subject, all cats, instead of being based on an idea *about* cats.

THE ARGUMENTATIVE EDGE

Find your thesis.

The *about*-ness puts an argumentative edge on the subject. When you have something to say *about* cats, you have found your underlying idea. You have something to defend, something to fight about: not just "Cats," but "The cat is really a person's best friend." Now the hackles on all dog people are rising, and you have an argument on your hands. You have something to prove. You have a thesis.

"What's the big idea, Mac?" Let the impudence in that time-honored demand remind you that the most dynamic thesis is a kind of affront to somebody. No one will be very much interested in listening to you deplete the thesis "The dog is a person's best friend." Everyone knows that already. Even the dog lovers will be uninterested, convinced they know better than you. But the cat. . . .

So it is with any unpopular idea. The more unpopular the viewpoint and the stronger the push against convention, the stronger the thesis and the more energetic the essay. Compare the energy in "Democracy is good" with that in "Communism is good," for instance. The first is filled with platitudes, the second with plutonium. By the same token, if you can find the real energy in "Democracy is good," if you can get down through the sand to where the roots and water are, you will have a real essay, because the opposition against which you generate your energy is the heaviest in the world: boredom. Probably the most energetic thesis of all, the greatest inner organizer, is some tired old truth that you cause to jet with new life, making the old ground green again.

To find a thesis and to put it into one sentence is to narrow and define your subject to a workable size. Under "Cats" you must deal with all felinity from the jungle up, carefully partitioning the eons and areas, the tigers and tabbies, the sizes and shapes. The minute you proclaim the cat the friend of humanity, you have pared away whole categories and chapters, and need only think up the arguments sufficient to overwhelm the opposition. So, put an argumentative edge on your subject—and you will have found your thesis.

Simple exposition, to be sure, has its uses. You may want to tell someone how to build a doghouse, how to can asparagus, how to follow the outlines of relativity, or even how to write an essay. Performing a few exercises in simple exposition will no doubt sharpen your insight into the problems of finding orderly sequences, of considering how best to lead your readers through the hoops, of writing clearly and accurately. It will also illustrate how much finer and surer an argument is.

You will see that picking an argument immediately simplifies the problems so troublesome in straight exposition: the defining, the partitioning, the narrowing of the subject. Not that you must be constantly pugnacious or aggressive. I have overstated my point to make it stick. Actually, you can put an argumentative edge on the flattest of expository subjects. "How to build a doghouse" might become "Building a doghouse is a thorough introduction to the building trades, including architecture and mechanical engineering." "Canning asparagus" might become "An asparagus patch is a course in economics." "Relativity" might become "Relativity is not so inscrutable as many suppose." Literary subjects take an argumentative edge almost by nature. You simply assert what the essential point of a poem or play seems to be: "*Hamlet* is essentially about a world that has lost its values." You assume that your readers are in search of clarity, that you have a loyal opposition consisting of the interested but uninformed. You have given your subject its edge; you have limited and organized it at a single stroke. Pick an argument, then, and you will automatically be defining and narrowing your subject, and all the partitions you don't need will fold up. Instead of dealing with things, subjects, and pieces of subjects, you will be dealing with an idea and its consequences.

Sharpen your thesis.

Come out with your subject pointed. Take a stand, make a judgment of value. Be reasonable, but don't be timid. It is helpful to think of your thesis, your main idea, as a debating question—"Resolved: Welfare payments must go"—taking out the "Resolved" when you actually write the subject down. But your resolution will be even stronger, your essay clearer and tighter, if you can sharpen your thesis even further—"Resolved: Welfare payments must go because————." Fill in that blank, and your worries are practically over. The main idea is to put your whole argument into one sentence.

Try, for instance: "Welfare payments must go because they are making people irresponsible." I don't know at all if that is true, and neither will you until you write your way into it, considering probabilities and alternatives and objections, and especially the underlying assumptions. In fact, no one, no master sociologist or future historian, can tell absolutely if it is true, so multiplex are the causes in human affairs, so endless and tangled the consequences. The basic assumption—that irresponsibility is growing—may be entirely false. No one, I repeat, can tell absolutely. But by the same token, your guess may be as good as another's. At any rate, you are now ready to write. You have found your *logos*.

Now you can put your well-pointed thesis-sentence on a card on the wall in front of you to keep from drifting off target. But you will now want to dress it for the public, to burnish it and make it comely. Suppose you try:

> **Welfare payments, perhaps more than anything else, are eroding personal initiative.**

But is this fully true? Perhaps you had better try something like:

> **Despite their immediate benefits, welfare payments may actually be eroding personal initiative and depriving society of needed workers.**

This is really your thesis, and you can write that down on a scrap of paper too.

EXERCISE

1 Below I have listed a series of topics about which you might write. Transform each into an assertion, a thesis. Start by trying to transform some of the topics into debating propositions. For example, "Welfare payments" becomes, "Resolved: Welfare payments must go." Having done that, you might take it a step further by supplying a reason. For example, "Resolved: Welfare payments must go because they are sapping people's initiative." Now you have a clear thesis, although it may be a bit mechanical in form. All that remains is to dress it up for public appearance. "Welfare payments, perhaps more than anything else, are eroding personal initiative and destroying the work-instinct." Supply a thesis statement for each of the following:

1. Abortion laws
2. The appearance of our campus
3. Student housing
4. Weight lifting
5. Two-mile, cross-country run
6. Modern aristocracy
7. A novel you have read. For example, Joseph Heller's *Catch-22*
8. Unequal distribution of blacks and whites in occupational groups
9. Half-day sessions in elementary schools
10. The tourist trade

2 The following sentences are all thesis statements taken from actual students' papers. As you can see, the authors did not spot the built-in weaknesses. Explain what, if anything, you think wrong with each of these as thesis statements. Then revise them as best you can.

1. I think we should all insist on the retention of the present abortion laws.
2. The campus of ——— University (College) is unique in many ways.
3. With the increasing enrollment at this university (and with the larger number of married students) steps need to be taken to increase student housing.

4. From experience, I would believe that weight lifting can be help-ful to a growing young man in more ways than one.

5. The two-mile, cross-country run is one of the most challenging of track events. It requires speed, endurance, and strategy.

6. No matter how it used to be in this country, we have an aristocracy of money now.

7. Joseph Heller's *Catch-22* is not great literature. Indeed, the book is not really a novel at all; it is just a series of little stories.

8. I believe, and will try to show, that the unequal distribution of blacks and whites in occupational groups revealed in the last Census is the result of two problems: inferior education for blacks and discriminatory hiring by white employers.

9. Could half-day sessions in elementary schools provide the same quality of education as provided by full-day sessions?

10. Pynchon's *Gravity's Rainbow* is a fantastically interesting novel.

Believe in your thesis.

Notice how your assertion about welfare mellowed as you re-vised. And not because you have resorted to cheap tactics, though tactics may get you to the same place, but rather because you brought it under critical inspection, asking what is true in it: what can (and cannot) be assumed true, what can (and cannot) be proved true. And you have asked yourself where you stand.

You should, indeed, look for a thesis you believe in, something you can even get enthusiastic about. Arguing on both sides of a question, as debaters do, is no doubt good exercise, if one can stand it. It breaks up old ground and uncovers what you can and do believe, at least for the moment. But the argument without the belief will be hollow. You can hardly persuade anyone if you can't per-suade yourself. So begin with what you believe, and explore its validities.

Conversely, you must test your belief with all the objections you can think of, just as you have already tested your first proposi-tion about welfare payments. First, you have acknowledged the most evident objection—that the opposition's view must have some merit—by starting your final version with "Despite their immediate benefits. . . ." Second, you have gone a little deeper by seeing that in your bold previous version you had, with the words *are eroding,* begged the question of whether responsibility is in fact undergoing erosion; that is, you had silently assumed that responsibility *is* being eroded. This is one of the oldest fallacies and tricks of logic. To "beg the question," by error or intent, is to take for granted that which the opposition has not granted, to assume as already proved that which is yet to be proved. But you have saved yourself. You have changed *are eroding* to *may be eroding.* You have gone further in deleting the *perhaps more than anything else.* You have come closer to the truth.

You may wonder if it is not astoundingly presumptuous to go around stating theses before you have studied your subject from all angles, made several house-to-house surveys, and read everything ever written. A natural uncertainty and feeling of ignorance, and a misunderstanding of what truth is, can well inhibit you from finding a thesis. But no one knows everything. No one would write anything if he waited until he did. To a great extent, the writing of a thing is the learning of it.

So, first, make a desperate thesis and get into the arena. This is probably solution enough. If it becomes increasingly clear that your thesis is untrue, no matter how hard you push it, turn it around and use the other end. If your convictions have begun to falter with:

> **Despite their immediate benefits, welfare payments undermine initiative. . . .**

try it the other way around, with something like:

> **Although welfare payments may offend the rugged individual-ist, they relieve much want and anxiety, and they enable many a fatherless family to maintain its integrity.**

You will now have a beautiful command of the major objections to your new position. And you will have learned something about human fallibility and the nature of truth.

Persuade your reader.

Once you believe in your proposition, you will discover that proving it is really a venture in persuasion. *Rhetoric* is, in fact, the art of persuasion, of moving the reader to your belief. You have made a thesis, a hypothesis really—an opinion as to what the truth seems to be from where you stand, with the information you have. Belief has an unfolding energy. Write what you believe. You may be wrong, of course, but you will probably discover this as you probe for reasons, and can then reverse your thesis, pointed with your new conviction. The truth remains true, and you must at least glimpse it before you can begin to persuade others to see it. So follow your convictions, and think up reasons to convince your reader. Give him enough evidence to persuade him that what you say is probably true; find arguments that will stand up in the marketplace and survive the public haggle. You must find public reasons for your private convictions.

EXERCISE

3 Look over the thesis statements you devised in Exercise 1. Which is most likely to have the reader nodding in agreement even before he finishes the sentence? And which of your thesis statements seems to be most interesting and exciting? Which seems to have the best argumentative edge? After having identified the most interesting and the least interesting of your thesis statements, briefly explain what you think generates the greater interest in the one than in the other. The topics themselves? Your interest in the topics? The way you have stated the thesis? Try to be as specific as possible.

Two
Rhetoric and Persuasion

Public persuasion is rhetoric, and rhetoric may be suspect. Plato, in fact, detested the Sophists because they were mere rhetoricians: they taught young men not to seek the truth but to win arguments—all manner and no matter, so to speak. We still refer to empty language as "just rhetoric," and "rhetorical questions" are those that require no answers, empty questions, for effect only. Although this disparaging usage may be most familiar to you, it is the term's minor meaning, as your dictionary will show you. Rhetoric is indeed artifice, but it is rightly an art necessary to make clear a worthy purpose, the art of displaying the truth, language at its best.

RHETORIC AT GETTYSBURG

Let us look at a famous, and familiar, rhetorical event to clarify our ideas about rhetoric: "The Consecration of the National Cemetery at Gettysburg, Pa.," on November 19, 1863 (the last of the killed had been buried in September), when two very different speeches

15

presented much the same idea. Here we may see the rhetoric of two
masters, both of whom labored at their addresses, and we may see
how the soul of the occasion moves into the rhetoric of Lincoln's
short masterpiece, after only an occasional visit among the more
roundly rhetorical sentences of Edward Everett, the Orator of the
Day.

But we should not underestimate Everett, or we shall underestimate Lincoln, too. Preacher, professor of Greek, member of the
House of Representatives, governor of Massachusetts, minister to
Great Britain, president of Harvard, secretary of state, and senator,
Everett was the most distinguished orator of his time. By his oration
on George Washington, delivered in all parts of the country, he had
raised more than $100,000 to buy Mount Vernon for the nation.

Everett's two-hour analysis of the three-day battle at Gettysburg is still one of the best, but his style, alongside that of Lincoln's
two-minute dedication, seems enormously puffy:

> . . . whether this august republican Union, founded by some of
> the wisest statemen that ever lived, cemented with the blood of
> some of the purest patriots that ever died, should perish or
> endure. . . .
> . . . those who sleep beneath our feet, and their gallant comrades
> who survive to serve their country on other fields of danger. . . .

These two quotations, as you will already have noticed, were
echoed by Lincoln, who followed Everett on the program. Having
read the press release of Everett's oration in advance, Lincoln seems
to have remembered Everett's thoughts as he wrote out his own brief
dedicatory remarks:

> . . . whether that nation . . . can long endure.
> The brave men, living and dead, who struggled here . . .
> . . . shall not perish. . . .

Later, in Gettysburg, Lincoln reworked his address twice before the
ceremony. The first version, with his subsequent alterations, is on
pages 17 and 18. Lincoln, with his speech in hand, nevertheless
spoke mostly from memory and followed his text almost verbatim,
adding only *under God*, as his speaking moved him. You will notice

that Lincoln, like Everett, elevates his language rhetorically. In one place, indeed, he may have elevated a touch too much: Matthew Arnold told friends that he could never get beyond "dedicated to the proposition." And by itself the phrase, rhyming a little slushily with "nation," does indeed sound like good old sociological jargon in full flower.

But the fault is ever so slight, and it consorts unnoticed with the general rhetorical heightening the occasion required. Note Lincoln's slightly inverted order of words in the famous opening sentence, and the alliterative tying of words beginning in *f* and *s* and *c* — all elevating the language above the ordinary. Note his repetitions, some merely emphatic, some worked for extra meaning — especially *lives-live,* and *dedicated,* which came only after revision. Note the new "fitting and proper" sentence, where the purely rhetorical need of bringing the paragraph to rest demands the redundant comfort of a cliché. Finally, notice how Lincoln dignifies and intensifies his thought by echoing the biblical "threescore years and ten" — the traditional span of a human life — to resonate his idea of the uncertain life of the nation at that moment, a nation that had perhaps already outlived its divinely appointed time in its present, ominous, internal war. "Eighty-seven years ago" would have seemed too short, too insignificant, and Lincoln would have lost not only the biblical solemnity but also the idea of the span of life — of birth, life, and death — which he beautifully elaborates in the first sentence with *fathers, brought forth,* and *conceived,* and in the last with *new birth of freedom,* as the life cycle starts again.

I have bracketed the portions Lincoln deleted as he revised, and I have underlined his additions. The phrase *who fought here* and the word *advanced* (indicated in italics) he added for publication at some time after the event.

> **Four score and seven years ago our fathers brought forth [,up]on this continent, a new nation, conceived in [liberty] Liberty, and dedicated to the proposition that ["]all men are created equal.["]**
> **Now we are engaged in a great civil war, testing whether that nation, or any nation so conceived, and so dedicated, can long endure. We are met on a great battle-field of that war. We have come to dedicate a portion of [it] that field, as a final resting place for those who [died here, that the] here gave their**

lives that that nation might live. [This we may, in all propriety do.] It is altogether fitting and proper that we should do this.

But, in a larger sense, we can not dedicate — we can not consecrate — we can not hallow — this ground. The brave men, living and dead, who struggled here, have [hallowed] consecrated it, far above our poor power to add or detract. The world will little note, nor long remember what we say here [; while], but it can never forget what they did here. It is [rather] for us, the living [to stand here ‖ we here be dedicated], rather, to be dedicated here to the unfinished work which they *who fought here* have thus far so nobly [carried on] *advanced*. It is rather for us to be here dedicated to the great task remaining before us — that from these honored dead we take increased devotion to that cause for which they [here] gave the last full measure of devotion — that we here highly resolve that these dead shall not have died in vain — that [the] this nation, under God, shall have a new birth of freedom — and that government of the people, by the people, for the people, shall not perish from the earth.*

There, indeed, is rhetoric. Coming after Everett's two hours of orotundity, it has always seemed simplicity unadorned, the homespun prose of Honest Abe, the noble backwoodsman. But note again the rhetorical force accumulating behind the word *dedicated,* used (with *dedicate*) six times in the ten sentences. The whole purpose was to *dedicate* a national cemetery. The nation, which the Civil War was cruelly testing, had been *dedicated* to the equality of men. We who have come to *dedicate* a portion of that battlefield cannot match the personal *dedication* of those who died there. We must again *dedicate* ourselves to equally shared freedom. Lincoln has punned in a serious way to extract from the word its shades of meaning and to emphasize the essential democratic ideal, which requires the dedication of all. He briefly works a similar rhetorical emphasis with the word *devotion,* before his final rhetorical repetition and parallel — *of the people, by the people, for the people* — alliterating beautifully and meaningfully with the *perish* he had borrowed from Everett.

* *Abraham Lincoln's Gettysburg Address: The First and Second Drafts Now in the Library of Congress* (Washington, D.C.: U.S. Government Printing Office, 1950), as compared against Lincoln's final fair copy — his fifth and last holograph, known as the "Bliss" copy (Joseph Tausek, *The True Story of the Gettysburg Address* [New York: Lincoln MacVeagh, The Dial Press, 1933], facsimile fold-out facing p. 36).

Here also we can see how a command of grammar takes its rhetorical effect. Grammar is necessary, of course, merely to steer clear of any error that would throw the audience off track, or lose its respect. But Lincoln uses his grammar rhetorically as well, not only in the slightly heightened inversion at the beginning (*brought forth on this continent a new nation*) but in a number of grammatical parallels: his contrast of *remember what we say here* as against *forget what they did here,* for instance. But the grammatical parallels with which he closes are the most striking; two triple parallels, one within the other, achieving a magnificent and moving finality. He puts equivalent thoughts into the same grammatical structure, again accumulating an emphasis: we are to resolve (1) that these dead shall not have died in vain, (2) that this nation shall have a new birth, (3) that democratic government shall not perish. And within this third parallel we learn, again in a triple grammatical parallel, that government of the people (any government at all) is, in a democracy, government *by* the people, but more especially *for* the people, as grammar effects the rhetorical point.

Behind both rhetoric and grammar is logic, since rhetoric accents the logical point, and grammar puts it in logical order. Grammar, logic, and rhetoric, the first three of the seven liberal arts, formed the basic *trivium* ("three roads, meeting") of education for over two thousand years, from old Roman schools almost down to our own day. Lincoln here exhibits their union, probably through insight, since his formal schooling was nil. Here he works straight through a logical unfolding from the Liberty in which the nation began, through the war over secession and liberty not achieved because some men were slaves and some thought themselves at liberty to own slaves, and on to the new birth of freedom that will reaffirm the original political ideal. The grammar, logic, and rhetoric are here inseparable, fused together by Lincoln's deep conviction. Perhaps the truly right message is the best rhetorical device after all, and the truth the best persuader.

But even the simple truth needs a vehicle. It cannot just hover in midair, like a disembodied glow. It must arrive in some procession, preceded by a few heralds and attended by visible evidence. Hence the rhetorical heightening, the biblical allusion and metaphor, the parallels, the repetitions, the emphases, in what is sometimes taken as Lincoln's simple, and simply moving, statement.

ATTITUDE

Writing well is a matter of conviction. You learn in school by exercises, of course; and exercises are best when taken as such, as body-builders, flexions and extensions for the real contests ahead. But when you are convinced that what you write has meaning, that it has meaning for you — and not in a lukewarm, hypothetical way, but truly — then your writing will stretch its wings and have the whole wide world in range. For writing is simply a graceful and articulate extension of the best that is in you. Writing well is not easy. It does not come naturally, though your natural endowments will certainly help. It takes unending practice, each essay a polished exercise for the next to come, each new trial, as T. S. Eliot says, a new "raid on the inarticulate."

In writing, you clarify your own thoughts. Indeed, you probably grasp them for the first time. Writing is thinking. The process of writing not merely transcribes but actually creates thought, and generates your ability to think. Through writing, you discover thoughts you hardly knew you had; through writing, you come to know what it is that you know. All kinds of forgotten impressions, lost facts, and surprising updrafts of words and knowledge support your flight. As you test your thoughts against their opposites, as you answer the questions rising in your mind, your conviction grows. You learn as you write. In the end, after you have rewritten and rearranged for your best rhetorical effectiveness, your words will carry your readers with you to see as you see, to believe as you believe, to understand your subject as you now understand it.

Don't take yourself too seriously.

Take your subject seriously — if it is a serious subject — but take yourself with a grain of salt. Your attitude is the very center of your prose. If you take yourself too importantly, your tone will go hollow, your sentences will go moldy, your page will go fuzzy with *of's* and *which's* and nouns clustered densely in passive constructions. In your academic career, the worst dangers lie immediately ahead. Freshmen usually learn to write tolerably well, but from the sophomore to the senior year the academic damp frequently sets in, and by graduate school you can often cut the gray mold with a cheese knife.

You must constantly guard against acquiring the heavy, sober-sided attitude that makes for wordiness and its attendant vices of obscurity, dullness, and anonymity. Do not lose your personality and your voice in the monotone of official prose. You should work like a scholar and scientist, but you should write like a writer, one who cares about the economy and beauty of language, and has some individual personality. Your attitude, then, should form somewhere between a confidence in your own convictions and a humorous distrust of your own rhetoric, which can so easily carry you away. You should bear yourself as a member of the human race, knowing that we are all sinners, all redundant, and all too fond of big words. Here is an example from—I blush to admit—the pen of a professor:

> The general problem is perhaps correctly stated as inadequacy of nursing personnel to meet demands for nursing care and services. Inadequacy, it should be noted, is both a quantitative and qualitative term and thus it can be assumed that the problem as stated could indicate insufficient numbers of nursing personnel to meet existing demands for their services; deficiencies in the competencies of those who engage in the various fields of nursing; or both.

Too few good nurses, and a badly swollen author—that is the problem. "Nursing personnel" may mean nurses, but it also may mean "the nursing of employees," so that the author seems to say, for a wildly illogical moment, that someone is not properly pampering or suckling people for the necessary services. And the ponderous jingle of "deficiencies in the competencies" would nearly do for a musical comedy. The author is taking herself too seriously and taking her readers almost nowhere.

Consider your readers.

If you are to take your subject with all the seriousness it deserves and yourself with as much skeptical humor as you can bear, how are you to take your readers? Who are they, anyway? Hypothetically, your vocabulary and your tone would vary all the way from Skid Row to Oxford as you turn from social work to Rhodes Scholarship; and certainly the difference of audience would reflect itself somewhat in your language. Furthermore, you must indeed sense your audience's capacity, its susceptibilities and prejudices, if you are to win even a hearing. No doubt our language skids a bit when down on the Row, and we certainly speak different tongues with our friends, and with the friends of our parents.

But the notion of adjusting your writing to a whole scale of audiences, though attractive in theory, hardly works out in practice. You are *writing,* and the written word presupposes a literate norm that immediately eliminates all the lower ranges of mere talk. Even when you speak, you do not so lose your identity as to pass for a total illiterate. You stand on your own linguistic feet, in your own linguistic personality, and the only adjustment you should assiduously practice in your writing, and in your speaking as well, is the upward one toward verbal adulthood, a slight grammatical tightening and rhetorical heightening to make your thoughts clear, emphatic, and attractive.

Consider your audience a mixed group of intelligent and reasonable adults. You want them to think of you as well informed and well educated. You wish to explain what you know and what you believe. You wish to persuade them pleasantly that what you know is important and what you believe is right. Try to imagine what they might ask you, what they might object to, what they might know already, what they might find interesting. Be simple and clear, amusing and profound, using plenty of illustration to show what you mean. But do not talk down to them. That is the great flaw in the slumming theory of communication. Bowing to your readers' supposed level, you insult them by assuming their inferiority. Thinking yourself humble, you are actually haughty. The best solution is simply to assume that your readers are as intelligent as you. Even if they are not, they will be flattered by the assumption. Your written language, in short, will be respectful toward your subject, considerate toward your readers, and somehow amiable toward human failings.

THE WRITTEN VOICE

Make your writing talk.

That the silent page should seem to speak with the writer's voice is remarkable. With all gestures gone, no eyes to twinkle, no notation at all for the rise and fall of utterance, and only a handful of punctuation marks, the level line of type can yet convey the writer's voice, the tone of his personality.

To achieve this tone, to find your own voice and style, simply try to write in the language of intelligent conversation, cleared of all the stumbles and weavings of talk. Indeed, our speech, like thought, is amazingly circular. We can hardly think in a straight line if we try. We think by questions and answers, repetitions and failures; and our speech, full of *you know's* and *I mean's,* follows the erratic ways of the mind, circling around and around as we stitch the simplest of logical sequences. Your writing will carry the stitches, not the loopings and pauses and rethreadings. It should be literate. It should be broad enough of vocabulary and rich enough of sentence to show that you have read a book. It should not be altogether unworthy to place you in the company of those who have written well in your native tongue. But it should nevertheless retain the tone of intelligent and agreeable conversation. It should be alive with a human personality—yours—which is probably the most persuasive rhetorical force on earth. Good writing should have a voice, and the voice should be unmistakably your own.

Suppose your spoken voice sounded something like this (I reconstruct an actual response in one of my classes):

> Well, I don't know, I like Shakespeare really, I guess—I mean, well, like when Lear divides up his kingdom like a fairy tale or something, I thought that was kind of silly, dividing his kingdom. Anyone could see that was silly if you wanted to keep your kingdom, why divide it? But then like, something begins to happen, like a real family, I mean. Cordelia really gets griped at her older sisters, I mean, like all older sisters, if you've ever had any. There's a kind of sibling rivalry, you know. Then she's kind of griped at her father, who she really loves, but she thinks, I mean, like saying it right out spoils it. You can't really speak right out, I mean, about love, well, except sometimes, I guess, without sounding corny.

Your written voice might then emerge from this with something of the same tone, but with everything straightened out, filled in, and polished up:

> The play begins like a fairy tale. It even seems at first a little abstract and silly. A king has three daughters. The two elder ones are bad; the youngest is good. The king wishes to keep his kingdom in peace, and keep his title as king, by dividing his kingdom in a senseless and almost empty ceremonial way. But very soon the play seems like real life. The family seems real, complete with sibling rivalry. It is the king, not the play, who is foolish and senile. The older daughters are hypocrites. Cordelia, the youngest, is irritated at them, and at her father's foolishness. As a result, she remains silent, not only because she is irritated at the flattering words of her sisters, but because anything she could say about her real love for her father would now sound false.

You might wish to polish that some more. You might indeed have said it another way, one more truly your own. The point, however, is to write in a tidy, economical way that wipes up the lapses of talk and fills in the gaps of thought, and yet keeps the tone and movement of good conversation, in your own voice.

EXERCISE

1 To find your own modern voice, translate the following passage from Walton's *The Compleat Angler** (1653) into modern English and your own idiom. Try to say as economically and accurately as possible what he is saying, as if you were talking to, or writing to, one of your own contemporaries.

> The Chub, though he eat well thus dressed, yet as he is usually

---

* Izaak Walton and Charles Cotton, *The Compleat Angler, or The Contemplative Man's Recreation*, ed. James Russell Lowell (Boston; Little, Brown, and Company, 1889), pp. 66–67.

dressed he does not: he is objected against, not only for being full of small forked bones, dispersed through all his body, but that he eats waterish, and that the flesh of him is not firm; but short and tasteless. The French esteem him so mean, as to call him *un Vilain*; nevertheless he may be so dressed as to make him very good meat: as, namely, if he be a large Chub, then dress him thus: —

First scale him, and then wash him clean, and then take out his guts; and to that end make the hole as little and near to his gills as you may conveniently, and especially make clean his throat from the grass and weeds that are usually in it, for if that be not very clean, it will make him to taste very sour. Having so done, put some sweet herbs into his belly; and then tie him with two or three splinters to a spit, and roast him, basted often with vinegar, or rather verjuice and butter, with good store of salt mixed with it.

Being thus dressed, you will find him a much better dish of meat than you, or most folk, even than Anglers themselves, do imagine; for this dries up the fluid watery humor with which all Chubs do abound.

But take this rule with you, that a Chub newly taken and newly dressed is so much better than a Chub of a day's keeping after he is dead, that I can compare him to nothing so fitly as to cherries newly gathered from a tree, and others that have been bruised and lain a day or two in water. But the Chub being thus used and dressed presently, and not washed after he is gutted, — for note, that, lying long in water, and washing the blood out of any fish after they be gutted, abates much of their sweetness, — you will find the Chub, being dressed in the blood and quickly, to be such meat as will recompense your labor and disabuse your opinion.

Don't apologize.

"In my opinion," the beginner will write repeatedly, until he seems to be saying "It is only *my* opinion, after all, so it can't be worth much." He has failed to realize that his whole essay represents his opinion — of what the truth of the matter is. Don't make your essay a letter to Diary, or to Mother, or to Teacher, a confidential report of what happened to you last night as you agonized upon a certain question. *"To me,* Robert Frost is a great poet" — this is really writing about yourself. You are only confessing private convictions. To find the "public reasons" often requires no more than a trick of grammar: a shift from *"To me,* Robert Frost is . . ." to "Robert Frost is . . . ," from *"I thought* the book was good" to "The book is good," from you and your room last night to your subject and what it *is.* The grammatical shift represents a whole change of viewpoint, a shift from self to subject. You become the informed adult, showing the reader around firmly, politely, and persuasively.

Once you have effaced yourself from your thesis, once you have erased *to me* and *in my opinion* and all such signs of amateur terror, you may later let yourself back into the essay for emphasis or graciousness: "Mr. Watson errs, I think, precisely at this point." You can thus ease your most tentative or violent assertions, and show that you are polite and sensible, reasonably sure of your position but aware of the possibility of error. Again: the reasonable adult. But it is better to omit the "I" altogether than to write a junior auto-biography of your discoveries and doubts.

You go easy on the *I,* in short, to keep your reader focused on your subject. But you can use the *I* as much as you like to *illustrate* your thesis, once established, using a personal experience among several other pieces of evidence, or even all by itself. Take, for instance, the thesis "The thrilling high-speed ride, if survived, will probably open the teen-ager's eyes to the dynamics of the group." You could then write all the rest of your essay illustrating that thesis with a personal anecdote, beginning your second paragraph with "Once three friends and I borrowed my dad's car to go to a drive-in." This is the point: use the *I* to *illustrate,* or for rhetorical politeness, but not to apologize or to limit your subject to yourself alone. *Generalize* your opinions and emotions. Change "I cried" to "The book is very moving." But your personal happenings can nicely illustrate your thesis with an immediate and specific example.

Plan to rewrite.

As you write your weekly assignments and find your voice, you will also be learning to groom your thoughts, to present them clearly and fully, to make sure you have said what you thought you said. Good writing comes only from rewriting. Even your happy thoughts will need resetting, as you join them to the frequently happier ones that a second look seems to call up. Even the letter-perfect paper will improve almost of itself if you simply sit down to type it through again. You will find, almost unbidden, sharper words, better phrases, new figures of speech, and new illustrations and ideas to replace the weedy patches not noticed before.

Allow yourself time for revision. After you have settled on something to write about, plan for at least three drafts—and try to manage four. Thinking of things to say is the hardest part at first. Even a short assignment of 500 words seems to stretch ahead like a Sahara. You have asserted your central idea in a sentence, and that leaves 490 words to go. But if you step off boldly, one foot after the other, you will make progress, find an oasis or two, and perhaps end at a run in green pastures. With longer papers, you will want some kind of outline to keep you from straying, but the principle is the same: step ahead and keep moving until you've arrived. That is the first draft.

The second is a penciled correction of the first. Of course, if the first has been really haphazard, you will probably want to type it again, rearranging, dropping a few things, adding others, before you can do much detailed work with a pencil. But the second, or pen-ciled, draft is where you refine and polish, checking your dubious spellings in the dictionary, sharpening your punctuation, clarifying your meaning, pruning away the deadwood, adding a thought here, extending an illustration there—running in a whole new paragraph on an inserted page. You will also be tuning your sentences, care-fully adjusting your tone until it is clearly that of an intelligent, rea-sonable person at ease with his knowledge and his audience.

Here is my penciled draft of the paragraph above, as it appeared on my first typescript:

```
                              ed correction              Of course,
        The second is a penciling of the first. ∧ If

    the first has been really haphazard, you will prob-
                                               a few
        ably want to type it again, rearranging, dropping, ∿
        things, adding others,
        filling out, before you can do much detailed work
                                                ed
        with a pencil.  But the second, or pencil, draft is
```

where you refine and polish, checking your *dubious* spelling, *3 in a dictionary*

sharpening your punctuation, ~~clearing up~~ *clarifying* your mean-

ing, ~~clearing out~~ *pruning away* the deadwood, adding a thought

here, extending an ~~explanation~~ *illustration* there--~~you may need~~ *perhaps*

~~arrows leading you to~~ *using* the back of the page to write a

whole new paragraph. You will also be tuning your

sentences, ~~sophisticating~~ *carefully adjusting* your tone ~~into~~ that of the *until it is clearly*

intelligent, reasonable person ~~perfectly~~ at ease with

his knowledge and his audience.

Your third draft is a smoothing of all this for public appearance. Still other illustrations and better phrases will suggest themselves as you get your penciled corrections into order. My penciled paragraph, above, stood up unusually well. I chose it, in fact, because most of my other paragraphs are so crisscrossed and scarred, draft after draft, that their evolution would be too complicated to represent in any practical way. For a classroom paper, three drafts, with several rereadings of the first and the second, are usually adequate. But, if you have time, a fourth draft will do no harm. Reading aloud will frequently pick up errors, lapses in punctuation, and infelicities of phrase. You may have to retype a page of your most polished draft, as a brilliant idea hits you at last, or a terrible sentence finally rears its fuzzy head. Furthermore, your instructor will probably require revisions after he has marked your paper, as my own editor's marking is, at this very moment, requiring me to cross out half a line and to write this sentence above it and over into the crowded margin. (The editor, like your instructor, was devilishly right, of course; I had not completed my thought; and now the printer has graciously covered my awkward tracks.)

Here is a passage from a student's paper that has gone the full course. First you see the student's initial draft, with his own corrections on it. Next you see the passage after a second typing, as it was returned by the instructor with his marks on it. Then you see the final revision, handed in again, as this particular assignment required:

First Draft

In a college education, students should be al-
choose
lowed to ~~make~~ their own course. ~~Too many~~ *All the* requirements, *they*
must take   discourage
~~are discouraging to~~ people's creativity, and they can-
they are
not learn anything ~~which is~~ not motivated ~~for him~~ to
R   *restrict*
learn. ~~With~~ requirements, their freedom to choose
and their eagerness to learn. They are only discouraged
~~what he is interested in is taken away~~ by having to
in which they can see no
study dull subjects like German, ~~which he is not in-~~
relevance to their interests.
~~terested in.~~

The Paper, with Instructor's Markings

In a college education, students <u>should be</u>   *can you get rid of the passive?*

<u>allowed</u> to choose their own curricula and select

redundant? their own courses. All the <u>requirements</u> they must take

relevant? stifle their <u>creativity</u>. Moreover, they <u>cannot learn</u>   *true?*

anything they are not motivated to learn. Require-

ments restrict their freedom to choose and their

eagerness to explore the subjects they are interested

activate in. <u>They are only discouraged by</u> having to study

dull subjects like German, in which they can see no

relevance.

Revised Paper

Students should choose their own education,
their own curricula, their own courses. Their education is really theirs alone. Every college re-
quirement threatens to stifle the very enthusiasms

upon which true education depends. Students learn best when motivated by their own interests, but, in the midst of a dozen complicated requirements, they can hardly find time for the courses they long to take. Requirements therefore not only restrict their freedom to choose but destroy their eagerness to explore. Dull subjects like German, in which they can see no relevance anyway, take all their time and discourage them completely.

MECHANICS

Type, or write, on 8 1/2-by-11-inch paper. Use one side only. Keep your type clean of fuzz and your handwriting neat. Unless otherwise instructed, follow the customs of publication by putting your name and identifications in the upper *left* corner:

```
Charles Meckman
English 123
Paper No. 6
October 12, 1984
```

Next, center your title about three inches from the top of your first page (not numbered). Put it in regular roman (*not* italics) or in capitals. Place no period after the title.

```
    Hooked on People Young
    HOOKED ON PEOPLE YOUNG
```

Put titles of books in italics by underlining them; put titles of poems and other "quoted" phrases in quotation marks:

```
The Problem of Time in Faulkner's The Sound and the
    Fury
Heaven in Frost's "After Apple Picking"
They All Said "Nuts"
```

Leave an inch and a half of margin on the left, and an inch on the right, to give your instructor some room for marks. Double-space your typewriting, and leave space in your handwriting: you and your instructor may want to put in a word above the line, with a caret (∧) to show where it goes. Start your paragraphs five letter-spaces in from your margin. See "Indentation" and "Quotation Marks" (pp. 56–57, 432–435) for details about how to space your quotations. Also see the sample paper in Chapter 14 for other elements and numbering of pages.

A FIRST PAPER

Now you have surveyed the problem of how to get an essay started. You find a subject that interests you. You turn it into a thesis by affirming something about it. You evolve your written voice as you think up points and illustrations to make your thesis persuasive. We have seen that rhetoric is a persuasive refining of language, and that style is rhetoric individualized and perfected. We have considered the attitude from which a good style springs: a serious engagement with your subject, a pleasant arrangement with your audience, a humorous effacement of yourself. And we have seen that revision is not only necessary and inevitable but positively creative as it brings your thoughts fully alive and makes them persuasive.

Now with the concepts and the style in hand, we need a framework, a structure, to put them in. This we shall look at in the next chapter. But let us close with a student's paper to illustrate the points of this chapter as it looks ahead to the structural points of the next. In it you can see the mechanics of typing, spacing, quoting, and so forth. The author has made a few small last-minute corrections in pencil, which are perfectly acceptable. Her writing is a little wordy and awkward. She is a little uncertain of her language. This is her first paper, and she has not yet fully discovered her own written voice. But it is an excellent beginning. It shows well how a personal experience produces a publicly valid thesis, then turns

around to give that thesis its most lively and specific illustration.
The assignment had asked for a paper of about five hundred words
on some book (or movie, or TV program) that had proved personally
meaningful. Even a memorable experience would do—fixing a car,
or building a boat, or being arrested. The aim of the assignment
was to generalize from a personally valuable experience and to explain to others how such an experience can be valuable to them.

Emily Maddox
English 123
Paper No. 1
September 15, 1977

ON FINDING ONESELF IN NEW GUINEA

Opposing View

Reading for pleasure is not considered to be
popular. Young adults prefer the "boob tube," the
television set with which they have spent so many
childhood hours. Too many attractions beckon them
away from the books ~~which~~ *that* the teacher recommended to
the class for summer reading. One's friends come by
in their automobiles to drive down for a coke. The
kids go to the moving pictures, or to the beach, and
the book one had intended to read remains on the shelf,
or pr*o*bably *in* the library, where one has not yet been
able to find the time to go. Nevertheless, a book

Thesis can furnish real enjoyment.

Generalized Support

The reader enjoys the experience of being in
another world. While one reads, one forgets that one
is in one's own room. The book has served as a magic

carpet to ~~take~~ *transport* one to India, or Africa, or Sweden,
or even to the cities and areas of one's own country
where one has never been. It has also transported
one into the lives of people with different experiences and problems, from which one can learn to solve
one's own problems of the future. The young person,
in particular, can learn by the experience of reading
what it is like to be a complete adult.

A book is able to help the young person to mature even further, and change one's whole point of
view. Growing up in New Guinea by Margaret Mead is
a valuable experience for this reason. I found the
book on our shelf, after having seen Margaret Mead
on TV. I was interested in her because the teacher
had referred to her book entitled Coming of Age in
Samoa. I was surprised to find this one about New
Guinea. I thought it was a mistake. I opened it and
read the first sentence:

*Personal
Experience*

> The way in which each human infant is
> transformed into the finished adult, into the
> complicated individual version of his city and
> his century, is one of the most fascinating
> studies open to the curious minded.

The idea that the individual is a version of his city
and his century was fascinating. I started reading
and was surprised when I was called to dinner to
learn that two hours had passed. I could hardly eat
my dinner fast enough so that I could get back to New
Guinea.

From this book, I learned that different cultures
have very different conceptions about what is right

*Thesis
Restated*

and wrong, in particular about the sex relations and
the marriage ceremony, but that people have the same
problems all over the world, namely the problem of
finding one's place in society. I also learned that
books can be more enjoyable than any form of pleasure. Books fascinate the reader because while one
is learning about other people and their problems,
particularly about the problem of becoming a full
member of society, one is also learning about one's
own problems.

Three
Basic
Structure

BEGINNING, MIDDLE, AND END

As Aristotle long ago pointed out, works that spin their way along through time need a beginning, a middle, and an end to give them the stability of spatial things like paintings and statues. You need a clear beginning to give your essay character and direction so the reader can tell where he is going and can look forward with expectation. Your beginning, of course, will set forth your thesis. You need a middle to amplify and fulfill. This will be the body of your argument, the bulk of your essay. You need an end to let readers know that they have arrived and where. This will be your final paragraph, a summation and reassertion of your theme.

Give your essay the three-part *feel* of beginning, middle, and end. The mind likes this triple order. Three has always been a magic number. The woodcutter always has three sons or three daughters; even the physical universe has three dimensions. Many a freshman's essay has no structure and leaves no impression. It is all chaotic middle. It has no beginning, it just begins; it has no end, it just stops, fagged out at two in the morning.

The beginning must feel like a beginning, not like an accident. It should be at least a full paragraph that lets your reader gently into the subject and culminates with your thesis. The end, likewise, should be a full paragraph, one that drives the point home, pushes the implications wide, and brings the reader to rest, back on the tonic chord to give a sense of completion. When we consider paragraphing in the next chapter, we will look more closely at beginning paragraphs and end paragraphs. The "middle" of your essay, which constitutes its bulk, needs further structural consideration now.

MIDDLE TACTICS

Arrange your points in order of increasing interest.

Once your thesis has sounded the challenge, your reader's interest is probably at its highest pitch. He wants to see how you can prove so outrageous a thing, or to see what the arguments are for this thing he has always believed but never tested. Each step of the way into your demonstration, he is learning more of what you have to say. But, unfortunately, his interest may be relaxing as it becomes satisfied: the reader's normal line of attention is a progressive decline, arching down like a wintry graph. Against this decline you must oppose your forces, making each successive point more interesting, so that your reader's interest will continue at least on the horizontal, with no sag, and preferably with an upward swing:

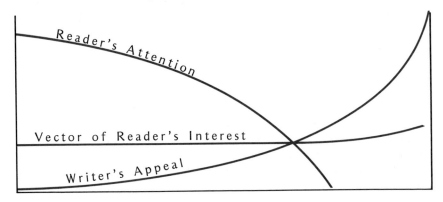

Reader's Attention

Vector of Reader's Interest

Writer's Appeal

This is the basic principle for organizing the middle of your essay. Save your best till last. It is as simple as that.

Here, for example, is the middle of a short, three-paragraph essay developing the thesis that "Working your way through college is valuable." The student arranged his three points in an ascending order of interest:

> The student who works finds that the experience is worth more than the money. First, he learns to budget his time. He now uses the time he would otherwise waste to support himself, and he studies harder in the time he has left because he knows it is limited. Second, he makes real and lasting friends on the job, as compared to the other casual acquaintances around the campus. He has shared rush hours, and nighttime cleanups with the dishes piled high, and conversation and jokes when business is slow. Finally, he gains confidence in his ability to get along with all kinds of people, and to make his own way. He sees how businesses operate, and how waitresses, for instance, can work cheerfully at a really tiring job without much hope for the future. He gains an insight into the real world, which is a good contrast to the more intellectual and idealistic world of the college student.

Again, each successive item of your presentation should be more interesting than the last, or you will suddenly seem anticlimactic. Actually, minor regressions of interest make no difference so long as the whole tendency is uphill and your last item clearly the best. Suppose, for example, you were to undertake the cat thesis. You decide that four points would make up the case, and that you might arrange them in the following order of increasing interest: (1) cats are affectionate but make few demands; (2) cats actually look out for themselves; (3) cats have, in fact, proved extremely useful to society throughout history in controlling mice and other plaguey rodents; (4) cats satisfy some human need for a touch of the jungle, savagery in repose, ferocity in silk, and have been worshiped for the exotic power they still seem to represent, even dozing on the banister. It may be, as you write, thinking of things, that you will find Number 1 developing attractive or amusing instances, and perhaps even virtually usurping the whole essay. Numbers 2, 3, and 4 should then be moved ahead as interesting but brief preliminaries. Your middle structure, thus, should range from least important to most important, from simple to complex, from narrow to broad, from pleasant to hilarious, from mundane to metaphysical—whatever "leasts" and "mosts" your subject suggests.

EXERCISE

1 In the following exercise you will find groups of information and ideas haphazardly arranged. Rewrite the statements with the information arranged in an ascending order of interest and importance. Then, in a sentence or two, explain your reasons for using that order.

1. We are now being made to realize the negative aspects of the technological "progress" of the twentieth century: 50,000 highway deaths per year, air and water pollution, the population explosion, nuclear warfare, loss of privacy.

2. Four different levels of government are investigating the effectiveness of the methadone treatment for heroin addiction. State, national, county, and city governments have all instituted research programs within the last year.

3. The psychological effects of the Depression are observable in an increase in the frequency of mental breakdown, an increase in the suicide rate, and a decrease in the birth rate.

4. Although most classrooms have tile floors, carpeting is actually better in several ways. First, if you figure maintenance into the total cost of floor covering, carpeting is cheaper than tile; second, carpeting is more aesthetically pleasing than tile; and third, carpeting serves a useful acoustical function, absorbing the noise of scuffing feet and scooting chairs.

5. This car not only looks sporty, but is also equipped for sporty performance. It has dual exhausts, four-speed gear box, heavy-duty springs and shocks, high-back bucket seats, vinyl roof, a 390cc engine, heavy-duty cooling system, power disc brakes, corduroy upholstery trim, rally accent stripes.

6. An all-volunteer army may be undesirable because it tends to draw from a limited segment of the population, to create an elitist military

caste such as those in Hitler's Germany and in tsarist Russia, and to cost more. But it does away with the draft.

7. Marijuana should be legalized because people are going to use it whether it is legalized or not. Legalizing it would make a sensible distinction between hard and soft drugs, would allow authorities to control the quality of the drugs available for sale, would eliminate criminal profiteering, and would prevent numbers of people from becoming cynical violators of the law.

8. If you have gotten along without a credit card until now, applying for one is really a mistake. If you have one, you might lose it or have it stolen, and then you might be liable for the expenses run up by someone else using your card. Then there are the interest charges. Few people realize that the interest on most credit cards is 18 percent a year. And obviously, if you have a credit card, you are going to spend more than if you were using cash.

9. Talking about scientific knowledge today, she identified three of its characteristics. First, this knowledge is not within the reach of most of us. Second, this knowledge is mostly new. And, finally, this knowledge has become almost the exclusive property of a very small group of scientists and engineers.

Acknowledge and dispose of the opposition.

Your cat essay, because it is moderately playful, can proceed rather directly, throwing only an occasional bone of concession to the dogs, and perhaps most of your essays, as you discuss the Constitutional Convention or explain a poem, will have no opposition to worry about. But a serious controversial argument demands one organizational consideration beyond the simple structure of ascending interest. Although you have taken your stand firmly as a *pro,* you will have to allow scope to the *con*'s, or you will seem not to have thought much about your subject. The more opposition you can manage as you carry your point, the more triumphant you will seem, like a high-wire artist daring the impossible.

This balancing of *pro*'s against *con*'s is one of the most fundamental orders of thought: the dialectic order, which is the order of argument, one side pitted against the other. Our minds naturally swing from side to side as we think. In dialectics, we simply give one side an argumentative edge, producing a thesis that cuts a clear line through any subject: "This is better than that." The basic organizing principle here is to get rid of the opposition first, and to end on your own side. Probably you will have already organized your thesis sentence in a perfect pattern for your *con-pro* argument:

> **Despite their many advantages, welfare payments. . . .**
> **Although dogs are fine pets, cats. . . .**

The subordinate clause (pp. 139–141) states the subordinate part of your argument, which is your concession to the *con* viewpoint; your main clause states your main argument. As the subordinate clause comes first in your thesis-sentence, so with the subordinate argument in your essay. Sentence and essay both reflect a natural psychological principle. You want, and the reader wants, to get the opposition out of the way. And you want to end on your best foot. (You might try putting the opposition last, just to see how peculiarly the last word insists on seeming best, and how, when stated last by you, the opposition's case seems to be your own.)

Get rid of the opposition first. This is the essential tactic of argumentation. You have introduced and stated your thesis in your beginning paragraph. Now start your Middle with a paragraph of concession to the *con*'s:

> **Dog-lovers, of course, have tradition on their side. Dogs are indeed affectionate and faithful. . . .**

And with that paragraph out of the way, go to bat for the cats, showing their superiority to dogs in every point. In a very brief essay, you can even use the opposition at the very beginning of your Beginning, using it to introduce your thesis itself and really getting rid of it right at the start, as in the essay in Exercise 4, at the end of this chapter (p. 46). But usually your beginning paragraph will lead up to your thesis more or less neutrally, and you will attack your opposition head-on in paragraph two, as you launch into your Middle.

Again, if the opposing arguments seem relatively slight and brief, you can get rid of them all together in one paragraph before you get down to your case. Immediately after your beginning, which has stated your thesis, you write a paragraph of concession: "Of course, security is a good thing. No one wants people begging." And so on to the end of the paragraph, deflating every conceivable objection. Then back to the main line: "But the price in moral decay is too great." The structure might be diagramed something like the scheme shown in Diagram I.

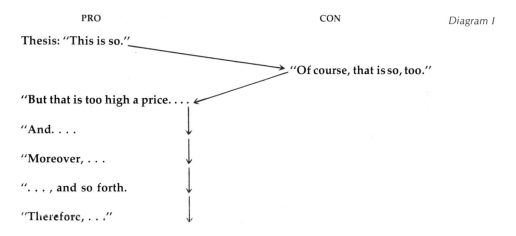

PRO CON *Diagram I*

Thesis: "This is so."

"Of course, that is so, too."

"But that is too high a price...."

"And...."

"Moreover,..."

"..., and so forth.

"Therefore,..."

If the opposition is more considerable, demolish it point by point, using a series of *con*'s and *pro*'s, in two or three paragraphs, before you steady down to your own side. Each paragraph can be a small argument that presents the opposition, then knocks it flat — a kind of Punch-and-Judy show: "We must admit that.... But..." And down goes the poor old opposition again. Or you could swing your argument through a number of alternating paragraphs: first your beginning, the thesis, then a paragraph to the opposition *(con)*, then one for your side *(pro)*, then another paragraph of *con*, and so on. The main point, again, is this: get rid of the opposition first. One paragraph of concession right after your thesis will probably handle most of your adversaries, and the more complicated argumentative swingers, like the one analyzed in Diagram II on page 42, will develop naturally as you need them.

You will notice that *but* and *however* are always guides for the *pro*'s, serving as switches back to the main line. *But, however,* and

Nevertheless are the basic *pro's.* *But* always heads its turning sentence (not followed by a comma); *Nevertheless* usually does (followed by a comma). I am sure, however, that *however* is always better buried in the sentence between commas. "However, . . ." is the habit of heavy prose. *But* is for the quick turn; the inlaid *however* for the more elegant sweep.

The structural line of your argument might look like the scheme shown in Diagram II.

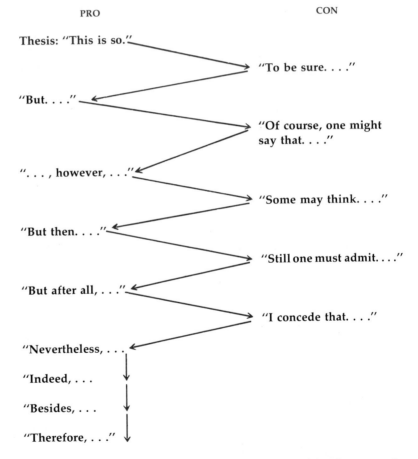

Diagram II   PRO   CON

Thesis: "This is so."

"To be sure. . . ."

"But. . . ."

"Of course, one might say that. . . ."

". . . , however, . . ."

"Some may think. . . ."

"But then. . . ."

"Still one must admit. . . ."

"But after all, . . ."

"I concede that. . . ."

"Nevertheless, . . .

"Indeed, . . .

"Besides, . . .

"Therefore, . . ."

We might diagram an actual *pro-con* argument like the example in Diagram III.

PRO   CON   *Diagram III*

Thesis: "Marijuana should
be legalized."

To be sure, soft
drugs can lead to hard
drugs. . . .

But most users of
marijuana seek only mild
pleasures among a group
of friends. . . .

Of course, one might
argue that marijuana only
prolongs the groupiness
of adolescence. . . .

People at every age,
however, seek support
from their peers. . . .

I concede that legal-
izing marijuana invites
certain serious risks. . . .

Nevertheless, the
present punishment and
its social consequences far
exceed these risks. . . .

Indeed, the law
could eliminate many dan-
gers by controlling quality.
. . .

Besides, legality
would eliminate the
profiteers. . . .

Therefore, legalizing
marijuana would solve
more problems than its
illegality now creates. . . .

EXERCISES

2 To strengthen your feeling for argumentative opposition, write three *con*-and-*pro* thesis sentences, beginning "Although. . . ."

3 In the exercise that follows, you will find a series of general assertions. Supply one argument *against* and one argument *for* each proposition. Then combine the statements into one thesis-sentence that includes not only the assertion, but also the reasons against and for it.

EXAMPLE.   Assertion: Movies should not be censored.
Con: Children should not be exposed to obscene and explicitly sexual images on the screen.
Pro: Obscenity is far too subjective a thing for any person to define for anyone else.
Thesis Statement: Although it is probably undesirable for young people to be exposed to scenes of explicit sex in films, movies still should not be censored because obscenity is so subjective a thing that no one can legitimately serve as censor for the rest of us.

1. Assertion: Discussion classes are superior to lectures.
2. Assertion: Rapid and convenient transit systems must be built in our cities.
3. Assertion: The federal government should subsidize large companies forced near bankruptcy.
4. Assertion: Medical schools should reduce the time required for a degree in general medicine from four years to two.
5. Assertion: States should prohibit the sale of beverages in nonreturnable containers.
6. Assertion: A guaranteed annual income would not wipe out poverty for all Americans.
7. Assertion: As exercise, golf is a waste of time.
8. Assertion: Rear-engine cars are dangerous.
9. Assertion: College students should study a foreign language.

Run comparisons point by point.

After blasting the opposition first, only one argumentative principle remains: *run your comparisons point by point.* Don't write all about sheep for three pages, then all about goats. Every time you say something about a sheep, say something comparable about a goat, pelt for pelt, horn for horn, beard for beard. Otherwise your essay will fall in two, and you will need to repeat all your sheep points when you get down to goats, and at last begin the comparison. The tendency to organize comparisons by halves is so strong that you will probably find you have fallen into it unawares, and in rewriting you will have to reorganize everything point for point — still arranging your pairs of points from least important to most. Finally, the most interesting comparison aims to demonstrate a superiority, that is, has a thesis — "Resolved: Sheep are more useful than goats."

Of course, comparing and contrasting two poems, two stories, two ballplayers, is an essential process of thought, an essential way to understanding. You may wish simply to set two similars, or dissimilars, side by side to illustrate some larger point — that excellence may come in very different packages, for instance. Comparing and contrasting can illuminate the unfamiliar with the familiar, or it can help you discover and convey to your readers new perspectives on things well known — two popular singers, two of Shakespeare's sonnets, two nursery rhymes. I gained this kind of insight by putting Lincoln beside Everett, for example, discovering things in the Gettysburg Address I had never noticed or known before. But, whether or not you are presenting one side as superior to the other, the structural tactics are the same: illuminate by comparing point for point, as long as the comparison illuminates.

Now, let us say, you have almost finished your essay. You have found a thesis. You have worked it into a decent beginning. You have then worked out a convincing middle, with your arguments presented in a sequence of ascending interest; you have used up all your points and said your say. You and your argument are both exhausted. But don't stop. You need an end, or the whole thing will unravel in your reader's mind. You need to buttonhole him in a final paragraph, to imply "I told you so" without saying it, to hint at the whole round experience he has just had, and to leave him convinced, satisfied, and admiring. One more paragraph will do it: beginning, middle, *and* end.

EXERCISE

4 In the exercise that follows, you will find an essay in which the author advances his thesis point by point. First, state the thesis, then number and identify the arguments both for and against the thesis. Also identify as *con* or *pro* the words or phrases the author uses to mark the switch from one side of the argument to the other. List the arguments for and against the assertion, and make another double list, headed "Pro" and "Con," of the writer's transitional devices.

I should start by admitting that as little as five years ago carpeted classrooms would rightly have seemed too fanciful and expensive. The carpeting then available would have been costly, difficult to maintain, and would have required frequent replacement. Now, however, because of improved materials, the arguments in favor of extensive carpeting seem a great deal more plausible. New indoor-outdoor synthetics — stain resistant, fade resistant, durable, and inexpensive — have made carpeting seem much less a luxury than a reasonable, even desirable, alternative to tile floors. Briefly, there seem to be three central arguments in favor of carpeting.

First, of course, carpeting is attractive. Now, admittedly, modern technology offers a great variety of attractively colored tiles, and the days of the drab, institutional grays, greens, and browns in tile are — happily — over. But, even though tile may approach carpeting in terms of color, it still has a hard and unattractive texture. Carpeting, on the other hand, is colorful, attractive to touch, and comfortable to walk on. It goes a long way toward creating a pleasant atmosphere all of us would like to work in, both in and out of class. Richly colored carpeting, such as the bold reds often used in banks, restaurants, department stores, and commercial offices, would make our facilities far less "institutional." Bright carpeting can easily make attractive an area that would otherwise seem Spartan and sterile. In short, carpeting seems desirable simply because it is more attractive to look at and walk on than tile.

The second argument in favor of carpeted classrooms is essentially pragmatic: carpeting serves a useful acoustical function. Of course, the flexible backing and roughened texture of modern tiles make them far less noisy than those of just a few years ago. Both tiles and carpets have improved significantly. Carpeting, however, is a superior dampener of sound; it cuts noise from crowded hallways, absorbs annoying background noise in classrooms—scuffing feet, scooting chairs, coughs—and makes busy space less noisy and, therefore, much more practical. In industry, if not in schools, one frequently finds carpeting in busy areas because it reduces noise.

A final argument in favor of carpeting is that, over a period of time, carpeting is no more expensive than tile. Certainly, carpeting costs more than tile, and it does need eventual replacement. But carpeting costs much less to maintain than tile, which needs frequent washing, waxing, and dusting. The new synthetic carpets resist stains and fading. An ordinary vacuum cleaner will keep them in shape. But the tile floor, unfortunately, needs frequent scrubbing and waxing if it is not to look dull and yellow with accumulated wax. This process is laborious and slow, and, in large institutions, it requires expensive scrubbing machines. In short, tile costs less than carpeting to install. But count in the maintenance, and carpeting becomes a legitimate economic alternative to tile.

Were it not for the obvious advantages in appearance and acoustics of carpeting over tile, one could perhaps argue fairly in favor of conventional flooring. After all, the costs over a very long period, say twenty or thirty years, are genuinely unpredictable. We simply haven't yet accumulated enough experience with the new synthetics, and perhaps over a quarter of a century carpets will prove more expensive. Perhaps we will discover that, after a decade or so, the savings in maintaining carpets will evaporate. To this point, however, our experience with synthetic materials is essentially affirmative. And so, given the clear edge carpeting has over tile aesthetically and acoustically, and given its apparent economic justification, carpeting for classrooms seems completely sensible.

Four
Paragraphs

THE STANDARD PARAGRAPH

A paragraph is a structural convenience—a building block to get firmly in mind. I mean the standard, central paragraph, setting aside for the moment the peculiarly shaped beginning paragraph and ending paragraph. You build the bulk of your essay with standard paragraphs, with blocks of concrete ideas, and they must fit smoothly. But they must also remain as perceptible parts, to rest your reader's eye and mind. Indeed, the paragraph originated, among the Greeks, as a resting place and place-finder, being first a mere mark (*graphos*) in the margin alongside (*para*) an unbroken sheet of handwriting—the proofreader's familiar ¶. You have heard that a paragraph is a single idea, and this is true. But so is a word, usually; and so is a sentence, sometimes. It seems best, after all, to think of a paragraph as something you use for your reader's convenience, rather than as some granitic form laid down by molten logic.

The writing medium determines the size of the paragraph. Your average longhand paragraph may look the same size to you as a typewritten one, and both may seem the same size as a paragraph in a book. But the printed page might show your handwritten paragraph so short as to be embarrassing, and your typewritten paragraph barely long enough for decency. Handwriting plus typewriting plus insecurity equals inadequate paragraphs. Your first impulse may be to write little paragraphs, often only a sentence to each. If so, you are not yet writing in any medium at all.

Journalists, of course, are habitually one-sentence paragraphers. The narrowness of the newspaper column makes a sentence look like a paragraph, and narrow columns and short paragraphs serve the rapid transit for which newspapers are designed. A paragraph from a book might fill a whole newspaper column with solid lead. It would have to be broken—paragraphed—for the reader's convenience. On the other hand, a news story on the page of a book would look like a gap-toothed comb, and would have to be consolidated for the reader's comfort.

Plan for the big paragraph.

Imagine yourself writing for print, but in a book, not a newspaper. Force yourself to four or five sentences at least, visualizing your paragraphs as about all of a size. Think of them as identical rectangular frames to be filled. This will allow you to build with orderly blocks, to strengthen your feel for structure. Since the beginner's problem is usually one of thinking of things to say rather than of trimming the overgrowth, you can do your filling out a unit at a time, always thinking up one or two sentences more to fill the customary space. You will probably be repetitive and wordy at first —this is our universal failing—but you will soon learn to fill your paragraph with clean and interesting details. You will get to feel a kind of constructional rhythm as you find yourself coming to a resting place at the end of your customary paragraphic frame.

Once accustomed to a five-sentence frame, say, you can then begin to vary the length for emphasis, letting a good idea swell out beyond the norm, or bringing a particular point home in a paragraph short and sharp—even in one sentence, like this.

The paragraph's structure, then, has its own rhetorical message. It tells the reader visually whether or not you are in charge of your subject, and are leading him confidently to see what you already know. Tiny, ragged paragraphs display your hidden uncertainty, unless clearly placed among big ones for emphasis. Brief opening and closing paragraphs sometimes can emphasize your thesis effectively, but usually they make your beginning seem hasty and your ending perfunctory. So aim for the big paragraph all the way, and vary it only occasionally and knowingly, for rhetorical emphasis.

Find a topic sentence.

Looked at as a convenient structural frame, the paragraph reveals a further advantage. Like the essay itself, it has a beginning, a middle, and an end. The beginning and the end are usually each one sentence long, and the middle gets you smoothly from one to the other. Since, like the essay, the paragraph flows through time, its last sentence is the most emphatic. This is your home punch. The first sentence holds the next most emphatic place. It will normally be your *topic sentence,* stating the small thesis of a miniature essay, something like this:

> *Jefferson believed in democracy because of his fearless belief in reason.* **He knew that reason was far from perfect, but he also knew that it was the best faculty we have. He knew that it was better than all the frightened and angry intolerances with which we fence off our own back yards at the cost of injustice. Thought must be free. Discussion must be free. Reason must be free to range among the widest possibilities. Even the opinion we hate, and have reasons for believing wrong, we must leave free so that reason can operate on it, so that we advertise our belief in reason and demonstrate a faith unafraid of the consequences — because we know that the consequences will be right. Freedom is really not the aim and end of Jeffersonian democracy: freedom is the means by which democracy can rationally choose justice for all.**

If your topic sentence covers everything within your paragraph, your paragraph is coherent, and you are using your paragraphs with maximum effect, leading your reader into your community block by block. If your end sentences bring him briefly to rest, he will know where he is and appreciate it.

BEGINNING PARAGRAPHS: THE FUNNEL

State your thesis at the END of your beginning paragraph.

Your beginning paragraph should contain your main idea, and present it to best advantage. Its topic sentence is also the *thesis sentence* of your entire essay. The clearest and most emphatic place for your thesis sentence is at the *end*—not at the beginning—of the beginning paragraph. If you put it first, you will have to repeat some version of it as you bring your beginning paragraph to a close. If you put it in the middle, the reader will very likely take something else as your main point, probably whatever the last sentence contains. The inevitable psychology of interest, as you move your reader through your first paragraph and into your essay, urges you to put your thesis last—in the last sentence of your beginning paragraph.

Think of your beginning paragraph, then, not as a frame to be filled, but as a funnel. Start wide and end narrow:

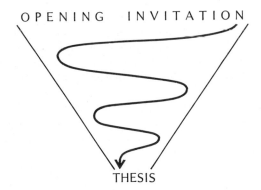

OPENING   INVITATION

THESIS

If, for instance, you wished to show that learning to play the guitar pays off in friendship, you would start somewhere back from your specific thesis with something more general—about music, about learning, about the pleasures of achievement, about guitars: "Playing the guitar looks easy," "Music can speak more directly than words,"

"Learning anything is a course in frustration." You can even open with something quite specific, *as long as it is more general than your thesis:* "Pick up a guitar, and you bump into people." A handy way to find an opener is to take one word from your thesis—*learning, play,* or *guitar,* for instance—and make a sentence out of it. Say something about it, and you are well on your way to your thesis, three or four sentences later.* Your opening line, in other words, should look forward to your thesis, should be something to engage interest easily, something to which most readers would assent without a rise in blood pressure. (Antagonize and startle if you wish, but beware of having the door slammed before you have a chance, and of making your thesis an anticlimax.) Therefore: broad and genial. From your opening geniality, you move progressively down to smaller particulars. You narrow down: from learning the guitar, to its musical and social complications, to its rewards in friendship (your thesis). Your paragraph might run, from broad to narrow, like this:

> **Learning anything has unexpected rocks in its path, but the guitar seems particularly rocky. It looks so simple. A few chords, you think, and you are on your way. Then you discover not only the musical and technical difficulties, but a whole unexpected crowd of human complications. Your friends think you are showing off; the people you meet think you are a fake. Then the frustrations drive you to achievement. You learn to face the music and the people honestly. You finally learn to play a little, but you also discover something better. You have learned to make and keep some real friends, because you have discovered a kind of ultimate friendship with yourself.**

Now, that paragraph turned out a little different from what I anticipated. I overshot my original thesis, discovering, as I wrote, a thesis one step farther—an underlying cause—about coming to friendly terms with oneself. But it illustrates the funnel, from the broad and general to the one particular point that will be your essay's main idea, your thesis. Here is another example:

> **The environment is the world around us, and everyone agrees it needs a cleaning. Big corporations gobble up the**

* I am grateful to James C. Raymond, of the University of Alabama, for this helpful idea.

countryside and disgorge what's left into the breeze and streams. Big trucks rumble by, trailing their fumes. A jet roars into the air, and its soot drifts over the trees. Everyone calls for massive action, and then tosses away his cigarette butt or gum wrapper. The world around us is also a sidewalk, a lawn, a lounge, a hallway, a room right here. Cleaning the environment can begin by reaching for the scrap of paper at your feet.

In a more argumentative paper, organized by *pro*'s and *con*'s, you can sometimes set up your thesis effectively by opening with the opposition, as we have already noted (p. 40):

> Shakespeare begins *Romeo and Juliet* with ominous warnings about fate. His lovers are "star-crossed," he says: they are doomed from the first by their contrary stars, by the universe itself. They have sprung from "fatal loins." Fate has already determined their tragic end. The play then unfolds a succession of unlucky and presumably fated accidents. Nevertheless, we soon discover that Shakespeare really blames the tragedy not on fate but on human stupidity and error.

EXERCISE

1 Below is a list of thesis-sentences. Choose one (or its opposite), or make one of your own on the same pattern. Then back off from it at least four or five sentences, and write a funnel-like beginning paragraph leading your reader down to it: your thesis, the last sentence of your beginning funnel. EXAMPLE, with thesis italicized, follows:

> The coal operators will tell you that stripping is cheaper and more efficient than conventional mining. Their 250-cubic-yard drag-lines, their 200-cubic-yard shovels, their 50-ton trucks, can rip the top off a mountain and expose a whole seam of coal in a fraction of the time it takes to sink a shaft. "It is cheaper," they will say, "to bring the surface to the coal than to bring the coal to the surface." And of course they are right; in a sense it is cheaper. But visit Eastern Kentucky and look at the real price we pay for stripped coal. Visit a stripped area and you will see that, no matter how low the price for a truckload of stripped coal, *the real price for strip-mining has to be reckoned in terms of blighted land, poisoned streams, and stunted human lives.*

1. Although motivated by proper concern for the public welfare, the FCC's ban of cigarette advertising on television is ineffective and discriminatory.

2. Although currently exempt, camper buses and vans should face the same federal safety requirements as automobiles.

3. Despite the evident advantages of artificial turf in football stadiums, it is dangerous and should, therefore, be banned.

4. Even though durable and convenient, tape cassettes reproduce sound with only mediocre fidelity.

5. Legalizing off-track betting may annoy some citizens, but, because it would weaken the underworld, we should support it.

MIDDLE PARAGRAPHS

Make your middle paragraphs full, and use transitions.

The middle paragraph is the standard paragraph, the little essay in itself, with its own little beginning and little end. But it must also declare its allegiance to the paragraphs immediately before and after it. Each topic sentence must somehow hook onto the paragraph above it, must include some word or phrase to ease the reader's path: a transition. You may simply repeat a word from the sentence that ended the paragraph just above. You may bring down a thought left slightly hanging in air: "Smith's idea is different" might be a tremendously economical topic sentence with automatic transition. Or you may get from one paragraph to the next by the usual steppingstones, like *but, however, nevertheless, therefore, indeed, of course.* One brief transitional touch in your topic sentence is usually sufficient.

The topic sentences in each of the following three paragraphs by James Baldwin contain neat transitions. I have just used an old standby myself: repeating the words *topic sentence* from the close of my preceding paragraph. Baldwin has just described the young people of Harlem who have given up, escaping into day-long TV, or the local bar, or drugs. He now begins his next paragraph with

And the others, a strong and natural transition, referring back, reinforced with the further transitional reference *all of these deaths.* In the next paragraph, *them* does the trick; in the last, *other* again makes the transition and sets the contrast. The paragraphs are nearly the same length, all cogent, clear, and full. No one-sentence paragraphing here, no gaps, but all a vivid, orderly progression:

> <u>**And the others**</u>, who have avoided <u>**all of these deaths**</u>, get up in the morning and go downtown to meet "the man." They work in the white man's world all day and come home in the evening to this fetid block. They struggle to instill in their children some private sense of honor or dignity which will help the child to survive. This means, of course, that they must struggle, stolidly, incessantly, to keep this sense alive in themselves, in spite of the insults, the indifference, and the cruelty they are certain to encounter in their working day. They patiently browbeat the landlord into fixing the heat, the plaster, the plumbing; this demands prodigious patience; nor is patience usually enough. In trying to make their hovels habitable, they are perpetually throwing good money after bad. Such frustration, so long endured, is driving many strong, admirable men and women whose only crime is color to the very gates of paranoia.

Topic Sentence with Transition

End Sentence: the Point

> One remembers <u>**them**</u> from another time — playing handball in the playground, going to church, wondering if they were going to be promoted at school. One remembers them going off to war — gladly, to escape this block. One remembers their return. Perhaps one remembers their wedding day. And one sees where the girl is now — vainly looking for salvation from some other embittered, trussed, and struggling boy — and sees the all-but-abandoned children in the streets.

Topic Sentence with Transition

End Sentence: the Point

> Now I am perfectly aware that there are <u>**other**</u> slums in which white men are fighting for their lives, and mainly losing. I know that blood is also flowing through those streets and that the human damage there is incalculable. People are continually pointing out to me the wretchedness of white people in order to console me for the wretchedness of blacks. But an itemized account of the American failure does not console me and it should not console anyone else. That hundreds of thousands of white people are living, in effect, no better than the "niggers" is not a fact to be regarded with complacency. The social and

Topic Sentence with Transition

End Sentence:
the Point

moral bankruptcy suggested by this fact is of the bitterest, most terrifying kind.*

Here are the four points to remember about middle paragraphs. First, think of the middle paragraph as a miniature essay, with a beginning, a middle, and an end. Its beginning will normally be its topic sentence, the thesis of this miniature essay. Its middle will develop, explain, and illustrate your topic sentence. Its last sentence will drive home the idea. Second, see that your paragraph is coherent, not only flowing smoothly but with nothing in it not covered by the topic sentence. Third, make your paragraphs full and well developed, with plenty of details, examples, and full explanations, or you will end up with a skeletal paper with very little meat on its bones. Fourth, remember transitions. Though each paragraph is a kind of miniature essay, it is also a part of a larger essay. Therefore, hook each paragraph smoothly to the paragraph preceding it, with some transitional touch in each topic sentence.

INDENTATION

You indent your topic sentence, of course, to signal your paragraph's beginning—usually five letterspaces from your margin. When you want to illustrate a point with a sizable quotation, you indent it twice your original amount from the margin, omitting quotation marks and single-spacing your quotation to simulate insets in smaller print. Also give an extra line of space above and below your quotation, to distinguish it even more clearly from your own text. (See Chapter 14 for good examples.) With short-lined poetry, you will probably need to indent even more, to center it attractively within the frame of your paragraph. To keep your paragraph clear as a whole, try to conclude, after the inset quotation, by coming back out to the margin with a sentence or two of your own. With a

* From "Fifth Avenue Uptown: A Letter from Harlem," in *Nobody Knows My Name* (New York: Dial Press, 1961), pp. 59–61. Copyright © 1960 by James Baldwin. Reprinted by permission of Dial Press. (Originally published in *Esquire*.)

very long quotation, however, which may take up a full block of paragraphing, and more, you had best let the paragraph go at that, and start again with your own text in a new paragraph.

For clear paragraphing with long quotations, which you may want to introduce with no more than a single topic sentence of your own, try to make that introductory sentence long enough to come back out to the margin, making the opening notch of your paragraph clearly visible to your reader. If your quotation itself begins as a paragraph, indent it *one more* full indentation (three, in all, from your margin), to show your reader just how it stands in *its* original text (see p. 33 for an example). A glance at the paragraphs I have been quoting in these pages will also show how this looks. But notice that the printer, since he is using smaller type and boldface print to distinguish the blocks of quotation, indents the whole quotation only the normal paragraph-value. You, however, will indent the whole thing *twice* (plus a third time for a quoted paragraph-beginning), since you cannot reduce the size of your typewriting and should not reduce the size of your handwriting, to spare your reader's eyes.

One more point: if you are quoting and insetting blocks of poetry, you may need "hanging indentation" for the longer lines, indenting their endings under the line-head to keep the line standing clear—perhaps even several times, as you would in quoting Walt Whitman's "There Was a Child Went Forth":

```
There was a child went forth every day,
And the first object he looked upon he became,
And that object became part of him for the day
     or a certain part of the day,
Or for many years or stretching cycles of years.
The early lilacs became part of this child,
And grass and white and red morning glories,
     and white and red clover, and the song
     of the phoebe-bird,
And the third-month lambs . . .
```

Indented Quotation

Hanging Indentation

Hanging Indentation

When quoting poetry in your running text, however, you enclose it in quotation marks, and indicate the line-end with a virgule (slant): "That is no country for old men, the young / In one another's arms. . . ."

EXERCISE

2 Pick a topic sentence from those listed below, or make a similar one of your own, and develop from it a full middle paragraph, remembering the four points: (1) the miniature essay, with beginning, middle, and end; (2) coherence; (3) fullness; (4) transition. Your paragraph should seem to be taken from the middle of a longer paper. You will have to imagine what comes before and after, supplying a transitional *But, Another aspect of, also,* and the like. EXAMPLE, with transitional touch italicized:

TOPIC SENTENCE: The fashions current in the early 1970's suggest an urge to get back to a simpler and more secure past.

    The fashions current in the early 1970's suggest *the same* urge *we have already seen in films and music* to get back to a simpler and more secure past. For the more stylish dressers among us, the Sunday supplements and fashion magazines are featuring 1920's, 1930's, and 1940's styles in both men's and women's clothing. On the street, you can see fashionable women in broad-shouldered and boxy suits, middy blouses, or "sensible shoes" with ugly, clomping heels, all clearly echoing the past. Or you can see modish men wearing huge bow ties for the first time in thirty years. And you see them wearing the wide lapels, fitted waists, flared trousers, and patterned shirts of the 1920's and 1930's. Even for the anti-Establishment or Bohemian dressers among us, the styles current in the early 1970's reflect the urge to get back to the past. Bibbed overalls, work shirts, clodhoppers, bandannas, wide belts, and Western hats, all conjure up images of a frontier past. Undergraduates go to class dressed like "sod-busters," trappers, or miners fresh from the Virginia City of the 1880's. And in any city park you can find a guitar player whose long hair, beard, and fringed leather jacket would make him appear completely at home in the turn-of-the-century West. It is as if all of us, from the solid Establishment to the Bohemian youth-culture, are seeking by our dress to recapture a more simple and secure past. It is as if we are trying to escape the complexity of the 1970's by costuming ourselves in the styles of the past. We are like children who escape by playing dress-up.

1. No matter what the advertisements promise, the X-rated movie usually turns out to be dull and wearisome; it turns out to be two hours of heavy breathing.

2. The computer has contributed to the modern sense of alienation.

3. If the filibuster is supposed to guarantee respect for minority opinion, it usually turns out to be a flagrant waste of time.

4. The new sense of black pride is our increasing awareness of black accomplishments in the past.

5. If women are discriminated against in schools and in industry, they are far more discriminated against in the military.

END PARAGRAPHS: THE INVERTED FUNNEL

Reassert your thesis.

If the beginning paragraph is a funnel, the end paragraph is a funnel upside down: the thought starts moderately narrow—it is more or less the thesis you have had all the time—and then pours out broader and broader implications and finer emphases. The end paragraph reiterates, summarizes, and emphasizes with decorous fervor. This is your last chance. This is what your reader will carry away—and if you can carry *him* away, so much the better. All within decent intellectual bounds, of course. You are the person of reason still, but the person of reason supercharged with conviction, sure of your idea and sure of its importance.

The final paragraph conveys a sense of assurance and repose, of business completed. Its topic sentence should be some version of your original thesis sentence, since the end paragraph is the exact structural opposite and complement of the beginning one. Its transitional word or phrase is often one of finality or summary—*then, finally, thus,* and *so:*

So, the guitar is a means to a finer end.
The environment, then, is in our lungs and at our fingertips.

The paragraph would then proceed to expand and elaborate this revived thesis. We would get a confident assertion that both the music and the friendships are really by-products of an inner alliance;

we would get an urgent plea to clean up our personal environs and strengthen our convictions. One rule of thumb: the longer the paper, the more specific the summary of the points you have made. A short paper will need no specific summary of your points at all; the renewed thesis and its widening of implications are sufficient.

Here is an end paragraph by Sir James Jeans. His transitional phrase is *for a similar reason.* His thesis was that previous concepts of physical reality had mistaken surfaces for depths:

> **The purely mechanical picture of visible nature fails for a similar reason. It proclaims that the ripples themselves direct the workings of the universe instead of being mere symptoms of occurrences below; in brief, it makes the mistake of thinking that the weather-vane determines the direction from which the wind shall blow, or that the thermometer keeps the room hot.***

Here is an end paragraph by Charles Wyzanski, Jr. His transitional phrase is *Each generation,* since he has been talking of the perpetual gap. His thesis was that differences, including those between generations, have stimulated life to higher modes:

> **Each generation is faced with a challenge of making some kind of sense out of its existence. In advance, it knows from the Book of Job and the Book of Ecclesiastes and the Greek drama that there will be no right answer. But there will be forms of answer. There will be a style. As ancient Greece had the vision of *arete* (the noble warrior), as Dante and the Medievalists had the vision of the great and universal Catholic Church, even as the founding fathers of the American Republic had the vision of the new order which they began, so for the young the question is to devise a style—not one that will be good *semper et ubique,* but one for our place and our time, one that will be a challenge to the very best that is within our power of reach, and one that will make us realize, in Whitehead's immortal terms, that for us the only reality is the process.†**

Here is an end paragraph of Professor Richard Hofstadter's. His transitional word is *intellectuals,* carried over from the preceding

---

* *The New Background of Science* (Cambridge: Cambridge University Press, 1933), p. 261.

† "A Federal Judge Digs the Young," *Saturday Review,* July 20, 1968, p. 62.

paragraphs. His thesis was that intellectuals should not abandon their defense of intellectual and spiritual freedom, as they have tended to do, under pressure to comform:

> **This world will never be governed by intellectuals—it may rest assured. But *we* must be assured, too, that intellectuals will not be altogether governed by this world, that they maintain their piety, their longstanding allegiance to the world of spiritual values to which they should belong. Otherwise there will be no intellectuals, at least not above ground. And societies in which the intellectuals have been driven underground, as we have had occasion to see in our own time, are societies in which even the anti-intellectuals are unhappy.***

*"Democracy and Anti-intellectualism in America," *Michigan Quarterly Review*, 59 (1953), 295.

EXERCISE

3 Now try the inverted funnel, in which your topic sentence is some version of the thesis with which you began, and your final paragraph broadens its implications outward to leave the reader fully convinced and satisfied. Using the thesis-sentences in Exercise 1, write two ending paragraphs for imaginary papers. EXAMPLE, with the rephrased thesis (its topic sentence) italicized, and some of the evidence from the paper's middle summarized for emphasis:

> *So, at last, we should add up the real costs of strip-mining; we should admit that the ultimate price of coal is far too high if we must rape the land, poison the streams, and wreck human lives to mine it.* For after the drag-lines have gone, even after the coal itself has been burned, the bills for strip-mining will keep coming in. So far, following the expedient path, we have laid bare more than 2,600 square miles of our land, and we show no signs of stopping. Every year we strip an additional 50,000 acres. Just as we cut down our forests in the nineteenth century and fouled our air in the twentieth, we still blunder along toward ecological and social disaster. Isn't it time to stop?

THE WHOLE ESSAY

You have now discovered the main ingredients of a good essay. You have learned to find and to sharpen your thesis in one sentence, to give your essay that all-important argumentative edge. You have learned to arrange your points in order of increasing interest, and you have practiced disposing of the opposition in a *pro-con* structure. You have seen that your beginning paragraph should look like a funnel, working from broad generalization to thesis. You have tried your hand at middle paragraphs, which are almost like little essays with their own beginnings and ends. And finally, you have learned that your last paragraph should work like an inverted funnel, broadening and embellishing your thesis.

Some students have pictured the essay as a Greek column, with a narrowing beginning paragraph as its top, or capital, and a broadening end paragraph as its base. Others have seen it as a keyhole,* (see the diagram opposite). But either way, you should see a structure, with solid beginning and end, supported by a well-shaped middle. The student's essay that follows illustrates this structure. The assignment, early in the semester, had been to find something in the newspaper from which to develop a thesis, and then to illustrate that thesis with (1) the newspaper item and (2) a personal experience. Again, the writer's language has not fully ripened (I crossed out *like* and *slow* in the third paragraph and put *as* and *slowly* in the margin, for instance). But he had grasped the basic ideas of structure: a thesis well set (though it may wobble a little), and a good sense of Beginning, Middle, and End.

* Mrs. Fran Measley of Santa Barbara, California, has devised for her students a mimeographed sheet to accompany my discussion of structure and paragraphing — to help them to visualize my points, through a keyhole, as it were. I am grateful to Mrs. Measley to be able to include it here.

A LESSON IN PRESTIGE

Broad Subject

Cars are a necessity in American society today, but they are also for pleasure. The many advertisements in magazines, with their shiny cars, and roomy

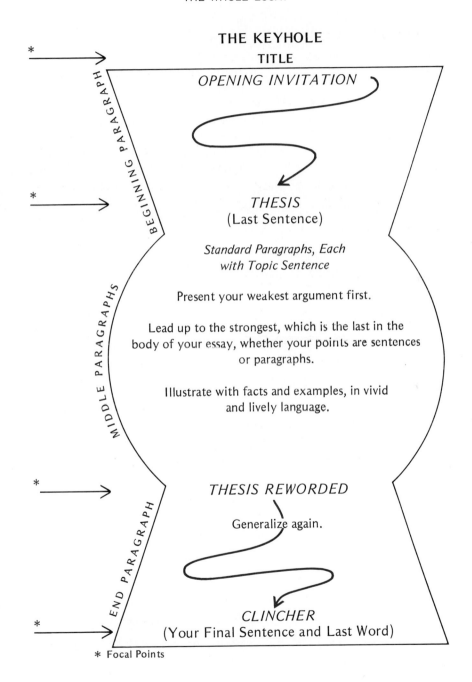

THE KEYHOLE

TITLE

OPENING INVITATION

THESIS
(Last Sentence)

*Standard Paragraphs, Each
with Topic Sentence*

Present your weakest argument first.

Lead up to the strongest, which is the last in the
body of your essay, whether your points are sentences
or paragraphs.

Illustrate with facts and examples, in vivid
and lively language.

THESIS REWORDED

Generalize again.

CLINCHER
(Your Final Sentence and Last Word)

BEGINNING PARAGRAPH

MIDDLE PARAGRAPHS

END PARAGRAPH

* Focal Points

interiors, and beautiful women, emphasize only the
pleasure and not the necessity. A car represents
power and social prestige as well as the pleasure of
driving, and the teen-ager acquires some of that
power and prestige when he borrows the family car.
What he may not realize is that he is also borrowing
danger, and that the car can teach a very expensive

Thesis lesson in social prestige.

Topic Almost every newspaper will list some automo-
Sentence bile accident. Drunk driving is very often listed as
one of the main causes. But statistics show that
young people are frequently involved, even when
alcoholic beverages are not involved. Last night,
The Star Gazette reported a head-on collision in
Middle: which two people aged forty-eight and fifty-three
General were killed, but the ages of the occupants of the
other car, all five of which were also killed, were
all between seventeen and twenty-one. The driver
was aged twenty-one. No one even needs to guess
which car was traveling at high speed and which car
was to blame.

Middle: The real fault, however, was not the speed, but
Personal the social prestige that was the cause of the speed.
I know this from my own experience. I borrowed the
family car once, probably just ~~like~~ as the driver of the
death car had done. I told my father that I only
wanted to pick up three friends and go down for a
Coke, which was really the truth. But we got to
driving around, and the question of how fast the job

would go came up, and I was soon on a ride I will
never forget. I hit 100 on a straightaway, and then
we hit a slight drop in the road. We were sailing
through the air, and the pit of my stomach practically
dropped down to the road where we weren't. We came
down going straight ahead, and careened around, but
didn't spin off or hit anything. We were all shaking and thanking God, and we drove home pretty slow*ly*
and didn't say very much.

The power of prestige can throw caution out the   *Thesis*
window. I did not really want to do it, but the   *Restated*
prestige of driving a nice big car kept me from saying I was afraid and would not do it. The same kind
of fear of not being cool about cars kept the other
occupants from saying anything. I am just thankful
that my dad never knew how close he was to losing
his new car and that I and my friends were not added
to those statistics in the newspaper the next day.
But I learned how powerful and stupid the idea of   *The Point*
prestige really is.

Five
Handling
the
Middle

From the first, we have been looking at what is usually called the deductive order of presentation: first, the thesis, then a "leading away from" it *(de-ducere)*, as you take your reader through an explanation of it, point by point.   This is indeed the basic structure of argument: beginning assertion, middle demonstration, and ending reassertion. In this structure, you have seen the simple and complex *con*'s and *pro*'s of your middle tactics, and the one psychological principle that underlies all possible arrangements of your middle points — the order of ascending interest, the saving of best for last.   Since ascending interest is obviously not limited to argument alone, we shall now look at some of those other possibilities.   There are orders other than *con*-and-*pro,* and climaxes other than those of battle.   The less pugnacious your subject, the less need for assertion and opposition. Your subject may indeed demand, or quietly suggest, other ways of arranging your entire middle section.   The possibilities, inherited more or less with the universe around us, seem to be these several orders: space, time, cause and effect, problem and solution, comparisons and contrasts, natural divisions, induction, deduction, and deduction-induction.

THE ORDER OF SPACE

Arranging details in some kind of tour through space is as natural as walking. When your subject dwells upon physical space—the layout of a campus, for instance—you literally take your reader with you. You simply organize your entire middle section by starting at the gate and conducting him in an orderly progress down the mall or around the quadrangle. Or you show him a rooming house floor by floor, from the apartment by the entry to the garret four flights up, where the graduate student lives on books and cheese. A city's slum or its crowded parking, a river's pollution, a mountain's trees from valley to timberline—any spatial subject will suggest a convenient route, from bottom to top, or top to bottom, left to right, east to west, center to periphery. You will instinctively use a series of spatial signals: *on the right, above, next, across, down the slope.* Your concern is to keep your progress orderly, to help your reader see what you are talking about.

This is exactly the way that Oliver Statler, in his *Japanese Inn,* takes us to the place he loves:

> On this day, I have already progressed along the old Tokaido Road to the village of Yui. A new highway has been built a few hundred yards inland to avoid the congested main street of the village, but leaving Yui it swings back to the shore and runs between the sea wall on my left and the sheer face of Satta Mountain on my right.
>
> It is here, as I drive almost into the sea, that my spirits always quicken, for only Satta Mountain divides Yui from Okitsu, the next village, where my inn lies. . . . I notice men and women diving around the off-shore rocks, sharp knives in hand, hunting for abalone. Beyond them, fishing boats dot Suruga Bay. . . .
>
> At the highest point of the pass, where the path breaks out of the pines and into the open, there is a breath-taking view, and anyone who finds himself there must turn to drink it in. He faces the great sweep of Suruga Bay and the open Pacific beyond, while waves break into flowers on the rocks far beneath his feet. Yui lies on the shore at his left and Okitsu at his right. Beyond Yui, bathed in mist far off on the left, looms the moun-

tainous coast of Izu. Beyond Okitsu, on the right, is one of the loveliest sights in Japan, for the harbor that lies there is protected by a long arm of curving black sand, covered with ancient and twisted pines. This is the fabled beach of Miho. . . .*

* Oliver Statler, *Japanese Inn* (New York: Pyramid Books, Random House, 1962), pp. 14–16. Copyright © 1961, Oliver Statler.

EXERCISE

1 In the following descriptive passages, you will find a number of specific spatial signals. Make a running list of these for each passage. Your list for the first passage would begin like this: *right front—Just a few inches in front—right half—halfway.* . . . Then write a brief explanation of what else the author does to lead your eye spatially around what he is describing, explaining why you think the author chose the particular order he did. What is the logic of his organization?

1. The tread on the right front tire was completely worn away, leaving a smooth surface broken only in places by the frayed tire-cord sticking through the rubber. The rim had been dented in several places, and the hub cap was missing. Of the original five, only four lugnuts held the wheel to the car. Just a few inches in front of the tire, badly bent, was the right half of the front bumper. Much of its chrome had been eaten away by rust, and in one place the metal had been ripped almost halfway through. The fender wasn't much better off. Several sections of the metal were just gone, and what metal remained was covered by highly oxidized and chipped blue paint. Where the headlight had once been mounted, there was now only a rusty hole, and the headlight was precariously fixed to the fender with two metal straps and some masking tape. The turn signal had been broken, and a bare bulb stuck up through the top of the fender. All along the length of the fender where it joined the body there was a corroded and muddy line of rotten metal.

   Resting between the front fenders and covering the engine was a sharply creased and bent hood. In the front, the hood ornament had long since been ripped away, leaving only two rusty holes where it had once been mounted. One of the windshield wipers had disappeared entirely, and the other sagged along the edge of the windshield, half of its rubber segment worn off. The windshield was crazed and clouded with water that had seeped in through the cracks.

2. The Bay of Nukuheva . . . is an expanse of water not unlike in figure the space included within the limits of a horseshoe. It is, perhaps, nine miles in circumference. You approach it from the sea by a narrow entrance, flanked on either side by two small twin islets which soar conically to the height of some five hundred feet. From these the shore recedes on both hands, and describes a deep semi-circle.

   From the verge of the water the land rises uniformly on all sides, with green and sloping acclivities, until from gentle rolling hillsides and moderate elevations it insensibly swells into lofty and majestic heights, whose blue outlines, ranged all around, close in the view. The beautiful aspect of the shore is heightened by deep and romantic glens, which come down to it at almost equal distances, all apparently radiating from a common center, and the upper extremities of which are lost to the eye beneath the shadow of the mountains. Down each of these little valleys flows a clear stream, here and there assuming the form of a slender cascade, then stealing invisibly along until it bursts upon the sight again in larger and more noisy waterfalls, and at last demurely wanders along to the sea.*

   * Herman Melville, *Typee: A Peep at Polynesian Life During Four Months Residence in a Valley of the Marquesas* (New York: The New American Library of World Literature, Inc., 1964), p. 37.

3. The schoolhouse was a log hut, where Colonel Wheeler used to shelter his corn. It sat in a lot behind a rail fence and thorn bushes, near the sweetest of springs. There was an entrance where a door once was, and within, a massive rickety fireplace; great chinks between the logs served as windows. Furniture was scarce. A pale blackboard crouched in the corner. My desk was made of three boards, reinforced at critical points, and my chair, borrowed from the landlady, had to be returned every night. Seats for the children —these puzzled me much. I was haunted by a New England vision of neat little desks and chairs, but, alas! the reality was rough plank benches without backs, and at times without legs. They had the one virtue of making naps dangerous,—possibly fatal, for the floor was not to be trusted.*

   * W. E. B. DuBois, *The Souls of Black Folk, Essays and Sketches.* (Chicago: A. C. McClurg and Company, 1903), p. 57.

4. A few yards from the bench was a high wire fence, too high to leap over, with a curving overhang that made climbing it impossible. Beyond it, a stream—an ordinary, lazy little stream with spring wildflowers along the banks—with nothing to indicate that it divided two worlds. Possibly it was once a river, for its banks were sharply cut and steep. Two Chinese women, in rough gray work-clothes and black buns shining, eased their way down its sides in silence, gathering wild yellow lantana. They had an audience: on the other side of the stream a soldier in mustard-colored uniform idly watched them. The sweltering, shrieking harbor of Hong Kong, with its shops of brocade and jade, its opulent hotels and highrise apartments, its tin-shack squatters and child beggars, lay to the southeast only two hours' train distance away. It could have been at the other end of the earth.*

   * Lisa Hobbs, *I Saw Red China* (New York: McGraw-Hill Book Company, 1966), pp. 1-2. Used with permission of McGraw-Hill Book Company.

5. SCENE. The back room and a section of the bar of Harry Hope's saloon on an early morning in summer, 1912. The right wall of the back room is a dirty black curtain which separates it from the bar. At rear, this curtain is drawn back from the wall so the bartender can get in and out. The back room is crammed with round tables and chairs placed so close together that it is a difficult squeeze to pass between them. In the middle of the rear wall is a door opening on a hallway. In the left corner, built out into the room, is the toilet with a sign "This is it" on the door. Against the middle of the left wall is a nickel-in-the-slot phonograph. Two windows, so glazed with grime one cannot see through them, are in the left wall, looking out on a backyard. The walls and ceiling once were white, but it was a long time ago, and they are now so splotched, peeled, stained and dusty that their color can best be described as dirty. The floor, with iron spittoons placed here and there, is covered with sawdust. Lighting comes from single wall brackets, two at left and two at rear.

   There are three rows of tables, from front to back. Three are in the front line. The one at left-front has four chairs; the one at center-front, four; the one at right-front, five. At rear of, and half between, front tables one and two is a table of the second row with five chairs. A table, similarly placed at rear of front tables two and three, also has five chairs. The third row of tables, four chairs to one and six to the other, is against the rear wall on either side of the door.*

   * Eugene O'Neill, *The Iceman Cometh* in *Selected Plays of Eugene O'Neill* (New York: Random House, Inc., 1969), p. 620.

THE ORDER OF TIME

Like space, time is a natural organizer, ancient and simple. Hour follows hour, day follows day, year follows year, life follows life. Again, you simply take your reader along the natural sequence of what happens—to us, or to nations, or to any items in experience or experiment. We understand processes most clearly by tracking the way they move through time, even processes complicated by other, simultaneous events:

> **And when this wheel turns, that lever tips the food into the trough.**
>
> **While this conveyor moves into the oven, the other one is bringing the chassis to point B.**
>
> **And all the time he talked, his hands were moving the shells and flicking the invisible pea.**

Any event, whether a football game or the inauguration of a president, can be best perceived as you have perceived it—through time—and you can bring your reader to perceive it by following the sequence of things as they happened, stepping aside as necessary to explain background and simultaneous events, guiding your reader along with temporal signposts: *at the same time, now, when, while, then, before, after, next, all the time.*

As Audubon, the nineteenth-century naturalist, describes in his *Ornithological Biography* the passenger pigeon and its astounding flights in masses a mile wide and one hundred and eighty miles long, he naturally presents his observations through the order of time. I have underlined the temporal words in one of his paragraphs:

> **As soon as the pigeons discover a sufficiency of food to entice them to alight, they fly round in circles, reviewing the country below. During their evolutions, on such occasions, the dense mass which they form exhibits a beautiful appearance, as it changes direction, now displaying a glistening sheet of azure, when the backs of the birds come simultaneously into view, and anon, suddenly presenting a mass of rich deep purple. They then pass lower, over the woods, and for a moment are lost among the foliage, but again emerge, and are seen gliding aloft.**

They now alight, but the next moment, as if suddenly alarmed, they take to wing, producing by the flappings of their wings a noise like the roar of distant thunder, and sweep through the forests to see if danger is near. Hunger, however, soon brings them to the ground. When alighted, they are seen industriously throwing up the withered leaves. . . .

You can most clearly explain any kind of development or decline — the civil rights movement, the decay of a neighborhood — by taking your reader up or down the path of time. Following the natural order of events, from past to present, is most usual and probably best. You can sometimes gain dramatic effect, however, by beginning with the present and moving back to former insignificance or splendor, as in describing a battered tenement that was once the mayor's mansion. But you will do your reader a favor by keeping to your order, whether forward or backward, and not reversing it inadvertently somewhere along the way.

Time and space, as the physicists tell us, are functions of one another. You need space to represent time; you need time to cover space. Since your aim is to bring your reader to see what you have seen, you will frequently feel the need to mix the orders of time and space in your presentation, stopping your local history to show your reader a building floor by floor, for example.

Here is a remarkable passage from the concluding chapter of D. H. Lawrence's *The Plumed Serpent,* in which you may profitably observe the orders of space and time blended to perfection. Lawrence first describes his dreamlike Mexican scene in spatial terms, as if it were a spacious and timeless Grecian frieze. Then he moves through time, bringing us to see and feel its stately process. Notice how the implied *now,* the *then,* and the *and at last* fall into natural sequence in the second paragraph, the "timed" paragraph:

Space　　　**A black boat with a red-painted roof and a tall mast was moored to the low breakwater-wall, which rose about a yard high, from the shallow water. On the wall stood loose little groups of white-clad men, looking into the black belly of the ship. And perched immobile in silhouette against the lake, was a black-and-white cow, and a huge monolithic black-and-white bull. The whole silhouette frieze motionless, against the far water that was coloured brown like turtle doves.**

> It was near, yet seemed strange and remote. Two peons fixed a plank gangway up to the side of the boat. <u>Then</u> they began to shove the cow towards it. She pawed the new broad planks tentatively, <u>then</u>, with that slow Mexican indifference, she lumbered unwillingly on to the gangway. They edged her slowly to the end, where she looked down into the boat. <u>And at last</u>, she dropped neatly into the hold.*

Time

This passage continues with undiminished magic for several pages, until the enchanted boat moves slowly off across the lake—"across the waters, with her massive, star-spangled cargo of life invisible." And Lawrence has in fact organized his entire chapter on a span of spaciously slackened time, entitling it "Here!" and implying the somehow static "and now" of deep experience. He has done what you yourself can do. He has taken his reader along the natural orders of both space and time, as his own perception of his subject has suggested them, simply keeping the orders orderly for his reader.

*Copyright 1926 by Alfred A. Knopf, Inc., and renewed in 1954 by Frieda Lawrence Ravagli.

EXERCISE

2 As in Exercise 1, make a running list of the specific words or phrases that signal movement through time in each of the two extended passages that follow — *at the same time, when, then, after,* and so forth — and then follow that list with a brief comment on the effectiveness of the temporal arrangement. Does the author need few or many such signals? How else does he guide us through the flow of time?

1. The battle was joined at 3:48 P.M. in a sullen afternoon. Steaming hard, the two battle cruiser forces made contact off the Skagerrak. Hipper immediately reversed course to draw Beatty back upon the main body of the High Seas Fleet. Beatty, always aggressive, followed hard, despite the fact that four fast battleships of his command were well out of range astern. The battle opened at ranges varying from 10,000 to 17,000 yards, with the British ships clear

against the western skyline, the German ships dull shapes in the mist to the east. Superior German gunnery and defects in the designs of the British battle cruisers quickly told.

By 4 P.M. *Tiger* had been hit, and *Lion*, Beatty's Flagship, had received its fourth hit from *Lützow*. Q. Turret blew up. Major F. J. W. Harvey of the Royal Marines—both legs severed—ordered the handling room crew to flood the magazines and saved the ship with his dying words. At 4:30 *Indefatigable* disappeared in a terrible sheet of flame and smoke; only two of her crew survived. At 4:06 Sir Hugh Evan-Thomas, with Beatty's four fast battleships, got into the fight at 19,000 yards range, and a 15-inch shell from *Barham* cut through *Von der Tann*'s armor and 600 tons of water flooded into the German ship.

The running fight stood on to the south at twenty-three knots as Hipper led Beatty toward the High Seas Fleet. The *Queen Mary* died at 4:26; a column of smoke mushroomed a thousand feet high and great fluttering clouds of paper, bodies, limbs, turret armor, and a lifeboat were hurled high into the air. Nine men out of 1,275 survived.

Princess Royal took a German salvo and a signalman on *Lion*'s flag bridge mistakenly reported her blown up.

Beatty, imperturbable, turned to his flag captain: "Chatfield, there seems to be something wrong with our bloody ships today. Turn two points to port [toward the Germans]."

At 4:50, as the dusk was coming down soon after Scheer's main battle fleet had been sighted, Beatty reversed course to the north, falling back upon Jellicoe in a running fight. Evan-Thomas's tough battleships brought up the rear and gave as good as they received. By 6 P.M. all of *Von der Tann*'s guns were out of action, her decks a shambles; *Seydlitz* was afire; *Lützow* and *Derfflinger* seriously damaged.

The sun was low before the main fleets met at last about 6:15 P.M. Squarely across Scheers course, capping the T of his column, lay the might and majesty of England—*King George V* and *Ajax*; *Iron Duke* and *St. Vincent*; *Tremeraire* and *Marlborough*; *Agincourt* and *Collingwood*; and a host of others bearing proud and ancient names and flying the cross of St. George.

The range was shortened now to 11,000 to 16,000 yards and the British had the advantage of the fading light. At 6:36 Scheer simultaneously reversed the course of his entire fleet—turning southward away from the gaping jaws of the British crescent. But not before he drew blood again; *Invincible*, British battle cruiser, joined the growing company of the departed. Scheer turned north again to the assault at 6:55, partly to try to succor the sinking light cruiser *Wiesbaden* and to aid the crippled *Lützow*. But not for long. His van was the focus for the broadsides of no fewer than thirty-three major British ships. It was too much. Scheer turned again to southward, covering his retirement with a torpedo attack upon the British battleships. Jellicoe, the cautious, turned his battleships *away* from the torpedoes of the retreating Germans and the main fight was over.*

* Hanson W. Baldwin, *World War I: An Outline History* (New York: Harper & Row, Publishers, 1962), pp. 89-92. Copyright © 1962 by Hanson W. Baldwin. Reprinted by permission of Harper & Row, Publishers, Inc.

2. On the evening of the first of March, 1932, an event took place which instantly thrust everything else, even the grim processes of Depression, into the background of American thought — and which seemed to many observers to epitomize cruelly the demoralization into which the country had fallen. The baby son of Colonel and Mrs. Charles A. Lindbergh was kidnapped — taken out of his bed in a second-story room of the new house at Hopewell, New Jersey, never to be seen again alive.

Since Lindbergh's flight to Paris nearly five years before, he had occupied a unique and unprecedented position in American life. Admired almost to the point of worship by millions of people, he was like a sort of uncrowned prince; and although he fiercely shunned publicity, everything he did was so inevitably news that the harder he tried to dodge the limelight, the more surely it pursued him. Word that he had been seen anywhere was enough to bring a crowd running; he was said to have been driven at times to disguise himself in order to be free of mobbing admirers. He now occupied himself as a consultant in aviation; late the preceding summer he and his wife, the former Anne Morrow, had made a "flight to the Orient" which Mrs. Lindbergh later described in lovely prose; and since his meeting with Dr. Alexis Carrel late in 1930 he had begun experiments in the construction of perfusion pumps which were to bring him a high reputation as a biological technician. His new house at Hopewell, remote and surrounded by woods, had been built largely as a retreat in which the Lindberghs could be at peace from an intrusive world.

And now, suddenly, this peace was shattered. Within a few hours of the discovery that the Lindbergh baby's bed was empty — the blankets still held in place by their safety pins — a swarm of police and newspaper men had reached the house and were trampling about the muddy grounds, obliterating clues. And when the

news broke in the next morning's newspapers, the American people went into a long paroxysm of excitement.*

> * Frederick Louis Allen, *Since Yesterday: The Nineteen-Thirties in
> America* (New York: Harper & Row, Publishers), pp. 67-68. Copyright 1939;
> 1940 by Harper and Row, Publishers, Inc. By permission of the publishers.

THE ORDER OF CAUSE AND EFFECT

In the order of cause and effect, sequence has moved from a
merely physical unfolding of space or time into the human domain
of the rational. The *what* of space and time has become the *why* of
existence — or rather, some of our answers to the *why*. *Because* is the
impulse of your thinking here: "Such and such is so *because. . . .*"
You think back through a train of causes, each one the effect of something prior; or you think your way into the future, speculating about
the possible effects of some present cause. In other words, you
organize your explanation in one of two ways:

I. You state a general effect, then deal with its several causes.

II. You state a general cause, then deal with its possible effects.

In Arrangement I, you know the effect (a lost football game, or the
solar system, let us say), and you speculate as to causes. In Arrangement II, you know the cause (a new restriction, or abolishing nuclear
weapons, let us say), and you speculate as to the effects. Arrangement I concerns the past, as you look back for causes; Arrangement
II concerns the future, as you look ahead for effects. Within each arrangement your proportions will vary, depending on where you
want your reader's concern — with causes or with effects.

ARRANGEMENT I: Look for general conditions
and immediate causes.

In Arrangement I, you look over the past for possible causes of
the event you are trying to explain, but you need not, of course, go
back to the beginning of time. You need not trace the quarterback's

bad pass clear back to Newton's laws of motion and gravity. You will find that causes separate into, first, several *conditions*—a weak defense, strong opponents, a wet field, a series of disheartening breaks—and, second, one or two *immediate causes*—an unblocked tackler, a slip in the mud. Your thesis from such an analysis would probably be: "Not quarterback Smith, but an unusual concentration of bad luck, lost us the game." Now, since your introductory paragraph and thesis have told the reader all he will care to know about the dismal *effect* (the lost game), you will give your middle over entirely to *immediate causes* and *conditions*. The best plan is probably to write a descriptive paragraph that lets your reader see the *immediate causes* (the unblocked tackler, the slip, the bad pass, the interception), and then to organize the *conditions* partly by chronology, partly by ascending order of interest, something like this:

1. **The bad weather [of least interest]**
2. **The breaking of the star's arm during practice early in the season**
3. **The previous games unexpectedly lost**
4. **The other side's unusually strong team**
5. **The train's delay, which further tired and disheartened the players**

Your concluding paragraph would return again to your thesis ("unusual bad luck") and some reminder of *immediate causes* (the bad pass).

You will probably notice, as you try to explain causes and effects, that they do not always run in a simple linear sequence, one thing following another, like a row of falling dominoes. Indeed, mere sequence is so famously untrustworthy in tracing causes that one of the classical errors of thought has been named *post hoc, ergo propter hoc* ("after this, therefore because of this"). It is wrong, in other words, to suppose that *A* caused *B* because *A* preceded *B*. The two may have been entirely unrelated. But the greatest danger in identifying causes is to fasten upon a single cause while ignoring others of equal significance. Both your thinking and your persuasiveness will be better if you do not insist, to the exclusion of all else, that Jones's failure to block the tackler lost the game.

In the lost ball game, you were interested in explaining causes, and you organized your middle entirely around *causes,* handling *effects* only in your beginning and end. But sometimes your interest will lie with *effects.* When describing a slum problem, for instance, you might in a single sentence set aside the causes as irrelevant, as water over the dam, as so much spilt milk: "perhaps caused by inefficiency, perhaps by avarice, perhaps by the indifference of Mayor Richman." Your interests, as I have said, will dictate your proportions of cause and effect. You might well write an essay that balances the slum's causes and effects in equal proportions: a paragraph each on inefficiency, avarice, and the mayor's indifference, then a paragraph each on ill health, poor education, and hopelessness.

In the following example, in three paragraphs, I have begun and ended with the *effect* (the peculiar layout of a town). First, I located the *immediate cause* (cattle) as my thesis, and then, in the middle paragraph, I moved through the cause and its *conditions* up to the *effect* again—the town as it stands today:

North of the Tracks

Effect

If you drive out west from Chicago, you will notice something happening to the towns. After the country levels into Nebraska, the smaller towns are built only on one side of the road. When you stop for a rest, and look south across the broad main street, you will see the railroad immediately beyond. All of these towns spread northward from the tracks. Why? As

Cause

you munch your hamburger and look at the restaurant's murals, you will realize that the answer is cattle.

Conditions

These towns were the destinations of the great cattle-drives from Texas. They probably had begun at the scattered watering places in the dry land. Then the wagon-trails and, finally, the transcontinental railroad had strung them together. Once the railroad came, the whole southwest could raise cattle for the slaughterhouses of Chicago. The droves of cattle came up from the south, and all of these towns reflect the traffic: corrals beside the tracks to the south, the road for passengers and wagons paralleling the tracks on the northern side, then, along the road, the row of hotels, saloons, and businesses, with the town spreading northward behind the businesses.

The cattle-business itself shaped these one-sided Nebraska towns. The conditions in which this immediate cause took root were the growing population in the East and the railroad that connected the plains of the West, and Southwest, with the tables of New York. The towns took their hopeful being north of the rails, on the leeward side of the vast cattle drives from the south. The trade in cattle has now changed, all the way from Miami to Sacramento. But the great herds of the old Southwest, together with the transcontinental railroad and man's need to make a living, plotted these Western towns north of the tracks.

Cause

Effect

ARRANGEMENT II: Look for future effects, but be reasonable.

Arrangement II is rarer, and more conjectural. Your order of presenting cause and effect is reversed. You are looking to the future. You state a known cause (a new restriction on dormitory hours) or a hypothetical cause ("If this restriction is passed"), and then you speculate about the possible, or probable, effects. Your procedure will then be much the same as before. But for maximum persuasiveness, try to keep your supposed effects, which no one can really foresee, as nearly probable as you can. Occasionally, of course, you may put an improbable hypothetical cause to good use in a satiric essay, reducing some proposal to absurdity: "If all restrictions were abolished. . . ." "If no one wore clothes. . . ." Or the improbable *if* may even help clarify a straightforward explanation of real relationships, as in the following excerpt from *Time* magazine's report on Fred Hoyle, the British astronomer and mathematician who has been modifying Newton's gravity and Einstein's relativity. The paragraph states the general condition, proposes its hypothetical cause with an *if*, then moves to the effects, first in temporal order and then in order of human interest:

The masses, and therefore the gravity, of the sun and the earth are partly due to each other, partly to more distant objects such as the stars and galaxies. According to Hoyle, if the universe were to be cut in half, local solar-system gravitation would double, drawing the earth closer to the sun. The pressure in the sun's center would increase, thus raising its temperature, its generation of energy, and its brightness. Before being seared into a lump of charcoal, a man on earth would find his weight increasing from 150 to 300 lbs.

EXERCISE

3 Below is a list of statements about the population of the United States, some general, some particular. First arrange them in a suitable order for Arrangement I (pp. 76–79), then arrange them again in a suitable order for Arrangement II (pp. 79–80). Remember that subordinate points should also follow the order of ascending importance.

1. An expanding population quickly expends resources and energy for new housing, and often neglects existing housing.
2. The annual death rate has declined slightly since 1940 (a decrease of slightly over one death per thousand of population).
3. Rapidly increasing population over-strains the classrooms in public schools, and has already forced enlarged classes and, in some instances, half-day sessions.
4. Despite our more recent concern and awareness, the total population of the United States has continued to increase alarmingly since the mid-1940's.
5. The annual birth rate per thousand of population has declined (15.6 in 1972 compared with the 1960 rate of 23.7). Nevertheless, 3.3 million babies were born in 1972, almost exactly the same number as twenty years previously.
6. An increasing population strains college facilities; the number of college students doubled between 1960 and 1970 and may be half again as large by 1980.
7. Immigration has gradually increased in recent years (385,000 in 1972 compared with 292,000 in 1964).
8. An expanding population forces cities to fill land once used for recreation and crops with shopping centers, streets, and houses.
9. A rapidly expanding population eventually crowds more people into less space, increasing their vulnerability to disease, to squalor, and to strife.

THE ORDER OF PROBLEM AND SOLUTION

In the order of problem and solution, you are again exploiting a natural order. You describe the problem for your reader; you then suggest solutions. This order serves well even for historical subjects. The Panama Canal, for instance, posed problems of politics, geology, and human survival. Your thesis would state the threefold problem; your middle would show its three solutions, one by one. Or you might choose a more obviously balanced approach, making your thesis "The Canal posed three major problems," and then organizing your middle in two equal parts:

I. The problems
   A. Difficulties of agreement between a small government and a large one
   B. Difficulties with variations in terrain and differing sea levels
   C. Yellow fever
II. The solutions
   A. The Canal Zone, sovereignty, payments
   B. Distance, lakes, and locks
   C. General Gorgas and the mosquito

This topic could expand into a considerable essay, complete with footnotes, but it also might turn out nicely in three paragraphs, based on articles in the *Encyclopaedia Britannica:*

Digging the Panama Canal

Dig this! The idea of the Panama Canal is almost as old as Columbus. When the Spanish explorers finally conceded that any passage westward to China, which Columbus had sought, was blocked by two continents and a thin isthmus, the idea of a canal was born. In 1550, Antonio Galvão began the long argument for a canal through Nicaragua, Panama, or Darien. When the United States opened the canal on August 15, 1914, the dreams of almost four centuries came true, and mountainous problems had been solved. Ultimately, the canal had posed three major problems.

Subject

Thesis

Problem 1

Solution to 1

Problem(s) 2

Solutions to 2

Problem 3

Solution to 3

Thesis Restated

Politics, geology, and human survival had confronted canal-planners from the beginning. A French company, organized in 1880 to dig the canal, repeatedly had to extend its treaties at higher and higher prices as the work dragged on. Uneasy about the French, the United States made treaties with Nicaragua and Costa Rica to dig along the other most feasible route. This political threat, together with the failure of the French and the revolt of Panama from Colombia, finally enabled the United States to buy the French rights and negotiate new treaties, which, nevertheless, continue to cause political trouble to this day. Geology also posed its ancient problems: how to manage torrential rivers and inland lakes; whether to build a longer but more enduring canal at sea level, or a shorter, cheaper, and safer canal with locks. Economy eventually won, but the problem of yellow fever and malaria, which had plagued the French, remained. By detecting and combating the fever-carrying mosquito, William Gorgas solved these ancient tropical problems. Without him, the political and geological solutions would have come to nothing.

In the end, of course, all three problems are human, as the canal answered the ancient human dream of a westward passage to China. Political tensions are nothing but human competition, and geology succumbs to human drives. And to dig a canal through the jungle, man had to triumph over the mosquito. The victories over the terrain and the mosquito remain virtually complete. But the ancient commercial impulse, which launched the idea of the canal in the first place, and the political tensions, which include the worldwide launching of larger navies with atomic submarines, continue to surround the old incision across the Isthmus of Panama.

Any problem and its solutions can produce an essay along these lines—choosing a college, or something to wear (if you want to be light-hearted), making an apartment or a commune work, building the Eiffel Tower or the pyramids.

EXERCISE

4 Using the order of problem and solution, write a two- or three-paragraph paper in which you describe some particularly interesting architectural or engineering accomplishment. Choose any topic you wish. For example, how did architects design the high-rise buildings in San Francisco so that they would withstand the shock of the severe earthquakes of 1971? Or how did medieval man make a suit of armor? Or how do you plan to convert your VW bus into a camper that will sleep four people? In the first paragraph, state the problem. Then go on to describe how the problem could be, or was, solved. Here, for example, is one student's paper:

NOTHING PRIMITIVE ABOUT IT

Stonehenge, the gigantic prehistoric construction on Salisbury Plain in England, cannot fail to fascinate us with a number of nearly unanswerable questions. How long has it been there? Who built it? Why? But of the questions Stonehenge raises, none is more intriguing than "*How* was it built?" How did these primitive people, whose *Thesis* only tools were rock, bone, or crudely fashioned sticks, who had not yet even discovered the wheel, manage to transport the huge rocks, *Problem 1* most of them more than twenty feet in length and weighing over thirty tons, more than twenty miles overland? And by what ingenuity did they manage, having transported the rocks, to stand them on end and *Problem 2* support them so that now, thousands of years later, most of them still stand? What primitive engineering geniuses were these?

Transporting the stones from their original site at Marlborough Downs, some twenty miles to the north of Stonehenge, must have *Solutions* been, by any of the possible means, a very slow process. One pos- *to 1* sibility is that hundreds of men, some pulling on the rock, some cutting down trees and filling in holes as they went, simply dragged the stones over the bare ground. Or perhaps they used snow or mud to "grease" the path. Foot by foot, and day by day, they may have dragged the rocks all the way from Marlborough Downs to Stonehenge. Another guess is that these primitive men, even though they had not yet invented the wheel, knew about using logs as rollers. If so, perhaps they mounted each stone on a sledge, and rolled the sledge slowly forward, workmen placing logs in its path as it moved. Such a method, while a good deal easier than dragging the rock along the ground, would still have required as many as seven or eight hundred men, and perhaps as much as a decade to move all the stones. A third possibility is that the stones were moved along riverbeds, the shallow water helping to buoy the weight, and the muddy banks helping to slide the weight along. Though much less direct than the overland route, the riverbed route would have provided these primitive men with a relatively clear path that ran approximately halfway from the stones' point of origin to their final location. Of course, the point is that any of these three means of transporting the stones must have been an incredibly laborious task, occupying as many as a thousand men, year after year after year.

Solutions to 2

Lifting the stones into an upright position, once they had been transported, was another triumph of ingenuity and brute strength. Apparently, the workmen dug closely fitted holes where they wanted the stones eventually to stand. Probably they cut away one side of the hole, the side nearest the stone, to form a ramp. Perhaps they also lined the hole with wooden skids. Then gradually they eased the stone down the ramp until it rested in a tilted position at the bottom of the hole. Next, they used brute strength, some men pushing, some pulling on primitive ropes, to raise the rock into a vertical position. If we suppose each man lifted only his own weight, say 150 pounds, it might have taken as many as 400 men to stand the stones upright. Finally, while some workers held the rock in position, others quickly filled in the excavation left by the ramp. For many months afterward they probably refilled and pounded the dirt until it was completely firm. The fact that most of the rocks are still standing after thousands of years is testimony of their planning and their workmanship.

Thesis Restated

We may never know quite why these primitive men chose to build Stonehenge, or who the men were. We may never know where they came from, or where they went. In Stonehenge, however, they have left a testament to their perseverance and their ingenuity Clearly, they rivaled any of the builders of the ancient world.

THE ORDER OF COMPARISON AND CONTRAST

Comparison and contrast is another basic order of thought, another natural means of organizing the middle of your essay, or the whole of it, or an occasional muscular paragraph. I have already mentioned the essential tactics, with the sheep and the goats, in

Chapter 3, and we shall look at these tactics again when we talk about ways to develop paragraphs in the next chapter. The process is indeed recurrent. It may be the very basis of thought itself, or at least one of the primary elements. All knowledge involves comparing things for their similarities and noticing their contrasting differences. We group all people together as People, and then tell them apart as individuals.

We instinctively know our friends in this way, for instance. Two of them drift side by side in our thoughts. We are comparing them. They are both boys; they are the same age and stature; we like them both. But one bubbles up like a mountain spring, and the other runs deep. Their appearances, mannerisms, and tastes match their contrasting personalities. One's room is messy; the other's is neat. One races his car; the other collects stamps. We compare the similar categories—looks, habits, hobbies, goals—and contrast the differences. In the process, we have come to know both friends more completely.

Your thoughts will intuitively pair the items and contrast them. You simply organize your comparing-contrasting essay along this pattern of thought. Let me repeat. Make your comparisons point by point, nose for nose, hobby for hobby, to keep your reader comfortably in touch with the similarities and differences. Do not write all about sheep and then all about goats. The reader cannot see the contrasting points unless they are side by side.

Of course, when writing about people or other familiar things—houses, towns, stadiums—you can risk writing a complete sketch of one for a paragraph or so, followed by an equivalent sketch of the other, because we are accustomed to thinking in these terms, and your reader can keep the details easily in mind:

> My father is tall, blond, and outgoing. He works hard and plays hard. He does everything at a cheerful run, whether he is off to a sales conference or off to the golf course with his usual foursome on Saturday mornings. As a boy . . . .
> My mother is almost completely the opposite. She is small and quiet. Even her dark brown hair, which is naturally wavy, has a certain repose about it. She has a pleasant smile, and bursts into laughter at my father's jokes, but she never stirs up fun on her own. She never seems to hurry. She hums at her work, and the house seems to slip into order without effort.

> She likes to play bridge with a few close friends, but she is just
> as happy with a book. As a girl . . . .

On less familiar ground, however, the principle of contrasting point by point is imperative. If you were to compare and contrast two short stories—Hemingway's "My Old Man" and Sherwood Anderson's "I Want to Know Why," for instance—you would be tempted to follow your first impulse, describing Hemingway's story for a page or two, then turning to Anderson with Hemingway comfortably behind you, and your reader wondering where you are. Don't fall into this familiar trap. Establish in your Beginning that the stories are similar, and therefore worthy of comparison: both are about horse racing; both are about young boys who painfully discover the ways of the world. You may wish to use a purely expository thesis, asserting simply that the comparison illuminates both stories, perhaps in some particular way. But you will go farther and deeper, and be more interesting, I am convinced, if you can see your way to asserting, and demonstrating through your comparison, that one is better than the other, perhaps "But Hemingway's story ultimately proves deeper than Anderson's." Now work your way through the Middle, point by point, contrasting the differences. Though both boys are young, Anderson's is somewhat older and more independent. In both stories, horse racing is corrupt, but Hemingway's gamblers are much more cynical. And so on, item by item, with brief illustrations of each in turn.

The underlying principle in comparing and contrasting is, again, contrasting point by point. If you can choose a side, so that your comparison takes on an argumentative edge, your essay will probably take on additional meaning and depth, as you seek to prove your thesis.

> Sheep are more useful than goats.
> Tom is really a better person than Bill.
> Hemingway's story is deeper than Anderson's.
> Zuñi society was superior to that of the more powerful Apaches.

EXERCISE

5 Here are two famous poetic birds, Shelley's skylark ("To a Skylark") and
Yeats's bird of hammered gold ("Sailing to Byzantium"). Write a paragraph comparing and contrasting the two, point for point, beginning with a
topic sentence that covers your comparative or contrastive aim (something
like "Both . . . are really imaginary" or "X's bird is more —————— than Z's"):

> Hail to thee, blithe spirit!
> Bird thou never wert,
> That from Heaven, or near it,
> Pourest thy full heart
> In profuse strains of unpremeditated art.
>
> *Shelley*

> . . . such a form as Grecian goldsmiths make
> Of hammered gold and gold enameling
> To keep a drowsy emperor awake,
> Or set upon a golden bough to sing
> To lords and ladies of Byzantium
> Of what is past, or passing, or to come.*
>
> *Yeats*

* From *Collected Poems* (New York: Macmillan Publishing Co.). Copyright
1928 by Macmillan Publishing Co., Inc., renewed 1956 by Georgie Yeats. Reprinted with permission of Macmillan, M. B. Yeats, Miss Anne Yeats, and Macmillan
of London & Basingstoke.

THE ORDER OF NATURAL DIVISIONS

Many subjects fall into natural or customary partitions, which
supply you with a kind of dialectic contrast not necessarily hostile,
and even blandly jointed, like a good roast of pork, ready for carving:
freshman, sophomore, junior, senior; Republicans, Democrats; right,
middle, left; legislative, executive, judicial. Similarly, any manu-

facturing process, or any machine, will already have distinct steps and parts. These customary divisions will help your reader, since he knows something of them already. Describe the Democratic position on inflation, and he will naturally expect your description of the Republican position to follow. If no other divisions suggest themselves, you can often divide your essay into a consistent series of parallel answers, or "reasons for," or "reasons against" — something like this:

A broad liberal education is best:
I. It prepares you for a world of changing employment.
II. It enables you to function well as a citizen.
III. It enables you to make the most of your life.

EXERCISES

6 Here are a number of topics that fall conveniently into natural divisions. For each topic, list the divisions that occur to you.

1. Causes affecting the rate at which a population grows.
2. Levels of government.
3. The "lunatic-fringe."
4. The early stages of space technology.
5. Undersea exploration.
6. Geological eras.
7. Mathematics in public schools.
8. Governmental response to the Depression.
9. Defrauding insurance companies.
10. Inequities in the tax structure.

7 List five topics of your own and indicate the natural divisions of those topics that would help you organize an essay.

INDUCTIVE ORDER

Induct means "to lead in"; *deduct* means "to lead away from." With inductive order, you simply lead your reader in — by successive questions and their dismissal, or partial answers — to your main and conclusive point. "Is it this? Well, no." "Then may it be this? No, not exactly this either." "Then how about this? Ah, yes, this seems to be it." The deductive order, beginning with your thesis and then explaining it, is much more usual, and usually clearer. But the inductive order has suspense, a kind of intellectual excitement, if you can keep your answer from slipping out.

Inductive order probably works best for short essays, since you must keep the cat in the bag, and you can't keep him in too long. You simply use a question for your thesis-sentence and then simulate for your reader the train of thought by which you arrived at a conclusion, as I did in the following passage:

> . . . **What does Walt Whitman mean when he says "I celebrate myself"?**
>
> **Can he be simply an egotist? The pronoun "I" dominates his writing. "I will effuse egotism, and show it underlying all," he writes. He speaks of generations of Americans passing with "faces turned sideways or backward toward me to listen, / With eyes retrospective toward me." He loves to see the smoke of his own breath, and to hear the beating of his own heart. Yet this egotism is somehow not offensive. He is something more than a simple egotist.**
>
> **Perhaps he takes himself as the common man, since his "I" represents others as well as himself: "I am of old and young, of the foolish as much as the wise,/ . . . Maternal as well as paternal, a child as well as a man." All men and women are his equals, his brothers and sisters, and he says a great deal about democracy. We soon realize that Whitman could not have done many of the things the "I" claims to have done. The "I" has been at sea with John Paul Jones; he is an artillery man in a bombarded fort; he has been a trapper, a fisherman off Newfoundland. The "I," then, is both the actual Whitman and his imaginative identification of himself with all walks of American life.**
>
> **But the "I" seems even more than this. The "I" has slept**

Thesis Question

Possible Answer Rejected

Partial Answer

*Complete
Answer*

for ages, has evolved upward through the eons, has been carried in a dinosaur's mouth. He has subsumed in himself all the ideas of God: "Taking myself the exact dimensions of Jehovah, / Lithographing Kronos, Zeus his son, and Hercules his grandson. . . ." Like the hawk, he sounds his "barbaric yawp over the roofs of the world." He dissolves into the next fold of the future, and waits for us somewhere up ahead. The "I" is now the spirit of life itself. So when Whitman celebrates himself, he is also celebrating the spirit of democracy and the Life Force, which are evident to him no less in geological history than in the men and women and blades of grass around him, and in his own present breathing and heartbeat.

This will give you an idea of inductive order. You may well use a short inductive section in a longer essay, especially for dismissing the opposition's arguments by putting them as questions ("Do we want unlimited freedom?") and then reducing them to absurdities. But, as I say, a wholly inductive essay is usually short, and you won't even find many of these.

EXERCISE

8 Write a paragraph in which you start with a question, and then, dismissing partial answers, lead your reader to your main and conclusive point. ("What is A? It might be B, and I know a lot of people think it is C, but I think it is really D.") Here is an example taken from an interview with a man reminiscing about his experiences during the Depression:

Topical Question

Answer 1

Answer 2

Answer 3

What was the worst thing about the Depression? Well, I don't know. I guess for some folks it was losing their savings. For us that wasn't so bad. I only had about $400 in the McLain County Bank when it closed and I got some of that back later, about 10 cents on the dollar. Then too, being out of work was rough for a lot of people. But even that wasn't so bad for me. I lost my job with the coal company in 1931, but we lived on a farm. And with that and some odd jobs I picked up, I managed to keep pretty busy until I got a steady job again. Of course, I know a lot of people didn't have enough to eat or enough to wear during the Depression. For us that wasn't too bad. We grew most of our own food, and my wife is pretty handy at sewing, so we got by. Nothing very fancy, you understand, but we managed. No, I guess for us the worst thing about the Depression was we got to feeling after a while that times just weren't ever going to get better. It just went on too long. For us, things got a little rough in 1931 and they stayed pretty rough until I got a job with the Highway Commission in 1938. Seven years is a long time to keep hoping. It just went on so long. *Main Answer (Thesis)*

DEDUCTIVE ORDER

Deductive is the opposite of inductive, of course — a leading *away* from your general proposition. Like its inductive counterpart, deductive order is the writer's imitation of a way of thought. Inductively, putting two and two together, we think our way into a general truth: "four." Deductively, we think out the consequences of a general truth, thinking *away* from the idea of four to find its relevance for this or that particular two or one. Deductive logic, as we shall see in Chapter 10, has become a specialized procedure of thought. But, for the present, the large-to-small order of deduction will help to fix in mind the most common, useful, and dependable way of arranging an essay, as I have indicated from the beginning. You set down your thesis, your general proposition, then *explain* it in detail and at length. The mode of induction is question and partial answer; the mode of deduction is assertion and explanation. As we have seen, however, the usual deductive order does not simply begin with your Big Idea and then dwindle down to nothing. You start with your thesis, then jump down to your smallest small and work progressively uphill until you again reach your thesis, which is now restated as your conclusion and rounded off in a concluding paragraph.

In short, the deductive order of presentation is the normal one we have been talking about all along. To change your little inductive essay on Whitman into a deductive one, you would simply make your thesis an assertion to be demonstrated rather than a question to be answered: "Whitman's 'I' represents not only Whitman himself, but also the spirit of democracy and the Life Force." You would then proceed with the same evidence, and in the same general order, from actual Whitman, through democracy, to the great force of life itself. Rather than the question that opened your second paragraph, you would assert: "At first, Whitman may strike the reader as a simple egotist." Rather than the tentative "Perhaps" that opened your third paragraph, you would assert: "We soon discover that Whitman's 'I' represents others, as well as himself."

EXERCISE

9 Take your inductive paragraph from the previous exercise, turn the order around, and expand your paragraph into a brief deductive essay, with thesis to be demonstrated rather than question to be answered. You will probably find that in switching from induction to deduction your paper will expand almost by itself, as you fill out your thoughts and explanations for your reader. EXAMPLE:

Topic

 For most Americans, the stock market crash was not the worst thing about the Depression. True, it carried away billions of dollars of investors' money, but relatively few of us felt directly affected. Few of us owned stock, and for most of us the market collapse was something that happened to other people, not to us. Of course, as we found out, the stock market collapse was only the trigger, and soon more and more Americans found their lives directly affected. By 1932, 25 percent of the work force was without jobs. Yet, for many Americans, the worst thing about the Depression was not the bank closures, or being out of work, or even shortages of food and clothing. For many of us,

Thesis

the worst thing about the Depression was that it lasted so long we almost gave up hoping that times would ever get better. George Harris of Wellsburg, West Virginia, is a good example of how the Depression hit most of us.

Demonstration

 In 1931, Mr. Harris had a job with the Green Coal Company as a tender on a boat that pushed coal barges up and down the Ohio River. His income was generally pretty good, and Mr. Harris had managed to buy a small farm just outside town. But cutbacks in industrial production, particularly in the production of steel, soon forced cutbacks in coal mining as well. And in August of 1931 Mr. Harris was laid off. The next year, in 1932, the McLain County Bank closed, and with it went the only savings the Harrises had, $400, although later he did manage to collect 10 percent of his lost savings. And so for the next seven years Mr. Harris bounced from job to job. Whatever he could get: a few days here, a few days there. He was thus able to hold onto his small farm, and on it he raised most of the food for the Harris family for the next seven years. Mrs. Harris, too, helped to cut corners by making most of the family's clothes, and by repairing things when they wore out. In this way, taking it one day at a time, and living as simply and as frugally as possible, the Harrises managed to get by until, in 1938, Mr. Harris once again got a secure and well-paying job with the County Road Commission.

So the Harrises are a good example of how the Depression hit *Restatement* many Americans. They lost some savings, they lost their jobs, they had to tighten their belts, but they managed to get by. For them, the worst thing about the Depression was not the deprivation; it was simply that the Depression went on year after year. As Mr. Harris says, "Seven years is a long time to keep hoping. It just went on so long."

DEDUCTIVE–INDUCTIVE ORDER

Actually, you can write a good essay about halfway between the inductive and deductive modes. The basic framework is deductive, a general thesis followed by its successive explanations in ascending order of interest and importance. But the inner movement is mostly inductive, a fairly large number of questions replacing the assertions that would otherwise guide the progress, section by section. You may set the mode very easily by putting your thesis as a broadly general question.

The more direct the question, the more purely inductive the essay. You launch a completely inductive essay when your questioning thesis asks for one specific answer among the several possibilities you will entertain and reject before letting the reader know your answer: "Is Whitman an egotist?" ("Not really"); "Should we make welfare payments?'' (''Yes''). The more your question suggests your answer, the more deductive you become: ''Is Whitman something more universal than a mere egotist?''; ''Are welfare payments really the socialistic and bureaucratic evil they are so often said to be?''

Virginia Woolf's famous essay ''How Should One Read a Book?'' is an almost perfect example of the deductive-inductive mode, as both her title and her thesis suggest. Even her questioning title implies an unstated deductive assertion: ''One should read a book, and read it the right way.'' Her thesis, also a question, likewise implies an unstated deductive assertion, which her essay proceeds to illustrate: ''How are we to bring order into this multitudinous chaos and so get the deepest and widest pleasure from what we read?'' Her thesis-question does not say exactly *how* — her essay proceeds to fill in the answer somewhat inductively — but the question clearly suggests that we must bring order from chaos to achieve the deep and wide pleasure she sees as the purpose of reading. A thesis-question similar to Woolf's may get you a very nice deductive-inductive essay:

> **How should one plan a vacation?**
> **What is the greatest reward in sports?**
> **What makes an effective teacher?**

You may also set the deductive-inductive mode by trimming a fully explicit thesis to get something of the open-endedness of a question. You simply trim the full-blown thesis at both ends, cutting away from the beginning the concessive ''Although . . .'' and from the end the explanatory ''because. . . .'' Your most completely stated thesis might be:

> **Although welfare payments may offend the rugged individualist, we should nevertheless have a system of welfare payments because they relieve much want and anxiety, and they enable many a fatherless family to maintain its integrity.**

To remake this a thesis for a partially inductive essay, you simply trim it to something like: **All in all, we need some system to help those in need.** You then proceed with a series of questions, or open-ended assertions, supplying the answers and *because*'s as you go:

a. But what about the threat to our ideal of self-sufficiency?
b. Private organizations already provide a number of charitable services.
c. But what about the actual needs of fatherless, poor families?
d. Can our affluent society care for its less fortunate members?

And so on, until you have reached and dealt with the want, anxiety, and frustration that are the center of your submerged but emerging thesis.

EXERCISE

10 Here are two essays in which the internal movement is essentially inductive. That is, the stress tends to fall at the end of the essay rather than at the beginning. In one of the two essays, however, an initial deductive framework helps to clarify the writer's central proposition, to give us a preview of the thesis before the paper's conclusion drives home his main idea. Read the two essays, and then answer the questions that follow.

THE SIGNS OF A GOOD GOVERNMENT

When, therefore, one asks what in absolute terms is the best government, one is asking a question which is unanswerable because it is indeterminate; or alternatively one might say that there are as many good answers as there are possible combinations in the absolute and relative positions of peoples.

But if it is asked by what signs one can tell whether a given people is well or badly governed, that is another matter; and the question of fact can be answered.

Even so, it is not really answered, because everyone will want to answer it in his own way. Subjects prize public tranquillity; citizens the freedom of the individual — the former prefer security of possessions, the latter security of person; subjects think the best government is the most severe, citizens that it is the mildest; the former want crimes to be punished, the latter want them prevented; subjects think it is a good thing to be feared by their neighbours, citizens prefer to be ignored by them; the former are satisfied so long as money circulates, the latter demand that the people shall have bread. But even if there were agreement on these and suchlike points, should we be any more advanced? Moral dimensions have no precise standard of measurement; even if we could agree about signs, how should we agree in appraisal?

For myself, I am always astonished that people should fail to recognize so simple a sign, or be so insincere as not to agree about it. What is the object of any political association? It is the protection and the prosperity of its members. And what is the surest evidence that they are so protected and prosperous? The numbers of their population. Then do not look beyond this much debated evidence. All other things being equal, the government under which, without external aids like naturalization and immigration, the citizens increase and multiply most, is infallibly the best government. That under which the people diminishes and wastes away is the worst. Statisticians, this is your problem: count, measure, compare.*

HOW CITIES OR STATES PREVIOUSLY INDEPENDENT MUST BE GOVERNED AFTER OCCUPATION

When those states which have been accustomed to live in freedom under their own laws are acquired, there are three ways of trying to keep them. The first is to destroy them, the second to go and live therein, and the third to allow them to continue to live under their own laws, taking a tribute from them and creating within them a new government of a few which will keep the state friendly to you. For since such a government is the creature of the prince it will know that it cannot exist without his friendship and authority and is thus certain to do its best to support him, and a city accustomed to freedom can be more easily held through its citizens than in any other way if it is desired to preserve it. Here we have the examples of the Spartans and the Romans. The Spartans held Athens and Thebes and created in both a government of a few; nonetheless they lost them. The Romans, in order to hold Capua, Carthage, and Numantia, razed them and did not lose them. They tried to keep Greece in the same way the Spartans had, permitting the country to be free under its own laws, but in this they were not successful inasmuch as they were compelled to destroy many cities of that province in order to hold it, for in truth there is no sure way of holding them other than by their ruin. And whoever becomes master of a city accustomed to living in freedom and does not

---

* Jean-Jacques Rousseau, *The Social Contract,* translated by Maurice Cranston (Baltimore, Penguin Books Inc., 1968), pp. 129–130. Reprinted by permission of A. D. Peters and Company Ltd., London.

destroy it may expect to be destroyed by it himself, for it has always as an incentive to rebellion the name of liberty and its own ancient laws which neither time nor favors received can cause the citizens to forget. And whatever action be taken or provision be made, as long as the inhabitants are not separated or dispersed, that name and those laws are never forgotten but provide a rallying point in every emergency, as is shown by the case of Pisa after many years of subjection to the Florentines. Cities or provinces used to living under a prince are accustomed to obedience, and when the ruling house becomes extinct they are unable to agree on a successor and, having no experience of self-government, they are slow in taking up arms and so with greater ease a prince may overcome them and feel secure in his possession of them. In republics there is greater life, greater hatred, more desire of vengeance, and the memory of their ancient liberty gives them no rest; so the safest way is either to extinguish them or go and live in them.*

1. What is Rousseau's thesis?

2. Do you find any anticipations of the thesis in the paper's opening section? If so, what are they?

3. What is Machiavelli's thesis?

4. What anticipations of his thesis do you find in his opening section?

5. Which of these two seems to be the deductive-inductive essay?

* Niccolo Machiavelli, *The Prince*, translated and edited by Thomas G. Bergin (Northbrook, Ill.: AHM Publishing Corporation, 1947), pp. 12–13. Copyright © 1947 by AHM Publishing Corporation. Reprinted by permission of AHM Publishing Corporation.

Six
Using the Major Rhetorical Modes

By now you probably have the general idea of paragraphing pretty well in mind. You have seen the funnel of the beginning paragraph and the inverted funnel of your essay's end. You are now probably accustomed to the idea of the "middle" paragraph as a standard frame—to be filled, and to be adjusted as needed—with its little thesis, its topic sentence, at the beginning, and its little conclusion at the end. Now some further rhetorical considerations may be helpful.

COHERENCE

Check your writing for clarity and coherence.

Does your paragraph really run smoothly from first sentence to last? The *topic sentence* is your best assurance that subsequent sentences will indeed fall into line, and it is the first point to check when you look back to see if they really do. Many a jumbled and misty paragraph can be unified and cleared by writing a broader topic sentence. Consider this disjointed specimen:

> **Swimming is healthful. The first dive into the pool is always cold. Tennis takes a great deal of energy, especially under a hot sun. Team sports, like basketball, baseball, and volleyball, always make the awkward player miserable. Character and health go hand in hand.**

What is all that about? From the last sentence, we can surmise something of what the writer intended. But the first sentence about swimming in no way covers the paragraph, which treats several sports not in the least like swimming, and seems to be driving at something other than health. The primary remedy, as always, is to find the paragraph's thesis and to devise a topic sentence that will state it, thus covering everything in the paragraph. Think of your topic sentence as a roof—covering your paragraph and pulling its lines and contents together.

POOR COVERAGE   GOOD COVERAGE

The first dive. Tennis. Basketball, baseball, volleyball. Character and health.

Swimming. The first dive. Tennis. Basketball, baseball, volleyball. Character and health.

Suppose we leave the paragraph unchanged for the moment, adding only a topic sentence suggested by our right-hand diagram. It will indeed pull things together:

> *Sports demand an effort of will and muscle that is healthful for the soul as well as the body.* **Swimming is healthful. The first dive into the pool is always cold. Tennis takes a great deal of energy, especially under a hot sun. Team sports, like**

Topic Sentence

basketball, baseball, and volleyball, always make the awkward
player miserable.   Character and health go hand in hand.

But the paragraph is still far from an agreeable coherence.   The
islands of thought still need some bridges.   Gaining coherence is
primarily a filling in, or a spelling out, of submerged connections.
You may fill in with (1) thought and (2) specific illustrative detail;
you may spell out by tying your sentences together with (3) transitional tags and (4) repeated words or syntactical patterns.   Let us
see what we can do with our sample paragraph.

From the first, you probably noticed that the writer was thinking in pairs: the pleasure of sports is balanced off against their difficulty; the difficulty is physical as well as moral; character and health
go hand in hand.   We have already indicated this doubleness of
idea in our topic sentence.   Now to fill out the thought, we need
merely expand each sentence so as to give each half of the double
idea its due expression.   We need also to qualify the thought here and
there with *perhaps, often, some, sometimes, frequently, all in all,* and
the like.   As we work through the possibilities, more specific detail
will come to mind.   We have already made the general ideas of *character* and *health* more specific with *will, muscle, soul,* and *body* in our
topic sentence, and we shall add a touch or two more of illustration,
almost automatically, as our imagination becomes more stimulated
by the subject.   We shall add a number of transitional ties like *but,
and, of course, nevertheless,* and *similarly.*   We shall look for chances
to repeat key words, like *will,* if we can do so gracefully; and to repeat
syntactical patterns, if we can emphasize similar thoughts by doing
so, as with *no matter how patient his teammates . . . no matter how heavy
his heart,* toward the end of our revision below (the original phrases
are in italics):

Topic
Sentence

**Sports demand an effort of will and muscle that is health-
ful for the soul as well as the body.** *Swimming is* **physically**
healthful, **of course, although it may seem undemanding and
highly conducive to lying for hours inert on a deck chair in the
sun.   But** *the first dive into the pool is always cold:* **taking the
plunge always requires some effort of will.   And the swimmer
soon summons his will to compete, against himself or others,
for greater distances and greater speed, doing twenty laps where
he used to do one.   Similarly,** *tennis takes* **quantities** *of energy,*

physical and moral, *especially* when the competition stiffens *under a hot sun. Team sports, like basketball, baseball, and volleyball,* perhaps demand even more of the amateur. *The awkward player* is miserable when he strikes out, or misses an easy fly, or an easy basket, no matter how patient his teammates. He must drive himself to keep on trying, no matter how heavy his heart. Whatever the sport, a little determination can eventually conquer one's awkwardness and timidity, and the reward will be more than physical. *Character and health* frequently *go hand in hand.*

Accustom yourself to the transitional tags.

We have already looked at some of the transitional bridges, first those that take you from the *pro* side of your argument to the *con* and back, and then those that, paragraph by paragraph, connect the paths of your thought from start to finish. Now let us simply summarize the common transitional possibilities, since any and all contribute importantly to the inner coherence of your paragraphs.

TRANSITIONS		USES
1. and or, nor also moreover	furthermore indeed in fact first, second . . .	You are adding something. *And* can be a good sentence-opener, when used with care.
2. for instance for example for one thing	similarly likewise	Again you are adding, and illustrating or expanding your point.
3. therefore thus so and so hence consequently	finally on the whole all in all in other words in short	You are adding up consequences, summarizing minor points to emphasize a major point.
4. frequently occasionally in particular in general	specifically especially usually	You are adding a qualifying point or illustration.

TRANSITIONS		USES
5. of course no doubt doubtless	to be sure granted (that) certainly	You are conceding a point to the opposition, or recognizing a point just off your main line.
6. but however yet on the contrary	not at all surely no	You are reversing or deflecting the line of thought, usually back to your own side.
7. still nevertheless notwith- standing		You return the thought to your own side after a concession.
8. although though whereas		You are attaching a concession to one of your points. Do not use *while* for *whereas; while* means, basically, "during the time that," and is thus ambiguous unless restricted to time.
9. because since for		You are connecting a *reason* to an assertion.
10. if provided in case	unless lest when	You are qualifying and restricting a more general idea.
11. as if as though even if		You are glancing at tentative or hypothetical conditions that strengthen and clarify your point.
12. this that these those who whom he she	it they all of them few many most several	These relative and demonstrative words (adjectives and pronouns) tie things together, pointing back as they carry the reference ahead. But be sure there can be no mistaking the specific word to which each refers.

You should use tags like these economically, of course. You should vary them, and avoid switching your argument back and forth so frequently that you spoil your paragraph's coherence. The more various the transitional tags at your command, the more flexible your resources. Keep an eye open for unusual ones. A rare *contrariwise, mind you,* or *egad* may give you just the right turn of humor or irony. But remember, these tags may easily become wordy. Make them work, or retire them with your revising pencil.

Lead your reader with specific details.

Transitional tags help the reader around the turns, but specific details give him solid footing. He needs to step from detail to detail, or his progress will not be coherent. Your topic sentences are generalizations. Your reader now needs to feel the support of facts, the specific items, numbers, quotations, men, and women, that illustrate your general points. Mr. George Ramsey of Sacramento, California, likes to give his classes his Ramsey Test of Specifics. "Look at your paragraph, class," he says, "and score one point for each capital letter on a name of a person or place; score one point for each direct quotation; score one point for any numbers; and score one point for each example or illustration." Scores are frequently zero. All generalization. No specific details whatsoever. The reader has nothing under his feet at all.

The following paragraph by Loren Eiseley would score about 10 or so. He has been writing of Alfred Russel Wallace's and Charles Darwin's conflicting views as to the evolution of man's brain, and has just referred to the small-brained humanoid apes:

> These apes are not all similar in type or appearance. They are men and yet not men. Some are frailer-bodied, some have great, bone-cracking jaws and massive gorilloid crests atop their skulls. This fact leads us to another of Wallace's remarkable perceptions of long ago. With the rise of the truly human brain, Wallace saw that man had transferred to his machines and tools many of the alterations of parts that in animals take place through evolution of the body. Unwittingly, man had assigned to his machines the selective evolution which in the animal changes the nature of its bodily structure through the ages.

Man of today, the atomic manipulator, the aeronaut who flies faster than sound, has precisely the same brain and body as his ancestors of twenty thousand years ago who painted the last Ice Age mammoths on the walls of caves in France.*

To illustrate his opening generalization that "these apes are not similar," Eiseley adds the specific details of *frailer-bodied, great bone-cracking jaws,* and *massive gorilloid crests atop their skulls.* Rather than merely stating his general point about man and machines, he goes on to illustrate specifically with *the atomic manipulator* and *the aeronaut who flies faster than sound.* Notice that he does not say *manipulators* or *aeronauts,* plural, but takes *the* single and specific *aeronaut* and lets him illustrate the whole range of what man can do with machines. Notice especially how he extends his closing general idea into specific detail: not merely "ancestors," but ancestors of specifically *twenty thousand years ago;* not merely "lived," let us say, but *who painted,* and not merely "pictures," but *the last Ice Age mammoths,* and specifically on *walls* in specific *caves* in one specific country, *France.* The point is to try to extend each of your generalizations by adding some specific detail to illustrate it. Don't stop with *awkward player:* go on to *when he strikes out, or misses an easy fly, or an easy basket.*

Write about what you know and feel.

In the end, the coherence of your paragraphs and your essay comes from your own coherence of thought, your knowledge warmed by your own conviction, your own gaiety or sadness, admiration or scorn, enthusiasm or distaste—together with a sympathetic sense of the details your reader needs to know as you lead him to see things as you see them. The mature writer often produces such coherence by second nature. His topic sentences are frequently oblique, covering only part of his thought, but catching his total

---

* "The Real Secret of Piltdown," in *The Immense Journey* (New York: Random House, Inc., 1955). © Copyright 1955 by Loren C. Eiseley.

mood to perfection. His paragraphs, brimming with his subject, as he is, flow in effortless coherence. Nothing seems out of place, or out of order. We could easily sum up his paragraph in one topic sentence, because the effect is single and coherent; but he himself, in the full mood of his knowledge, has not found it necessary to spell his meaning out all at once, in a single sentence. Consider the topic sentences and the coherence of these two paragraphs by Katherine Anne Porter, the first with topic sentence, the second without, but both perfectly coherent. She is writing about Sylvia Beach of Shakespeare and Company, Beach's Paris bookshop, famous in the twenties as the gathering place for such notables as James Joyce and Ernest Hemingway.

> The bookshop at 12 Rue de l'Odéon has been closed ever since the German occupation, but her rooms have been kept piously intact by a faithful friend, more or less as she left them, except for a filmlike cobweb on the objects, a grayness in the air, for Sylvia is gone, and has taken her ghost with her. All sorts of things were there, her walls of books in every room, the bushels of papers, hundreds of photographs, portraits, odd bits of funny toys, even her flimsy scraps of underwear and stockings left to dry near the kitchen window; a coffee cup and small coffeepot as she left them on the table; in her bedroom, her looking glass, her modest entirely incidental vanities, face powder, beauty cream, lipstick. . . .
>
> Oh, no. She was not there. And someone had taken away the tiger skin from her bed—narrow as an army cot. If it was not a tiger, then some large savage cat with good markings; real fur, I remember, spotted or streaked, a wild woodland touch shining out in the midst of the pure, spontaneous, persevering austerity of Sylvia's life: maybe a humorous hint of some hidden streak in Sylvia, this preacher's daughter of a Baltimore family brought up in unexampled highmindedness, gentle company, and polite learning; this nervous, witty girl whose only expressed ambition in life was to have a bookshop of her own. Anywhere would do, but Paris for choice. God knows modesty could hardly take denser cover, and this she did at incredible expense of hard work and spare living and yet with the help of quite dozens of devoted souls one after the other; the financial and personal help of her two delightful sisters and the lifetime savings of her mother, a phoenix of a

Topic Sentence

Spatial Details

Transitional Fragment

Biographical Details

mother who consumed herself to ashes time and again in aid of her wild daughter.*

Certainly these two paragraphs are filled coherently with Porter's impression of the living personality, now dead. In spite of its length, the first sentence serves perfectly as topic sentence, especially in its final, subordinate clause: "Sylvia is gone, and has taken her ghost with her." She is indeed gone, though somehow the gray shreds of her ghost seem still to hang about hauntingly. After the topic sentence, the details fall into spatial place as the visitor walks through the apartment and we walk with her: first the living room, it seems, lined with its books, then the books in every room, then the kitchen, then the bedroom. The ellipsis (. . .) is Porter's own, not mine, as the meditation drifts off from details to some general impression of Sylvia Beach and of the strange vanity into which death turns all personal vanities.

The next paragraph has no topic sentence, rationally formulated, but it continues the general idea of life's oddly pathetic efforts, as, with a dramatic transition, Porter's mind comes back from its elliptical drift into the mystery of personality: "Oh, no. She was not there." And then a detail that perfectly represents the softness, wildness, and austerity of Sylvia Beach's spirit: a tiger skin on an army cot of a bed. A complete topic sentence for the paragraph would be something like: "All that strange compound of modesty, femininity, wildness, and austerity, all the unusual power that commanded a lifetime of sacrifices from herself and others, is gone."

Katherine Anne Porter's way is simpler—the quiet exclamation, the repeated fact of absence, the tiger skin, the narrow bed—and the paragraph proceeds with perfect coherence. Try an occasional topic-sentenceless paragraph yourself, for dramatic effect, if your subject moves you. But if you suspect that your paragraph is not coherent, make for it the best topic sentence you can, and then pull your sentences into line with transitions, filling in specific details, and perhaps throwing out a few things too. In sum, all paragraphs, like all writing, should be smoothly coherent, as you lead your reader along.

* "Paris: A Little Incident in the Rue de l'Odéon," *Ladies' Home Journal,* August 1964, p. 54. Copyright © 1964 by Katherine Anne Porter. Reprinted by permission of Cyrilly Abels, Literary Agent.

Now we shall look at particular kinds of paragraphs, in the fundamental rhetorical modes of description, narration, and exposition, all of which must sustain the same coherent flow.

EXERCISES

1 Write down the first four sentences that come to mind on any convenient topic: ice-skating, women's lib, early marriage, dieting, baseball. Then make a topic sentence for them that will assert a covering attitude or precept. Next make a full paragraph by filling the gaps with sentences, phrases, transitions, qualifiers and specific details — rearranging where you can gain clarity or achieve ascending interests. Hand in both your original group of four sentences and your finished paragraph.

2 Read the following paragraph from W. E. B. DuBois's *The Souls of Black Folk*, in which he describes Georgia's "Black Belt" (a name referring to the soil, not the people) as he saw it in 1903, and then answer the following questions:

It is a land of rapid contrasts and of curiously mingled hope and pain. Here sits a pretty blue-eyed quadroon hiding her bare feet; she was married only last week, and yonder in the field is her dark young husband, hoeing to support her, at thirty cents a day without board. Across the way is Gatesby, brown and tall, lord of two thousand acres shrewdly won and held. There is a store conducted by his black son, a blacksmith shop, and a ginnery. Five miles below here is a town owned and controlled by one white New Englander. He owns almost a Rhode Island county, with thousands of acres and hundreds of black laborers. Their cabins look better than most, and the farm, with machinery and fertilizers, is much more business-like than any in the county, although the manager drives hard bargains in wages. When now we turn and look five miles above, there on the edge of town are five houses of prostitutes, — two of blacks and three of whites; and in one of the houses of the whites a worthless black boy was harbored too openly two years ago; so he was hanged for rape. And here, too, is the high whitewashed fence of the "stockade," as the county prison is called; the white folks say it is ever full of black criminals, — the black folks say that only colored boys are sent to jail, and

they not because they are guilty, but because the State needs criminals
to eke out its income by their forced labor.*

1. What is most interesting about this paragraph?

2. What is the topic sentence of the paragraph?

3. How does DuBois use detail to support his topic sentence? Be
   specific.

4. Is there a consistent order of the details in the paragraph? Give
   examples to support your answer.

5. What transitional tags are there?

6. Does DuBois repeat key terms? If so, which and where?

7. Is the point of view consistent? If so, describe it.

8. Does the author interrupt his paragraph with parenthetical comments?

9. What do you think are the clearest evidences of coherence within
   this paragraph?

    *W. E. B. DuBois, *The Souls of Black Folk, Essays and Sketches* (Chicago:
A. C. McClurg & Co., 1903), pp. 125–126.

3 Supply a paragraph from your own writing, one from a paper you have
already done, or, if you wish, a new one, but choose one you think rather
good, one you think coherent. Then answer the following questions:

1. What is most interesting about this paragraph?

2. What is the topic sentence of the paragraph?

3. How do you use details to support your topic sentence?

4. Is there a consistent order of the details in the paragraph?

5. What transitional tags were there?

6. Do you repeat key terms?

7. Is the point of view consistent?

8. Do you interrupt your paragraph with parenthetical comments?

9. What do you think are the clearest evidences of coherence within
   this paragraph?

4 Write two paragraphs on the model of those by Katherine Anne Porter
(pp. 105–106), providing the first with a complete topic sentence and the
second with an oblique, dramatic one, like "Ah, yes." "Too late."
"Well."

DESCRIPTIVE PARAGRAPHS

Put your perceptions into words.

Description is essentially spatial. When your subject concerns a campus, or a failing business district, you may want to write your middle as some orderly progress through space, and your paragraphs virtually as units of space: one paragraph for the intersection, one for the first building, one for the second, one for the tattered cigar store at the end of the block. Within a paragraph, you simply take your reader from one detail to the next in order. Your topic sentence summarizes the total effect: "The Whistler Building was once elegant, three stories of brick with carved stone pediments." Then your paragraph proceeds with noteworthy details in any convenient spatial order: first the sagging front door, then the windows to the left, then those to the right, then the second floor's windows, with their suggestion of dingy apartments, then those of the third, which suggest only emptiness.

The best spatial description follows the perceptions of a person entering or looking at the space described, as with the imaginary visitor in this description by R. Prawer Jhabvala of a modern house in India:

> Our foreign visitor stands agape at the wonderful residence his second host has built for himself. No expense has been spared here, no decoration suggested by a vivid taste omitted. There are little Moorish balconies and Indian domes and squiggly lattice work and an air-conditioner in every window. Inside, all is marble flooring, and in the entrance hall there is a fountain lit up with green, yellow, and red bulbs. The curtains on the windows and in the doorways are of silk, the vast sofa-suites are upholstered in velvet, the telephone is red, and huge vases are filled with plastic flowers.*

This procedure may be seen in elaborate extension, paragraph after paragraph, at the beginning of Thomas Hardy's *The Return of the Native*, in which we are moved into the setting from a great dis-

* *Encounter*, May 1964, pp. 42–43.

tance, as if, years before moving pictures, we are riding a camera-man's dolly.

Description frequently blends space and time, with the ob-server's perceptions unifying the two as he moves through them, and takes his readers with him. You pick out the striking features, show-ing the reader what would strike him first, as it did you, then pro-ceeding to more minute but no less significant details. This is the usual way of describing people, as in this paragraph (by the anony-mous reporter for the *New Yorker's* "Talk of the Town") about an actual Englishman, whose odd occupation is mending the broken eggs brought to him by bird's-egg collectors:

> **Colonel Prynne, who is sixty-seven, lives and carries on his singular pursuit in a rambling, thatch-roofed, five-hundred-year-old cottage in the tiny village of Spaxton, Somerset, and there, on a recent sunny afternoon, he received us. A man of medium build who retains a military carriage, he was sprucely turned out in a brown suit, a tan jersey vest, a green shirt and tie, and tan oxfords. He has a bald, distinctly egg-shaped head, wears a close-cropped mustache and black shell-rimmed glasses, and seems always to have his nose tilted slightly upward and the nostrils faintly distended, as if he were sniffing the air. After taking us on a rather cursory tour of his garden, which is as neat and well tended as its owner, he remarked crisply that it was time to get cracking, and we followed him indoors, past an enormous fireplace, which burns five-foot logs, and up a flight of stairs to a room that he calls his studio.***

You may use a descriptive paragraph to good effect in almost any kind of essay, as you illustrate by a detailed picture—the face of a town, the face of a drifter—the physical grounds for your con-victions. For this, the paragraph makes an extremely convenient and coherent unit.

* *The New Yorker,* May 23, 1964, p. 37.

EXERCISES

5 Write a paragraph describing a unit of space, taking your reader from the outside to the inside of your own home, for instance, or dealing with some interesting spatial unit as in the following paragraph from a student's paper.

> The courtyard of the hotel at Uxmal was a wonderfully cool and welcome surprise after the sweaty bus trip out from Mérida. Surrounding the whole yard was a large *galería,* its ceiling blocking out the few rays of the sun that managed to filter through the heavy plantings that filled the yard. Overhead, along the *galería,* ceiling fans quietly turned, and underfoot the glazed tile floors felt smooth and delightfully cool even though the temperature on the road had pushed up past 100 degrees. Airy wicker chairs lined the railing, and just a few feet away, flowering jungle plants rose almost to the top of the stone arches on the second floor. Under the branches of a tall tree in the middle of the courtyard, out beyond the rail and the thick plantings, raised tile walkways crisscrossed the yard, bordered all along by neatly cultivated jungle flowers. And right in the middle of the yard, at the base of the big tree, a small waterfall splashed down over mossy rocks into a tiny bathing pool. The splashing water, the shade, the cool tile, all made the road outside seem very far off indeed.

6 Write a one-paragraph description of a person, blending space and time, as in the paragraph on Colonel Prynne (p. 110), including details of appearance, as well as surroundings.

NARRATIVE PARAGRAPHS

Narrate to illustrate.

Time is the essence of narrative. The narrative paragraph merely exploits convenient units of time. Narrative is the primary business of fiction, of course, but occasionally an expository essay will give over its entire middle to a narrative account of some event that illustrates its thesis. Of this kind is George Orwell's great essay "Shooting an Elephant." Orwell's thesis is that imperialism tyrannizes over the rulers as well as the ruled. To illustrate it, he tells of an incident during his career as a young police officer in Burma, when he was compelled, by the expectations of the watching crowd, to shoot a renegade elephant. Here is a narrative paragraph in which Orwell reports a crucial moment; notice how he mixes external events and snippets of conversation with his inner thoughts, pegging all perfectly with a topic sentence:

> But I did not want to shoot the elephant. I watched him beating his bunch of grass against his knees, with that preoccupied grandmotherly air that elephants have. It seemed to me that it would be murder to shoot him. At that age I was not squeamish about killing animals, but I had never shot an elephant and never wanted to. (Somehow it always seems worse to kill a *large* animal.) Besides, there was the beast's owner to be considered. Alive, the elephant was worth at least a hundred pounds; dead, he would only be worth the value of his tusks, five pounds, possibly. But I had got to act quickly. I turned to some experienced-looking Burmans who had been there when we arrived, and asked them how the elephant had been behaving. They all said the same thing: he took no notice of you if you left him alone, but he might charge if you went too close to him.*

Orwell is simply giving us an account of events, and of his inner thoughts, as they happened, one after the other. Almost any kind of essay could use a similar paragraph of narrative to illustrate a point.

But to select details and get them in order is not so simple as it may seem. Here are four of the most common flaws in narrative paragraphs, against which you may check your own first drafts:

I. INSUFFICIENT DETAIL. A few words, of course, can tell what happened: "I saw an accident." But if the reader is to feel the whole sequence of the experience, he needs details, and many of them. He

---

also needs in the first sentence or two some orientation to the general scene—a topic sentence of setting and mood. The following is the opening of a narrative paragraph from an essay that has already logically discussed its thesis that "haste makes waste." It is not a bad beginning, but a few more details, as we shall see in a moment, would help us know where we are, and at what time of day or night:

> **The sky was very dark. People were walking quickly in all directions. . . .**

II. DETAILS OUT OF ORDER. The writer of the dark-sky paragraph went on in her next two sentences with additional detail:

> **The sky was very dark. People were walking quickly in all directions. The trees were tossing and swaying about. The air felt heavy, and lightning flickered here and there behind the gray sky.**

But, clearly, the further details are out of order. Although she has said the trees were moving, the air seems to have remained still. She eventually rearranged these details, but not before committing another error.

III. COMMENTS BREAKING INTO THE NARRATIVE FLOW. Our dark-sky student went on to intrude an editorializing comment, and a clever one at that. But she would have been better off letting her details *imply* the moral of the story. Here is her paragraph, revised after conference, with the opening details of setting filled and re-arranged, but with the intruding comment, which she actually deleted, left in italics to illustrate the fault:

> **One day, going home from school, I came to understand for the first time how costly haste can be. The sky was very dark, and people were walking quickly across the streets through the afternoon traffic. The air was heavy, and lightning flickered here and there behind the overcast. Suddenly a soft wind moved through the trees, setting them tossing and sway-ing; and then came a great gust, sending leaves and papers scurrying, and rattling shop signs. Wet splotches the size of quarters began to dapple the sidewalk; and then it started to pour. Everyone began to run in a frenzied scramble for shelter.**

People should not lose their heads at the very time they need them most. **At the street corner ahead of me, two girls, running from different directions, crashed together. A boy riding a bicycle slammed on his brakes to avoid them, and he went skidding, out of control, into the middle of the street. A car caught him squarely. Next day, still stunned, I read in the paper that he had died on the way to the hospital.**

IV. SHIFTING VIEWPOINT. The effect of a shift of viewpoint is about the same as that of the intruding comment. The narrative flow is broken. The author seems to have jumped out of his original assumptions, from one location to another, as the italicized sentence shows:

> **My boys of Tent Five were suddenly all piling on top of me on the shaky bunk. I didn't feel much like a counselor, but at least I was keeping them amused. The giggling heap on top of me seemed happy enough. It was organized recreation time, and they seemed pretty well organized.** *The Chief hurried across the camp ground, wondering what was going on over there, and issuing a silent death warrant for the counselor of Five.* **I looked out through a wiggly chink in the heap and saw the Chief in the doorway, with his face growing redder and redder.**

The writer of this paragraph has let his imagination shift from his recollected location on the bunk, beneath the heap of boys, to his reconstruction of what must have been going on in the Chief's head, out on the campground. Similar unwarranted shifts occur when you have been writing *he,* and suddenly shift to *they,* or when you unwittingly shift your tenses from present to past, or past to present.

EXERCISES

7 Write a paragraph in which you blend the incidents and thoughts of a crucial moment, as in Orwell's paragraph on p. 112.

8 Write two paragraphs that would be part of a longer essay, using the fol-

lowing excerpt from Alfred Kazin's *Starting Out in the Thirties* as a model (notice the effective topic sentence in both paragraphs).

The dinner was not a success. I kept trying to see everything through Ferguson's eyes, and I felt that everything looked very strange to him. For the first time, I had brought into our home someone from "outside," from the great literary world, and as Ferguson patiently smiled away, interrupted only by my mother's bringing in more and more platters and pleading with him to *eat something,* I tried to imagine his reactions. We all sat around him at the old round table in the dining room—my father, my little sister, and myself—and there poor Ferguson, his eyes bulging with the strain and the harsh bright lights from the overhead lamp, his cheeks red with effort, kept getting shoveled into him cabbage and meatballs, chicken, meat loaf, endless helpings of seltzer and cherry soda; and all the while I desperately kept up a line of chatter to show him that he was not completely isolated, our cousin Sophie sat at the table silently staring at him, taking him in. In our boxlike rooms, where you could hear every creak, every cough, every whisper, while the Brooklyn street boiled outside, there was a strangled human emotion that seemed to me unworthy of Ferguson's sophistication, his jazz, his sardonic perch on Union Square. But as Sophie sat at the table in her withdrawn silence, my sister stared wide-eyed at the visitor, my mother bustlingly brought in more platters, and my father explained that he had always followed and admired the *New Republic*—oh, ever since the days of Walter Lippmann and Herbert Croly!—I felt, through Ferguson's razor-sharp eyes, how dreary every-thing was. My father kept slurping the soup and reaching out for the meat with his own fork; since I had warned him that Ferguson would expect a drink, he self-consciously left the bottle of whiskey on the table and kept urging our visitor all through the meal to take another drink. My mother, who did not have even her personal appreciation of the *New Republic* to regale Ferguson with, had nothing to do but bring food in, and after a while Sophie took to her room and barri-caded herself in.

So the meal which I had so much advertised in advance—which I had allowed Ferguson to believe would be exotic, mysterious, vaguely Levantine—passed at last, and after he had charmingly said good-by to my parents and I walked him back to the subway at Rock-away Avenue, he studied me quietly for a moment and said, "What the hell was so exotic about that?"...*

* Boston: Little, Brown and Company, 1965, pp. 45–57. Copyright © 1962, 1965 by Alfred Kazin. By permission of Little, Brown and Co. in association with The Atlantic Monthly Press.

EXPOSITORY PARAGRAPHS

Develop most paragraphs by illustration.

The standard way of developing paragraphs, as I have already suggested, is by illustration. You begin with your topical assertion. You follow with three or four sentences of illustration. You round off with some concluding sentence or phrase. After your topic sentence, you may well fill your whole paragraph with a single illustration, as does Albert Schweitzer in this paragraph from his "The Evolution of Ethics":

> For the primitive man the circle of solidarity is limited to those whom he can look upon as his blood relatives—that is to say, the members of his tribe, who are to him his family. I am speaking from experience. In my hospital I have primitives. When I happen to ask a hospitalized tribesman, who is not himself bedridden, to render little services to a bedridden patient, he will consent only if the latter belongs to his tribe. If not, he will answer me candidly: "This, no brother for me," and neither attempts to persuade him nor threats will make him do this favor for a stranger.*

Or you may illustrate your topical assertion with several parallel examples:

> The undercurrent of admiration in hatred manifests itself in the inclination to imitate those we hate. Thus every mass movement shapes itself after its specific devil. Christianity at its height realized the image of the antichrist. The Jacobins practiced all the evils of the tyranny they had risen against. Soviet Russia is realizing the purest and most colossal example of monopolistic capitalism. Hitler took the Protocols of the Wise Men of Zion for his guide and textbook; he followed them "down to the veriest detail."†

Your illustration may also be hypothetical, as it frequently is

---

* *The Atlantic Monthly*, November 1958, p. 69. Copyright © 1958 by The Atlantic Monthly Company, Boston, Mass. Reprinted with permission.

† Eric Hoffer, *The True Believer* (New York: Harper & Row, Publishers, 1951), pp. 94–95.

in scientific explanation. "Suppose you are riding along in a car," the scientist will say, as he tries to convey the idea of relative motion. "You drop a baseball straight down from your hand to the floor between your feet." And he continues by explaining that this vertical drop describes a long slanting line in relation to the line of the rapidly receding highway beneath the car. After this paragraph, he might have an additional one for each new aspect of relativity, illustrating each by the same dropped ball in its relation to curves in the road, the earth itself, the sun, and to whatever hypothetical platforms he may wish to put into orbit. You may also use a hypothetical illustration, as we have already seen in discussing cause and effect, to reduce to absurdity an opponent's hidden implications. Suppose someone has proposed enhancing the democratic process by installing "Yes-No" switches on our TV sets, all to be recorded by computer in Washington. You could develop a sarcastic paragraph of suppositions, somewhat along these lines: "This would mean that any child could vote, and we could put little pictures, cleverly devised, on the tiny voting machines."

EXERCISE

9 Write two illustrative paragraphs, using the same topic sentence for both. In the first paragraph, illustrate by one extended example, as in the paragraph from a student's paper below. In the second paragraph, illustrate the same point by several different examples. This student would have shortened his illustration from Marlowe, then added similar examples from Shakespeare, Jonson, Kyd, and so forth.

But if the Elizabethan playwright had to be anything, he had to be a showman who could entertain and delight his audiences with the kinds of spectacle they loved so well. Witness, for example, Christopher Marlowe, whose play *The Tragical History of Doctor Faustus* was one of the most popular plays ever presented upon the Elizabethan stage. The play begins with the protagonist, Dr. Faustus, acquiring supernatural powers by signing a pact with the devil, Mephistopheles, who first appears before the audience "in the shape of a dragon." *Topic Sentence*

Illustration

From that point on, as Faustus exercises his magical power, the stage is filled with showy and miraculous scenes, one after the other. Elaborately costumed angels, clowns, and devils appear. A Pope, Helen of Troy, an Emperor, and The Seven Deadly Sins, all troop across Marlowe's stage. The ghost of Alexander the Great shows up. There are pantomimes, dances, and songs in quick succession. And the sound effects must be exciting too, for fireworks are exploded on stage several times during the play. But, best of all, from the Elizabethan point of view, there is a good lot of violence and vulgar sexual humor sprinkled throughout. Oh, of course, the play ends piously enough: Faustus loses his soul for having bargained with the devil. But for two hours, at least, Marlowe gave Faustus—and his Elizabethan audience—a heady excursion through all the pleasures of this world. The fact that the play was enormously popular and frequently revived on the Elizabethan stage is good evidence that Marlowe knew what his audiences wanted and gave it to them.

Develop by citing authority.

Of course, citing authorities has certain pitfalls, as we shall see when we consider straight and crooked thinking in Chapter 10. Dishonesty here is all too easy. Mention no more than "science" or "doctors," and you have already persuaded your reader unfairly, unless you go on to bring in the evidence and make the connection clear. "Science" and "doctors" are very persuasive authorities. Until the Federal Communications Commission barred the practice in 1974, TV actors donned laboratory coats to intone their claims for soaps and gasoline. To avoid unfair persuasion, cite your authorities as specifically as possible, and in the area of their authoritative competence. Citing Einstein to support a point of grammar, for example, would probably be persuasive, but certainly unfair, since Einstein was a physicist, not a grammarian, though he wrote superbly well.

Make your appeal to authority honest, and your citation explicit, quoting directly, for your reader's benefit, when the quotation is sharp and not too long. In the following paragraph, W. T. Stace cites Alfred North Whitehead, one of the twentieth century's most noted philosophers, to support his point, and he does so by epitomizing a number of Whitehead's writings in one telling quotation:

> For . . . the past three hundred years there has been grow-
> ing up in men's minds, dominated as they are by science, a new
> imaginative picture of the world. The world, according to this
> new picture, is purposeless, senseless, meaningless. Nature is
> nothing but matter in motion. The motions of matter are gov-
> erned, not by any purpose, but by blind forces and laws. Na-
> ture on this view, says Whitehead — to whose writings I am in-
> debted in this part of my paper — is "merely the hurrying of
> material, endlessly, meaninglessly." You can draw a sharp
> line across the history of Europe dividing it into two epochs of
> very unequal length. The line passes through the lifetime of
> Galileo. European man before Galileo — whether ancient pagan
> or more recent Christian — thought of the world as controlled
> by plan and purpose. After Galileo, European man thinks of it
> as utterly purposeless.*

> * "Man Against Darkness," *The Atlantic Monthly*, September 1948, p. 54.

EXERCISE

10 Write a paragraph in which you drive home your point with a quotation
from some authority — a well-known columnist, *Time* magazine, one of
your textbooks. Here is an example from a student's paper on the ghetto
riots in the summer of 1967:

> But the real cause of the riots seems to go much deeper than that.   *Topic*
> It has to do with the whole history of white-black relations in this   *Sentence*
> country and is, strictly speaking, neither the consequence of a peculiar
> set of events in the summer of 1967 nor the result of a freakish and iso-
> lated accident. It was not the heat, it was not an incident of police
> brutality, it was not militant agitation that caused the riots, though all
> these things perhaps contributed. Rather, it was the long unchanged
> pattern of attitude and behavior of most white Americans toward
> black Americans that caused the violent summer of 1967. It was, as
> the Kerner Commission Report maintains, race prejudice that caused   *Authority Cited*

the riots. If the heat, or police, or agitators, provided the spark, none-theless, as the Commission Report states, "White racism is essentially responsible for the explosive mixture which has been accumulating in our cities since the end of World War II."*

* Report of the National Advisory Commission on Civil Disorders (New York: Bantam Books, Inc., 1969), p. 203.

Develop by comparisons.

With a comparison, you help your reader grasp your subject by showing how it is like something familiar. Your topic sentence asserts the comparison, and then your paragraph unfolds the comparison in detail:

> School spirit is like patriotism. Students take their school's fortunes as their own, defending and promoting them against those of another school, as citizens champion their country, right or wrong. Their school is not only their alma mater but their fatherland as well. Like soldiers, they will give their utmost strength in field games and intellectual contests for both personal glory and the greater glory of the domain they represent. And, in defeat, they will mourn as if dragged in chains through the streets of Rome.

Here is E. B. White describing Thoreau's *Walden* by analogy, a form of comparison that is really an extended metaphor:

Analogy

> Thoreau's assault on the Concord society of the mid-nineteenth century has the quality of a modern Western: he rides into the subject at top speed, shooting in all directions. Many of his shots ricochet and nick him on the rebound, and throughout the melee there is a horrendous cloud of inconsistencies and contradictions, and when the shooting dies down and the air clears, one is impressed chiefly by the courage of the rider and by how splendid it was that somebody should have ridden in there and raised all that ruckus.*

* "A Slight Sound at Evening," in *The Points of My Compass* (New York: Harper & Row, Publishers, 1962), p. 17.

That is probably as long as an analogy can effectively run. One paragraph is about the limit. Beyond that, the reader may tire of it.

EXERCISE

11 Develop a paragraph by some humorous but apt comparison like E. B. White's on p. 120. You might find a helpful model in Mark Twain's two extended analogies—comparisons that clarify the unfamiliar by bringing the familiar alongside:

But I am wandering from what I was intending to do, that is, make plainer than perhaps appears in the previous chapters some of the peculiar requirements of the science of piloting [a Mississippi steamboat]. First of all, there is one faculty which a pilot must incessantly cultivate until he has brought it to absolute perfection. *Topic Sentence* Nothing short of perfection will do. The faculty is memory. He cannot stop with merely thinking a thing is so and so, he must *know* it, for this is eminently one of the "exact" sciences. With what scorn a pilot was looked upon in the old times, if he ever ventured to deal in that feeble phrase "I think," instead of the vigorous one, "I know!" One cannot easily realize what a tremendous thing it is to know every trivial detail of twelve hundred miles of river and know it with absolute exactness. If you will take the longest street in New York and *Comparison* travel up and down it, conning its features patiently until you know every house and window and lamppost and big and little sign by heart, and know them so accurately that you can instantly name the one you are abreast of when you are set down at random in that street in the middle of an inky black night, you will then have a tolerable notion of the amount and the exactness of a pilot's knowledge who carries the Mississippi River in his head. And then, if you will go on until you know every street-crossing, the character, size, and position of the crossing-stones, and the varying depth of mud in each of these numberless places, you will have some idea of what the pilot must know in order to keep a Mississippi steamer out of trouble. Next, if you will take half of the signs in that long street and *change their places* once a month, and still manage to know their new positions accurately on dark nights, and keep up with these repeated changes

without making any mistakes, you will understand what is required
of a pilot's peerless memory by the fickle Mississippi.

Comparison

   I think a pilot's memory is about the most wonderful thing in
the world. To know the Old and New Testaments by heart and be able
to recite them glibly, forward or backward, or begin at random anywhere in the book and recite both ways and never trip or make a mistake, is no extravagant mass of knowledge and no marvelous facility,
compared to a pilot's massed knowledge of the Mississippi and his
marvelous facility in the handling of it. I make this comparison deliberately, and believe I am not expanding the truth when I do it.
Many will think my figure too strong but pilots will not.*

   * Mark Twain, *Life on the Mississippi,* in *The Portable Mark Twain,* ed.
Bernard De Voto (New York: Viking Press, Inc., 1956), pp. 109–111.

Develop by contrasts.

   Your comparisons present helpful illustrations of your subject
by emphasizing similarities. Contrasts, on the other hand, compare
similar things to emphasize their differences—West Germany as
against East Germany, for example—usually to persuade your reader
that one is in some or most ways better than the other.

   The problem in paragraphing such "comparative contrasts" is
exactly what we have already seen with the sheep and goats in Chapter 3 and the more extended discussion in Chapter 5 (pp. 84–86): the
problem of keeping both sides before the reader, of not talking so
long about West Germany that your reader forgets all about East
Germany. Again, the rule is to run your contrasts point by point,
and this you may do in one of two ways: (1) by making a topic sentence to cover one point—agriculture, let us say—and then continuing your paragraph in paired sentences, one for the West, one for the
East, another for the West, another for the East, and so on; or (2) by
writing your paragraphs in pairs, one paragraph for the West, one
for the East, using the topic sentence of the first paragraph to govern
the second, something like this:

*Topic
Sentence*

   **West Germany's agriculture is far ahead of the East's.
Everywhere about the countryside, one sees signs of prosperity.**

Trucks and tractors are shiny. Fences are mended and in order.   *West*
Buildings all seem newly painted, as if on exhibit for a fair.
New Volkswagens buzz along the country roads. The annual
statistics spell out the prosperous details . . . .

    East Germany, on the other hand, seems to be dropping   *Contrast*
progressively behind. The countryside is drab and empty. On
one huge commune, everything from buildings to equipment
seems to be creaking from rusty hinges . . . . The statistics are
equally depressing . . . .

In an extended contrast, you will probably want to contrast some
things sentence against sentence, within single paragraphs, and to
contrast others by giving a paragraph to each. Remember only to
keep your reader sufficiently in touch with both sides.

    Here is a paragraph in which the writer illustrates his point (a
seaman's sense of the weather) by contrasting it to something more
familiar (the landsman's inattention to the weather):

    This was a sullen, dripping morning with wet, woolly
clouds smothering the land and sea. Every few minutes, Mike
or I would go up on deck and peer at the sky, wondering
whether it would clear later and give us a decent day. In New   *Contrast*
York, I am like most people, only marginally aware of the
weather. Before going out of my apartment, I want to know
what the temperature is and whether it is raining, but I don't
experience weather in any real sense; it is only an interim sensa-
tion, a transient state, known briefly between the enduring
reality of interiors — living room, subway, stores, offices, the
library. On the Sound, the situation is reversed; the sky and the   *Topic*
air and the things they contain are the real world, and the interiors of boats and buildings are only burrows that one crawls
into for brief periods to comfort oneself. The sailor is forever
intensely aware of the sky, immense and enveloping. On the
Sound, as on the open sea, one is in, under, and of the sky; one's
eyes constantly search its vastness to know whether it means
well or ill. When the sky changes, the man under it finds that
his mood changes accordingly. Yet the moment he steps ashore,
he becomes detached. The sky is now a thing apart.*

* Morton M. Hunt, "The Inland Sea," *The New Yorker,* September 5, 1964,
pp. 57–58.

EXERCISE

12 (A) Write a paragraph developed by contrasts, running your comparative contrasts point by point, as "students" are contrasted with "athletes" in this paragraph:

> The most essential distinction between athletics and education lies in the institution's own interest in the athlete as distinguished from its interest in its other students. Universities attract students in order to teach them what they do not already know; they recruit athletes only when they are already proficient. Students are educated for something which will be useful to them and to society after graduation; athletes are required to spend their time on activities the usefulness of which disappears upon graduation or soon thereafter. Universities exist to do what they can for students; athletes are recruited for what they can do for the universities. This makes the operation of the athletic program in which recruited players are used basically different from any educational interest of colleges and universities.*

> *Harold W. Stoke, "College Athletics, Education or Show Business?" *Atlantic Monthly*, March 1954, pp. 46–50. Copyright © 1954 by The Atlantic Monthly Company, Boston, Mass. Reprinted with permission.

(B) Write two paragraphs contrasting something like high school and college, small town and city, football and baseball, men and women — the first paragraph describing one, the second the other, and the two using parallel contrasting terms, as in the example contrasting a mother and father on pp. 85–86, or the two Germanys on pp. 122–123. If your subject does not readily provide parallel contrasting terms, you might follow the lead of the freer contrast from a student's paper below.

Topic Sentence
First Subject

In fact, in some respects the commercials are really better than the shows they sponsor. The commercials are carefully rehearsed, expertly photographed, highly edited and polished. They are made with absolute attention to detail and to the clock. One split-second over time, one bad note, one slightly wrinkled dress and they are done over again. Weeks, even months, go into the production of a single sixty-second commercial.

The Contrast

The shows, on the other hand, are slapped together hastily by writers and performers who have less than a week to put together an hour show. Actors have little time to rehearse, and often the pieces of a show are put together for the first time in front of the camera.

Lighting, sound reproduction, and editing are workmanlike, but un-polished; a shadow from an overhead microphone on an actor's face causes no real concern in the control room. A blown line or a muffed cue is "just one of those things that happen." In all, it often takes less time and money to do an hour show than to do the four sixty-second commercials that sponsor it.

Develop by definition.

I concede that definition may sometimes unduly oppress your reader by telling him what he already knows, or what he can easily gather from your context. I know to my despair that a definition from a dictionary, especially to get an essay started, has been a device most dismally hackneyed by generations of desperate students. I know that you should, if possible, avoid the necessity of definition, and the big subjects that demand it. Nevertheless, an occasional bout with a big subject is good for the sinews, and you will certainly need to clarify for your reader your particular emphasis in dealing with the likes of "Love," "Loyalty," or "Happiness."

Richard Hofstadter, for instance, found it necessary in his essay "Democracy and Anti-intellectualism in America" to devote a number of paragraphs to defining both *democracy* and *intellectual*, each paragraph clarifying one aspect of his term. Coming early in his essay, after he has set his thesis and surveyed his subject, his section of definition begins with the following paragraph:

> But what is an intellectual, really? This is a problem of definition that I found, when I came to it, far more elusive than I had anticipated. A great deal of what might be called the jour-neyman's work of our culture—the work of engineers, physi-cians, newspapermen, and indeed of most professors—does not strike me as distinctively intellectual, although it is certainly work based in an important sense on ideas. The distinction that we must recognize, then, is one originally made by Max Weber between living *for* ideas and living *off* ideas. The intel-lectual lives for ideas; the journeyman lives off them. The engineer or the physician—I don't mean here to be invidious—

needs to have a pretty considerable capital stock in frozen ideas to do his work; but they serve for him a purely instrumental purpose: he lives off them, not for them. Of course he may also be, in his private role and his personal ways of thought, an intellectual, but it is not necessary for him to be one in order to work at his profession. There is in fact no profession which demands that one be an intellectual. There do seem to be vocations, however, which almost demand that one be an anti-intellectual, in which those who live off ideas seem to have an implacable hatred for those who live for them. The marginal intellectual workers and the unfrocked intellectuals who work in journalism, advertising, and mass communication are the bitterest and most powerful among those who work at such vocations.*

Try different kinds of definition.

Your subject will prompt you in one of two ways, toward inclusiveness or toward exclusiveness. Hofstadter found that he needed to be inclusive about the several essentials in *democracy* and *intellectual*—terms used commonly, and often loosely. Inclusiveness is the usual need, as you will find in trying to define *love* or *loyalty* or *education.* But you may sometimes need to move in the opposite direction, toward exclusiveness, as in sociological, philosophical, or scientific discussion, when you need to nail your terms firmly to single meanings: "By *reality,* I mean only that which exists in the physical world, excluding our ideas about it."

Such exclusive defining is called *stipulative,* since you stipulate the precise meaning you want. But you should avoid the danger of trying to exclude more than the word will allow. If you try to limit the meaning of the term *course* to "three hours a week a semester," your discussion will soon encounter courses with different hours; or you may find yourself inadvertently drifting to another meaning, as you mention something about graduating from an "engineering course." At any rate, if you can avoid the sound of dogmatism in your stipulation, so much the better. You may well practice some disguise, as with *properly speaking* and *only* in the following stipula-

* *The Michigan Quarterly Review,* LIX (1953), p. 282. Copyright © 1953 by the University of Michigan.

tive definition: "Properly speaking, the *structure* of any literary work is only that framelike quality we can picture in two, or three, dimensions."

Definitions frequently seem to develop into paragraphs, almost by second nature. A sentence of definition is usually short and crisp, seeming to demand some explanation, some illustration and sociability. The definition, in other words, is a natural topic sentence. Here are three classic single-sentence kinds of definition that will serve well as topics for your paragraphs:

I. DEFINITION BY SYNONYM. A quick way to stipulate the single meaning you want: "Virtue means moral rectitude."

II. DEFINITION BY FUNCTION. "A barometer measures atmospheric pressure" — "A social barometer measures human pressures" — "A good quarterback calls the signals and sparks the spirits of the whole team."

III. DEFINITION BY SYNTHESIS. A placing of your term in striking (and not necessarily logical) relationship to its whole class, usually for the purposes of wit: "The fox is the craftiest of beasts" — "A sheep is a friendlier form of goat" — "A lexicographer is a harmless drudge" — "A sophomore is a sophisticated moron."

Here are three more of the classic kinds of definition, of broader dimensions than the single-sentence kinds above, but also ready-made for a paragraph apiece, or for several. Actually, in making paragraphs from your single-sentence definitions, you have undoubtedly used at least one of these three kinds, or a mixture of them all. They are no more than the natural ways we go in trying to define our meanings.

IV. DEFINITION BY EXAMPLE. The opposite of *definition by synthesis.* You start with the class ("crafty beasts") and then give an example of a member or two ("fox" — plus monkey and raccoon). But of course you would go on to give further examples or illustrations — accounts of how the bacon was snitched through the screen — that broaden your definition beyond the mere naming of class and members.

V. DEFINITION BY COMPARISON. You just use a paragraph of comparison (which we have already considered on page 120) to expand and explain your definition. Begin with a topic sentence something like: "Love is like the sun." Then extend your comparison on to the end of the paragraph (or even separate it, if your cup runneth over, into several paragraphs), as you develop the idea: love is like the sun because it too gives out warmth, makes everything bright, shines even when it is not seen, and is indeed the center of our lives.

VI. DEFINITION BY ANALYSIS. This is Hofstadter's way, a searching out and explaining of the essentials in terms used generally, loosely (and often in ways that emphasize incidentals for biased reasons), as when it is said that an *intellectual* is a manipulator of ideas.

Cover all the angles.

You may find that in a defining paragraph—or a defining essay—you have said all you wish to say as you clarified what a thing *is*. Nevertheless, in your preliminary sketching, try jotting down also what it *is not*. You can indeed build some good paragraphs (or parts of paragraphs, or parts of essays) by spelling out the *not*'s, especially if you can thus set aside or qualify (as Hofstadter does) such popular misconceptions as "the intellectual is a manipulator of ideas." You might come up with something like: "Love is not greed. It is no mere lust for gold or beefsteak or people of the opposite sex, although some component of greed has caused the popular misconception. We all declare, on occasion, that we love a good steak, and we mean it. But certainly this usage is only incidental to the real meaning of love as most of us understand it, fundamentally and seriously."

Here are four good steps to take in reaching a thorough definition of something, assuring that you have covered all the angles. Consider:

1. What it *is not like*.

2. What it *is like*.

3. What it *is not*.

4. What it *is*.

This program can produce a good paragraph of definition:

> **Love may be many things to many people, but, all in all,**
> **we agree on its essentials. Love is not like a rummage sale, in** *1*
> **which everyone tries to grab what he wants. It is more like a** *2*
> **Christmas, in which gifts and thoughtfulness come just a little**
> **unexpectedly, even from routine directions. Love, in short, is** *3*
> **not a matter of seeking self-satisfaction; it is first a matter of** *4*
> **giving and then discovering, as an unexpected gift, the deepest**
> **satisfaction one can know.**

The four steps above can also furnish four effective paragraphs, which you would present in the same order of ascending interest and climax.

Beware of cracks in your logic.

Defining is, of course, a way of classifying your concepts and of keeping your headings straight. Elucidation is your major concern; rigorous logical precision is not always necessary (although rhetorical precision, the subject of the next chapter, is). Nevertheless, you should be aware of some pitfalls, and some standard precautions:

1. Avoid echoing the term you are defining. Do not write "Courtesy is being courteous" or "Freedom is feeling free." Look around for synonyms: "Courtesy is being polite, being attentive to others' needs, making them feel at ease, using what society accepts as good manners." You can go against this rule to great advantage, however, if you repeat the *root* of the word meaningfully: "Courtesy is treating your girl like a princess in her *court.*"
2. Don't make your definitions too narrow—except for humor ("professors are only disappointed students"). Do not write: "Communism is subversive totalitarianism." Obviously, your definition needs more breadth, something about sharing property, and so forth.
3. Don't make your definition too broad. Do not go uphill in your terms, as in "Vanity is pride" or "Affection is love." Bring the definers down to the same level: "Vanity is a kind of frivolous personal pride"—"Affection is a mild and chronic case of love."

EXERCISES

13 Write a paragraph defining something by telling: (1) what it is not like, (2) what it is like, (3) what it is not, and, finally, (4) what it is. See pp. 128–129.

14 Write two independent paragraphs, each defining some term. Use a single-sentence definition (synonym, function, or synthesis) as the topic sentence of the first (see p. 127). Use a broader definition (example, comparison, or analysis) in your second paragraph (see pp. 127–128). Here are two examples:

Term

Definition by Synthesis

As the sun was going down, we saw the first specimen of an animal known familiarly over two thousand miles of mountain and desert — from Kansas clear to the Pacific Ocean — as the "jackass rabbit." He is well named. He is just like any other rabbit, except that he is from one third to twice as large, has longer legs in proportion to his size, and has the most preposterous ears that ever were mounted on any creature *but* a jackass. When he is sitting quiet, thinking about his sins, or is absent-minded or unapprehensive of danger, his majestic ears project above him conspicuously; but the breaking of a twig will scare him nearly to death, and then he tilts his ears back gently and starts for home. All you can see, then, for the next minute, is his long gray form stretched out straight and "streaking it" through the low sage-brush, head erect, eyes right, and ears just canted a little to the rear, but showing you where the animal is, all the time, the same as if he carried a jib. Now and then he makes a marvelous spring with his long legs, high over the stunted sage-brush, and scores a leap that would make a horse envious. Presently he comes down to a long, graceful "lope," and shortly he mysteriously disappears. He has crouched behind a sage-bush, and will sit there and listen and tremble until you get within six feet of him, when he will get under way again. But one must shoot at this creature once, if he wishes to see him throw his heart into his heels, and do the best he knows how. He is frightened clear through, now, and he lays his long ears down on his back, straightens himself out like a yard-stick every spring he makes, and scatters miles behind him, with an easy indifference that is enchanting.*

* Mark Twain, *Roughing It* (New York: Holt, Rinehart and Winston, 1964), pp. 12–13.

Black Power means, for example, that in Lowndes County, *Term*
Alabama, a black sheriff can end police brutality. A black tax assessor
and tax collector and county board of revenue can lay, collect, and
channel tax monies for the building of better roads and schools serving
black people. In such areas as Lowndes, where black people have a
majority, they will attempt to use power to exercise control. This is
what they seek: control. When black people lack a majority, Black *Definition*
Power means proper representation and sharing of control. It means *by Analysis*
the creation of power bases, of strength, from which black people can
press to change local or nation-wide patterns of oppression — instead
of from weakness.

It does not mean *merely* putting black faces into office. Black *What It Is Not*
visibility is not Black Power. Most of the black politicians around the
country today are not examples of Black Power. The power must be
that of a community, and emanate from there. The black politicians
must start from there. The black politicians must stop being representatives of "downtown" machines, whatever the cost might be in
terms of lost patronage and holiday handouts.*

* Stokely Carmichael and Charles V. Hamilton, *Black Power, the Politics of
Liberation in America* (New York: Random House, 1967), p. 15.

Writing Seven Good Sentences

All this time you have been writing sentences, as naturally as breathing, and perhaps with as little variation. Now for a close look at the varieties of the sentence. Some varieties can be shaggy and tangled indeed. But they are all offshoots of the simple active sentence, the basic English genus *John hits Joe,* with action moving straight from subject through verb to object.

This subject-verb-object sentence can be infinitely grafted and contorted, but there are really only two general varieties of it: (1) the "loose, or strung-along," in Aristotle's phrase, and (2) the periodic. English naturally runs "loose." Our thoughts are by nature strung along from subject through verb to object, with whatever comes to mind simply added as it comes — a word order happily acquired from French as a result of the Norman Conquest. The loose sentence puts its subject and verb early. But we can also use the periodic sentence characteristic of our German and Latin ancestry, a sentence in which ideas hang in the air like girders until all interconnections are locked by the final word, at the period: *John, the best student in the class, the tallest and most handsome, hits Joe.* A periodic sentence, in other

132

words, is one that suspends its grammatical completion until the end, usually with subject and verb widely separated, and the verb as near the end as possible.

So we have two varieties of the English sentence, partly because its old Germanic oak was first limbered by French and then cured by Latin, but mostly because (as Aristotle observed of Greek) the piece-by-piece and the periodic species simply represent two ways of thought: the first, the natural stringing of thoughts as they come; the second, the more careful contrivance of emphasis and suspense.

THE SIMPLE SENTENCE

Use the simple active sentence, loosely periodic.

Your best sentences will be hybrids of the loose and the periodic. First, learn to use active verbs (*John* HITS *Joe*), which will keep you within the simple active pattern with all parts showing (subject-verb-object), as opposed to verbs in the passive voice (*Joe* IS HIT *by John*), which put everything backwards and use more words to say the same thing: IS HIT *by John* is "passive voice" because it makes the real doer, John, seem to be inactive, or "passive," resting at the end of the sentence instead of starting the action, right at the beginning. Then learn to give your native strung-along sentence a touch of periodicity and suspense.

Any change in normal order can give you unusual emphasis, as when you move the object ahead of the subject:

> **That I like.**
> **The house itself she hated, but the yard was grand.**
> **Nature I loved; and next to Nature, Art.**
> **The manuscript, especially, he treasured.**

You can vary the subject-verb-object pattern more gently by interruptive words and phrases, so that the meaning gathers excitement from the delay. The *especially* does more for the manuscript than the words themselves could manage: the phrase postpones the already postponed subject and predicate. Put the phrase last, and the emphasis fades considerably; the speaker grows a little remote: "The manuscript he treasured, especially." Put the sentence in normal order—"He especially treasured the manuscript"—and we are, in fact, back to normal.

We expect our ideas one at a time, in normal succession—*John hits Joe*—and with anything further added, in proper sequence, at the end—*a real haymaker.* Change this fixed way of thinking, and you immediately put your reader on the alert for something unusual. Consequently, some of your best sentences will be simple active ones sprung wide with phrases coloring subject, verb, object, or all three, in various ways. You may, for instance, effectively complicate the subject:

> King Lear, proud, old, and childish, probably aware that his grip on the kingdom is beginning to slip, devises a foolish plan.
>
> To come all this way, to arrive after dark, and then to find the place locked and black as ink was almost unbearable.

Or the verb:

> She made her way, carefully at first, then confidently, then with reckless steps, along the peak of the smoldering roof.
>
> A good speech usually begins quietly, proceeds sensibly, gathers momentum, and finally moves even the most indifferent audience.

Or the object:

> He finally wrote the paper, a long desperate perambulation, without beginning or end, without any guiding idea—without, in fact, much of an idea at all.
>
> Her notebooks contain marvelous comments on the turtle in the back yard, the flowers and weeds, the great elm by the drive, the road, the earth, the stars, and the men and women of the village.

These are some of the infinite possibilities in the simple active sentence as it delays and stretches and heightens the ordinary expectations of subject-verb-object.

EXERCISES

1 Give each of the following sentences a touch of periodicity by changing the normal word order, by adding interruptive words or phrases, or by complicating one of the three principal elements of the sentence: the subject, the verb, the object.

EXAMPLE. She made her way along the smoldering roof.
She made her way, carefully at first, then confidently, then with reckless steps, along the peak of the smoldering roof.

1. Commune residents are often escapees from solidly middle-class families.
2. Old friends are often shocked and embarrassed when they meet after years of separation and find they now have little in common.
3. Some firemen began carrying guns when they were frightened by the chaos of the riots.
4. The bottleneck in education is that the teacher can listen and respond to no more than one student at a time.
5. The car wheezed to a stop.
6. The editorial in the *New York Times* suggested that tight control of governmental spending might check inflation.
7. It was wholly unlike his father to give up without trying.
8. The inspector discovered a window that had been forced open.
9. We certainly remember that first night in the new house!
10. The escaped convict offered only token resistance and allowed himself to be captured and disarmed after a short chase by a private citizen.
11. William Faulkner died of a heart attack on July 6, 1962.
12. The *Scientific American* customarily devotes its September issue to a single, unified topic.
13. We must note that some parents have misgivings about the schools.
14. The house sits at the edge of town in the middle of large grounds.

2 Cull through your papers and find five of your own simple sentences. Revise them as in Exercise 1, handing in your original sentences paired with their revisions.

COMPOUND AND COMPLEX SENTENCES

Learn the difference between compound and complex sentences.

You make a compound sentence by linking together simple sentences with a coordinating conjunction (*and, but, or, nor, yet*) or with a colon or a semicolon. You make a complex one by hooking lesser sentences onto the main sentence with *that, which, who*, or one of the many other subordinating connectives like *although, because, where, when, after, if*. The compound sentence *coordinates*, treating everything on the same level; the complex *subordinates*, putting everything else somewhere below its one main self-sufficient idea. The compound links ideas one after the other, as in the basic simple sentence; the complex is a simple sentence elaborated by clauses instead of merely by phrases. The compound represents the strung-along way of thinking; the complex frequently represents the periodic.

Avoid simple-minded compounds.

Essentially the compound sentence *is* simple-minded, a set of clauses on a string—a child's description of a birthday party, for instance: "We got paper hats and we pinned the tail on the donkey and we had chocolate ice cream and Randy sat on a piece of cake and I won third prize." *And . . . and . . . and.*

But this way of thinking is necessary, even in postgraduate regions. It is always useful simply for pacing off related thoughts, and for breaking the staccato of simple statement. It often briskly connects cause and effect: "The clock struck one, and down he run." "The solipsist relates all knowledge to his own being, and the demonstrable commonwealth of human nature dissolves before his dogged timidity." The *and* can link causes with all sorts of different effects and speed, can bring in the next clause as a happy afterthought or a momentous consequence. Since the compound sentence is built on the most enduring of colloquial patterns—the simple sequence of things said as they occur to the mind—it has the pace, the immediacy, and the dramatic effect of talk. Hemingway, for instance, often gets all the numb tension of a shell-shocked mind by reducing his character's thoughts all to one level, in sentences something like this: "It was a good night and I sat at a table and . . . and . . . and . . . ."

With *but* and *or*, the compound sentence becomes more thoughtful. The mind is at work, turning its thought first one way then another, meeting the reader's objections by stating them. With semicolon and colon (or, if the clauses are very short, with comma), the compound grows more sophisticated still:

> **John demands the most from himself; Pete demands.**
> **I came, I saw, I conquered.**
> **Economic theorists assume a common man: he commonly wants**
> **more than he can supply.**

Think of the compound sentence in terms of its conjunctions — the words that yoke its clauses — and of the accompanying punctuation. Here are three basic groups of conjunctions that will help you sort out and punctuate your compound thoughts.

GROUP I. *The three common coordinating conjunctions:* and, but, *and* or (nor). *Put a comma before each.*

> **I like her, and I don't mind saying so.**
> **Art is long, but life is short.**
> **Win this point, or the game is lost.**

GROUP II. *Conjunctive adverbs:* therefore, moreover, however, nevertheless, consequently, furthermore. *Put a semicolon before, a comma after, each.*

> **Nations indeed seem to have a kind of biological span like**
> **human life, from rebellious youth, through caution, to decay;**
> **consequently, predictions of doom are not uncommon.**

GROUP III. *Some in-betweeners* — yet, still, so — *which sometimes take a comma, sometimes a semicolon, depending on your pace and emphasis.*

We long for the good old days, yet we never include the disadvantages.
People long for the good old days; yet they rarely take into account the inaccuracy of human memory.
The preparation had been halfhearted and hasty, so the meeting
was wretched.
Rome declined into the pleasures of its circuses and couches; so
the tough barbarians conquered.

Try compounding without conjunctions.

Though the conjunction usually governs its compound sentence, two powerful coordinators remain—the semicolon and the
colon. These strong punctuations can replace both the , and and
the period. The semicolon coordinates by contrasts; the colon, by
amplification. You will notice in the preceding sentence how the
semicolon pulls the contrasting clauses together for close inspection,
so closely, in fact, that we can drop the verb in the second clause,
substituting a comma, and so tighten the contrast still further. For
contrasts, the semicolon is the prince of coordinators.

Contrast

The dress accents the feminine; the pants suit speaks for freedom.
Golf demands the best of time and space; tennis, the best of
personal energy.
The government tries to get the most out of taxes; the individual
tries to get out of the most taxes.

The colon similarly pulls two "sentences" together without blessing
of conjunction, period, or capital. But it signals contrast, not amplification: the second clause explains the first.

Amplification

A house with an aging furnace costs more than the asking price
suggests: ten dollars more a month in fuel means about eighty
dollars more a year.
A growing population means more business: more business
will exhaust our supply of ores in less than half a century.
Sports at any age are beneficial: they keep your pulses hopping.

EXERCISES

3 Write six compound sentences, two with *and*, two with *but*, two with *or (nor)*. Try to get as grand a feeling of consequence as possible with your *and*'s: "Empires fall, and the saints come marching in."

4 Write five compound sentences using conjunctive adverbs, on the pattern: "_____; therefore, _____." Punctuate carefully with semicolon and comma.

5 Write five compound sentences in which the link is the semicolon alone. Try for meaningful contrasts.

EXAMPLE. The county wants the new expressway; the city wants to renew its streets.

6 Write five compound sentences in which the link is a colon. Try to make the second half of the compound explain the first.

EXAMPLE. His game was ragged: he went into sand traps four times, and into the trees five.

Learn to subordinate.

You probably write compound sentences almost without thinking. But the subordinations of the complex usually require some thought. Indeed, you are ranking closely related thoughts, arranging the lesser ones so that they bear effectively on your main thought and clarify their connections to it. You must first pick your most important idea. You must then change the thoughtless coordination of mere sequence into various forms of subordination—ordering your lesser thoughts "sub," or below, the main idea. The childish birthday sentence, then, might come out something like this:

After paper hats and chocolate ice cream, after Randy's sitting on a piece of cake and everyone's pinning the tail on the donkey, I WON THIRD PRIZE.

Subordinating by Adverbs "After"

You do the trick with connectives—with any word, like *after* in the preceding sentence, indicating time, place, cause, or other qualification:

> *If* **they try,** *if* **they fail,** THEY ARE STILL GREAT *because* **their spirit is unbeaten.**

You daily achieve subtler levels of subordination with the three relative pronouns *that, which, who,* and with the conjunction *that. That, which,* and *who* connect thoughts so closely related as to seem almost equal, but actually each tucks a clause (subject-and-verb) into some larger idea:

*Relative
Pronouns*

> **The car,** *which* **runs perfectly, is not worth selling.**
> **The car** *that* **runs perfectly is worth keeping.**

*Conjunctive
"That"*

> **He thought** *that* **the car would run forever.**
> **He thought [***that* **omitted but understood] the car would run forever.**

But the subordinating conjunctions and adverbs *(although, if, because, since, until, where, when, as if, so that)* really put subordinates in their places.   Look at *when* in this sentence of E. B. White's from *Charlotte's Web:*

Adverbs

> **Next morning** *when* **the first light came into the sky and the sparrows stirred in the trees,** *when* **the cows rattled their chains and the rooster crowed and the early automobiles went whispering along the road, Wilbur awoke and looked for Charlotte.**

Here the simple *when,* used only twice, has regimented five subordinate clauses, all of equal rank, into their proper station below that of the main clause, "Wilbur awoke and looked for Charlotte." You can vary the ranking intricately and still keep it straight:

Conjunctions

> *Although* **some claim** *that* **time is an illusion,** *because* **we have no absolute chronometer,** *although* **the mind cannot effectively grasp time,** *because* **the mind itself is a kind of timeless presence almost oblivious to seconds and hours,** *although* **the time of our solar system may be only an instant in the universe at large,** WE STILL CANNOT QUITE DENY *that* **some progression of universal time is passing over us,** *if* **only we could measure it.**

Complex sentences are, at their best, really simple sentences gloriously delayed and elaborated with subordinate thoughts. The following beautiful and elaborate sentence from the Book of Common Prayer is all built on the simple sentence "draw near":

> Ye who do truly and earnestly repent you of your sins, and are in love and charity with your neighbors, and intend to lead a new life, following the commandments of God, and walking from henceforth in his holy ways, draw near with faith, and take this holy sacrament to your comfort, and make your humble confession to Almighty God, devoutly kneeling.

Even a short sentence may be complex, attaining a remarkably varied suspense. Notice how the simple statement "I allowed myself" is skillfully elaborated in this sentence by the late Wolcott Gibbs of the *New Yorker:*

> Twice in my life, for reasons that escape me now, though I'm sure they were discreditable, I allowed myself to be persuaded that I ought to take a hand in turning out a musical comedy.

Once you glimpse the complex choreography possible within the dimensions of the simple sentence, you are on your way to developing a prose capable of turns and graceful leaps, one with a kind of intellectual health that, no matter what the subject or mood, is always on its toes.

EXERCISES

7 Here are some pairs of sentences. Convert them into complex sentences, trying to use a variety of subordinators.

　　1. He couldn't go on. He was just too tired.

　　2. The crime commission recommended a number of such programs. Federal funds have been made available for putting them into operation.

3. We can probably never perfect the process beyond its present state. We should still try.

4. Most schools are just now starting courses in computers for freshmen. To evaluate those programs will take several years.

5. On small farms labor was not specialized. On medium farms, labor was partially specialized. But large farms carefully divided their workers into teams of specialists.

6. Few recipients of social security benefits can actually live on that income alone. Most supplement their incomes with savings or by selling the possessions of a lifetime.

7. We desperately need more judges and more staff. Courts are as much as twenty-six months behind schedule, with little hope of catching up.

8. A large reduction in the prime interest rate is not likely. House seekers, therefore, must choose either mortgages with interests as high as nine percent, or no purchases.

9. Within the past three years, jobs open to recent graduates have steadily shrunk. As a result, students are increasingly challenging the curriculum to provide them marketable skills.

10. An independent candidate for President has little chance of becoming a serious contender. He cannot rely upon large party machinery, and he has little money for advertising.

11. Two motorists were killed last night when their car hit a guard rail, overturned, and caught fire. Police were unable to determine the cause of the accident.

12. Plants can obtain the elements necessary for photosynthesis from water in the soil and from carbon dioxide in the air. Nevertheless, they need many other elements.

13. Federal control of prices could have encouraged a switch to lead-free gasolines. The government could have legislated against higher prices for gasoline without lead additives.

14. You may be familiar with our facilities and resources already. If not, simply fill out the enclosed form and return it to us, and we will send you a free brochure.

15. True scientific knowledge is no longer accessible to the majority of us. We wish it were, but it just isn't. It's too complicated for most of us.

8 Supply five pairs of simple sentences from your previous papers, and subordinate one to the other so as to revise the pairs into complex sentences.

9 Write a one-hundred-word sentence *with only one independent clause and with everything else subordinated.* You can get started with a string of parallel clauses: "When I get up in the morning, when I look at my bleary eyes in the mirror, when I think of the paper still to be done . . . ," or "After . . . , after . . . , after . . . ." See how far you can run on before you must bring in your main subject and verb.

Try for still closer connections: modify.

Your subordinating *if*'s and *when*'s have really been modifying —that is, limiting—the things you have attached them to. But there is a smoother way. It is an adjectival sort of thing, a shoulder-to-shoulder operation, a neat trick with no need for shouting, a stone to a stone with no need for mortar. You simply put clauses and phrases up against a noun, instead of attaching them with a subordinator. This sort of modification includes the following constructions, all using the same close masonry: (1) appositives, (2) relatives understood, (3) adjectives-with-phrase, (4) participles, (5) absolutes.

APPOSITIVES. Those phrases about shoulders and tricks and stones, above, are all in apposition with *sort of thing*, and they are grammatically subordinate to it. The phrases are nevertheless nearly coordinate and interchangeable. They are compressions of a series of sentences ("It is an adjectival sort of thing. It is a neat trick . . . ," and so forth) set side by side, "stone to stone." Mere contact does the work of the verb *is* and its subject *it*. English often does the same with subordinate clauses, omitting the *who is* or *which is* and putting the rest directly into apposition. "The William who is the Conqueror" becomes "William the Conqueror." "The Jack who is the heavy hitter" becomes "Jack the heavy hitter." These, incidentally, are called "restrictive" appositions, because they restrict to a particular designation the nouns they modify, setting this William and this Jack apart from all others (with no separating commas). Similarly, you can make nonrestrictive appositives from nonrestrictive clauses, clauses that simply add information (between commas). "Smith, who is a man to be reckoned with, . . ." becomes "Smith, a man to be reckoned with, ..." "Jones, who is our man in Liverpool, . . ." becomes "Jones, our man in Liverpool, ..." Restrictive or nonrestrictive, close contact makes your point with economy and fitness.

RELATIVES UNDERSTOOD.   You can often achieve the same economy, as I have already hinted, by omitting any kind of relative and its verb, thus gaining a compression both colloquial and classic:

> A compression [that is] both colloquial and classic. . . .
> The specimens [that] he had collected. . . .
> The girl [whom] he [had] left behind. . . .

But be careful after verbs of feeling and seeing; omitting *that* may lead to confusion: "She felt his ears were too big."   "He saw her nose was too small."

ADJECTIVES-WITH-PHRASE.   This construction is also appositive and adjectival.   It is neat and useful:

> **The law was passed,** *thick with provisions and codicils, heavy with implications.*
> **There was the lake,** *smooth in the early air.*

EXERCISES

10 Streamline the following sentences by using appositives wherever you can.

1. The security guard, who must have been a very frightened man, fired point-blank into the crowd.

2. Professor Stanley, who is now associate vice-president and director of business operations, has been named a vice-president at the University of Nebraska.

3. The book, which has been a best seller for several months, will be made into a movie.

4. American social mores have undergone staggering changes since

the early 1950's. These changes are so great in quality and number as to constitute a virtual revolution.

5. The Globe Theatre, which was immediately acclaimed the best designed and appointed playhouse in London, was completed in 1599.

11 Eliminate relatives and their accompanying verbs from the following sentences:

1. The freeze on wages and prices that was announced by the President shocked European investors.

2. *Pygmalion,* which had first been popular as a play, and which had later been rewritten as a popular musical comedy, was finally done as a movie.

3. Although Picasso executed the original design, he had nothing to do with erecting the sculpture which is now standing in front of the Hancock Building in Chicago.

4. The studded tire, which has long been popular for winter driving in some states, is now being outlawed in many states because of damage to roads.

5. Because of the recession, the renovation that we had all hoped for has been postponed.

6. Students who are now being admitted to the master's program will not have to pass the foreign language proficiency test that has always been required in the past.

12 In the following sentences, move the adjectival phrases next to the noun they modify, separating the two with a comma.

1. The young girl cowered in the corner. There was pure terror in her eyes.

2. This construction is also appositional and adjectival. It is a neat trick for the beginning writer to remember.

3. Its deck was splintered and peeling. Its rigging was nearly all frayed and rotted. The boat obviously hadn't been cared for at all.

4. Griswell had neither eaten nor slept, and when he stumbled into the bar he was trembling with fatigue.

5. The ladder was sagging with his weight, and at last it collapsed.

6. The commission's final report will probably not be ready for Friday's meeting. After all, the report is over three hundred pages long and has more than seventy charts.

7. The street in Lawrence was completely familiar to Andrews. It was firmly rooted in his memory even after three years in the Army.

8. The narrator in *Autobiography of an Ex-Colored Man* was so light-skinned that he could easily pass for white, and when he finally decided to give up his black identity, he found it easy to do. Still, the choice left him bitter and embarrassed.

PARTICIPLES. Participles—verbs acting as adjectives—are extremely supple subordinators. Consider these three coordinate sentences:

He finally reached home. He discovered how tired he was. He went to bed without reading his mail.

Change the main verbs into present participles, and you can subordinate two of the sentences to the other, economizing on excess *He's*, balancing incidentals, and emphasizing the main point. You simply use the participles as adjectives to modify the subject *he:*

Finally *reaching* **home,** *discovering* **how tired he was, he went to bed . . . .**

The past participle has the same adjectival force:

Dead to the world, *wrapped* **in sweet dreams,** *untroubled* **by bills, he slept till noon.**

You will appreciate how like the adjective is the participle when you notice that *dead,* in the sentence above, is in fact an adjective, and that the participles operate exactly as it does.

Beware of dangling participles. They may trip you, as they have tripped others. The participle, with its adjectival urge, may grab the first noun that comes along, with shocking results:

Bowing to the crowd, the bull caught him unawares.
Observing quietly from the bank, the beavers committed several
  errors in judgment.
Squandering everything on beer, the money was never paid.
By bending low, the snipers could not see the retreating squad.
Tired and discouraged, half the lawn was still uncut.
What we need is a list of teachers broken down alphabetically.

Simply move the participle next to its intended noun or pronoun;
you will have to supply this word if inadvertence or the passive voice
has omitted it entirely.   You may also save the day by changing a
present participle to a past:

Observed quietly from the bank, the beavers. . . .
Squandered on beer, the money. . . .

Or you may choose elaboration by giving your participle a subject of
its own within the phrase:

Every cent squandered on beer, the money was never paid.

Here is a sentence from Jane Austen's *Persuasion* that illustrates
the adjectival and subordinating power of the participle — *delighted*
twice modifying *She* and subordinating everything to the one basic
four-word clause that begins the sentence:

She always watched them as long as she could, delighted to
fancy she understood what they might be talking of, as they
walked along in happy independence, or equally delighted to
see the Admiral's hearty shake of the hand when he encountered
an old friend, and observe their eagerness of conversation when
occasionally forming into a little knot of the navy, Mrs. Croft
looking as intelligent and keen as any of the officers around her.

This sentence ends so gracefully because, with the phrase *Mrs. Croft
looking,* it achieves the ultimate in participial perfection — the ablative
absolute, which we will consider in the next section.

EXERCISES

13 Keeping an eye out for dangling participles, revise the following sentences by transforming as many verbs as reasonably possible into participles.

1. Apparently the boxer thought the bell had sounded. He dropped his guard, and he was immediately knocked out.

2. He settled in to a Bohemian life in the French quarter. He started publishing in all the appropriate little magazines. And at last he found himself presiding over a colony of artists and writers.

3. The prisoners were obviously angered by the news that no guards were fired. They felt cheated and betrayed. And so on August 4 they seized three guards as hostages to force the warden to reconsider.

4. Trumbo was blacklisted in Hollywood; he was vilified in the press; and he was forced to write scripts under an assumed name until nearly 1960.

5. In the 1970's, men are beginning to become peacocks again; they dress in flamboyant colors. They wear elaborate hair styles, and for the first time in two hundred years they are starting to use false hair, perfumes, and even makeup.

6. The student-designed rocket functioned perfectly. It rose one hundred miles above the earth, flew for ten minutes, traveled some fifty miles down range, and splashed down precisely on target.

14 Write five sentences with dangling participles, with a remedy for each.

ABSOLUTES. The absolute phrase has a great potential of polished economy. Many an absolute is simply a prepositional phrase with the preposition dropped:

> **He ran up the stairs, [with]** *a bouquet of roses under his arm,* **and rang the bell.**
> **She walked slowly, [with]** *her camera ready.*

But the ablative absolute (*ablative* means "removed") is absolutely removed from grammatical connection with the main clause, modifying only by proximity. If you have had some Latin, you will probably remember this construction as some kind of brusque condensation, something like *"The road completed,* Caesar moved his camp." But it survives in the best of circles. Somewhere E. B. White admits to feeling particularly good one morning, just having brought off an especially fine ablative absolute. And it is actually more common than you may suppose. A recent newspaper article stated that "the Prince has fled the country, *his hopes of a negotiated peace shattered."* The *hopes shattered* pattern (noun plus participle) marks the ablative absolute. The idea might have been more conventionally subordinated: "since his hopes were shattered" or "with his hopes shattered." But the ablative absolute accomplishes the subordination with economy and style.

Take a regular subordinate clause: *"When* the road *was* completed." Cut the subordinator and the finite verb. You now have an ablative absolute, a phrase that stands absolutely alone, shorn of both its connective *when* and its full predication *was: "The road completed,* Caesar moved his camp." Basically a noun and a participle, or noun and adjective, it is a kind of grammatical shorthand, a telegram: *ROAD COMPLETED CAESAR MOVED* — most said in fewest words, speed with high compression. This is its appeal and its power.

> **The cat stopped, its** *back arched, its eyes frantic.*
> **The whole economy,** *God willing,* **soon will return to normal.**
> *All things considered,* **the plan would work.**
> **The** *dishes washed,* **the** *baby bathed* **and** *asleep,* **the last** *ashtray emptied,* **they could at last relax.**

It is certainly a construction you should use with caution. It can sound exactly like a bad translation. But able writers come to it sooner or later, whether knowingly or through discovering for themselves the horsepower in a subordinate clause milled down to its absolute minimum of noun and participle, or noun and adjective, or even noun and noun. Hemingway uses it frequently. Here is one of the noun-noun variety at the end of a sentence about pistols in *To Have and Have Not:* ". . . their only *drawback the mess* they leave for relatives to clean up." And here are two noun-participle ones *(he playing* and *the death administered),* in a passage that will serve as a closing illustration of how a complex sentence can subordinate as many as 164 words to the 7 of its one main clause ("They will put up with mediocre work"):

*Subordinating
Conjunction*

Main Clause

Relatives

Participles

Absolutes

If the spectators know the matador is capable of executing a complete, consecutive series of passes with the muleta in which there will be valor, art, understanding and, above all, beauty and great emotion, THEY WILL PUT UP WITH MEDIOCRE WORK, cowardly work, disastrous work because they have the hope sooner or later of seeing the complete faena; the faena that takes a man out of himself and makes him feel immortal while it is proceeding, that gives him an ecstasy, that is, while momentary, as profound as any religious ecstasy; moving all the people in the ring together and increasing in emotional intensity as it proceeds, carrying the bullfighter with it, he playing on the crowd through the bull and being moved as it responds in a growing ecstasy of ordered, formal, passionate, increasing disregard for death that leaves you, when it is over, and the death administered to the animal that has made it possible, as empty, as changed, and as sad as any major emotion will leave you.*

*Reprinted by permission of Charles Scribner's Sons from *Death in the Afternoon,* pp. 206–207. Copyright 1932 Charles Scribner's Sons; renewal copyright © 1960 Ernest Hemingway.

EXERCISE

15 Try turning prepositional phrases and subordinate clauses in the following sentences into absolutes.

1. With examinations coming and with the temperature dropping, students are beginning to show up at the health service with all sorts of nebulous ailments, most of them purely imagined.

2. Ted left the room, leaving his things still scattered over the floor.

3. Even though the tank was filled with gas and the ignition was working perfectly, the engine still wouldn't start.

4. Even though the stock market had collapsed, and fifteen percent of the workers were jobless, Hoover nonetheless felt the economy would eventually right itself without tinkering.

5. With mud splattered all over her stockings, she looked as if she had been out playing in puddles.

6. When his three minutes were up, he deposited another quarter.

PARALLEL CONSTRUCTION

Use parallels to strengthen equivalent ideas.

Hemingway's 171-word sentence could not have held together without parallel construction. No complex sentence can hold up very long without it. Actually, Hemingway's "that is" after "ecstasy" makes a false parallel, throwing his sentence briefly out of line (he should have used "which is" or something like "an ecstasy as profound, though momentary, as any . . ."). You have also seen examples of parallel ranking in White's *when* sentence (p. 140) and in the sentence that followed, dealing with time. The sentence about the cat and the one about the relaxing couple (p. 149) have shown you ablative absolutes laid parallel.

Paralleling can be very simple. Any word will seek its own kind, noun to noun, adjective to adjective, infinitive to infinitive. The simplest series of things automatically runs parallel:

shoes and ships and sealing wax
I came, I saw, I conquered
to be or not to be
a dull, dark, and soundless day
mediocre work, cowardly work, disastrous work

But they very easily run out of parallel too, and this you must learn to prevent. The last item especially may slip out of line, as in this series: "friendly, kind, unobtrusive, and *a bore*" (boring). The noun *bore* has jumped off the track laid by the preceding parallel adjectives. Your train of equivalent ideas should all be of the same grammatical kind to carry their equivalence clearly—to strengthen it: either parallel adjectives, *friendly, kind, unobtrusive,* and *boring,* or all nouns, *a friend, a saint, a diplomat,* and *a bore.* Your paralleling articles and prepositions should govern a series as a whole, or should accompany *every* item:

> a hat, a cane, a pair of gloves, and a mustache
> a hat, cane, pair of gloves, and mustache
> by land, by sea, or by air
> by land, sea, or air

Verbs also frequently intrude to throw a series of adjectives (or nouns) out of parallel:

> He thought the girl was *attractive, intelligent,* **and** *knew* how to make him feel needed.
> He thought the girl was *attractive, intelligent,* **and** *sympathetic,* knowing how to make him feel needed.

Here is an example from one of my students that illustrates how faulty paralleling obscures equivalent ideas:

> He stated two ways in which man could hope to continue survival. (1) World citizenship, or 2) destroying most of the inventions that man is uncertain of and go back to where we can understand ourselves and progress.

The most glaring error is the period and the capitalized *World.* This not only seems to start a new sentence and leaves the reader hanging in air at the end, still waiting for a verb to complete the thought, but also breaks the two parallel solutions away from the *two ways* that have set them up. A colon and small *w* will pull the sentence together, and a full parenthesis at "(2)" will make the parallel visibly equivalent. Next, we must bring the ideas themselves to the surface as equals by putting them into the same kind of grammatical slot: using either two nouns, as in the first solution below, or two participles, as in the second:

> (1) world citizenship, or (2) destruction . . .
> (1) seeking world citizenship, or (2) destroying . . .

But the sentence goes farther out of parallel still: *go back* needs to be parallel with *destroying* (or *destruction*, if you choose the noun). And what are we to make of that blurred parallel at the end? Are we to understand *ourselves* and the nature of *progress* (two nouns)? Or are we to *go back* and then begin to *progress* all over again (two verbs)? We do not know to which of the two choices *progress* is parallel, nor whether to accent it as a verb or a noun. Parallel construction would have told us. I found out by asking the student. The solution we worked out, with parallel ideas underlined, was this:

> He stated two ways in which man could hope to survive: (1) <u>creating</u> some kind of world government, or (2) <u>destroying</u> most of our inventions, <u>going back</u> to where we can understand ourselves as simple human beings, and <u>beginning</u> the painful history of progress all over again.

The speaker, of course, was arguing for world government (not *citizenship*), and he saw the present nuclear predicament as so threatening that the only parallel alternative to world government was scrapping everything and beginning again. We discovered that *creating* was the thought really parallel to *destroying*. By searching out the parallel ideas and putting them into grammatically equivalent structures, we brought the writer's idea clearly up to visibility where both he and I could understand it fully for the first time. Actually, only by first reaching for the grammatical parallels did we discover the really crucial parallel between *creating* and *destroying*.

Repeat your paralleling connectives.

When your series consists of phrases or of clauses, you should repeat the preposition or conjunction introducing them, to ensure clarity:

> *By* weeks of careful planning, *by* intelligence, *by* thorough training, and *by* a great deal of luck. . . .
> *Since* all things are not equal, *since* consequences cannot be foreseen, *since* we live but a moment. . . .
> He looked *for* clean fingernails and polished shoes, *for* an air of composure and a quick wit.

Watch the paralleling of pairs.

Pairs should be pairs, not odds and ends. Notice how the faulty pairs in these sentences have been corrected:

> She liked *the lawn and gardening* (the lawn and the garden).
> They were *all athletic or big men on campus* (athletes or big men on campus).
> They wanted *peace without being disgraced* (peace without dishonor).
> She liked *to play well and winning before a crowd* (to play well and to win; playing well and winning).
> He was *shy but a creative boy* (shy but creative).

Check your terms on both sides of your coordinating conjunctions *(and, but, or)* and see that they match:

> Orientation week seems both worthwhile [adjective] and necessary
>   ~~a necessity~~ [noun].

>   that
> He prayed that they would leave and /\   the telephone would not ring.

Learn to use paralleling coordinators.

The sentence above about "Orientation week" has used one of a number of useful (and tricky) parallel constructions: *Both/and; either/or; not only/but also; not/but; first/second/third; as well as.* This last one is similar to *and,* a simple link between two equivalents, but it often causes trouble:

> One should take care of one's physical self [noun] *as well as* being [participle] able to read and write.

Again, the pair should be matched: "one's *physical self* as well as one's *intellectual self,*" or one's physical *self* as well as one's *ability* to read and write"—though this second is still slightly unbalanced, in rhetoric if not in grammar.   The best cure would probably extend the underlying antithesis, the basic parallel:

> **One should take care of one's physical self as well as one's intellectual self, of one's ability to survive as well as to read and write.**

With the *either/or*'s and the *not only/but also*'s you continue the principle of pairing.   The *either* and the *not only* are merely signposts of what is coming: two equivalents linked by a coordinating conjunction *(or* or *but)*.   Beware of putting the signs in the wrong place—too soon for the turn.

> Either he is an absolute piker or a fool.
>
> Neither in time nor space. . . .
>
> He not only likes the girl, but the family, too.

In these examples, the thought got ahead of itself, as in talk.   Just make sure that the word following each of the two coordinators is of the same kind, preposition for preposition, article for article, adjective for adjective—for even with signs well placed, the parallel can skid:

> **The students are not only organizing [present participle] social**
>   **discussing**
> **activities, but also are ~~interested~~ [passive construction] in political questions.**

Put identical parts in parallel places; fill in the blanks with the same parts of speech: "not only _____, but also _____."   You similarly parallel the words following numerical coordinators:

> **However variously he expressed himself, he unquestionably thought, first, *that* everyone could get ahead; second, *that* workers generally were paid more than they earned; and, third, *that* laws enforcing a minimum wage were positively undemocratic.**
>
> **For a number of reasons he decided (1) that he did not like it, (2) that she would not like it, (3) that they would be better**

Numerical Coordinators

> off without it. [Note that the parentheses around the numbers operate exactly as any parentheses, and need no additional punctuation.]
> My objections are obvious: (1) it is unnecessary, (2) it costs too much, and (3) it won't work.

In parallels of this kind, *that* is usually the problem, since you may easily, and properly, omit it when there is only one clause and no confusion:

> . . . he unquestionably thought everyone could get ahead.

If second and third clauses occur, as your thought moves along, you may have to go back and put up the first signpost:

> that
> . . . he unquestionably thought ∧ everyone could get ahead, that workers . . . , and that laws. . . .

Enough of *that.* Remember simply that equivalent thoughts demand parallel constructions. Notice the clear and massive strategy in the following sentence from the concluding chapter of Freud's last book, *An Outline of Psychoanalysis.* Freud is not only summing up the previous discussion, but also expressing the quintessence of his life's work. He is pulling everything together in a single sentence. Each of the parallel *which* clauses gathers up, in proper order, an entire chapter of his book (notice the parallel force in repeating *picture,* and the summarizing dash):

> The picture of an ego which mediates between the id and the external world, which takes over the instinctual demands of the former in order to bring them to satisfaction, which perceives things in the latter and uses them as memories, which, intent upon its self-preservation, is on guard against excessive claims from both directions, and which is governed in all its decisions by the injunctions of a modified pleasure principle—this picture actually applies to the ego only up to the end of the first period of childhood, till about the age of five.

Such precision is hard to match. This is what parallel thinking brings—balance and control and an eye for sentences that seem intellectual totalities, as if struck out all at once from the uncut rock. Francis Bacon also can seem like this (notice how he drops the verb after establishing his pattern):

> For a crowd is not company, and faces are but a gallery of pictures, and talk but a tinkling cymbal, where there is no love. Reading maketh a full man; conference a ready man; and writing an exact man.

And the balance can run from sentence to sentence through an entire passage, controlled not only by connectives repeated in parallel, but by whole phrases and sentences so repeated, as in this passage by Macaulay:

> To sum up the whole: we should say that the aim of the Platonic philosophy was to exalt man into a god. The aim of the Baconian philosophy was to provide man with what he requires while he continues to be man. The aim of the Platonic philosophy was to raise us far above vulgar wants. The aim of the Baconian philosophy was to supply our vulgar wants. The former aim was noble; but the latter was attainable.

EXERCISES

16 Review the discussion of parallel coordinators on pages 154–156. Then write two sentences apiece for each of the following sets of coordinators. Try different parts of speech, but keep your parallels true by filling the blanks in any one sentence with the same parts of speech.

> both _____ and _____
> either _____ or _____
> not only _____ but also _____
> (1) _____ , (2) _____ , (3) _____
> _____ as well as _____

17 Correct the faulty parallelism in the following sentences from students' papers, and clean up any wordiness you find.

1. Twain seems eventually to become completely cynical, seemed to doubt even that any human life could be happy.

2. The Hemingway hero is a man who moves from one affair to another, who seeks adventure, enjoys bullfights, did a great deal of drinking, who was involved in activities we all wish we could try at least once.

3. In this way not only the teacher needs to be concerned with the poorest student, but every class member helped.

4. A student follows not only a special course of training, but among his studies and social activities finds a liberal education.

5. Either the critics attacked the book for its triteness, or it was criticized for its lack of organization.

6. By driving carefully, by making sure the engine was tuned, keeping the tires carefully filled, we were able to increase the gas mileage by about 18 percent.

7. When they go to church, it is only because they have to go and not of their own desire.

8. Many people argue that the so-called virtues of man belong to the age of chivalry, and they do not apply to the present.

9. This is not only the case with the young voters of the United States but also of the adult ones.

10. Certain things are not actually taught in the classroom. They are learning how to get along with others, to depend on oneself, and managing one's own affairs.

11. Not only did he delight in youth, but he had an almost pathological fear of growing old.

12. Knowing Greek and Roman antiquity is not just learning to speak their language but also their culture.

13. I think fraternities are sociable as well as the dormitories.

14. We have seen that Wright was always fascinated by violence, that he had often seen violence first-hand, and he was himself a potentially violent person.

18 **(A)** In the following famous sentence of Bacon's, straighten the faulty parallels and fill out all the phrasing implied by them:

Histories make men wise; poets witty; the mathematics subtle; natural philosophy deep; moral grave; logic and rhetoric able to contend.

(B) Now write three sentences on the Baconian pattern: "Jack would eat no fat; his wife no lean; the old dog only soup . . . ; the young. . . ."

19 Write an imitation, or a parody, of the following passage from Samuel Johnson, matching him sentence for sentence and phrase for phrase ("Of genius, that power which constitutes a ball player. . . ." "Of glamour, that power which constitutes an actress. . . ."):

> Of genius, that power which constitutes a poet; that quality without which judgement is cold and knowledge is inert; that energy which collects, combines, amplifies, and animates — the superiority must, with some hesitation, be allowed to Dryden. It is not to be inferred that of this poetical vigour Pope had only a little, because Dryden had more, for every other writer since Milton must give place to Pope; and even of Dryden it must be said that if he has brighter paragraphs, he has not better poems. Dryden's performances were always hasty, either excited by some external occasion, or extorted by domestick necessity; he composed without consideration, and published without correction. What his mind could supply at call, or gather in one excursion, was all that he sought, and all that he gave. The dilatory caution of Pope enabled him to condense his sentiments, to multiply his images, and to accumulate all that study might produce, or chance might supply. If the flights of Dryden therefore are higher, Pope continues longer on the wing. If of Dryden's fire the blaze is brighter, of Pope's the heat is more regular and constant. Dryden often surpasses expectation, and Pope never falls below it. Dryden is read with frequent astonishment, and Pope with perpetual delight.

THE LONG AND SHORT OF IT

Your style will emerge once you can manage some length of sentence, some intricacy of subordination, some vigor of parallel, and some play of long against short, of amplitude against brevity. Try the very long sentence, and the very short. The best short sentences are meatiest:

To be awake is to be alive.
A stitch in time saves nine.
The mass of men lead lives of quiet desperation.
The more selfish the man, the more anguished the failure.

The fragment is close to conversation. It is the laconic reply, the pointed afterthought, the quiet exclamation, the telling question. Try to cut and place it clearly (usually at beginnings and ends of paragraphs) so as not to lead your reader to expect a full sentence, or to suspect a poor writer:

> **But no more.**
> **First, a look behind the scenes.**
> **No, not really.**
> **Enough of that.**

The fragment, of course, usually counts as an error. The reader expects a sentence and gets only a fragment of one: you leave him hanging in air, waiting for the second shoe to fall, or the voice to drop, with the thought completed, at the period. The *rhetorical* fragment—the effective and persuasive one—leaves him satisfied: *Of course.* The *grammatical* fragment leaves him unsatisfied: *When the vote was counted.* A question hangs in the air: *what* happened? who won? who got mad? Here is a paragraph with rhetorical fragments placed at the surest and most emphatic places, beginning and end, with a faulty grammatical fragment, to illustrate the difference, still wandering in the middle (all fragments in italics):

> *Not quite.* **The battle, as it proved, still had two bloody hours to run. B Company, presumed lost by allies and enemy alike, had finally worked through the jungle and flanking outposts, virtually intact.** *Tired but fully equipped.* **They now brought the full force of surprise and weaponry to bear on the attackers' weakened right flank. The attack turned to meet the surprise. The defenders, heartened, increased their pressure. Reinforcements by helicopter completed the flaming drama.** *Curtains for the assault on Won Thang.*

That floating fragment in the middle needs to be attached to the sentence of which it is really a part, either the one before or the one following:

EITHER: B Company, presumed lost by allies and enemy alike, had finally worked through the jungle and flanking outposts, virtually intact, tired but fully equipped.
OR: Tired but fully equipped, they now brought the full force . . .

But the point here about rhetorical fragments is to use their short, conversational staccato as one of your means to vary the rhythm of your long and longer sentences, playing long against short.

The conversational flow between long and short makes a passage move. Study the subordinations, the parallels, and the play of short and long in this elegant passage of Virginia Woolf's — after you have read it once for sheer enjoyment. She is writing of Lord Chesterfield's famous letters to Philip Stanhope, his illegitimate son:

But while we amuse ourselves with this brilliant nobleman and his views on life we are aware, and the letters owe much of their fascination to this consciousness, of a dumb yet substantial figure on the farther side of the page.	*Subordinate* *Long*
Philip Stanhope is always there.	*Short*
It is true that he says nothing, but we feel his presence in Dresden, in Berlin, in Paris, opening the letters and poring over them and looking dolefully at the thick packets which have been accumulating year after year since he was a child of seven.	*Long*
He had grown into a rather serious, rather stout, rather short young man.	*Short*
He had a taste for foreign politics.	*Shorter*
A little serious reading was rather to his liking.	*Longer*
And by every post the letters came — urbane, polished, brilliant, imploring and commanding him to learn to dance, to learn to carve, to consider the management of his legs, and to seduce a lady of fashion.	*Long*
He did his best.	*Short*
He worked very hard in the school of the Graces, but their service was too exacting.	*Longer*
He sat down halfway up the steep stairs which lead to the glittering hall with all the mirrors.	
He could not do it.	*Short*
He failed in the House of Commons; he subsided into some small post in Ratisbon; he died untimely.	*Parallel*

He left it to his widow to break the news which he had lacked the heart or the courage to tell his father — that he

had been married all these years to a lady of low birth, who had
borne him children.

Short　　　　　　**The Earl took the blow like a gentleman.　His letter to his**
Longer　　　　**daughter-in-law is a model of urbanity.　He began the educa-**
　　　　　　tion of his grandsons . . . .*

Those are some sentences to copy.　We immediately feel the rhythmic
play of periodic and loose, parallel and simple, long and short.　Such
orchestration takes years of practice, but you can always begin.

* *The Second Common Reader,* p. 81.　Copyright, 1932, by Harcourt Brace Jovanovich, Inc.; renewed, 1960, by Leonard Woolf.　Reprinted by permission of Harcourt
Brace Jovanovich, Inc., the Author's Literary Estate and The Hogarth Press, Ltd.

EXERCISES

20 Write a paragraph beginning and ending with a deliberate rhetorical fragment, and containing one or two clearly faulty grammatical ones, on the
model of the paragraph on page 160.

21 Write an imitation of the passage from Virginia Woolf on pages 161–162,
choosing your own subject but matching the patterns, lengths, and
rhythms of her sentences, sentence for sentence, if you can.　At any rate,
aim toward effective rhythms of long and short.

Eight
Correcting Wordy Sentences

Now let us contemplate evil — or at least the innocently awful, the bad habits that waste our words, fog our thoughts, and wreck our delivery. Our thoughts are naturally roundabout, our phrases naturally secondhand. Our satisfaction in merely getting something down on paper naturally blinds us to our errors and ineptitudes. Writing is devilish. It hypnotizes us into believing we have said what we meant, when our words actually say something else: "Every seat in the house was filled to capacity." Two ways of expressing your thought, two clichés, have collided: *every seat was taken* and *the house was filled to capacity*. Cut the excess wordage, and the absurd accident vanishes. Good sentences come from constant practice in correcting the bad.

Count your words.

The general sin is wordiness. We put down the first thought that comes, we miss the best order, and we then need lengths of *is*'s, *of*'s, *by*'s and *which*'s — words virtually meaningless in themselves —

to wire our meaningful words together again. Look for the two or three words that carry your meaning; then see if you can rearrange them to speak for themselves, cutting out all the little useless wirings:

> **This is the young man who was elected to be president by the class.** [The class elected this young man president. *7 words for 14*]

See if you can't promote a noun into a verb, and cut overlaps in meaning:

> **Last week, the gold stampede in Europe reached near panic proportions.** [Last week, Europe's gold rush almost *stampeded.* *7 words for 11*]

When you convert the noun, *stampede,* into a verb, *stampeded,* you suddenly discover that you have already said "near panic proportions" and you can drop it entirely: stampedes *are* panics. The ungrammatical *near* (which, incidentally, should be either *nearly* or *almost*) is usually a symptom of wordiness, probably because it reveals a general inattention to meanings: the writer is not, as his word seems to say, visualizing a hand reaching near something called "panic."

The basic cure for wordiness is to count the words in any suspected sentence—and to make each word count. If you can rephrase to save even one word, your sentence will be clearer. And seek the active verb: *John* HITS *Joe.*

EXERCISES

1 Clear up the blurred ideas, and grammar, in these sentences from students' papers and official prose, making each word say what it means, and counting your words to make sure your version has fewer.

1. Tree pruning may be done in any season of the year.
2. After reading a dozen books, the subject is still as puzzling as ever.

3. The secret teller vote used in the past was this time a recorded teller vote.

4. I awoke at midnight, my bones aching and my back felt as if it were being pricked with electric needles.

5. The courses listed herein are those which meet the college level requirements which were stated above.

6. Summer is a time in which more engines overheat than any other.

7. Records can be used in the Audio Room by individual students for their suggested listening assignments.

8. My counter was for refunds for which the customer had already paid for.

9. Entrance was gained by means of the skylight.

10. The reason we give this test is because we are anxious to know whether or not you have reflexes that are sufficiently fast to allow you to be a safe worker.

2 From magazines, newspapers, or your own papers, collect ten sentences you can improve. Cut excess words, promote nouns to verbs, convert to active voice, and generally economize by attending to what the words say. Hand in the wordy sentences with your revisions, indicating the number of words saved.

Avoid the passive voice.

I have already mentioned the passive voice, and will return to it again (pp. 193–195), but it is more wordy and deadly than most people imagine, or it would not be so persistent:

It was voted that there would be a drive for the cleaning up of the people's park. [*passive voice — 17 words*]
We voted a drive to clean up the people's park. [*active voice — 10 words*]

The passive voice puts the cart before the horse: the object of the action first, then the harnessing verb, running backwards, then the driver forgotten, and the whole contraption at a standstill. The passive voice is simply "passive" action, the normal action backwards: object-verb-subject (with the true subject usually forgotten) instead of subject-verb-object — *Joe was hit by John* instead of *John hit Joe.*

The passive voice liquidates and buries the active individual, along with most of the awful truth. Our massed, scientific, and bureaucratic society is so addicted to it that you must constantly alert yourself against its drowsy, impersonal pomp. The simple English sentence is active; it *moves* from subject through verb to object: "The dean's office has turned down your proposal." But the impersonal bureau usually emits instead a passive smokescreen, and the student sees no one at all to help him:

> **It has been decided that your proposal for independent study is not sufficiently in line with the prescribed qualifications as outlined by the college in the catalog.**

Committees always write this way, and the effect on academic writing, as the professor goes from committee to desk to classroom, is astounding. "It was moved that a meeting would be held," the secretary writes, to avoid pinning the rap on anybody. So writes the professor, so writes the student.

I reluctantly admit that the passive voice has certain uses. It can, in a string of active sentences, give mere variety, although phrasal and clausal variations are better. It can also vary the emphasis, and the interest, by inverting normal order. *Joe was hit by John* throws selective light on Joe, by inverting regular consequences and distinguishing him from all other unfortunates, and it gives John a certain dubious distinction too. The passive voice can, indeed, eliminate the doer with meaningful effect. *Joe was hit.* ("I was sunk." "It was done.")

In fact, your meaning sometimes demands the passive voice; the agent may be better under cover—insignificant, or unknown, or mysterious. The active "Shrapnel hit him" seems to belie the uncanny impersonality of "He was hit by shrapnel." The broad forces of history similarly demand the passive: "The West was opened in 1848." Moreover, you may sometimes need the passive voice to place your true subject, the hero of the piece, where you can modify him conveniently: *Joe was hit by John, who, in spite of all. . . .* And sometimes it simply is more convenient: "This subject-verb-object sentence can be infinitely contorted." You can, of course, find a number of passive constructions in this book, which preaches against them, because they can also space out a thought that comes too fast and thick. In trying to describe periodic sentences, for instance (p. 132), I changed "until all interconnections lock in the final word" (active) to ". . . are locked by the final word" (passive). The *lock* seemed too tight, especially with *in,* and the locking seemed contrary to the way buildings *are built.* Yes, the passive has its uses.

But it is wordy. It puts useless words in a sentence. Its dullness derives as much from its extra wordage as from its impersonality. *Joe was hit by John* says no more than *John hit Joe,* but takes 66 percent more words! The passive's inevitable *was* and *by* do nothing but connect; worse, all the *was*'s and *by*'s and *has been*'s actually get in the way of the words carrying the meaning, like underbrush slowing you down and hiding what you want to see.

The best way to prune is with the active voice, cutting the passive and its fungus as you go. Notice the effect on the following typical, and actual, samples:

> PASSIVE: Public concern *has* also *been given* a tremendous impetus *by* the findings of the Hoover Commission on the federal government, and "little Hoover" commissions to survey the organizational structure and functions of many state governments *have been established.*
> ACTIVE: The findings of the Hoover Commission on federal government *have* also greatly stimulated public concern, and many states *have established* "little Hoover" commissions to survey their governments. [*27 words for 38*]

> PASSIVE: The algal mats *are made up of* the interwoven filaments of several genera.
> ACTIVE: The interwoven filaments of several genera *make up* the algal mats. [*11 words for 13*]

> PASSIVE: Many of the remedies *would* probably *be shown to be* faith cures.
> ACTIVE: Many of the remedies *are* probably faith cures. [*8 words for 12*]

> PASSIVE: Anxiety and emotional conflict *are lessened* when latency sets in. The total personality *is oriented* in a repressive, inhibitory fashion so as to maintain the barriers, and what Freud has called "psychic dams," against psychosexual impulses.
> ACTIVE: When latency sets in, anxiety and emotional conflict *subside.* The personality *inhibits* itself, maintaining its barriers—Freud's "psychic dams"—against psychosexual impulses. [*22 words for 36*]

The passive voice, simply in its wordiness, is always a bit unclear even on the surface; but, if it eliminates the real subject of the verb, as it usually does, it is intrinsically unclear as well. "This passage has been selected because . . . ," the student will write, and the reader cannot tell who did the selecting. Does he mean that he, the writer, has picked it, or does he describe some process of natural or popular selection? We surmise he means himself, of course; but why doesn't he say so, and save a word, and avoid confusion? "I selected this passage because . . . ."

Any form of the verb *is* may reveal that you have a passive construction. Our language must use some form of *is* so frequently in stating that things *are* and in forming its compound verbs *(is falling, were playing)* that you should drop as many *is*'s and *was*'s as possible, simply to avoid monotony. But when they are—as they often are— signs of the passive voice, you can also avoid rigor mortis by replacing your *is*'s with active verbs, along with their true subjects, the real doers of the action.

To be, itself, frequently ought not to be:

> He seems [to be] upset about something.
> She considered him [to be] perfect.
> This appears [to be] difficult.

Above all, keep your sentences awake by not putting them into those favorite stretchers of the passivists, *There is . . . which, It is . . . that,* and the like:

> Moreover, [there is] one segment of the population [which]
>   never seeks employment.
> [There are] many women [who] never marry.
> [There] is nothing wrong with it. [Nothing is . . . .]
> [It is] his last book [that] shows his genius best.
> [It is] this [that] is important.

The bracketed words can disappear without a ripple. Furthermore, *It is* frequently misleads your reader by seeming to mean something specific *(beer,* in the following example):

> Several members voted for beer. *It is* hard to get *it* through
>   some people's heads that minors can't buy it.
> REVISED: Some people never learn that minors can't buy it.

Cut every *it* not referring to something. Next to activating your passive verbs, and cutting the passive *there is*'s and *it is*'s, perhaps nothing so improves your prose as to go through it systematically also deleting every *to be*, every *which, that, who,* and *whom* not needed for utter clarity or for spacing out a thought. All your sentences will feel better.

EXERCISES

3 Write five sentences in the passive voice, and change each to its active equivalent.

4 Recast these sentences in the active voice, clearing out all passive constructions, saving as many words as you can, and indicating the number saved:

1. The particular topic chosen by the instructor for study in his section of English 2 must be approved by the Steering Committee. [Start with "The Steering Committee," and don't forget the economy of an apostrophe *s.* I managed 16 words for 22.]

2. Avoidance of such blunders should not be considered a virtue for which the student is to be commended, any more than he would be praised for not wiping his hands on the tablecloth or polishing his shoes with the guest towels. [Begin "We should not"; try *avoiding* for *avoidance.* I dropped *virtue* as redundant and scored 34 for 41.]

3. The first respect in which too much variation seems to exist is in the care with which writing assignments are made. ["First, care in assigning" — 8 for 21.]

4. The remaining variations that will be mentioned are concerned not with the assignment of papers but with the marking and grading of them. ["Finally, I shall mention" — 16 for 23.]

5. The difference between restrictives and nonrestrictives can also be better approached through a study of the different contours that mark the utterance of the two kinds of element than through confusing attempts to differentiate the two by meaning. ["One can differentiate restrictives" — I managed 13 for 38.]

5 Pick three obese and passive passages from your textbooks (including this one, if I have slipped). Change them to clean active sentences, indicating the number of words saved in each passage.

Beware the of-and-which disease.

The passive sentence also breaks out in a rash of *of*'s and *which*'s, and even the active sentence may suffer. Diagnosis: something like sleeping sickness. *With*'s, *in*'s, *to*'s, and *by*'s also inflamed. Surgery imperative. Here is a typical, and actual, case:

> Many biological journals, especially those *which* regularly publish new scientific names, now state *in* each issue the exact date *of* publication *of* the preceding issue. *In* dealing *with* journals *which* do not follow this practice, or *with* volumes *which* are issued individually, the biologist often needs *to* resort *to* indexes . . . *in order to* determine the actual date *of* publication *of* a particular name.

Note *of publication of* twice over, and the three *which*'s. The passage is a sleeping beauty. The longer you look at it the more useless little attendants you see. Note the inevitable passive voice *(which are issued)* in spite of the author's active efforts. The *of*'s accompany extra nouns, *publication* repeating *publish,* for instance. Remedy: (1) eliminate *of*'s and their nouns, (2) change *which* clauses into participles, (3) change nouns into verbs. You can cut more than a third of this passage without touching the sense (using 39 words for 63):

> Many biological journals, especially those regularly *publishing* new scientific names, now give the date of each preceding issue. With journals not *following* this practice, and with some books, the biologist must turn to indexes . . . *to date* a particular name.

I repeat: you can cut most *which*'s, one way or another, with no loss of blood. Participles can modify their antecedents directly, since they are verbal adjectives, without an intervening *which:* "a car *which was* going south" is "a car going south"; "a train *which is* moving" is "a moving train." Similarly with the adjective itself: "a song *which was* popular last year" is "a song popular last year"; "a person *who is* attractive" is "an attractive person." Beware of this whole crowd: *who are, that was, which are.*

If you need a relative clause, remember *that.* *Which* has almost completely displaced it in labored writing. *That* is still best for restrictive clauses, those necessary to definition: "A house that faces north is cool" (a participle would save a word: "A house facing north is cool"). *That* is tolerable; *which* is downright oppressive. *Which* should signal the nonrestrictive clause (the afterthought): "The house, which faces north, is a good buy." Here you need *which*. Even restrictive clauses must turn to *which* when complicated parallels arise. "He preaches the brotherhood of man *that* everyone affirms" elaborates like this: "He preaches the brotherhood of man *which* everyone affirms, *which* all the great philosophies support, but *for which* few can make any immediate concession." Nevertheless, if you need relatives, a *that* will often ease your sentences and save you from the *which*'s.

Verbs and their derivatives, especially present participles and gerunds, can also help to cure a string of *of*'s. Alfred North Whitehead, usually of clear mind, once produced this linked sausage: "Education is the acquisition *of* the art *of* the utilization *of* knowledge." Anything to get around the three *of*'s and the three heavy nouns would have been better: "Education instills the art of using knowledge"—"Education teaches us to use knowledge well." Find an active verb for *is the acquisition of,* and shift *the utilization of* into some verbal form: the gerund *using,* or the infinitive *to use.* Shun the *-tion*'s! Simply change your surplus *-tion*'s and *of*'s—along with your *which* phrases—into verbs, or verbals *(to use, learning).* You will save words, and activate your sentences.

EXERCISE

6 Eliminate the italicized words in the following passages, together with all their accompanying wordiness, indicating the number of words saved (my figures again are merely guides; other solutions are equally good).

1. *There is* a certain tendency to defend one's own position *which* will cause the opponent's argument to be ignored. [14 for 19]

2. *It is* the other requirements *that* present obstacles, some *of which* may prove insurmountable in the teaching of certain subjects. [13 for 20]

3. In the sort of literature-centered course being discussed here, *there is* usually a general understanding *that* themes will be based on the various literary works *that* are studied, the theory being *that* both the instruction in literature and *that* in writing will be made more effective by this interrelationship.   [26 for 50]

4. The person *whom* he met was an expert *who was* able to teach the fundamentals quickly.   [13 for 16]

5. They will take a pride *which is* wholly justifiable in being able to command a prose style *that is* lucid and supple.   [13 for 22]

Beware "the use of."

In fact, both *use,* as a noun, and *use,* as a verb, are dangerously wordy words.   Since *using* is one of our most basic concepts, other words in your sentence will already contain it:

He uses rationalization. [He rationalizes.]
He uses the device of foreshadowing. [He foreshadows.]
Through [the use of] logic, he persuades.
His [use of] dialogue is effective.

The utilization of and *utilize* are only horrendous extremes of the same pestilence, to be stamped out completely.

Break the noun habit.

Passive writing adores the noun, modifying nouns with nouns in pairs, and even in denser clusters — which then become official jargon.   Break up these logjams, let the language flow, make one noun of the pair an adjective:

Teacher militancy **is not as marked in Pittsburgh. [***Teachers* **are not so** *militant* **in Pittsburgh.** *7 words for 8*]

Or convert one noun to a verb:

> *Consumer demand* **is falling in the area of services.** [Consumers *are demanding* **fewer services.** *5 words for 9*]

Of course, nouns have long served English as adjectives, as in "*rail-road*," "*railroad* station," "*court*house," and "*noun* habit." But modern prose has aggravated the tendency beyond belief; and we get such monstrosities as *child sex education course,* whole strings of nothing but nouns. Education, sociology, and psychology produce the worst noun-stringers, the hardest for you not to copy if you take these courses. But we have all caught the habit. The nouns *level* and *quality* have produced a rash of redundancies. A meeting of "high officials" has now unfortunately become a meeting of "high-*level* officials." The "finest cloth" these days is always "finest *quality* cloth." Drop those two redundant nouns and you will make a good start, and will sound surprisingly original. You can drop many an excess noun:

WORDY	DIRECT
advance notice	notice
long in size	long
puzzling in nature	puzzling
of an indefinite nature	indefinite
of a peculiar kind	peculiar
in order to	to
by means of	by
in relation to	with
in connection with	with
1976-model car	1976 car

Wherever possible, find the equivalent adjective:

of great importance	important
highest significance level	highest significant level
government spending	governmental spending
reaction fixation	reactional fixation
teaching excellence	excellent teaching
encourage teaching quality	encourage good teaching

Or change the noun to its related participle:

advance placement	advanced placement
charter flight	chartered flight
uniform police	uniformed police
poison arrow	poisoned arrow

Or make the noun possessive:

reader interest	reader's interest
factory worker wage	factory worker's wage
veterans insurance	veterans' insurance

Or try a cautious *of*:

WRONG	RIGHT
color lipstick	color of lipstick
teaching science	science of teaching
production quality	quality of production
high quality program	program of high quality
significance level	level of significance
a Marxist-type program	a Marxist program *or*
	a Marxist type of program

Of all our misused nouns, *type* has become peculiarly pestilential and trite. Advertisers talk of *detergent-type cleansers* instead of *detergents;* educators, of *apprentice-type situations* instead of *apprenticeships;* newspapermen, of *fascist-type organizations* instead of *fascistic organizations.* Don't copy your seniors; write boldly. We have become a nation of hairsplitters, afraid of saying *Czechoslovakia's Russian tanks* for fear that the reader will think they really belong to Russia. So the reporter writes *Russian-type tanks,* making an unnecessary distinction, and cluttering the page with one more *type-type* expression. We have forgotten that making the individual stand for the type is the simplest and oldest of metaphors: "Give us this day our daily bread." A twentieth-century supplicant might have written "bread-type food."

The simple active sentence transmits the message by putting each word unmistakably in its place, a noun as a noun, an adjective as an adjective, with the verb—no stationary *is*—really carrying the mail.   Recently, after a flood, a newspaper produced this apparently succinct and dramatic sentence: **Dead animals cause water pollution.** (The word *cause,* incidentally, indicates wasted words.)   That noun *water* as an adjective throws the meaning off and takes 25 percent more words than the essential active message: **Dead animals pollute water.**   As you read your way into the sentence, it seems to say *dead animals cause water* (which is true enough), and then you must readjust your thoughts to accommodate *pollution.*   The simplest change is from *water pollution* (noun-noun) to *polluted water* (adjective-noun), clarifying each word's function.   But the supreme solution is to make *pollute* the verb it is, and the sentence a simply active message in which no word misspeaks itself.   Here are the possibilities, in a scale from most active and clearest to most passive and wordiest, which may serve to chart your troubles if you get tangled in causes and nouns:

> **Dead animals pollute water.**
> **Dead animals cause polluted water.**
> **Dead animals cause water pollution.**
> **Dead animals are a factor in causing the pollution of water.**
> **Dead animals are a serious factor in causing the water pollution situation.**
> **Dead farm-type animals are a danger factor in causing the post-flood clearance and water pollution situation.**

So the message should now be clear.   Write simple active sentences, outmaneuvering all passive eddies, all shallow *is*'s, *of*'s, *which*'s, and *that*'s, all overlappings, all rocky clusters of nouns: they take you off your course, delay your delivery, and wreck many a straight and gallant thought.

EXERCISES

7 Find in your textbooks two or three passages suffering from the *of*-and-*which* disease, the *the-use-of* contagion, and the noun habit ("which shows the effect of age and intelligence level upon the use of the reflexes and the emergence of child behavior difficulties") and rewrite them in clear English.

8 To culminate this chapter, clear up the wordiness, especially the italicized patches, in these two official statements, one from an eminent linguist, one from an eminent publisher.

1. The work *which is* reported *in this* study *is* an investigation *of* language *within* the social context *of* the community *in which it is spoken. It is* a study *of* a linguistic structure *which is* unusually complex, but no more than the social structure *of* the city *in which it* functions. [I tried two versions, as I chased out the *which*'s; 29 for 52, and 22 for 52.]

2. Methods *which are* unique to the historian *are illustrated* throughout the volume *in order to* show how history *is written* and how historians work. The historian's approach to his subject, *which* leads to the asking of provocative questions and to a new understanding of complex events, situations, and personalities *is probed.* The manner *in which* the historian reduces masses of chaotic fact—and occasional fancy—to reliable meaning, and the way *in which* he formulates explanations and tests them *is examined and clarified* for the student. *It is its* emphasis on historical method *which* distinguishes this book from other source readings in western civilization. The problems *which are examined* concern *themselves with* subjects *which are dealt with by* most courses in western civilization. [82 for 123]

Nine
Words

We began this course looking at the whole essay and finding it necessary to write paragraphs—beginning, middle, and end. Then we concentrated on sentences, the units of the paragraph—simple, compound, complex, long and short. Inevitably, we now seek to master the smallest, and most powerful, tool of our craft. Here, then, is the word. Sesquipedalian or short, magniloquent or low, Latin or Anglo-Saxon, Celtic, Danish, French, Spanish, Indian, Hindustani, Dutch, Italian, Portuguese, Choctaw, Swahili, Chinese, Hebrew, Turkish, Greek—English contains them all, a million words at our disposal, if we are disposed to use them. Although no language is richer than English, our expository vocabularies average probably fewer than eight thousand words. We could all increase our active vocabularies; we all have a way to go to possess our inheritance.

VOCABULARY

If you can increase your hoard, you increase your chances of finding the right word when you need it. Read as widely as you can, and look words up the second or third time you meet them. I once knew a man who swore he learned three new words a day from his reading by using each at least once in conversation. I didn't ask him about *polyphiloprogenitive* or *antidisestablishmentarianism*. It depends a little on the crowd. But the idea is sound. The bigger the vocabulary, the more various the ideas one can get across with it— the more the shades and intensities of meaning.

The big vocabulary also needs the little word. The vocabularian often stands himself on a Latin cloud and forgets the Anglo-Saxon ground—the common ground between him and his audience. So do not forget the little things, the *stuff, lint, get, twig, snap, go, mud, coax.* Hundreds of small words not in immediate vogue can refresh your vocabulary. The Norse and Anglo-Saxon adjectives in -*y* (*muggy, scrawny, drowsy),* for instance, rarely appear in sober print. The minute the beginner tries to sound dignified, in comes a misty layer of words a few feet off the ground and nowhere near heaven, the same two dozen or so, most of them verbs. One or two will do no harm, but any accumulation is fatal—words like *depart* instead of *go:*

accompany—go with	place—put
appeared—looked *or* seemed	possess—have
arrive—come	prepare—get ready
attempt—try	questioned—asked
become—get	receive—get
cause—make	relate—tell
cease—stop	remain—stay
complete—finish	remove—take off
continue—keep on	retire—go to bed
delve—dig	return—go back
discover—find	secure—get
locate—find	transform—change

I add one treasured noun: *manner—way.* The question, as always, is one of meaning. *Manner* is something with a flourish; *way* is the usual way. But the beginner makes no distinction, losing the normal *way,* and meaning, in a false flourish of *manners.* Similarly, "she *placed* her cigarettes on the table" is usually not what the writer means (*place* connotes *arrange).* *Delve* is something that happens only when students begin to meditate. *Get* and *got* may be too colloquial for constant use in writing, but a discreet one or two can limber many a stiff sentence. Therefore, use the elegant Latin and the commonplace Anglo-Saxon, tastefully fitted; but shun the frayed gentility of *secure* and *place* and *remain,* whose shades of meaning you can find in your dictionary.

Abraham Lincoln read the dictionary from cover to cover, and you really can browse it with pleasure, looking at the pictures and finding out about aardvarks and axolotyles, jerboas and jerkins. You can amaze yourself at the number of things *set* can mean. Best of all, you can look at a word's derivation and get a quick sense of our linguistic history, of families of words and ideas, of how some meanings have changed and some others have persisted through centuries and across continents. *Mid,* for instance, is still what it has been for the last five thousand years, persisting in most of the Indo-European languages all the way from Sanskrit to Old Norse and giving English a whole family of words from *middle* to *intermezzo.* Acquaintance with a family can make you feel at home. You can know and use a *ramp,* or a *rampage,* or a lion *rampant* familiarly, once you see the Old French for *climb* in all three. You can cut your meaning close to the old root, as in "He was *enduring* and *hard* as nails," where the Latin *durus* ("hard") has suggested its Anglo-Saxon synonym and given you a phrase your readers will like, though most of them won't know why. (Section A, "The English Language," of THE HANDBOOK, describes the many sources of our speech.)

Through the centuries, English has added Latin derivatives alongside the Anglo-Saxon words already there, keeping the old with the new: after the Anglo-Saxon *deor* (now *deer*) came the *beast* and then the *brute,* both from Latin through French, and the *animal* straight from Rome. Although we use more Anglo-Saxon in assembling our sentences *(to, by, with, though, is),* well over half our total vocabulary comes one way or another from Latin. The things of this world tend to be Anglo-Saxon *(man, house, stone, wind, rain):* the abstract qualities, Latin and French *(value, duty, contemplation).*

Our big words are Latin and Greek. Your reading acquaints you with them; your dictionary will show you their prefixes and roots. Learn the common prefixes and roots (see Exercises 1, 2, and 3 at the end of this section), and you can handle all kinds of foreigners at first encounter: *con-cession* (going along with), *ex-clude* (lock out), *pre-fer* (carry before), *sub-version* (turning under), *translate* (carry across), *claustro-phobia* (dread of being locked in), *hydro-*

phobia (dread of water) *ailuro-philia* (love of cats), *megalo-cephalic* (big-headed), *micro-meter* (little-measurer). You can even, for fun, coin a word to suit the occasion: *megalopede* (big-footed). You can remember that *intramural* means "within the (college) walls," and that "intermural sports," which is the frequent mispronunciation and misspelling, would mean something like "wall battling wall," a physical absurdity.

Besides owning a good dictionary, you should refer, with caution, to a thesaurus, a treasury of synonyms ("together-names"), in which you can find the word you couldn't think of; the danger lies in raiding this treasury too enthusiastically. Checking for meaning in a dictionary will assure that you have expanded, not distorted, your vocabulary.

EXERCISES

1 Browse your dictionary and find three families of words, like *ramp-rampage-rampant*. Give the root-idea of each family, and a word or two in definition of each word.

2 Make a permanent reference list by looking up in your dictionary each of the Latin and Greek prefixes and constituents listed below. Illustrate each with several English derivatives, and put in parentheses after each derivative its close literal English translation, as in these two examples:

> *con-* (with): convince (conquer with), conclude (shut with) concur (run with).
> *chron-* (time): chronic (lasting a long time), chronicle (a record of the time), chronometer (time-measurer).

LATIN: *a- (ab-), ad-, ante-, bene-, bi-, circum-, con-, contra-, di- (dis), e- (ex-), in- (two meanings), inter-, intra-, mal-, multi-, ob-, per-, post-, pre-, pro-, retro-, semi-, sub- (sur-), super-, trans-, ultra-.*

GREEK: *a- (an-), -agogue, allo-, anthropo-, anti-, apo-, arch-, auto-, batho-, bio-, cata-, cephalo-, chron-, -cracy, demo-, dia-, dyna-, dys-, ecto-, epi-, eu-, -gen, geo-, -gon, -gony, graph-, gyn-, hemi-, hepta-, hetero-, hexa-, homo-, hydr-, hyper-, hypo-, log-, mega-, -meter, micro-, mono-, morph-, -nomy, -nym, -pathy, penta-, -phag, phil-, -phobe (ia), -phone, poly-, pseudo-, psyche-, -scope, soph-, stero-, sym- (syn-), tele-, tetra-, theo-, thermo-, tri-, zoo-.*

3 Think up and look up seven or eight more words, or as many as you can (omitting mere parts of speech, like *acts, acted, acting*) to add to the list of derivations already started after each of the following Latin verbs and their past participles. Add a note to explain any particularly interesting one like *actuary* (an insurance expert), which will turn up in your first list.

agere, actus (do) — agent, act . . .
audire, auditus (hear) — audit . . .
capere, captus (seize) — capable . . .
cedere, cessus (go) — concede . . .
claudere, clausus (shut) — close, include . . .
currere, cursus (run) — recur, course . . .
dicere, dictus (say) — dictate . . .
ducere, ductus (lead) — produce . . .
facere, factus (make) — infect . . .
ferre, latus (carry) — infer, relate . . .
fidere, fisus (trust) — confide, Fido . . .
fundere, fusus (pour) — refuse, refund . . .
gradi, gressus (step) — grade, digressions . . .
ire, itus (go) — exit, tradition . . .
jacere, jactus (throw) — reject . . .
legere, lectus (choose, read) — legible, elect . . .
loqui, locutus (speak) — circumlocution . . .
mittere, missus (send) — permit, mission . . .
pellere, pulsus (drive) — impel, repulse . . .
pendere, pensus (hang) — depend, pension . . .
plicare, plicatus (fold) — implication, complex . . .
ponere, positus (put) — response, position . . .
portare, portatus (carry) — import . . .
rumpere, ruptus (break) — rumpus, erupt . . .
scribere, scriptus (write) — scribble, script . . .
sedere, sessus (sit) — sedentary, assess . . .
sentire, sensus (feel) — sense . . .
specere, spectus (look) — speculate . . .
tendere, tensus (stretch) — tend, tense . . .
tenere, tentus (hold) — content . . .
trahere, tractus (drag) — tractor . . .
venire, ventus (come) — convene, invent . . .
vertere, versus (turn) — diverting, verse . . .
videre, visus (see) — divide, visible . . .
vocare, vocatus (call) — vocation . . .

ABSTRACT AND CONCRETE

Every good stylist has perceived, in one way or another, the distinction between the abstract and the concrete. Tangible things — things we can touch — are "concrete"; their qualities, along with all our emotional, intellectual, and spiritual states, are "abstract." The rule for a good style is to be as concrete as you can, to illustrate tangibly your general propositions, to use *shoes* and *ships* and *sealing wax* instead of *commercial concomitants*. But this requires constant effort: our minds so crave abstraction we can hardly pin them down to specifics.

Abstraction, a "drawing out from," is the very nature of thought. Thought moves from concrete to abstract. In fact, *all* words are abstractions. *Stick* is a generalization of all sticks, the crooked and the straight, the long and the short, the peeled and the shaggy. No word fits its object like a glove, because words are not things: words represent ideas of things. They are the means by which we class eggs and tents and trees so that we can handle them as ideas — not as actual things but as *kinds* of things. A man can hold an egg in his hand, but he cannot think about it, or talk about it, unless he has some larger idea with which his mind, too, can grasp it, some idea like *thing,* or *throwing thing,* or *egg* — which classes this one white ellipsoid with all the eggs he has known, from ostrich to hummingbird, with the *idea* of egg. One word per item would be useless; it would be no idea at all, since ideas represent not items, but *classes* of items.

In fact, abstract words can attain a power of their own, as the rhetorician heightens attention to their meanings. This ability, of course, does not come easily or soon. First, and for the present, I repeat, you need to be as concrete as you can, to illustrate tangibly, to pin your abstractions down to specifics. But once you have learned this, you can move on to the rhetoric of abstraction, which is, indeed, a kind of squeezing of abstract words for their specific juice.

Lincoln does exactly this, as we have seen, when he concentrates on *dedication* six times within ten sentences — in his dedication at Gettysburg. Similarly, Eliot refers to "faces / Distracted from distraction by distraction" (*Four Quartets*). Abstractions can, in fact, operate beautifully as specifics: "As a knight, Richard the Lion-

Hearted was a *triumph;* as a king, he was a *disaster."* Actually, most of the rhetorical devices in Section E of THE HANDBOOK likewise concentrate on abstract essences:

> . . . tribulation works patience, and patience experience, and experience hope. (Rom. v.3–4.)
> The humble are proud of their humility.
> Care in your youth so you may live without care.

An able writer like Samuel Johnson can make a virtual poetry of abstractions, as he alliterates and balances them against each other (I have capitalized the alliterations and italicized the balances):

> Dryden's performances were always hasty, either *Excited* by some *External occasion,* or *Extorted* by some *domestic necessity;* he *ComPosed without ·Consideration,* and *Published without Correction.*

Notice especially how *excited* ("called forth") and *extorted* ("twisted out"), so alike in sound and form, so alike in making Dryden write, nevertheless contrast their opposite essential meanings. Johnson thus extorts the specific juice of each abstract word.

So before we disparage abstraction, we should acknowledge its rhetorical power; and we should understand that it is an essential distillation, a primary and natural and continual mental process. Without it, we could not make four of two and two. So we make abstractions of abstractions to handle bigger and bigger groups of ideas. *Egg* becomes *food,* and *food* becomes *nourishment.* We also classify all the psychic and physical qualities we can recognize: *candor, truth, anger, beauty, negligence, temperament.* But because our thoughts drift upward, we need always to look for the word that will bring them nearer earth, that will make our abstractions seem visible and tangible, that will make them graspable — mentioning a *handle,* or a *pin,* or an *egg,* alongside our abstraction, for instance. We have to pull our abstractions down within reach of our reader's own busily abstracting headpiece.

In short, we must pin our abstractions down with constant comparisons to the concrete eggs from which they sprang. I might have written that sentence — as I found myself starting to do: "Abstractions should be actualized by a process of constant comparisons with the concrete objects which they represent." But note what I have done to pull this down within reach. First, I have used *we* — that is, you and me, real people — and I have cut the inhuman passive voice to put us in the act. Then I have changed *actualize* to *pin down*, a visible action that, being commonplace and proverbial, makes us feel at home among the abstractions. I have replaced the abstract *by a process of* with its simpler abstract equivalent *with*. More important, I have made *eggs* stand for all objects — and note how easily our abstracters take this in. Furthermore, I have punned on *concrete*, making it, for a fleeting instant, into cement. How? By choosing *egg*, something that could really be made out of concrete, instead of *stick* (which I had first put there): a concrete stick is not much as a physical possibility. Finally, I have gone on to use *egg* also as a real egg by having the abstract ideas spring from it. Later, I almost changed *sprang* to *hatched*, but decided that this was too vivid. It would make the concrete egg too nearly real, and the picture of broken cement with fluffy abstractions peeping forth would have gotten in the way of the idea — that is, the disembodied abstract concept — I was trying to convey.

But the writer's ultimate skill perhaps lies in making a single object represent its whole abstract class. I have paired each abstraction below with its concrete translation:

> *Friendliness* **is the salesman's best asset.**
> *A smile* **is the salesman's best asset.**
>
> *Administration of proper proteins* **might have saved John Keats.**
> *A good steak* **might have saved John Keats.**
>
> **To** *understand* **the world by** *observing all of its geological details. . . .*
> **To** *see* **the world in** *a grain of sand. . . .*

EXERCISES

4 Write three sentences using abstractions concretely, as in "As a knight, Richard was a *triumph;* as a king, he was a *disaster.*"

5 Write three sentences in which a single concrete item represents its whole abstract class, as in *"A good steak* might have saved John Keats."

METAPHOR

As you have probably noticed, I have been using metaphors — the most useful way of making our abstractions concrete. The word is Greek for "transfer" *(meta* equals *trans* equals *across; phor* equals *fer* equals *ferry).* The idea is that of representing something as if it were something else, objects as if all of them were eggs, abstractions as if they were chickens that are also vaguely like flowers springing, thought as if it were rising steam. Metaphors illustrate, in a word, our general ideas. I might have written at length about how an idea is like an egg. I did, in fact, follow each declaration with an example, and I illustrated the point with a man holding an egg. But the metaphor makes the comparison at a stroke. I used our common word *grasp* for "understanding," comparing the mind to something with hands, *transferring* the physical picture of the clutching hand to the invisible mental act.

Almost all our words are metaphors, usually with the physical picture faded. *Transfer* itself pictures a physical portage. When the company *transfers* its men, it is sending them about the country as if by piggyback, or raft, or whatever. But mercifully the physical facts have faded — *transfer* has become a "dead metaphor" — and we can use the word in comfortable abstraction. Now, precisely because we are constantly abstracting, constantly letting the picture fade, you can use metaphor to great advantage — or disastrously, if your eyes aren't sharp. With metaphors, you avoid the nonpictorial quality of most of our writing; you make your writing both vivid and unique. As Aristotle said, the metaphor is clear, agreeable, and strange; like a solved riddle, it is the most delightful of teachers.

Metaphor seems to work at about four levels, each with a different clarity and force (and, as you will see, we must here distinguish between the general idea of "metaphor" as the whole process of transfer, and that specific thing called "a metaphor"). Suppose you wrote "She snorted, and tossed the red mane of her hair." You have transferred to a woman the qualities of a horse to make her appearance and personality vivid. You have chosen one of the four ways to make this transfer, which I shall simplify for clarity, and then discuss:

I. SIMILE: **She was** *like* **a horse.**
She stopped *as* **a horse stops.**
She stopped *as if* **she were a horse.**
II. METAPHOR: **She was a horse.**
III. IMPLIED METAPHOR: **She snorted and tossed her mane.**
IV. DEAD METAPHOR: **She bridled.**

I. SIMILE. The simile is the most obvious form the metaphor can take, and hence would seem elementary. But it has powers of its own, particularly where the writer seems to be trying urgently to express the inexpressible, comparing his subject to several different possibilities, no one wholly adequate. In *The Sound and the Fury,* Faulkner thus describes two jaybirds (my italics):

> **[they] whirled up on the blast** *like gaudy scraps of cloth or paper* **and lodged in the mulberries, . . . screaming into the wind that** *ripped* **their harsh cries onward and away** *like scraps of paper or of cloth* **in turn.**

The simile has a high poetic energy. D. H. Lawrence uses it frequently, as here in *The Plumed Serpent* (my italics):

> **The lake was quite black,** *like a great pit.* **The wind suddenly blew with violence, with a strange ripping sound in the mango trees,** *as if some membrane in the air were being ripped.*

II. METAPHOR. The plain metaphor makes its comparison in one imaginative leap. It is shorthand for "as if she were a horse"; it pretends, by exaggeration *(hyperbole),* that she *is* a horse. We move instinctively to this kind of exaggerated comparison as we try to convey our impressions with all their emotional impact. "He was a maniac at Frisbee," we might say, "a dynamo, a computer." The metaphor is probably our most common figure of speech: *the pigs, the swine, a plum, a gem, a phantom of delight, a shot in the arm.* It may be humorous or bitter; it may be simply and aptly visual: "The road was a ribbon of silver." Thoreau extends a metaphor through several sentences in one of his most famous passages:

> **Time is but the stream I go a-fishing in. I drink at it; but**
> **while I drink I see the sandy bottom and detect how shallow it**
> **is. Its thin current slides away, but eternity remains. I would**
> **drink deeper; fish in the sky, whose bottom is pebbly with stars.**

III. IMPLIED METAPHOR. The implied metaphor is even more widely useful. It operates most often among the verbs, as in *snorted* and *tossed,* the horsy verbs suggesting "horse." Most ideas can suggest analogues of physical processes or natural history. Give your television system *tentacles* reaching into every home, and you have compared TV to an octopus, with all its lethal and wiry suggestions. You can have your school spirit *fall below zero,* and you have implied that your school spirit is like temperature, registered on a thermometer in a sudden chill. In the following passage about Hawthorne's style, Malcolm Cowley develops his explicit analogy first into a direct simile *(like a footprint)* and then into the metaphor implying that phrases are people walking at different speeds:

> **He dreamed in words, while walking along the seashore or un-**
> **der the pines, till the words fitted themselves to his stride. The**
> **result was that his eighteenth-century English developed into a**
> **natural, a *walked,* style, with a phrase for every step and a comma**
> **after every phrase like a footprint in the sand. Sometimes the**
> **phrases hurry, sometimes they loiter, sometimes they march to**
> **drums.***

Cowley's implied metaphor about hurrying and loitering phrases is in fact a kind of extended pun, to illustrate the *walked* style he italicizes. You can even pun on the physical Latin components in our abstract words, turning them back into their original suggestions of physical acts, as in "The *enterprise* grabbed everything" (some beast or army is rushing in), for *enterprise* means in Latin something like "to rush in and grab." Too subtle? No, the contrast between *enterprise* and *grabbed* will please anyone, and the few who see it all will be delighted.

---

* *The Portable Hawthorne* (New York: The Viking Press, 1948).

IV. DEAD METAPHOR. *Enterprise* is really a dead metaphor, and the art of resuscitation is the metaphorist's finest skill. It comes from liking words and paying attention to what they say. The punster makes the writer, if he can restrain himself. Simply add onto the dead metaphor enough implied metaphors to get the circulation going again: *She bridled, snorting and tossing her mane. She bridled* means, by itself, in our usual nonpictorial parlance, nothing more than "reacted disdainfully." By bringing the metaphor back to life, we keep the general meaning but also restore the physical picture of a horse lifting its head and arching its neck against the bridle. This is exhilarating. We recognize *bridle* concretely and truly for the first time. We know the word, and we know the woman. We have an image of her, a posture vaguely suggestive of a horse.

Perhaps the best dead metaphors to revive are those in proverbial clichés. See what Thoreau does (in his *Journal*) with *spur of the moment:*

I feel the spur of the moment thrust deep into my side. The present is an inexorable rider.

Or again, when in *Walden* he speaks of wanting "to improve the nick of time, and notch it on my stick too," and of not being *thrown off the track* "by every nutshell and mosquito's wing that falls on the rails." In each case, he takes the proverbial phrase literally and physically, adding an attribute or two to bring the old metaphor back alive.

You can go too far, of course. Your metaphors can be too thick and vivid, and the obvious pun brings a howl of protest. Jane Austen disliked metaphors, as Mary Laselles notes (*Jane Austen and Her Art,* pp. 111–112), and reserved them for her hollow characters. I have myself sometimes advised scholars not to use them because they are so often overworked and so often tangled in physical impossibilities. "The violent population explosion has paved the way for new intellectual growth" looks pretty good—until you realize that explosions do not pave, and that new vegetation does not grow up through solid pavement. The metaphor, then, is your most potent device. It makes your thought concrete and your writing vivid. It tells in an instant how your subject looks to you. But it is dangerous. It should be quiet, almost unnoticed, with all details agreeing, and all absolutely consistent with the natural universe.

EXERCISES

6 Write two sentences illustrating each of the following (six sentences in all): (1) the simile, (2) the metaphor, (3) the implied metaphor.

7 Write a sentence for each of the following dead metaphors, bringing it to life by adding implied metaphorical detail, as in "She *bridled, snorting* and *tossing her mane,* or by adding a simile, as in "He was *dead* wrong, *laid out like a corpse on a slab.*"

dead center, pinned down, sharp as a tack, stick to, whined, purred, reflected, ran for office, yawned, take a course.

8 Revise the following sentences so as to clear up the illogical or unnatural connections in their metaphors and similes.

1. The violent population explosion has paved the way for new intellectual growth.
2. The book causes a shock, like a bucket of icy water suddenly thrown on a fire.
3. The whole social fabric will become unstuck.
4. They were ecstatic: they scaled the mountain and from here on out they could sail with the breeze.
5. His last week had mirrored his future, like a hand writing on the wall.
6. The recent economic picture, which seemed to spell prosperity, has wilted beyond repair.
7. They were tickled to death by the thunderous applause.
8. Stream-of-consciousness fiction has gone out of phase with the new castles in the air of fantasy.

ALLUSION

Allusions also illustrate your general idea by referring it to something else, making it take your reader as Grant took Richmond, making you the Mickey Mantle of the essay, or the Mickey Mouse. Allusions depend on common knowledge. Like the metaphor, they illustrate the remote with the familiar—a familiar place, or event, or personage. "He looked . . . like a Japanese Humphrey Bogart," writes William Bittner of French author Albert Camus, and we instantly see a face like the one we know so well (a glance at Camus' picture confirms how accurate this unusual allusion is). Perhaps the most effective allusions depend on a knowledge of literature. When Thoreau writes that "the winter of man's discontent was thawing as well as the earth," we get a secret pleasure from recognizing this as an allusive borrowing from the opening lines of Shakespeare's *Richard III:* "Now is the winter of our discontent / Made glorious summer by this sun of York." Thoreau flatters us by assuming we are as well read as he. We need not catch the allusion to enjoy his point, but, if we catch it, we feel a sudden fellowship of knowledge with him. We now see the full metaphorical force, Thoreau's and Shakespeare's both, heightened as it is by our remembrance of Richard Crookback's twisted discontent, an allusive illustration of all our pitiful resentments now thawing with the spring.

Allusion can also be humorous. The hero of Peter De Vries's *The Vale of Laughter,** for instance (not the biblical "vale of tears"), contemplates adultery but decides for home and honor:

> **If you look back, you turn into a pillar of salt. If you look ahead, you turn into a pillar of society.**

He alludes, of course, to Lot's wife, who looked back on the adulterous city of Sodom, against orders, and was turned into a pillar of salt (Gen. xix.26). De Vries begins his book with a wildly amusing allusion to Melville's already allusive beginning of *Moby Dick,* the archetypal whale-hunt. Melville's narrator says to call him "Ishmael," the biblical outcast (Gen. xvi.11–12). De Vries throws a devilish comma into Melville's opening sentence, then turns allusion into metaphor:

> **Call me, Ishmael. Feel absolutely free to. Call me any hour of the day or night at the office or at home, and I'll be glad to give you the latest quotation with price-earnings ratio and estimated dividend of any security traded in those tirelessly**

* Copyright © 1953, 1962, 1964, 1967 by Peter De Vries. The two following excerpts in the text are reprinted by permission of Little, Brown and Co.

tossing, deceptively shaded waters in which we pursue the elusive whale of Wealth, but from which we come away at last content to have hooked the twitching bluegill, solvency. And having got me, call me anything you want, Ish baby. Tickled to death to be of service.

EXERCISE

9 Write a sentence for each of the following, in which you allude either humorously or seriously to:

1. A famous modern celebrity ("She is the Sophia Loren of the class-room")
2. A famous historical person (Caesar, Napoleon, Catherine the Great, Victoria, Lincoln, Hitler)
3. A famous event (the Declaration of Independence, the Battle of Waterloo, landing on Plymouth Rock, the Battle of the Bulge, Vietnam, Custer's Last Stand)
4. A notable place (Athens, Rome, Paris, London Bridge, Jerusalem)
5. This famous passage from Shakespeare, by quietly borrowing some of its phrases:

> To be, or not to be—that is the question:
> Whether 'tis nobler in the mind to suffer
> The slings and arrows of outrageous fortune,
> Or to take arms against a sea of troubles,
> And by opposing end them.

DICTION

"What we need is a mixed diction," said Aristotle, and his point remains true twenty-three centuries and several languages later. The aim of style, he says, is to be clear but distinguished. For clarity, we need common, current words; but, used alone, these are commonplace, and as ephemeral as everyday talk. For distinction, we need words not heard every minute, unusual words, strange words, foreign words, metaphors; but, used alone, these become gibberish. What we need is a diction that weds the popular with the dignified, the clear current with the sedgy margins of language and thought.

Not too low, not too high; not too simple, not too hard—an easy breadth of idea and vocabulary. English is peculiarly well endowed for this Aristotelian mixture. The long abstract Latin words and the short concrete Anglo-Saxon ones give you all the range you need. For most of your ideas, you can find Latin and Anglo-Saxon partners. In fact, for many ideas, you can find a whole spectrum of synonyms from Latin through French to Anglo-Saxon, from general to specific—from *intrepidity* to *fortitude* to *valor* to *courage* to *bravery* to *pluck* to *guts*. You can choose the high word for high effect, or you can get tough with Anglo-Saxon specifics. But you do not want all Anglo-Saxon, and you must especially guard against sobriety's luring you into all Latin. Tune your diction agreeably between the two extremes.

Indeed, the two extremes generate incomparable zip when tumbled side by side, as in *incomparable zip, inconsequential snip, megalocephalic creep,* and the like. Rhythm and surprise conspire to set up the huge adjective first, then to add the small noun, like a monumental kick. Here is a passage from Edward Dahlberg's *Can These Bones Live,** which I opened completely at random to see how the large fell with the small (my italics):

> Christ walks on a *visionary sea;* Myshkin . . . has his ecstatic premonition of infinity when he has an *epileptic fit.* We know the inward size of an artist by his *dimensional thirsts. . . .*

This mixing of large Latin and small Anglo-Saxon, as John Crowe Ransom has noted, is what gives Shakespeare much of his power:

> This my hand will rather
> The multitudinous seas incarnadine,
> Making the green one red.

* Ann Arbor: University of Michigan Press, Ann Arbor Paperbacks, 1967, p. 80.

The short Anglo-Saxon *seas* works sharply between the two magnificent Latin words, as do the three short Anglo-Saxons that bring the big passage to rest, contrasting the Anglo-Saxon *red* with its big Latin kin, *incarnadine*. William Faulkner, who soaked himself in Shakespeare, gets much the same power from the same mixture. He is describing a very old Negro woman in *The Sound and the Fury* (the title itself comes from Shakespeare's *Macbeth*, the source of the *multitudinous seas* passage). She has been fat, but now she is wrinkled and completely shrunken except for her stomach:

> **. . . a paunch almost dropsical, as though muscle and tissue had been courage or fortitude which the days or the years had consumed until only the indomitable skeleton was left rising like a ruin or a landmark above the somnolent and impervious guts. . . .**

The impact of that short, ugly Anglo-Saxon word *guts*, with its slang metaphorical pun, is almost unbearably moving. And the impact would be nothing, the effect slurring, without the grand Latin preparation. "What we need is a mixed diction."

Beware of wordiness.

Wordiness, of course, is also an offense against good diction. In speaking of sentences earlier, I commended elaboration. But I also recommended deletion as so important that we have spent a whole chapter on it. A fully worded sentence, each word in place and pulling its weight, is a joy to see. But a sentence full of words is not. Words should count, I say again. And again, the best way to make them count is to count the words in each suspicious case. Suspect every *by*, every *of*, every *which*, every *is*. Any shorter version will be clearer. I once counted the words, sentence by sentence, in a thirty-page manuscript rejected as "too loose." In some sentences, I cut no more than one or two words. I rephrased many, but I think I cut no entire sentence. In fact, I added a considerable paragraph; and I still had five pages fewer, and a better essay. If you cut only one word from every sentence, you will in ten pages (if you average ten words a sentence) save your reader one whole page of uselessness and obstruction and wasted time.

Sentences can be too short and dense, of course. Many thoughts need explanation and an example or two. Many need the airing of *and*'s and *of*'s. Many simply need some loosening of phrase. In fact, colloquial phrasing, which is as clear and unnoticed as a clean window, is usually longer than its formal equivalent: *something to eat* as compared to *dinner*. By all counts, *dinner* should be better. It is shorter. It is more precise. Yet *something to eat* has social delicacy (at least as I am imagining the party). "Shall we have something to eat?" is more friendly than the more economical "Shall we have dinner?" We don't want to push our friends around with precise and economical suggestions. We want them at their ease, with the choices slightly vague. Consequently, when we write *what we are after* for *object* and *how it is done* for *method,* we give our all-too-chilly prose some social warmth. These colloquial phrases use more words, but they are not wordy if they pull with the rest of the sentence.

It all comes down to redundancy, the clutter of useless words and tangential ideas—"the accumulation of words that add nothing to the sense and cloud up what clarity there is," as Aristotle says. What we write should be easy to read. Too many distinctions, too many nouns, and too much Latin can be pea soup:

> **Reading is a processing skill of symbolic reasoning sustained by the interfacilitation of an intricate hierarchy of substrata factors that have been mobilized as a psychological working system and pressed into service in accordance with the purpose of the reader.**

This comes from an educator, with the wrong kind of education. He is saying:

> **Reading is a process of symbolic reasoning aided by an intricate network of ideas and motives.**

Try *not* to define your terms. If you do, you are probably either evading the toil of finding the right word, or defining the obvious:

> **Let us agree to use the word signal as an abbreviation for the phrase "the simplest kind of sign." (This agrees fairly well with the customary meaning of the word "signal.")**

Now, really! That came from a renowned semanticist, a student of the meanings of words. The customary meaning of a word *is* its meaning, and uncustomary meanings come only from careful punning. Don't underestimate your readers, as this semanticist did.

The definer of words is usually a bad writer. Our semanticist continues, trying to get his signals straight and grinding out about three parts sawdust to every one of meat. In the following excerpt, I have bracketed his sawdust. Read the sentence first as it was written; then read it again, omitting the bracketed words:

> **The moral of such examples is that all intelligent criticism [of any instance] of language [in use] must begin with understanding [of] the motives [and purposes] of the speaker [in that situation].**

Here, each of the bracketed phrases is already implied in the others. Attempting to be precise, the writer has beclouded himself. Naturally the speaker would be "in that situation"; naturally a sampling of language would be "an instance" of language "in use." *Motives* may not be *purposes,* but the difference here is insignificant. Our semanticist's next sentence deserves some kind of immortality. He means "Muddy language makes trouble":

> **Unfortunately, the type of case that causes trouble in practice is that in which the kind of use made of language is not transparently clear. . . .**

Clearly, transparency is hard. Writing is hard. It requires constant attention to meanings, and constant pruning. It requires a diction a cut above the commonplace, a cut above the inaccuracies and circumlocutions of speech, yet within easy reach. Clarity is the first aim; economy, the second; grace, the third; dignity, the fourth. Our writing should be a little strange, a little out of the ordinary, a little beautiful, with words and phrases not met every day but seeming as right and natural as grass. A good diction takes care and cultivation.

It can be overcultivated. It may seem to call attention to itself rather than to its subject. Suddenly we are aware of the writer at work, and a little too pleased with himself, reaching for the elegant cliché and the showy phrase. Some readers find this very fault with my own writing, though I do really try to saddle my maverick love of metaphor. If I strike you in this way, you can use me profitably as a bad example along with the following passage. I have italicized elements that individually may have a certain effectiveness, but that cumulatively become mannerism, as if the writer were watching himself gesture in a mirror. Some of his phrases are redundant; some are trite. Everything is somehow cozy and grandiose, and a little too nautical.

> *There's* little excitement *ashore* when merchant ships from *faraway* India, Nationalist China, or Egypt *knife through* the *gentle swells* of Virginia's Hampton Roads. This *unconcern* may simply reflect the *nonchalance* of people who live by *one of the world's great seaports.* Or perhaps *it's just that folk* who *dwell* in the *home towns* of atomic submarines and Mercury astronauts are not likely to be impressed by a visiting freighter, *from however distant a realm. . . . Upstream a bit* and also *to port,* the mouth of the Elizabeth River leads to Portsmouth and a major naval shipyard. *To starboard lies* Hampton, where at Langley Air Force Base the National Aeronautics and Space Administration prepares to send a man *into the heavens.**

* Robert Damron, "Hampton Roads," *Voyager,* July-August 1960, p. 124.

EXERCISES

10 Write a paragraph in which you mix your diction as effectively as you can, with the big Latin word and the little Anglo-Saxon, the formal word and just the right touch of slang, working in at least two combinations of the extremes, on the pattern of *multitudinous seas, diversionary thrust, incomparable zip,* underlining these for your instructor's convenience.

11 Here are some wordy, awkward, and flat passages from students' papers, with their wordage indicated in parentheses. Improve their diction by making their meaningful words count, cutting all the waste, and indicating your own wordage. Make it less, and grow rich with economy.

1. Machines are merely amplifiers of the abilities of workmen, and exist only as they can do man's bidding effectively. (19)

2. Clearly, the only way to deal with machines is to neither flee from them nor surrender to them, but to use them as means to ends appointed not by them but by ourselves. (33)

3. The question is pertinent today, and painfully practical, as people examine the premises of their personal morality. (17)

4. Civil disobedience, then, is not the product of a recalcitrant minority intent on abolishing law and order, but exists in consequence of and as an important integral part of the give-and-take in democratic adjustment. It serves as a kick in the pants for legislators and the unconcerned majority, making them aware of faults in the democratic system. (57, *give-and-take* counted as one word)

5. The criticism of the military in connection with the draft needs not be of only its character, which overshadowed the draft machinery, but also of its direct involvement with the selective service system. The draft, an institution created by Congress with the intention that it might be civilian-operated, administered by civilians for civilians, became what it was through the gradual infusion of the military. (64)

6. The ability to rapidly handle enormous amounts of data and make rapid decisions often enables the computer to do control applications, such as the generation of power at an electrical power plant. (32)

7. It is wrong to assume, although many criticisms are being raised against technology as it affects human values, that the author does not appreciate its great capacity for good. (29)

8. As the establishment filled with people, an air of stuffiness and a feeling of being uncomfortable permeated the room. (19)

9. This reviewer, after reading about a dozen reviews of the book, was struck by the lack of perception and openmindedness that the critics showed. (24)

10. With all the loud activity in the next apartment, the thinness of the walls became painfully apparent, and sleeping became impossible. (21)

11. The most essential prerequisite that any student group must have in order to be recognized as a power is a leader that acts both as a mouthpiece of the students' ideas and as an originator of students' strategy in their war against the administrators. (44)

12. When a student becomes a member of the Student Government

Council, it is expected that he give up much of his spare time for the council. However, it is not, or at least should not, be expected that he quit school to take on the responsibility of a council member. (50)

13. Another fact which is revealed by the census statistics is that 72.4 percent of the total nonwhite population lives in urban areas. (22)

14. A minority finds it difficult to progress in such a society due to the fact that a majority can perpetuate inequality by simply insuring that the vast majority of its members acquire the positions that pay the greater amounts of money and carry the greatest authority. (46)

15. There are two major results of the increasing mechanization of industry. One is a great reduction in the number of simple, repetitive jobs where all you need is your five senses and an untrained mind. The other result is a great increase in the number of jobs involved in designing, engineering, programming, and administering these automatic production systems. (58)

12 Write a TERRIBLE ESSAY. Have some fun with this perennial favorite, in which you reinforce your sense for clear, figurative, and meaningful words by writing the muddiest and wordiest essay you can invent, gloriously working out all your bad habits. Make it a parody of the worst kind of sociological and bureaucratic prose. Pick some trivial subject, like dripping faucets, and then write, in good essay form but with terribly abstract and jargonish language, *A Report of a Study of the Person Sociology and Night Loss Cost Economics of the Faucets Which Drip in the Second Floor North Corner Woman Dormitory Lavatory*, or some similarly inflated piece of nonsense. Here are the rules:

1. Put EVERYTHING in the passive voice.
2. Modify nouns *only* with nouns, preferably in strings of two or three, never with adjectives: *governmental spending* becomes *government level spending*; an *excellent idea* becomes *the excellence of conception of program*.
3. Use only big abstract nouns — as many *-tion's* as possible.
4. Use no participles: not *dripping faucets* but *faucets which drip,* and use as many *which's* as possible.
5. Use as many words as possible to say the least.
6. Work in as many trite and wordy expressions as possible: *needless to say, all things being equal, due to the fact that, in terms of, as far as that is concerned.*
7. Sprinkle heavily with *-wise*-type and *type*-type expressions, and say *hopefully* every three or four sentences.

8. Compile and use a basic terrible vocabulary: *situation, aspect, function, factor, phase, utilize, the use of,* and so on. The class may well cooperate in this.

One class has had great success with a three-paragraph terrible essay, incorporating each terrible error only once, and then all rewriting the winning worst essay into the best prose possible.

13 Refine your sense of diction and meanings still further by writing *irony:* meaning the opposite, or something different from what you say. Your Terrible Essay has been ironic, of course. You have seemed to say, "This is serious"; you have meant, "This kind of writing is nonsense." Such ironic oppositeness requires an understanding between author and reader. It is like a secret language in which two can talk and circumvent a third. I can say, "It was a fine day"; the uninitiated will think it really was, but you and I will know that it was not. The pleasure in the secret, furthermore, gives the truth an emphasis beyond that of bald statement. Alongside irony, plain statement seems uncouth. "It was a terrible day" seems young and petulant. "It was a fine day" is the voice of refined experience, a suggestion of tweed and teacups, Tobruk to El Alamein, tigers in Bengal, and never a hair turned. A few of the guests might think the day's shooting had been good, but the speaker and you and I would know—and enjoy the unperturbed secret, even secretly enjoy the disappointment because it made irony possible—that the day had been terrible.

So take a pose the opposite of your true standpoint, and let the ironic oppositeness come out through touches of exaggeration, understatement, absurdity, and the like. You might be against a raise in taxes, and write:

The popular clamor against the proposed raise in taxes is as short-sighted as it is unfounded. Purging the purse is good for the spleen. What does it matter that the present Drain Commissioner has wasted exactly a half-million dollars on a poorly conceived plan? What does it matter that our fine city council now finds it necessary to ask for a new bond and a new assessment to overhaul a drainage system just four years old? It matters not.

Or you might be for a new bond issue, and write:

The public has again expressed its infinite wisdom in voting down the recent bond issue. Stinginess is next to godliness, as my great-uncle used to say. It really does not matter that classrooms built for twenty are desperately trying to hold forty; or that our best teachers are leaving for Southfield and Adams and Middlebranch, and even Potfield, simply because they can no longer teach the numbers of students pouring into our beautiful Smith School—one of our most revered landmarks, by the way, and certainly the oldest.

But pick some subject relatively simple and close to your interests, something like the joys of learning languages by tape, Chinese made easy, happy college days, the beloved roommate, the eight o'clock class, our courteous age, chivalry is not dead, the joys of cooking, college—the home away from home. Write a brief, three- or four-paragraph essay, in usual form, but ironic in its stance and diction.

Ten.
Straight
and Crooked
Thinking

All along, you have been thinking and feeling your way into writing, and writing your way into feeling and thought. You have probably seen for yourself how writing can help you discover thought, how it can even seem to create thought, and how it can keep your thinking straight. In fact, we can think straight only on paper.

Our thinking is really not logical, but psychological, sometimes with almost no words at all. Louisa May Alcott once recorded her morning's activities as "having fun with my mind." This sounds attractive, but it probably involved no thinking—in any straight and logical way. Straight thinking is work, and our minds are really not built for it; or, rather, they are built too well for it.

The mind really is a wonder; from the data it has stored away, mostly on its own initiative, it will snap out an answer you can verify only after much careful work on paper. The answer may be wrong, because storage has been partial, wrongly weighted, or distorted by your subsurface yearnings and fears, or because remembrance has simply faded away. Again, only on paper, which holds

201

your thoughts steady enough to look at them, can you work out the fallacies.

The mind *is* a wonder; and much of its activity is, indeed, *wondering,* which is the beginning of thought. We actually think by a series of questions. What you finally produce on paper as an essay, an effort in straight thinking, is far different from the swinging pendulum of questions and answers that produced it. Nevertheless, your finished essay is an idealized analogue of your mental electronics. Your thesis is the answer your computer flashed in the beginning. Your reasoning and illustration are the stored mental data uncoiled and laid out reasonably straight, so we can see them.

So we can see them—here is the key to the power of written words. We want to see them as well as hear them; we want Space to collaborate with Time—so we may have time and space to think. The ancient world designated sight as the chief of the five senses— superior to hearing, smell, taste, and touch. And certainly most of us would still agree. We would probably rather be deaf than blind, and *light* is our commanding metaphor for intelligence (*illumination, enlightenment, throw light on the subject*). Because the spoken word, or the mind's idea, spins away as soon as it comes, we want to get it down on paper where it will stay put, where, by seeing it, we come to understand. Writing, then, is our basic straightener of thought.

WORDS AND THINGS

Learn the multiple meanings of words.

The first step to straight thinking is to understand the nature of words, which we have already considered at some length in the last chapter. Speech, in a sense, is virtually "wordless," since our meaningful utterances are words blended together in a fluid sweep of sound, with their meanings selected for us by their position and emphasis and pitch. You have probably heard about the difference between "HEzaLIGHThousekeeper" and "HEzalightHOUSEkeeper," and about the subtle differences in stress, pitch, and pause by which we select from a word's several meanings the one we want. When conversing, we enjoy a total context of understanding, complete with shrugs and *you know'*s, that makes individual words and sentences of minimal importance. We actually speak as much in fragments as in sentences, and we constantly repeat and circle, even after we know we have been understood. In a sense, the other person doesn't hear a word we say: he gets the meaning without necessarily noticing the words at all.

But on the silent printed page, you must place your words with care: the pitch, the stress, the general context of understanding — all the elements that free our speech from care — are gone. And the visible presence of words heightens our awareness of them *as* words. So much so, indeed, that we sometimes think them physical things, confusing them with the actual sticks and stones of this world.

Words are not things, nor are they symbols of things: words are symbols of our *ideas* of things. The primary fact about words, as I have already suggested (p. 182), is that they are the abstractions or generalizations by which we pick up the particular sticks of this world. A written word is a symbol for a generalization in our heads. Since we like our words to be as concrete as possible, the idea of generalization may bother us. But a word's function is to name a general class of things, or states, or thoughts, or whatever, and we want a word's limits no narrower. When I say *bed,* I mean the general idea of "bed." The physical bed you may picture will be different from mine, but we will understand each other sufficiently. You will get the general idea, and you will also know that I do not specifically mean your little bunk at the dorm, though I mean something like it.

So: words are symbols for our general ideas of things. They are classifiers not only of the sticks and stones of the physical world, but of all the qualities, movements, functions, and conditions we know — *cold, grateful, walk, marry, mother, president, slow, exactly.* Many words refer to nothing in the physical world, though we may infer the entity by its effects — *anger, confidence, peace,* for example; and many words seem to symbolize a kind of mental gesture, the grammar with which we connect our thoughts or describe the connections of the physical world, as with *of, by, in, with, when.*

Words, like other symbols, usually represent a multiplicity of things, not all closely related to each other. A *log* is something for cabins or hearths, a gadget towed behind a ship, or a book on its bridge. A *bridge* may be not only on a ship, but in someone's mouth, or across the Golden Gate (which has neither gold nor hinges). The skipper could take out his bridge while sailing under the bridge and playing bridge on the bridge. Context is usually sufficient to select the wanted meanings automatically from the unwanted. That words have varieties of meanings bothers no one but the theoreticians — or your readers, if you are careless.

Try a little punning.

To master words you must keep alert to all their possibilities of meaning. Hence the punster usually makes the good writer: he forestalls any diabolical misreading because he has already seen the possibility himself. He would never accidentally write: "The situation was explosive, and he was no match for it." Nor: "The girls were barely attractive." A certain devilish eye for meanings will keep your thinking straight, and save you from innocent damnation.

Words are full of deviltry. *Pale* means bloodless of complexion (from Latin *pallidus*); and *pale* means a region staked out for one's reign (from Latin *palus,* or stake). Add such homophones ("same-sounders") as *rain* and *reign* to *pail* (bucket) and *pale* (bloodless; region), and you can see what Shakespeare, that prince of punsters and master of meanings, could do when full of springtime, as in this, the best of all his songs, from *The Winter's Tale:*

> **When daffodils begin to peer,**
> **With heigh! the doxie over the dale —**
> **Why, then comes in the sweet o' the year,**
> **For the red blood reigns in the winter's pale.**

A good writer revels in multiple meanings, letting the ones he doesn't want just linger around the edge of the fun, to show that he knows them but decrees them temporarily insignificant.

A word acquires multiple meanings as it drifts into a new general usage and its specific meaning fades. A circle is a circle, but in expressions like *well known in artistic circles* the word has faded until it means no more than "group." It is a dead metaphor, ready for the touch of the good writer's pencil. The first user was making a metaphor (a *metonymy,* in fact; see Section E in THE HANDBOOK), in which he pictured admirers literally standing around an artist in a ring; he called them not people but a *circle,* naming them by something logically similar. In ordinary thoughtless parlance, we certainly do not see the circle; the physical, literal origin has faded. But the good writer will turn up the color a little, will bring the physical origin back for the reader to see: "The artist found in his circle a charmed protection from the world." Or he will at least prevent any unwanted physical or literal meanings, never writing, for instance, "The artist painted his circle." The writer's best control of a word's multiple meanings lies in respecting the essentially physical thing it says, and in keeping an impudent eye open for all transferred and metaphorical meanings.

EXERCISE

1 Find as many meanings as you can, in your head and dictionary, for each of the following words. EXAMPLE: *bridge—a structure over a river; false teeth; a card game; the navigating platform on a ship.*

Hatch, hitch, runs, fair, case, draft, lock, down, prove, club, grave, fashion, light, medium, joint, sole, cross, term, check

FACTS, AND DEGREES OF BELIEF

Write as close to the facts as possible.

Words may radiate several meanings, but they are your only means of lighting the facts for your reader. You cannot really present the "hard facts" themselves. You cannot reach through the page to hand out actual lumps of coal and bags of wheat. You can only tell *about* these things, and then persuade the reader to see them as you believe they should be seen. Let us now look briefly at the nature of fact, and of belief, opinion, and preference—all matters of concern in keeping your thinking straight, and in convincing your reader that you know what you are about.

Facts are the firmest kind of thought, but they are *thoughts* nevertheless — verifiable thoughts about the coal and wheat and other entities of our experience. The whole question of fact comes down to verifiability: things not susceptible of verification leave the realm of factuality. Fact is limited, therefore, to the kinds of things that can be tested by the senses (verified empirically, as the philosophers say) or by inferences from physical data so strong as to allow no other explanation. "Statements of fact" are assertions of a kind provable by referring to experience. The simplest physical facts — that a stone is a stone and that it exists — are so bound into our elementary perceptions of the world that we never think to verify them, and indeed could not verify them beyond gathering testimonials from the group. With less simple and tangible facts, verification is simply doing enough to persuade any reasonable person that the assertion of fact is true, beginning with what our senses can in some way check.

Measuring, weighing, and counting are the strongest empirical verifiers; assertions capable of such verification are the most firmly and quickly demonstrated as factual:

> **Smith is five feet high and four feet wide.**
> **The car weighs 2,300 pounds.**
> **Three members voted for beer.**

In the last assertion, we have moved from what we call physical fact to historical fact — that which can be verified by its signs: we have the ballots. Events in history are verified in the same way, although the evidence is scarcer the farther back we go.

Facts, then, are those things, states, or events of a kind susceptible of verification. Notice: *of a kind* susceptible of verification. Some perfectly solid facts we may never be able to verify. The place, date, and manner of Catullus's death; whether a person is guilty as accused or innocent as claimed — these may never be known to us, may never be established as "facts," because we lack the evidence to verify them. But we would not want to remove them from the realm of factuality; they are the *kind* of thing that could be verified, if only we could get at the evidence.

Believe what you write — but learn the nature of belief.

Facts, then, are things susceptible of verification. Belief presents an entirely different kind of knowledge: things believed true but yet beyond the reach of sensory verification — a belief in God, for instance. We may infer a Creator from the creation, a Beginning from the beginnings we see around us in the natural world. But a doubting Thomas will have nothing to touch or see; judging our inferences wrongly drawn, he may prefer to believe in a physical accident, or in a flux with neither beginning nor end. The point is that although beliefs are unprovable, they are not necessarily untrue, and they are not unusable as you discourse with your reader. You can certainly assert beliefs in your writing, establishing their validity in a tentative and partially probable way, so long as you do not assume you have *proved* them. State your convictions; support them with the best reasons you can find; and don't apologize. But, for both politeness and persuasion, you may wish to qualify your least demonstrable convictions with "I believe," "we may reasonably suppose," "perhaps," "from one point of view," and the like — unless the power of your conviction moves you beyond the gentilities, and you are writing heart to heart.

Don't mistake opinion for fact.

Halfway between fact and belief is opinion. An opinion is a candidate for fact, something you believe true but about whose verification you are still uncertain. All the facts are not in, you are not sure of the tests, and you may not be sure that there are tests; but you can at least present tentative verification. The difference between fact and opinion, then, is simply a difference in verifiableness. One opinion may eventually prove true, and another false; an opinion may strengthen, through verifying tests, into accepted fact, as with Galileo's opinion that the earth moved.

The testing of opinions to discover the facts is, indeed, the central business of straight thinking. When you assert something as fact, you indicate (1) that you assume it true and easily verified, and (2) that its truth is generally acknowledged. When you assert something as opinion, you imply some uncertainty about both these things. Here are two common opinions that will probably remain opinions exactly because of such uncertainty:

Girls are brighter than boys.
Men are superior to women.

Although these statements are in *kind* susceptible of verification, we know we will probably never verify them satisfactorily. We know that the necessary tests are difficult, not merely to administer and control, but to agree upon, and we know that the terms *brighter* and *superior* have a range of meaning hard to pin down. Even when agreeing upon the tests for numerical and verbal abilities, and for memory and ingenuity, we cannot be sure that we will not miss other kinds of brightness and superiority, or that our tests will measure these things in any thorough way. The range of meaning in our four other terms, moreover, is so wide as virtually to defy verification. We need only ask "At what age?" to illustrate how broad and slippery the terms *girls, boys, men,* and *women* really are.

Dispute your preferences with care.

Preferences are something else again. They are farther from proof than opinions — indeed, beyond the pale of proof. And yet they are more firmly held than opinions, because they are primarily subjective, sweetening our palates and warming our hearts. *De gustibus non est disputandum:* tastes are not to be disputed. So goes the medieval epigram, from the age that refined the arts of logic. You can't argue successfully about tastes, empirical though they be, because they are beyond empirical demonstration. Are peaches better than pears? Whichever you choose, your choice is probably neither logically defensible nor logically vulnerable. The writer's responsibility is to recognize the logical immunity of preferences, and to qualify them politely with "I think," "many believe," "some may prefer," and so forth.

But that preferences are subjective does not eliminate their general interest, nor remove them from discussion. Because they are immune, because they are strong, and because everyone has them, preferences have a certain "validity" that repays investigation. The medieval logicians notwithstanding, tastes are indeed worth disputing, because discussing them may lead to assertions demon-

strable enough to be, in some measure, persuasive. You will probably never convince a pear person, but you may make a fairly sound
case for peaches. I would guess that the annual consumption of
peaches exceeds that of pears three to one. And in a best-selling
cookbook, recipes for peaches outnumber those for pears three to
one. Of course, popularity is no criterion for quality; but a continued preference by large numbers of people, if you can establish
that as fact, shows that what had seemed a private preference actually has a public acceptance worth analyzing. Your private taste
for peaches may then translate into a perfectly demonstrable thesis:
"People seem to prefer peaches to pears." You could probably
make even a qualitative judgment stand up, with a thesis something
like: "Although chilled pears are delicious, Americans seem to consider peaches more satisfying, as the annual sales figures would
indicate."

So go ahead, dispute over tastes, and you may find some solid
grounds for them. Shakespeare *is* greater than Ben Jonson, his
friend and greatest competitor. Subjective tastes have moved all
the way up beside fact: the grounds for Shakespeare's margin of
greatness have been exhibited, argued, and explored over the centuries, until we accept his superiority, as if empirically verified.
Actually, the questions that most commonly concern us are beyond
scientific verification. But you can frequently establish your preferences as testable opinions by asserting them reasonably and without
unwholesome prejudice, and by using the secondary evidence that
other reasonable people agree with you in persuasive strength and
number.

ASSUMPTIONS AND IMPLICATIONS

Check your statements, root and branch.

Your statements spring from assumptions below the surface
and sprout all kinds of unwritten sprigs. These latter, the implications, you can more readily control. Actually, language is at its
best when implying more than it says. Irony, for instance, is a constant shadow-play of implication. When you say, "As an officer, he
certainly had command of his tailor," you clearly imply that he could

command little else. The danger in implications is in your not seeing them yourself. If you say "The demonstration was unfair to the management," you must face your implication that the management has been fair to the customers and the help. Keep your eyes open for where your words are pointing, and either trim the pointers or follow them out.

Language naturally looks ahead, so we look for our implications almost by second nature. But we do not naturally check our assumptions, because our whole lives rest on acquired assumptions we hardly think to question: love is better than hate; life is better than death; self-preservation is primary; giving your life for others is good; security is good; success is good; and so on and on. Many of our assumptions conflict, as when our approvals of selfless dedication and of self-sufficiency clash. Sacrifice can be truly selfless, or morbidly self-serving; and selfishness can have a certain forthright honesty that works not too badly in the social mix. As when you first shaped your thesis in Chapter 1, you should continue to check your assumptions to see what your readers, or your opponents, will take for granted, and what they will not grant until proved. If you assume, simply, that football builds character or that socialism ruins it, that some races are inferior or all men equal, you may find your platform shot from under you as the opposition hits the narrowness of your assumptions.

Assumptions and implications can be seen as different ends of the same idea. By assuming that football builds character, you may overlook your implications that other things do not and that "character" means, for you, only a healthy competitive tenacity and a measure of physical courage. Overlooking the full width of the term, you may assume its meaning too narrowly; "character" also means a sense of responsibility, honesty, and humanity, which, along with tenacity and courage, may come readily from other sources. If you acknowledge this breadth of assumption behind your term, you can very well go ahead with the case, arguing that football does indeed build character in certain ways. Perhaps you need merely change your thesis to something like: "Although no magical guarantee, football contributes certain valuable disciplines toward the development of character." You immediately show that you are neither claiming nor assuming more than the reasonable truth. You have found a solid premise.

Assumptions and implications have to do with your thesis, or with any subordinate assertion you make in demonstrating it. Your proof is what makes your assertions stick. Proof is just enough of evidence and reasoning to persuade your readers that what you are saying is true. Usually, as I have already said, all you need is common sense and enough delicacy not to shout "proved" too loudly. Anything within reason goes; but keep in mind the kinds of proving within reason, and the traps beyond reason.

EXERCISE

2 After each of the following assertions, write two or three short questions that will challenge its assumptions, questions like "Good for what? Throwing? Fertilizer?" For example: Girls are brighter than boys. "At what age? In chess? In physics?"

1. Men are superior to women.
2. The backfield made some mistakes.
3. Communism means violent repression.
4. Don't trust anyone over thirty.
5. All men are equal.
6. The big companies are ruining the environment.
7. Travel is educational.
8. Our brand is free of tar.
9. The right will prevail.
10. A long walk is good for you.

PROOF BEYOND LOGIC

Know your authorities.

An appeal to some authority to prove your point is really an appeal beyond logic, but not necessarily beyond reason. "Einstein said . . ." can silence many an objection, since we believe Einstein knew more about physical fact than anyone. "According to Freud" may win your point on human personality, as may an appeal to Winston Churchill or Matthew Arnold or H. W. Fowler on English usage. Shakespeare, the Bible, and Samuel Johnson can authenticate your claims about the ways of the world and the spirit.

Since authority has long since proved itself right, appeals to authority are not beyond reason. But they are beyond logic, because the logical proof that first established the authority has long since retired to the bookshelves. What Einstein said, we tend to take on faith, without demanding proof, which may well be beyond us. The greatest men in the field have accepted Einstein's logic and acknowledged his achievement. Who are we to question that? In this apparent infallibility, of course, reside the hazards of relying upon authority.

Appeals to authority risk four common fallacies. The first is in appealing to the authority outside of his field, even if his field is the universe. Although Einstein had a powerful intellect, we should not assume he knew all about economics too. Even if a chance remark of Einstein's sounds like the quantum theory of banking, you will do best to quote it only for its own rational merits, using Einstein's having said it only as a bonus of persuasive interest; otherwise, your appeal to his authority will seem naïve in the extreme. The good doctor, of the wispy hair and frayed sweater, was little known for understanding money.

The second fallacy is in misunderstanding or misrepresenting what the authority really says. Sir Arthur Eddington, if I may appeal to an authority myself, puts the case: "It is a common mistake to suppose that Einstein's theory of relativity asserts that everything is relative. Actually it says, 'There are absolute things in the world but you must look deeply for them. The things that first present themselves to your notice are for the most part relative.' "* If you appeal loosely to Einstein to authenticate an assertion that everything is "relative," you may appeal in vain—since *relative* means relative *to* something else, eventually to some absolute.

The third fallacy is in assuming that one instance for an authority represents him accurately. Arguments for admitting the

* *The Nature of the Physical World* (Ann Arbor: University of Michigan Press, 1958), p. 23.

split infinitive to equal status with the unsplit, for instance, often present split constructions from prominent writers. But they do not tell us how many splits a writer avoided, or how he himself feels about the construction. A friend once showed me a split infinitive in the late Walter Lippmann's column after I had boldly asserted that careful writers like Lippmann never split their infinitives. Out of curiosity, I wrote Mr. Lippmann; after all, he might have changed his tune. He wrote back that the split had been simply a slip, that he disliked the thing and tried to revise it out whenever it crept in.

The fourth fallacy is deepest: the authority may have faded. New facts have generated new ideas. Einstein has limited Newton's authority. Geology and radioactive carbon have challenged the literal authority of Genesis. Jung has challenged Freud; and Keynes, Marx.

The more eminent the authority, the easier the fallacy. Ask these four questions:

1. Am I citing him outside his field?
2. Am I presenting him accurately?
3. Is this instance really representative?
4. Is he still fully authoritative?

Do not claim too much for your authority, and add other kinds of proof, or other authorities. In short, don't put all your eggs in one basket; write as if you knew the market and the risks. Every appeal to authority is open to logical challenge.

EXERCISE

3 Each of the following statements contains at least one fallacious citation of authority. Identify it, and explain how it involves one or several of these reasons: "Outside Field," "Not Accurately Presented," "Not Representative," "Out of Date."

1. According to Charles Morton, a distinguished eighteenth-century theologian and schoolmaster, the swallows of England disappear to the dark side of the moon in winter.

2. Einstein states that everything is relative.

3. "Nucular" is an acceptable pronunciation of "nuclear." President Eisenhower himself pronounced it this way.

4. War between capitalists and communists is inevitable, as Karl Marx shows.

5. Giving LSD to everyone, including children, as Timothy Leary says, will greatly improve modern society.

6. The American economy should be controlled in every detail; after all, economist John Kenneth Galbraith comes out for control.

7. "Smooths are America's finest cigarette," says Joe Namath.

Handle persistences as you would authorities.

That the persistence of an idea constitutes a kind of unwritten or cumulative authority, is also open to logical challenge. Because a belief has persisted, the appeal goes, it must be true. Since earliest times, for example, man has believed in some kind of supernatural beings or Being. Something must be there, the persistence seems to suggest. But the appeal is not logical; the belief could have persisted from causes other than the actuality of divine existence, perhaps only from man's psychological need. As with authority, new facts may vanquish persistent beliefs. The belief that the world was a pancake, persistent though it had been, simply had to give way to Columbus and Magellan. For all this, however, persistence does have considerable validating strength. Shakespeare's supremacy, upheld now for three centuries, and by men of many nations, has considerable force in upholding the assertion that he is, so far, supreme. As with appeals to authority, appeals to persistence are most effective when acknowledged as *indications* of validity rather than as logical proofs and validities themselves.

Inspect your documentary evidence before using.

Documents are both authoritative and persistent. They provide the only evidence, aside from oral testimony, for all that we know beyond the immediate presence of our physical universe, with its physical remains of the past. Documents point to what has happened, as long ago as Nineveh and Egypt and as recently as the tracings on last hour's blackboard. But documents are only records or traces, not events themselves, and you must be wary of presenting them at face value. Documents vary in reliability. The inscription on tombstone and monument would seem a firmer testimonial than the name in a legend; the diplomat's diary firmer than the public announcement; the eyewitness's description firmer than the historian's summary. You must consider a document's historical context, since factuality may have been of little concern, as with stories of heroes and saints. You must allow, as with newspapers, for the effects of haste and limited facts. You should consider a document's author, his background, his range of knowledge and belief, his assumptions, his prejudices, his probable motives, his possible tendencies to suppress or distort the facts.

Finally, you should consider the document's data. Are the facts of a kind easily verifiable or easily collected? Indeed, can you present other verification? For example, numerical reports of population can be no more than approximations, and they are hazier the farther back you go in history, as statistical methods slacken. Since the data must have been selected from almost infinite possibilities, does the selection seem reasonably representative? Are your source's conclusions right for the data? Might not the data produce other conclusions? Your own data and conclusions, of course, must also face questioning.

Statistics are particularly persuasive data, and because of their psychological appeal, they can be devilishly misleading. To reduce things to numbers seems scientific, incontrovertible, final. But each "1" represents a slightly different quantity, as one glance around a class of 20 students will make clear. Each student is the same, yet entirely different. The "20" is a broad generalization convenient for certain kinds of information: how many seats the instructor will need, how many people are absent, how much the instruction costs per head, and so forth. But clearly the "20" will tell nothing about the varying characteristics of the students or the education. So present your statistics with some caution so that they will honestly show what you want them to show, and will not mislead your readers.

Averages and percentages can be especially misleading, carrying the numerical generalization one step farther from the physical facts. The truth behind a statement that the average student earns $10 a week could be that nine students earn nothing and one earns $100. A statement in an eminent professional journal that 73 percent of the "cultivated informants" in the North Central States say "ain't I" is actually reporting on a group of only 31 cultivated informants, a mere 11 of whom answered the question about "ain't I" —and only 8 of these used "ain't I." Dividing 8 by 11 does give .73. But put "73 percent" in print, and you seem to have scientific proof that 73 of every 100 cultivated persons say "ain't I," whereas the figure represents merely 8 people in a population of some 35 million. How many of 35 million persons are cultivated, and how we test for cultivation, are questions not easily answered. The statistic also ignores how often the "ain't I" people said "ain't" as against other possibilities, and whether humorously, or accidentally, and so forth. Be wary in presenting your statistics, especially when each number, so firm and final, can conceal variations beyond the reach of calipers and scales.

LOGICAL PROOF: INDUCTION

In Chapter 5, we considered induction and deduction as ways of leading your reader: *in*duction leads him through the evidence to the main point (*in + ducere,* "to lead"); *de*duction leads away from your thesis into the evidence that supports it. In logic, you simply follow one or the other of these directions, either toward or away from the Big Idea.

Induction is the way of science: one collects the facts and sees what they come to. Sir Francis Bacon laid down in 1620 the inductive program in his famous *Novum Organum, sive indicia vera de interpretatione naturae* ("The New Instrument, or true evidence concerning the interpretation of nature"). Bacon was at war with the syllogism; its abstract deductions seemed too rigid to measure nature's subtlety. His new instrument changed the entire course of thought. Before Bacon, the world had deduced the consequences of its general ideas; after Bacon, the world looked around and induced new generalizations from what it saw. Observed facts called the old ideas into question, and theories replaced "truths." As you probably know, Bacon died from a cold caught while stuffing a chicken's carcass with snow for an inductive test of refrigeration.

Induction has great strength, but it also has a basic fallacy. The strength is in taking nothing on faith, in having no ideas at all until the facts have suggested them. The fallacy is in assuming that the mind can start blank, with no prior ideas. Theoretically, Bacon had no previous ideas about refrigeration. Theoretically, he would ex- periment aimlessly until he noticed consistencies that would lead to the icebox. Actually, from experience, one would already have a hunch, a half-formed theory, that would suggest the experimental tests. Induction, in other words, is always well mixed with deduc- tion. The major difference is in the tentative frame of mind: in mak- ing a hypothesis instead of merely borrowing an honored assump- tion, and in keeping the hypothesis hypothetical, even after the facts seem to have supported it.

Use analogies to clarify, not to prove.

The simplest kind of induction is analogy: because this tree is much like that oak, it too must be some kind of oak. You identify the unknown by its analogy to the known. You inductively look over the similarities until you conclude that the trees are very similar, and therefore the same kind. Analogies are tremendously useful in- dications of likeness; analogy is virtually our only means of classifi- cation, our means of putting things into groups and handling them by naming them. Analogy also illustrates the logical weakness of induction: assuming that *all* characteristics are analogous after find- ing one or two analogous. We check a few symptoms against what we know of colds and flu, and conclude that we have a cold and flu; but the doctor will add to these a few more symptoms and conclude that we have a virulent pneumonia.

Similarity does not mean total identity, and analogies must al- ways make that shaky assumption, or clearly demonstrate that the mismatching details are unimportant. In your writing, you may use analogy with tremendous effect, since it is almost the very basis of knowledge. But watch out for the logical gap between *some* and *all*. Make sure that:

1. A reasonably large number of details agree.
2. These details are salient and typical.
3. The misfitting details are insignificant and not typical.

If the brain seems in some ways like a computer, be careful not to assume it is in all ways like a computer. Keep the analogy figurative: it can serve you well, as any metaphor serves, to illustrate the unknown with the known.

Look before you leap.

The hypothetical frame of mind is the essence of the inductive method, because it acknowledges the logical flaw of induction, namely, the *inductive leap*. No matter how many the facts, or how carefully weighed, a time comes when thought must abandon the details and leap to the conclusion. We leap from the knowledge that *some* apples are good to the conclusion: "[All] apples are good." This leap, say the logicians, crosses an abyss no logic can bridge, because *some* can never guarantee *all* — except as a general *probability*. The major lesson of induction is that *nothing* can be proved, except as a probability. The best we can manage is a *hypothesis,* while maintaining a perpetual hospitality to new facts that might change our theory. This is the scientific frame of mind; it gets as close to substantive truth as we can come, and it keeps us healthily humble before the facts.

Probability is the great limit and guarantee of the generalizations to which we must eventually leap. You know that bad apples are neither so numerous nor so strongly typical that you must conclude: "Apples are unfit for human consumption." You also know what causes the bad ones. Therefore, to justify your leap and certify your generalization, you base your induction on the following three conditions:

1. Your samples are reasonably numerous.
2. Your samples are truly typical.
3. Your exceptions are explainable, and demonstrably not typical.

The inductive leap is always risky because all the data may not be known. The leap might also be in the wrong direction: more than one conclusion may be drawn from the same evidence. Here, then, is where the inductive frame of mind can help you. It can teach you always to check your conclusions by asking if another answer might not do just as well. Some linguists have concluded that speech is superior to writing because speech has many more "signals" than writing. But from the same facts one might declare writing superior: it conveys the same message with fewer signals.

The shortcomings of induction are many. The very data of sensory observation may be indistinct. Ask any three people to tell how an accident happened, and the feebleness of human observation becomes painfully apparent. If the facts are slippery, the final leap is uncertain. Furthermore, your hypothesis, which must come early to give your investigation some purpose, immediately becomes a *deductive* proposition that not only will guide your selection of facts, but may well distort slightly the facts you select. Finally, as we have seen with statistics and averages, scientific induction relies heavily on mathematics, which requires that qualities be translated into quantities. Neither numbers nor words, those two essential generalizers of our experience, can adequately grasp all our particular diversities. The lesson of induction, therefore, is the lesson of caution. Logically, induction is shot full of holes. But it makes as firm a statement as we can expect about the physical universe and our experience in it. It keeps our feet on the ground, while it makes remarkable sense of our facts. The ultimate beauty of science is perhaps not that it is efficient (and it is), but that it is hypothetical. It keeps our minds open for new hypotheses. The danger lies in thinking it absolute.

LOGICAL PROOF: DEDUCTION

Establish your premise.

De-duction, as I have said, leads *away from* your premise, your basic assumption. A premise is a kind of weathered hypothesis, a general idea so well fitted and durable as to seem part of the natural order of things and beyond question: *life is essentially good,* for instance. Deductive reason characteristically operates in those areas of *values* and *qualities* where factual induction finds little to grasp. Induction starts with the particulars and sees what general proposition they make. Deduction, the only other possible way to reason, starts with the general proposition and sees what it implies for the particulars: granted that such and such is true, then these things also must be true. Both methods can fall down when the numbers or words they employ generalize too far from the skin of physical and mental actuality—which we can scarcely reach without them. Like induction, deduction can make some notorious mistakes. The greatest mistake may be in the premise itself. Since deductive reasoning *depends* on your premise—literally "hangs from" it—you must bolt your premise to solid assumptions, or your whole chain of logic will fall in a heap. First check your assumptions with an eye for termites; then attend to the logical linkage.

Deductive reasoning has produced the syllogism, the deducer's standard computer. We are sometimes put off by syllogisms, since they seem a ponderous device for producing what we already know. And when the input is faulty, they tell us that all men are Gerald Ford or that Republicans wear blue neckties. But if you take the syllogism as a machine to test your logical alignment, or to attack the illogic of your adversaries, you will certainly improve the quality of the thoughts you commit to paper.

The *standard categorical syllogism* tests the validity of your classifications—your "categories." When you prove that all men are Gerald Ford, something has gone wrong with your sorting: you should have "Ford" in some larger class, like "men," and not the other way around. A syllogism does its classifying in three steps, as with this famous example (the typeface differentiates the size of the classes):

All MEN are MORTAL CREATURES.   (major premise)
Socrates is a MAN.   (minor premise)
Therefore, *Socrates* is a MORTAL CREATURE.   (conclusion)

Socrates (the *minor term*) fits in the larger class of MEN (*middle term*), which fits in the still larger class of MORTAL CREATURES (*major term*).

The first step in classifying by syllogism is to construct a "categorical proposition"—an assertion containing a subject (S), a linking *is (are, were)*, and a predicate nominative (a noun or noun clause that completes the linking *is*), the "predicate term" or P. Your verb, I repeat, must be *is (are, were)* and no other; and it must be completed by a noun or noun clause (the predicate term, or P). Both your subject (S) and your predicate term (P) must be nouns or noun clauses. You must change "Socrates is mortal" (*noun-is-adjective*) to "Socrates is a mortal creature" (*noun-is-noun*); otherwise you cannot manipulate your predicate term in logical equivalence with your subject. Similarly, to put into a syllogism the assertion that "you can't teach an old dog new tricks," you must manufacture the categorical proposition: "All new tricks are things that you can't teach old dogs." Such prose is atrocious, of course, but syllogisms often must untune the language to get at the logic. If you need to state a syllogism directly in your writing, there it must stand, clumsy or not. But more often you use the syllogism to check a question of logic on the side, and what appears in your paper will be a recasting of the same idea in your best-tuned language.

Now, there are only four kinds of categorical propositions:

    I. All students are pragmatists.
   II. No students are pragmatists.
  III. Some students are pragmatists.
  IV. Some students are not pragmatists.

As you have seen with Socrates, a syllogism has three propositions: (1) a major premise, (2) a minor premise, and (3) a conclusion. Our Socrates-syllogism takes its three propositions from category I ("Socrates" is naturally "all Socrates"). Furthermore, a syllogism always uses three and only three terms: a MAJOR term, a *minor* term, and a MIDDLE term. The syllogism must always begin with the major premise (1), which contains the MAJOR term and the MIDDLE term. It must then assert the minor premise (2), which must contain the *minor* term and, again, the MIDDLE term. Thus the MIDDLE term appears in both major and minor premises to help relate the *minor* term to the MAJOR term. That relationship is finally expressed in the conclusion (3), which must always state the *minor* term as its subject (S) and the MAJOR term as its predicate term (P), and which must not mention the MIDDLE term at all.

Unfortunately, classification by size does not work out so neatly in syllogisms using propositions of categories II, III, and IV. In these, size of class may be irrelevant. Your minor class could well be larger than your major, as in the conclusion "No men [minor] are workhorses [major]," or "Some girls [minor] are sophomores [major]"; the world obviously contains more men than workhorses, and more girls than sophomores. Nevertheless, except for our negative statements, we tend to think uphill, putting smaller into larger ("Some sophomores are girls"), as the traditional terms themselves suggest: *minor* —————→ MAJOR.

As we have said, the syllogism aims to draw a valid conclusion that states the minor term as its subject (S) and the major term as its predicate term (P). It is extremely useful, then, *to think of the minor and major terms as S and P,* their eventual functions in the conclusion, *and to think of the middle term as M.* In other words, the syllogism first fits the P(redicate) to the M(iddle term), then the S(ubject) to the M(iddle term), and finally the S(ubject) to the P(redicate). The M is merely a means of getting the S correctly related to the P. By way of review, we may now use these symbols in setting down the basic constituents of the syllogism:

Major premise: P, M or M, P (major, middle; middle, major)
Minor premise: S, M or M, S (minor, middle; middle, minor)
Conclusion: S, P   (minor [subject], major [predicate])

The middle term (M) *always* appears in both major and minor premises; the conclusion *always* states that S is P.

Here are two exercises to help you label your terms. Go to the conclusion first and label your S and P. The remaining term will of course be your M.

_____

EXERCISES

4 Label the terms — P, M, and S — in the following syllogisms:

1. All knowledge is something useful. ("P" premise)
   Awareness of death is knowledge. ("S" premise)
   Therefore, awareness of death is something useful.

2. No human being is a perpetually happy person.
   All teachers are human beings.
   Therefore, no teacher is a perpetually happy person.

3. All poisonous plants are things to be avoided.
   Some things to be avoided are mushrooms.
   Therefore, some mushrooms are poisonous plants.

5 Supply the missing terms and labels (P, M, or S) for the following valid syllogisms.

1. All creatures capable of crime (M) are human beings (P).
   Criminals (S) are _____ (M).
   Therefore, criminals ( ) are human beings (P).

2. No fish (P) are mammals (M).
   Some _____ ( ) are sea creatures (S).
   Therefore, some _____ (S) are not fish (P).

3. All respecters of Marx (M) are potential Communists ( ).
   Some faculty members ( ) are respecters of Marx ( ).
   Therefore, some _____ ( ) are _____ ( ).

4. No _____ ( ) are great-grandmothers ( ).
   Girls ( ) are people under thirty (M).
   Therefore, no _____ ( ) are great-grandmothers ( ).

5. Some realists ( ) are idealists well seasoned (M).
   All _____ ( ) are _____ ( ).
   Therefore, some people of mature years ( ) are realists ( ).

6. No _____ ( ) is an astronaut ( ).
   All _____ ( ) are teenagers ( ).
   Therefore, no fifteen-year-old ( ) is an astronaut ( ).

7. All beasts of burden ( ) are _____ ( ).
   _____ ( ) are vegetarians ( ).
   Therefore, no tigers ( ) are _____ ( ).

8. _____ ( ) are carers for their young ( ).
   _____ ( ) are mammals ( ).
   Therefore, no fish ( ) are _____ ( ).

But labels are just a beginning.

Now, let's try a Category III syllogism:

> **Some Republicans (M) are Watergaters (P).**
> **Smith (S) is a Republican (M).**
> **Therefore, Smith (S) is a Watergater (P).**

How was that again? The syllogism follows the rules, but something has gone wrong. We have violated another principle of classification, a most important one, concerning the "distribution" of our classes.

Learn how to distribute your terms.

The question of *all* and *some* is at the center of classifying ideas in syllogisms. The rules for distributing and not distributing your terms—that is, for making them assert information about all members, or only some members, of a class—are a little tricky. A term is "distributed," logically, when it includes ("is distributed throughout") *all* members of the group it describes. In the syllogism on page 220, "All MEN" is *distributed;* "Some MEN" is undistributed. MORTAL CREATURES, *undistributed* because it asserts something about only those mortal creatures known as men. "Socrates" is *distributed,* because he is "all Socrates"; but "MAN" is *undistributed* because it asserts nothing about the entire class of man. Two rules ensure against faulty distribution:

1. Your middle term (M) *must* be distributed at least once.
2. Neither major term (P) nor minor term (S) may be distributed in the conclusion ("All") if it is undistributed ("Some") in its premise.

In our Republican syllogism, we have not kept our eyes on the *all* and *some.* Our middle term, Republicans (M), is not distributed in either premise: "Some Republicans are Watergaters" asserts nothing about *all* Republicans; and "Smith is a Republican" similarly asserts nothing about *all* Republicans. In short, we have fallen into that common fallacy known as "the undistributed middle."

Here are two simple summaries to help you check your distribution:

1. Distributed: "All" terms, and terms following negatives (*both* terms after "no" are distributed).
2. Undistributed: Any terms following "some" or "is."

EXERCISE

6 Copy out the following propositions. Over each term write "D" or "U" for "Distributed" or "Undistributed," and put a I, II, III, or IV after the proposition to indicate to which category it belongs.

1. All mice are warm-blooded creatures.
2. Some teenagers are voters.
3. Some men are not fighters.
4. No activist is a college president.
5. Some air creatures are not birds.
6. All motorists are potential killers.
7. No girls are varsity football players.

Check the six standard rules.

RULE 1.   Use only three terms, with no change in sense—no "All girls are *bright creatures;* stars are *bright creatures*" (a shift in meaning called the FALLACY OF FOUR TERMS).

RULE 2.   Distribute middle term (M) at least once, to avoid the common FALLACY OF THE UNDISTRIBUTED MIDDLE.

RULE 3.   Do not distribute your major term (P) nor minor term (S) in the conclusion ("All") *if undistributed* ("*Some*") *in its premise* (the FALLACY OF ILLICIT PROCESS).

RULE 4.   Use only one negative premise.

RULE 5.   If either premise is negative, the conclusion must be negative.

RULE 6.   If the conclusion is "particular" ("Some"), the syllogism may have only one "universal" ("All" or "No") premise.

EXERCISES

7 Evaluate the following syllogisms, indicating which fallacy each contains ("Four Terms," "Undistributed Middle," or "Illicit Process), or certify it "Valid."

1. All paper money is a medium of exchange.
   Some beads are a medium of exchange.
   Therefore, some beads are paper money.

2. All media of exchange are tokens of value.
   Some beads are a medium of exchange.
   Therefore, all beads are tokens of value.

3. All media of exchange are commercially useful.
   Some beads are a medium of exchange.
   Therefore, some beads are commercially useful.

4. No cheaters are fair people.
   All blonds are fair people.
   Therefore, no blonds are cheaters.

5. No trustworthy people are people over thirty.
   Some people over thirty are alcoholics.
   Therefore, no alcoholics are trustworthy people.

6. Some meat-eaters are reptiles.
   Some reptiles are constrictors.
   Therefore, some constrictors are meat-eaters.

7. No vegetarians are meat-eaters.
   Some reptiles are meat-eaters.
   Therefore, no reptiles are vegetarians.

8. Some puzzles are nervewrackers.
   All syllogisms are puzzles.
   Therefore, all syllogisms are nervewrackers.

9. All good cooks are seasoners.
   Some seasoners are not girls.
   Therefore, no girls are good cooks.

10. All good cooks are seasoners.
    Some girls are not seasoners.
    Therefore, no girls are good cooks.

8 Construct syllogisms on the following major premises.

1. All good cooks are seasoners.

2. No cheaters are fair people.

3. No trustworthy people are people over thirty.

4. Some puzzles are nervewrackers.

5. Some meat-eaters are reptiles.

Watch out for fallacies.

The syllogism helps to display our fallacies, but most of them you can detect by simply knowing they are lurking. Here are the most common:

1. EITHER-OR. You assume only two opposing possibilities: "either we abolish requirements or education is finished." Education will probably amble on, somewhere in between. Similarly, IF-THEN: "If I work harder on the next paper, then I'll get a better grade." You have overlooked differences in subject, knowledge, involvement, inspiration.

2. OVERSIMPLIFICATION. As with *either-or,* you ignore alternatives. "A student learns only what he wants to learn" ignores all the pressures from parents and society, which in fact account for a good deal of learning.

3. BEGGING THE QUESTION. A somewhat unhandy term: you assume as proved something that really needs proving. "Free all political prisoners" assumes that none of those concerned has committed an actual crime.

4. IGNORING THE QUESTION. The question of whether it is right for a neighborhood to organize against a newcomer shifts to land values and taxes.

5. NON SEQUITUR. ("It does not follow.") "He's certainly sincere; he must be right." "He's the most popular; he should be president." The conclusions do not reasonably follow from sincerity and popularity.

6. POST HOC, ERGO PROPTER HOC. ("After this, therefore because of this.") The non sequitur of events: "He stayed up late and

therefore won the race." He probably won in spite of late hours, and for other reasons.

EXERCISE

9 Name and explain the fallacy in each of the following:

1. Jones is rich. He must be dishonest.
2. He either worked hard for his money, or he is just plain lucky.
3. The best things in life are free, like free love.
4. Sunshine breeds flies, because when the sun shines the flies come out.
5. If they have no bread, let them eat cake. Cake is both tastier and richer in calories.
6. This is another example of American imperialism.
7. Smith's canned-soup empire reaches farther than the Roman empire.
8. *Chips* is America's most popular soap. It is clearly the best.
9. The draft is illegal. It takes young men away from their education and careers at the most crucial period of their lives. They lose thousands of dollars worth of their time.
10. Women are the most exploited people in the history of the world.
11. Two minutes after the accused left the building, the bomb exploded.

Eleven
Outlines

The first thing to grasp about outlines is that they seldom work out to the letter. The second is that they always help. The third is that the headings do not represent equal space in the finished essay: one heading may become two paragraphs and the next only two sentences. The fluid pressure of writing will always force revision of your best-laid plans. An incidental sentence may swell into an entire section; a scheduled section may end up scrapped. But an outline helps you lay things straight.

Outline to set your thoughts in order.

An outline helps you to spot gaps in your own argument and in the arguments of others, to test the relationships of parts, to certify a thesis, to validate an assertion. Outline your reading, and you will really grasp it. Outline the plan of your essay, and you straighten out your thinking for your reader to grasp.

We think and write largely by free association, but to explain these thoughts fully to our readers, and to ourselves, we need to discover and outline their logical pattern. With the logic down on paper, we can write from heading to heading, sure of our direction, and our order of ascending interest. We can push aside the good ideas constantly crowding in: our outline has already scheduled a place for them up ahead, each where it will be most logical and effective.

Suit the outline to the task.

Finding a firm, assertive thesis has already won much of your battle with logic. Beyond the thesis, your essay's length and its structural demands will suggest your choice from among the four kinds of outlines: (1) the jotted outline, (2) the topic outline, (3) the sentence outline, and (4) the paragraph outline. Argument, of course, demands more planning than does descriptive exposition. A *pro-con* structure demands more outlining than do the orders of time and space. A short paper of five hundred or a thousand words will need but the simplest of outlines: a thesis, and three or four headings arranged in any reasonable order of ascending interest, human, logical, or chronological. Longer papers require more detailed planning: exactly how much, you will eventually learn from experience.

Revise your outline.

Whatever the kind of outline you choose, your best procedure is to sketch the whole thing out in rough form first, aligning and refining your points later. After setting down your thesis, with your title boldly above it, rough out your main points, not bothering yet with the minor ones. Next, rearrange your main headings in some systematic sequence of ascending interest. Try to fix firmly on your main headings, or you may waste much time on subheadings that will vanish if your main heads shift. Then sketch in and arrange your subpoints under each of your main headings. Check to be sure each heading develops your thesis. Finally, rephrase your headings, keeping them concise, grammatically parallel, and properly coordinated and subordinated. If you do not word your headings in grammatical parallel, the logical relations between them will be unclear. Keep your headings brief, favoring the active voice; your outline will condition the language of your paper.

THE JOTTED OUTLINE

The jotted outline is the simplest—perhaps all you will need for a short paper. Even with these jotted headings, parallel phrasing helps keep your thinking straight. Here is a jotted outline for a paper against smoking:

The Wicked Cigarette

THESIS: **Despite certain hazy benefits, we must admit that cigarettes are bad for us.**
1. Social benefits—put you "in," give you something to do and say, make you feel mature (in charge of your own life).
2. Economic benefits—support a tremendous industrial network, from farmer to company to advertising agency to magazines and newspapers, providing thousands of livelihoods.
3. But moral hazards—become a habit controlling you, defeating your personal autonomy, making you "follow the pack."
4. Physical hazards—pose an unnecessary risk to the only heart and lungs you have.

Notice how easily you may now convert this outline into an essay. The subordinate clause in your thesis has set aside the concessions you must make to the opposition, and the main clause has asserted the main point. The jotted main headings fall neatly into place, each parallel grammatically, each a noun with its adjective ("social benefits"), each structurally equal, and the four effectively balanced —two for opposition, two for affirmation. The lesser elements of your explanation are also in parallel—*put, give, make,* for example—

to indicate equivalent treatment. Your paper's structure firmly before you, now you are free to write it out.

EXERCISES

1 Write an essay from the outline on smoking (p. 231), or, reversing the viewpoint, write one on the same pattern.

2 Read the following essay and then make a jotted outline that describes its structure. Use your own words to paraphrase the author's central idea and to state his supportive ideas. Do not simply quote sentences from the essay.

HOW A PRINCE SHOULD CONDUCT HIMSELF IN ORDER TO ACQUIRE PRESTIGE

Nothing brings a prince into greater respect than the undertaking of great enterprises and setting a glorious example. In our day we have Ferdinand of Aragon, the present King of Spain. He may almost be called a new prince for, from being a very weak king, he has risen in fame and glory to be the leading monarch in Christendom. If his actions be studied, they will all be found great and some of them really extraordinary. Shortly after ascending to the throne, he attacked Granada, and that undertaking was the foundation of his state. For first of all he carried on the siege at his leisure and without fear of interference, and he kept the attention of the barons of Castile fixed on this war and thus unlikely to consider changes in the state, so that, almost without their being aware of it, he acquired great prestige and authority over them. The money from the Church and from the people enabled him to pay the troops and, in the course of that long war, to lay the foundations for his own army, which has since won so much honor for him. Furthermore, in order to prepare for greater enterprises, and always making use of the pretext of religion, he adopted the piously cruel policy of driving the Moors from his kingdom and despoiling them; herein his conduct could not have been more admirable and extraordinary. Still with the same pretext he attacked Africa, made the campaign in Italy, and has recently turned on the French. Thus he has continually been weaving some great design, which has arrested and amazed the minds of his subjects and kept them absorbed in the development of his plans. His projects have arisen naturally one out of the other and thus have afforded no time for men to pause and organize against him.

A prince should also give a good example in the matter of internal government, as in the case of Messer Bernabò of Milan, rewarding or punishing, as the occasion arises, the citizens who do good or evil in the service of the state, but taking care that the rewards or punishments be such as to cause comment. Above all a prince should see to it that his every action may add to his fame of greatness or excellence.

A prince is also esteemed when he shows himself a true friend or a true enemy, that is, when, without reservation, he takes his stand with one side or the other. This is always wiser than trying to be neutral, for if two powerful neighbors of yours fall out they are either of such sort that the victor may give you reason to fear him or they are not. In either case it will be better for you to take sides and wage an honest war. In the first case, if you do not show your sympathies, you will be an easy prey for the winner to the delight and satisfaction of the loser, and you will have no reason to expect anyone to defend you or give you refuge. For the winner will not care for unreliable friends who may abandon him in adversity, and the loser will not welcome you since you were not willing to take up arms and share the hazards of his fortune.

When Antiochus, invited by the Aetolians, had passed over into Greece to drive out the Romans, he sent a spokesman to the Achaeans, who were the allies of the Romans, urging them to keep out of the war. The Romans on their part were urging the Achaeans to join them. The situation was discussed before the Council of the Achaeans, and when the legate of Antiochus attempted to persuade them to remain neutral, the Roman envoy replied: "As to the statement that it is best and most profitable to your state to take no part in our war, nothing is further from the truth, for if you do not come into it you will be the prize of the victors without any prestige left to you and with no hope of consideration." And it will always fall out that a party unfriendly to you will ask you to remain neutral and those who are friendly will ask you to join them in the war. Irresolute princes, in order to avoid present dangers, usually follow the path of neutrality and more often than not are ruined. But if the prince chooses his side boldly, and his ally wins, even though the latter be powerful and the prince at his mercy, nonetheless there is a bond of obligation and friendship, and mankind is never so faithless as to show ingratitude under such circumstances by turning on friends. Besides, victories are never so complete that the victor need have no caution or respect for justice. But if your ally be the loser then he will welcome you and, as long as he can, he will give you aid and thus you will have a companion in your ill fortune which may yet rise again.

As for the second case, when the two contestants are of such stature that you will have nothing to fear from the victor, it is even more prudent to take part in the war for you will accomplish the ruin of one with the aid of the other who, had he been wise, should rather have supported him. For with your aid he is sure to win and, winning, to put himself in your power. And here it may be noted that a prince should never ally himself with one more powerful to attack another unless absolutely driven by necessity, as in the abovementioned cases. For if your powerful ally wins, you are at his mercy, and princes should avoid as much as possible being at the mercy of another. The Venetians joined France against the Duke of Milan when they could well have dispensed with their ally, and from this alliance came their ruin. Yet there are times when there is no help for it, as in the case of the Florentines when the Pope and the Spanish sent their armies to attack Lombardy, and then a prince must join one of the parties for the reasons set forth in the preceding paragraphs.

Let no state think that it can always adopt a safe course; rather should it be understood that all choices involve risks, for the order of things is such that one never escapes one danger without incurring another; prudence lies in weighing the disadvantages of each choice and taking the least bad as good.

A prince too must always show himself a lover of value and quick to honor those who excel in the various arts. Furthermore, he should encourage his citizens and enable them to go about their affairs in tranquility whether in commerce, agriculture, or any other kind of activity, so that one man may not refrain from improving his possessions for fear lest they be taken from him, nor another hesitate to engage in commerce for fear of taxes. Rather should a prince reward such citizens and any others who may in any way enrich his state or his city. He should also, on the appropriate occasions, offer festivals and spectacles for the diversion of his people, and, since every city is divided into guilds or clans, he should be mindful of these groups and occasionally mingle with them, giving an example of his humanity and munificence, always preserving, however, the majesty of his dignity, for this should never be allowed to suffer in any way.*

* Niccolo Machiavelli, *The Prince,* translated and edited by Thomas G. Bergin (Northbrook, Ill.: AHM Publishing Corporation, 1947), pp. 65–68. Copyright © 1947 by AHM Publishing Corporation. Reprinted by permission of AHM Publishing Corporation.

THE TOPIC OUTLINE

The topic outline is the most common, an arranging of your jotted thoughts into heads and subheads, each rank in parallel phrasing. The major headings rise in ascending importance, but their minor headings descend in smaller and smaller components. You alternate numbers and letters proceeding from Roman numeral *I* through capital *A* to Arabic *1* and little *a,* until you reach, if you need them, parenthesized *(1)* and *(a)*. You indent equal heads equally, so that they fall in the same column, Roman under Roman, capital under capital, and so on:

```
I.  _____
    A.  _____
        1.  _____
        2.  _____
    B.  _____
        1.  _____
            a.  _____
                (1)  _____
                     (a)  _____
                     (b)  _____
                (2)  _____
            b.  _____
        2.  _____
II. _____
```

You will probably need no more than the Roman headings — *I, II, III* — with an *A, B,* and perhaps a *C* under each, but I have sketched the full system for you.

Check your outline for balance.

Ideally every *I* should have its *II,* every *A* its *B,* every *1* its *2,* since an unpaired heading suggests that it is a detail too small for separate treatment, really a part of the larger heading above. For instance:

POOR	GOOD
II. Value of cats	II. Value of cats as pets
A. As pets	
III. Kinds of cats	III. Kinds of cats
A. _____	A. _____
B. _____	B. _____

One of your first revisions should be to absorb any such unpaired heading into its related major heading. Then see that each heading is a noun (or noun phrase), with or without modifiers: "Benefits," for instance, or "Benefits to the individual." This will keep your outline parallel. You can signal your major turns by adding a *But* or *Nevertheless.*

Now for a topic outline of your projected essay on cigarettes. You have already read Thackeray's *Vanity Fair,* and you remember that Dobbin took out a cigar "and amused himself for half an hour with the pernicious vegetable." The phrase suggests a title that catches the subject exactly as you mean to treat it, straightforwardly but humorously. You will work in Thackeray himself later on, letting your reader in on the secret of your title as you cite an eminent man who apparently liked a cigar himself but knew the awful truth.

The Pernicious Vegetable

THESIS: **Although cigarettes have brought certain benefits to society, we must ultimately judge them harmful.**

I. Beneficial effects
  A. Benefits to society
    1. Income for the tobacco industry
      a. Farmers
      b. Wholesalers
      c. Retailers
    2. Income for the communications industry
      a. Advertising agencies
      b. Advertising media
    3. Income for the government
      a. National tax revenues
      b. State and local tax revenues
  B. Benefits to the individual
    1. Feeling of social ease and acceptance

      2. Feeling of self-responsibility
      3. Feeling of maturity

II.   **But: harmful effects**   *Logical*

    A.   **Income for criminal elements**   *Order*

         1. Vending-machine racketeers

         2. Narcotics and gambling racketeers

    B.   **Physical harm to the individual**   *Chronological*

         1. Historical opinions   *Order*

            a.   James I's condemnation of tobacco

            b.   Thackeray's characterization of the cigar

            c.   Edison's refusal to hire smokers

         2. Modern findings   *Order of*

            a.   Impairment of physical stamina   *Ascending*

               (1)   Views of athletes and coaches   *Interest*

               (2)   Personal experience in sports

            b.   Relation to heart disease

            c.   Relation to cancer

               (1)   Laboratory findings with animals

               (2)   Laboratory findings with human beings

                   (a)   Lip cancer

                   (b)   Laryngeal cancer

                   (c)   Lung cancer

    C.   **Moral harm to the individual**

         1. Surrender of one's individuality to the group

         2. Surrender of one's destiny to the habit

Notice two things about this outline. First, section II.B on "physical harm to the individual," itself in logical order, can freely organize its subordinate parts in chronological order: historical opinions, then modern findings. Moreover, the historical opinions themselves fall into chronological order, but the subheads under "modern findings" then revert effectively to the order of ascending interest. The point is this: each heading and subheading is parallel to its co-equal—*A* matches *B, 1* matches *2, a* matches *b.*

Second, notice that we have ended rather more with character than with cancer—an order opposite from that of our jotted outline back on page 231. Why? Strangely but inevitably, sheer length has changed the dynamics of our argument. For the shorter essay, "the only heart and lungs you have" seemed stronger than the equivalent business about losing individuality in habit. But in the plan for the longer essay, the laboratory details are now too extensive for a single climactic point. They have indeed moved to subordinate rank — (1) not 1, and not even *a*. Now the moral argument stands in higher rank, simpler and more lofty, a fitting climax before the concluding summation.

EXERCISE

3 Read the following essay and then develop a topic outline for it.

COUNTERFEIT MONEY

How to Detect Counterfeit Bills. — Years of experience have proved to the secret service that the best detector of counterfeit money is the properly trained human eye. The person who is best able to see the difference between the bogus bill and one that is genuine must know just what a genuine bill looks like. The only way such knowledge can be gained is through a careful examination of all parts of a genuine bill, and it is such a study that is advocated by the secret service to help Americans defend themselves against the counterfeiter.

The portion most difficult of good reproduction is the portrait on the face of every note. The portraits of famous Americans on United States paper money identify the denominations of the bills on which they appear, as follows:

$1	Washington	$50	Grant
$2	Jefferson (no longer issued)	$100	Franklin
		$500	McKinley
$5	Lincoln	$1,000	Cleveland
$10	Hamilton	$5,000	Madison
$20	Jackson	$10,000	Chase

The genuine portraits are lifelike and distinct, and the shading which characterizes the facial features consists of numerous delicately executed dots and dashes. The oval background surrounding each portrait comprises a series of tiny squares, formed by the crossing of very fine vertical and horizontal lines. On most counterfeits the portraits are defective in the shading in the face, and many of the little squares in the background are filled with ink or are flecked with white where the vertical and horizontal lines are broken. In the genuine portrait the eyes are always clear and expressive, but in most counterfeits they are dull, distorted or otherwise executed so that they do not compare favorably with the genuine.

These differences alone between the genuine and counterfeit portraits prompt the secret service advice to the individual to compare any questionable bill with another of the same type known to be genuine. Such a comparison will make evident any differences between the two to such an extent that if one is a counterfeit it can be classified as such.

Only three types of currency are in circulation in the United States—(1) federal reserve notes; (2) United States notes; and (3) silver certificates. The latter two are no longer issued. Part of the design of every genuine bill includes the treasury seal, a small circle edged with sharp points like the teeth of a saw, enclosing an angle square under which is a key and over which is a balance scale, all mounted upon a dotted white shield within the circle. Surrounding the design are the Latin words *Thesaur. Amer. Septent. Sigil.*, representing the "Seal of the Treasury of North America." On silver certificates the seal and the serial numbers are printed in blue; on United States notes they are in red, and on federal reserve notes, in green. Thus, the type of any bill may be quickly determined merely by the colour of the treasury seal and the serial numbers. In addition, the words "Silver Certificate," "United States Note" or "Federal Reserve Note," as the case may be, are engraved at the top center of the face of a bill.

On many counterfeits the sharp points around the outer edge of the treasury seal are blunt or broken. Here again, a comparison of the seal on a questionable bill with the seal on a genuine bill will show the difference.

The serial numbers of genuine United States paper money are printed in a distinctive type style, and numbering blocks of the kind used for this purpose cannot be obtained except by the bureau of engraving and printing. Therefore, in producing a counterfeit, the counterfeit must either use numbers unlike the genuine, or must try to copy the genuine numerals. In the first instance a comparison will show the difference in the style, and in the second instance the copies or imitated numbers are usually poorly spaced or crookedly aligned, so that a comparison will indicate they are not authentic.

The border design of every genuine bill includes an intricate lacelike network of fine white lines. The patterns for these lines are produced by a machine known as a geometric lathe, and the lines are technically called geometric lathework. In a genuine bill these lines are clear and unbroken, but on most bogus notes the border is too dark because many of the spaces between the lines are filled with black ink caused by inferior etching, or perhaps too light because the white lines are thicker than the genuine, creating a bleached appearance. . . .

How to Detect Counterfeit Coins. — The manufacture of spurious coins does not involve losses as great as those suffered by victims of counterfeit bills. This is due, of course, to the fact that there is a wide margin of difference between the value of metal money and the representative value of paper money.

The passer of counterfeit coins depends upon the carelessness of his victims in the same way as does the passer of counterfeit bills. Genuine silver coins [and alloy coins issued today] have a corrugated outer edge, known as the reeding. Consisting of evenly spaced ridges, this feature was included on silver coins originally to prevent unscrupulous persons from cutting or filing from the edges of the coins small bits of silver, which they would then sell for the intrinsic value of the metal so derived. Later, however, the reeded edges of silver coins formed considerable protection against counterfeiting since the corrugations on most bogus coins are only partially executed, unevenly spaced or entirely missing in places. Thus, a comparison of a questionable coin with one known to be genuine, or even a careful scrutiny of the ridges around a questionable coin, will usually indicate whether it is good or bad.

Most counterfeit coins are made of metal alloy which does not ring as clearly as genuine coins when dropped on a hard surface and which is usually much softer than silver. Therefore, questionable coins should be dropped on a hard surface to test their ring and should be cut with a knife to test their quality. If a coin sounds dull or is easily cut, it is undoubtedly a counterfeit.

It is also a fact that most counterfeit coins feel greasy, so it is wise to feel all coins, and if one feels slippery or greasy it should be further examined for defects in the reeding or other characteristics.*

* Frank J. Wilson, in *The Encyclopaedia Britannica* (Chicago: Encyclopaedia Britannica, Inc., 1970), Vol. 6, p. 646. Reprinted by permission, © *Encyclopaedia Britannica,* 14th edition (1970). A few sentences in this article have been modified here to bring the information it contains up to date.

THE SENTENCE OUTLINE

In the sentence outline, you phrase each heading as a complete sentence. Such an outline lays out the plan of your essay as no other can, giving the fullest statement of your ideas, and showing clearly and explicitly the logical relation of parts. Often a required procedure in the assigned research paper, the sentence outline is useful for leading you through organizational intricacies and saving you from logical snares. Because it forces you to think out your plan so thoroughly beforehand, a good sentence outline can speed the actual writing of any essay that depends greatly on logical structure. But outlining in sentences consumes your time—and therein lies the danger. The outlining may leave too little time for the writing. A few experiments in the form, however, should help you decide when to use it to your advantage.

A sentence outline for your cigarette essay would begin like this:

The Pernicious Vegetable

THESIS: **Although cigarettes have brought certain benefits to society, we must ultimately judge them harmful.**

    I. **These benefits are both social and personal.**

        A. **The most evident social benefit is the tremendous income generated from tobacco.**

            1. **A wide variety of people make a living in the tobacco industry.**

                a. **The growing, transplanting, and curing of tobacco supports thousands of farmers and farm workers in the United States alone.**

                b. **The wholesaling of tobacco is virtually an industry of its own.**

                c. **From cigarette stand to supermarket, money from cigarettes flows steadily into the cash register.**

Remember, each heading, whether in a jotted, topic, or sentence outline, will require widely differing amounts of space as you write out your essay. Heading *I* would probably also absorb heading *A,* as you started your paragraph:

> **These benefits are both social and personal, most evidently in the tremendous income generated from tobacco. Annual retail sales of cigarettes alone are estimated at . . . .**

Your next paragraph would probably also use headings *1* and *a* consecutively:

> **A wide variety of people make a living in the tobacco industry. The growing, transplanting, and curing of tobacco . . . .**

And then your next paragraph would probably begin with the wholesaling, run on through its associated trucking and railroading, and end with sentence *c* and the cash register.

EXERCISE

4 Develop a sentence outline for the following essay on limiting the Presidency of the United States to a single term.

The Hon. Mike Mansfield
United States Senator, Montana, Democrat
Senate Majority Leader
Testimony before the Senate Constitutional Amendments Subcommittee,
October 28, 1971.

I welcome the chance to express my views pertaining to the proposed Constitutional Amendment that would limit the Presidency to a single term of six years. I am particularly proud and pleased to join with the distinguished Senator from Vermont* in this endeavor which I personally regard as one of the most important reforms that our system of government could undergo.

---
* The Hon. George D. Aiken.

In recent years there have been a number of significant amendments to the Constitution of the United States. Correcting the matter of Presidential succession and particularly extending the franchise of the ballot to young adults 18, 19 and 20 years of age represent enormous steps forward: steps that protect and enhance immensely the Democratic processes of this Nation. In my judgment there is still another step that must be taken in this area of Constitutional evolution. It is only in providing a single Presidential term of six years, I believe, that this Nation will preserve for its highest office a sufficient degree of freedom and independence to function properly and adequately today and in the years ahead; years that will produce enormous trials and tensions on the national and global scale, some of which have yet to emerge.

By no means do I intend to imply that with this proposed amendment new ground is being broken or that a topic of first impression is here being raised. Indeed, the suggestion of a single six-year term has been with us ever since the delegates to the Constitutional Convention of 1787 thrashed over the question of a President's term and his eligibility for re-election. It is interesting to note that popular election was not considered with any great favor at all during the proceedings of that convention. But proposals limiting the tenure of the President were put forth and discussed. Ultimately none were approved and the question then became moot when the suggestion for an electoral college system gained the widest support.

Since the Constitution was ratified hundreds of amendments have been introduced in the Senate and House of Representatives proposing a change in Presidential tenure. More than 130 of these recommended a single term of six years. Twice, the House reported legislation providing for the six-year term. And in 1913, the Senate passed S.J. Res. 78 calling for a term of six years, but no action was taken by the other body. Presidents themselves have been most active in their support for the concept. Nearly 150 years ago Andrew Jackson recommended that the electoral college be abolished — also a good suggestion — that the President be elected by direct vote, and that he be limited to a single term of either four or six years. Presidents Hayes and Cleveland and William Howard Taft also offered the proposal. In more recent years on this issue I have followed the lead of the able and distinguished Senator from Vermont, the dean of the Republicans and a wise and prudent judge on all matters and particularly on those affecting the needs of democratic institutions in a rapidly changing world. That brings us up to today, and I must say that the merits of the proposal dictate its need now as never before.

It is just intolerable that a President of the United States — any

President, whatever his party—is compelled to devote his time, energy and talents to what can be termed only as purely political tasks. I do not refer solely to a President's own re-election campaign. To be sure a re-election effort and all it entails are burdens enough. But a President facing re-election faces as well a host of demands that range from attending to the needs of political office holders, office seekers, financial backers and all the rest, to riding herd on the day-to-day developments within the pedestrian partisan arena. Surely this amendment does not represent a panacea for these ills which have grown up with our system of democracy. But it would go far, I think, in unsaddling the Presidency from many of these unnecessary political burdens that an incumbent bears.

Clearly such a change to a very great extent would free the President to devote a far greater measure of his time to the enormous task of serving all of the people of this Nation as Chief Executive. More time would thus be provided for policy-making and policy-implementing, for program initiating and for shaping and directing the kind of Administration a President chooses. More time would be provided for the kind of experimentation that a successful Presidency requires; such experimentation has come too infrequently in recent years, and as a Nation we suffer from that inadequacy. . . .

To sum it up, what this amendment seeks is to place the office of the Presidency in a position that transcends as much as possible partisan political considerations of whatever nature and source. That it cannot do the job completely, I would agree. The man who achieves the office carries with him his full political heritage. But its adoption would do much, I think, to streamline the Presidency in a manner that ultimately will make the position more fully responsive to the concerns of all Americans.*

* *The Congressional Digest,* March 1972, pp. 80–84.

OUTLINES FOR READING

Outlining by sentences is additionally useful in analyzing the logical structure of a printed essay and coming to understand it. Having first read for the meaning, you outline for the structure. Your finished outline should convey the essence of both. Here is part of an essay by George Santayana on one of the world's great books, followed by an analytical sentence outline of it:

Cervantes

Cervantes is known to the world as the author of *Don Quixote,* and although his other works are numerous and creditable, and his pathetic life is carefully recorded, yet it is as the author of *Don Quixote* alone that he deserves to be generally known or considered. Had his wit not come by chance on the idea of the Ingenious Hidalgo, Cervantes would never have attained his universal renown, even if his other works and the interest of his career should have sufficed to give him a place in the literary history of his country. Here, then, where our task is to present in miniature only what has the greatest and most universal value, we may treat our author as playwrights are advised to treat their heroes, saying of him only what is necessary to the understanding of the single action with which we are concerned. This single action is the writing of *Don Quixote;* and what we shall try to understand is what there was in the life and environment of Cervantes that enabled him to compose that great book, and that remained imbedded in its characters, its episodes, and its moral.

There was in vogue in the Spain of the sixteenth century a species of romance called books of chivalry. They were developments of the legends dealing with King Arthur and the Knights of the Table Round, and their numerous descendants and emulators. These stories had appealed in the first place to what we should still think of as the spirit of chivalry: they were full of tourneys and single combats, desperate adventures and romantic loves. The setting was in the same vague and wonderful region as the Coast of Bohemia, where to the known mountains, seas, and cities that have poetic names, was added a prodigious number of caverns, castles, islands, and forests of the romancer's invention. With time and popularity this kind of story had naturally intensified its characteristics until it had reached the greatest extravagance and absurdity, and combined in a way the unreality of the fairy tale with the bombast of the melodrama.

Cervantes had apparently read these books with avidity, and was not without a great sympathy with the kind of imagination they embodied. His own last and most carefully written book, the *Travails of Persiles and Sigismunda,* is in many respects an imitation of them; it abounds in savage islands, furious tyrants, prodigious feats of arms, disguised maidens whose discretion is as marvelous as their beauty, and happy deliverances from intricate and hopeless situations. His first book also, the *Galatea,* was an embodiment of a kind of pastoral idealism: sentimental verses being interspersed with euphuistic prose, the whole describing the lovelorn shepherds and heartless shepherdesses of Arcadia.

But while these books, which were the author's favorites among his own works, expressed perhaps Cervantes's natural taste and ambition, the events of his life and the real bent of his talent, which in time he came himself to recognize, drove him to a very different sort of composition. His family was ancient but impoverished, and he was forced throughout his life to turn his hand to anything that could promise him a livelihood. His existence was a continuous series of experiments, vexations, and disappointments. He adopted at first the profession of arms, and followed his colors as a private soldier upon several foreign expeditions. He was long quartered in Italy; he fought at Lepanto against the Turks, where among other wounds he received one that maimed his left hand, to the greater glory, as he tells us, of his right; he was captured by Barbary pirates and remained for five years a slave in Algiers; he was ransomed, and returned to Spain only to find official favors and recognitions denied him; and finally, at the age of thirty-seven, he abandoned the army for literature.

His first thought as a writer does not seem to have been to make direct use of his rich experience and varied observation; he was rather possessed by an obstinate longing for that poetic gift which, as he confesses in one place, Heaven had denied him. He began with the idyllic romance, the *Galatea,* already mentioned, and at various times during the rest of his life wrote poems, plays, and stories of a romantic and sentimental type. In the course of these labors, however, he struck one vein of much richer promise. It was what the Spanish call the *picaresque;* that is, the description of the life and character of rogues, pickpockets, vagabonds, and all those wretches and sorry wits that might be found about the highways, in the country inns, or in the slums of cities. Of this kind is much of what is best in his collected stories, the *Novelas Exemplares*. The talent and the experience which he betrays in these amusing narratives were to be invaluable to him later as the author of *Don Quixote*, where they enabled him to supply a foil to the fine world of his poor hero's imagination.

We have now mentioned what were perhaps the chief elements of the preparation of Cervantes for his task. They were a great familiarity with the romances of chivalry, and a natural liking for them; a life of honorable but unrewarded endeavor both in war and in the higher literature; and much experience of Vagabondia, with the art of taking down and reproducing in amusing profusion the typical scenes and languages of low life. Out of these elements a single spark, which we may attribute to genius, to chance, or to inspiration, was enough to produce a new and happy conception: that of a parody on the romances of chivalry, in which the extravagances of the fables of knighthood should be contrasted with the sordid realities of life. This is done by the ingenious device of representing a country gentleman whose naturally generous mind, unhinged by much reading of the books of chivalry, should lead him to undertake the office of knight-errant, and induce him to ride about the country clad in ancient armor, to right wrongs, to succor defenseless maidens, to kill giants, and to win empires at least as vast as that of Alexander.

This is the subject of *Don Quixote*. But happy as the conception is, it could not have produced a book of enduring charm and well-seasoned wisdom, had it not been filled in with a great number of amusing and lifelike episodes, and verified by two admirable figures, Don Quixote and Sancho Panza, characters at once intimately individual and truly universal.*

This I would outline in sentences as follows, sharpening and spelling out the implications of Santayana's deductive-inductive thesis, gathered from reading the entire essay, making a completely deductive assertion, for clarity:

* Reprinted by permission of Charles Scribner's Sons from *Essays in Literary Criticism of George Santayana,* edited by Irving Singer. Copyright © 1956, Charles Scribner's Sons.

Cervantes

THESIS: Cervantes's chivalric idealism and realistic experience combined to produce his masterpiece, *Don Quixote,* which laughs at idealism only to endorse its realistic application.

I. Cervantes's chivalric romanticism was natural to him.
   A. He grew up when romances were in vogue.
   B. His own family, though poor, was ancient and presumably noble.
   C. He read romances avidly.
   D. His first and last writings were serious attempts at idealistic romance.
II. But, being poor, Cervantes led a harshly realistic and disappointing life.
   A. He experienced the hardships of a soldier abroad.
      1. As a private who saw service in several foreign campaigns, he was long stationed in Italy.
      2. He fought the Turks at Lepanto, suffering a wound that crippled his left hand.
      3. He was a captive of Algerian pirates for five years.
      4. Ransomed, he returned to Spain at the age of thirty-five to find neither recognition nor pay awaiting him.
   B. He turned to writing for his livelihood.
      1. He began with an idealistic romance, a kind of writing he continued throughout his life with little success.
      2. He tried the picaresque tale, the story of rogues and vagabonds.
III. From these two strains, the high and the low, came the idea for *Don Quixote* — a parodying of high chivalric romances through low situations.
IV. Cervantes's genius made this simple contrast great: he created two great characters to represent the two sides of the contrast.

Making a sentence outline really masters an essay for you. You discover the essay's parts; you summarize them into clear sentences; you work out their logical relations. You may indeed discover some logical lapses (Santayana, a professional philosopher, seems neatly coherent). You will certainly bring some of your author's points to sharper clarity as I have done with Santayana's thesis, for instance, to put the essay in a nutshell, and to make my outline clear.

To outline your reading, you first boil the essay down to its true thesis, in one sentence. Then you simply go through the essay, typing out a series of sentences that summarize the key ideas as they come along. Sometimes you use the author's words, but usually you compress them into a sentence of your own. The next step is to grade and group your sentences into what seem their major and minor hierarchies, and this may take considerable recasting, and reassigning of *A*'s for *I*'s, of *I*'s for *A*'s, and so forth. You may need to rearrange the order of sentences for a better flow of logic, so that you can see how the essay ought to have been, in its best possible form. Such an outline gets you into essay as nothing else will. You have made the writer's thoughts and their relationships your own, and may discover that even a professional is seldom perfect.

OUTLINING BY TOPIC SENTENCES

You can also outline a published essay paragraph by paragraph, to strengthen your ability to organize by topic sentences—as you also strengthen your grasp of the essay and of the essayist's own organizing skills. After formulating a thesis for some published essay, and also formulating a heading for its first section, if it does not already have one, you simply write a topic sentence for each paragraph, inserting other general headings for sections as necessary. Since your paragraphs are many and your headings few, a combination of roman and arabic is most convenient for numbering. A topic-sentence outline of Santayana's essay would begin like this:

> THESIS: **Cervantes's chivalric idealism and realistic experience combined to produce his masterpiece, *Don Quixote,* which laughs at idealism only to endorse its realistic application.**
>
> I. **Cervantes's chivalric romanticism was natural to him. [This is a general heading, not a paragraph.]**
>   1. **There was in vogue in the Spain of the sixteenth century a species of romance called books of chivalry.**
>   2. **Cervantes had apparently read these books avidly, and was not without a great sympathy for the kind of imagination they embodied.**

3. But the events of his life and the real bent of his talent drove him to a very different sort of composition.
4. His first thought as a writer was not to use his rich experience but to pursue his romantic longing.
5. We have now mentioned what were perhaps the chief elements of Cervantes's preparation for his great task.

This is the first section of Santayana's Middle. You will notice that our paragraph outline has covered in one section, as does the essay, what our sentence outline covers in two, as it makes the logic clear. I have used Santayana's own topic sentences, condensing only a little here and there. The last paragraph, as its topic sentence indicates, summarizes the points of the preceding four before moving on to describe the spark that animated the elements into a single work of genius.

EXERCISE

5 Develop a topic-sentence outline for the following excerpt from an essay on how classical music, as an institution, seems to inhibit the musicians who create it.

CONDUCTORS AND CRITICS

Musicians' major institutional enemies are conductors and critics. The performances of individual conductors always provoke comment. The conductor who can't maintain a beat, who loses his place, who "hams it up," who abuses his orchestra or a particular instrumentalist, or who loses control of his orchestra or of his temper will be the source of countless anecdotes that circulate through the international music community.

The musician regards the conductor as an arbitrary, capricious martinet whose knowledge of music is eclipsed by his egotism, megalomania, and flair for histrionics — qualities he can indulge to the fullest when he ascends the podium.

The nature of the conductor's position invites these responses, for the conductor is required to control, direct, and discipline simultaneously, in a public setting, as many as a hundred or more specialists, each of whom in his own specialty feels he is more competent than the conductor. Each will resent the discipline to which he is subjected, especially if it is administered unskillfully.

The instrumentalists tend to feel that the conductor gets the credit for a good performance, the performers the blame for a bad one. The conductor, of course, is better paid and is a celebrity. Thus the musician often perceives him as a social climber and a traitor to the art of music.

The conductor, on the other hand, is likely to feel that his instrumentalists are lazy, incompetent, and obstreperous. He may regard them as children who resist the discipline necessary to create an ensemble. If a firm hand is not used, he may reason, they can wreck the orchestra and destroy his own reputation. Both conductors and instrumentalists can cite instances of this having occurred.

Another institutional enemy of the musician is the critic. He is more the enemy of the soloist than of the orchestra member, but both regard him with caution. Whether or not they respect his judgment, they must respect his power. He has vast influence over the lay audience; he can wreck the career of a soloist, a conductor, or an entire orchestra. Musicians regard him as arbitrary and capricious to the extent they think, as they sometimes do, that he is bent on destroying a performer, conductor, or ensemble. Such professional paranoia is least common among members of the orchestra because they see each review as part of a campaign, with the cumulative effects being greater than a single battle. To the soloist, however, a bad and possibly unjust review or one based on an "off night" can be a Waterloo.

Musicians often view critics as frustrated performers whose failure as musicians has led them to merely talk and write about music and to compensate for their own inadequacies by attacking those musicians who have not given up. The musician sees criticism as an act of resentment against creation and creators. Nevertheless, the critic's opinions will be warmly applauded when he castigates the work of a rival performer or group.

The critic is usually considered superior to the music historian or musicologist, unless the latter happens to be working on specific problems of performance or on unearthing valuable lost manuscripts.*

* Joseph Pensman, "Classical Music and the Status Game," *Transaction*, 4, 9 (September 1967), 55–59. Copyright © 1967 by Transaction, Inc. Published by permission of Transaction, Inc.

FURTHER CONVENTIONS OF OUTLINING

Most of the outline's formal conventions have emerged during our survey, but some further details and reminders will be useful.

1. TITLE.   Keep your title independent of the text of your outline.   Do not number it in with the text; do not use it as a heading for subheads; do not refer to it by pronouns.   Do *not* do this:

I. The Advantages of the Bikini

A. Its convenience in packing

2. THESIS.   To keep your logical structure straight, make as explicit a deductive thesis as you can, even when you intend to write a more inductive essay, with less explicit thesis.   In outlining a printed essay, do the same, using verbatim only a thesis already clearly deductive and explicit.

3. CAPITALIZATION.   Capitalize only the first word of each heading (and other words normally capitalized).

4. PUNCTUATION.   Put periods after headings that are complete sentences, but not after merely phrasal headings.

5. HEADINGS.   For the topic outline, use all nouns (or noun phrases), with modifiers accompanying them, as needed.   Do not mix kinds of headings: some single nouns, some sentences, some fragments. Keep headings equivalent:

A. **Benefits to society**
B. **Benefits to the individual**
 1. **Feeling of social ease**
 2. **Feeling of self-responsibility**
  a. **James I's condemnation**
  b. **Thackeray's characterization**
  c. **Edison's refusal**

Now we have pretty well covered the structure of the essay, together with its verbal and rational dynamics, and you have developed your skills more than a little.   Let us now see, in the next chapter, how we can apply them, as Santayana did, toward understanding literature and other arts.

Writing About Literature

Writing about literature (or film or music or painting) is really no different from writing about life—though literature and life are distinctly different. Writing about either art or life is a way to discover meanings and then to deepen them for ourselves as we try to make them clear and meaningful to others. The significant difference lies not between literature and life, but between expository argument and literature, between the essay you write and the story, the essay you write and the poem.

An essay states its point; literature implies its point. Poem, short story, novel, play, or motion picture, each acts out in its particular way some underlying idea that probably remains unstated. Even the brief lyric poem is really a dramatized moment, a voice speaking intensely and beautifully from some larger drama, which is probably life itself. So, poem or novel, each enacts and demonstrates—each *presents,* or represents—something about life, but usually does not tell us exactly what. These are the *mimetic* arts— actions imitating life, grand mimickings of the human predicament.

So, to write about literature, you must first discover, and decide for yourself, what *it* is about. What point, or points, *does* it

253

imply, or act out? Poems make statements, of course, and characters in plays, novels, or films also make statements. A poem or a
character may even state the author's thesis explicitly. Even so,
you must select the stated thesis from all the other things said, and
then interpret it in the light of all the other statements, or of the
entire action. When Hamlet says "the readiness is all," we know
we have a thesis. Hamlet has found an important answer to both
his brooding inaction and his impetuosity. Yet, is it *the* thesis?
Perhaps—but certainly we need to qualify it with something about
murderous ambitions, about thinking too little and too much, about
appearance and reality, about the strange, dark web of thought and
circumstance in which all life in this play seems caught beyond
control.

Your first step, then, is to find the action's thesis, even though
—and precisely because—the writer may have bent his best efforts
to avoid stating a thesis or seeming to have one. The writer has
wanted to *dramatize* his problem, or his mood, not to state it flatly,
to display it in action, not merely to describe it. He has not wanted
to tack a moral to his tale. That is the reader's job: to find the one
idea toward which all these statements, all these moral and immoral
actions, point.

To write an essay about literature, then, you first try to discover
its point—or the significance of some part or feature—and assert
something *about* it, probably that this *is* the point, that this feature
is significant. *Your* thesis is an *aboutness* asserted.

EXPLICATION

Explication is an unfolding of meanings (from *ex,* "out," and
plicare, "to fold")—detail by detail, pleat by pleat. You unfold for
your reader what this play, or novel, or poem, is about. Your *aboutness* may be simply that the unfolding is necessary for full understanding, or it may find some commanding detail or pattern or metaphor and assert its preeminence, showing how all the others fit
under it. Poetry, intense and compressed, metaphoric and symbolic,

especially invites explication, invites an explanation and demonstration of what it is all about. But a scene or a passage in a novel
or play also may evoke a valuable explication as you argue for its
importance to the work as a whole in all its details and levels of
suggestion. You may not wish to, or need to, unfold everything.
But I shall now try my hand at the most thorough explication I can
manage, so you can see something of the range of possibilities—of
the questions you might ask and write about.

Here is an apparently simple poem by Robert Herrick:

Upon Julia's Clothes

Whenas in silks my *Julia* goes,
Then, then (me thinks) how sweetly flowes
That liquefaction of her clothes.

Next, when I cast mine eyes and see
That brave Vibration each way free;
O how that glittering taketh me!

Perhaps the first thing that strikes us, before we take in the two
statements very fully, is the smoothness of Herrick's meter and
rhymes. He is fitting his two sentences into a metrical frame as if
with no effort at all, talking in a perfectly easy way within a set of
artificial conditions few of us can manage without awkwardness,
like the person who walks a high-wire in a way the rest of us walk a
street. His skill furnishes part of our wonder and delight.

You will probably notice that Herrick's meter is iambic, far
and away the most usual of the meters, though modern poetry goes
predominantly for free verse, with no metrical pattern nor rhyme
(for more on meter, see pp. 264–266). But certainly a full explication
of Herrick's poem would note its metrical pattern and Herrick's
handling of it. He here writes two brief stanzas of three iambic
tetrameter (four beat) lines each, rhymed as triplets, or triads. His
iambic feet are unusually regular. *Julia* is certainly pronounced as
only two syllables ("Jul-ya"), and *glittering* is the only irregularity.
It could have been pronounced "glit-ring," of course, but reading it
as an irregularity, with a very light and quick extra syllable (giving
the line nine syllables rather than the regular eight) is so pleasing as

to seem right and smooth, especially as it echoes the heavy-light-light that the inverted foot gives the line-beginning. *O how/that glitt/ -ering tak* would scan $-\cup/\cup-/\cup\cup-/$, but it would read like a pleasant echo: $-\cup\cup/-\cup\cup/$. The poem has only two such inverted feet, which, as line-beginners, are so common to iambic writing as to be what we might call a regular variation. And both of these (*Next, when* and *O how*) come in the second stanza as the excitement rises. Another interesting variation is *Then, then,* which we would presumably read as two heavies $/--/$, a spondee, slowed even further by the comma. What looks like a redundancy, a mere line-filler (and it probably was), Herrick has made into a dramatic measuring out of expectation, or an emphasis on the very moment of the thrill. We will notice two other pleasing variations in pace: how Herrick's sentence twice "runs on" to the next line without stopping at the line-end, at *flowes/That liquefaction* and at *see/That brave Vibration*. These are his two key phrases similarly patterned, similarly set up with a rush of expectation. And we will notice how the last line of each stanza carries the punch.

Next, we will have enjoyed that unusual word, which has probably caught every reader's eye from 1648 to the present, *liquefaction*. Part of our pleasure comes from seeing how naturally Herrick has fitted a big, four-syllable, unpoetic word, directly from Latin, into his regular meter, and has made it poetry. And it is poetry because it climaxes those liquid *s*-sounds with which Herrick has prepared us: *Whenas, silks, goes, thinks, sweetly flowes.* Then the idea hits us: silks rubbing softly against each other would indeed rustle with a liquid sound, which the very name, *silks,* also suggests in its sound. Finally, Herrick may have intended that *liquefaction* would also bring the word *satisfaction* to mind by their similarity, an idea that has struck more than one of my students, since the sound itself is satisfying, and satisfaction is certainly what the young man wants, though he dare not say so, or even think so. *Liquefaction,* "turning something into water," completes the metaphor that Julia's silken clothes, from their sound as she moves, seem as if they were water. Her movement turns them into water, and their *liquefaction* suggests that the clothes might indeed sweetly flow away, leaving the imagination filled with actuality.

When we come to the second stanza, we realize something

further. The first stanza concerns sounds only. Julia is apparently approaching her admirer from behind, coming up a hall, let us say. He hears her. He knows it is she. She is dressed elegantly, perhaps for some gathering at court. The sound of her silks, flowing as she flows, epitomizes his thrill at her presence. And certainly she must be beautiful to look at. *Next,* he says, after savoring the sound of her approach, he must turn to look at her, almost as with an effort to face a brilliant light (*cast mine eyes*).

But what is a *brave Vibration* that is *each way free?* Well, we certainly know what a vibration is. Again the big Latin word is neatly fitted to the meter among its short Anglo-Saxon companions, and with an inner rhyming, or alliteration, of *brave* and *brations* (for a discussion of sounds, see page 214), and we know it is significant. And we certainly know what parts of a woman are apt to vibrate. *Brave* we must look up in the dictionary to discover a seventeenth-century meaning, still occasionally in use, which has nothing to do with courage. *Brave,* here, primarily means "splendid," suggesting both "excellence" and "resplendence," value and brightness. Yet the vibration is a little bold, too, a little courageous, to display such hidden beauty. *Vibration,* which Herrick capitalizes, apparently for emphasis, is also, in Latin, not only a quick shaking back and forth, but such a motion of human limbs, trembling in excitement, and of flames, lightning, or, especially significant here, the sea or other waters glittering with lights, as are Julia's silks, sparkling outward. But exactly what is producing those brave vibrations? Julia could be walking past her admirer, going away, and a rear view might certainly provide him with a brave vibration each way free. But again our explication needs history. Seventeenth-century portraits will show us that skirts were very full. We must further assure ourselves that *goes* in the first line meant "walks" not "departs." Julia is certainly *approaching,* as her admirer's first hearing, then seeing, clearly indicates. Julia's breasts, then, free under the silk in an age before the bra, must be furnishing the vibration, though her admirer—at least for the moment—is too much the gentleman (and too much the poet) to say so. Of course, her entire dress is "vibrating" to and fro with light, so we need not be anatomically specific. Nevertheless, the bright sheen of the silk, glittering as she moves, takes her admirer so powerfully precisely because it represents, as had the liquefaction earlier, the desired beauty beneath.*

Now we have just about explicated everything, down to the bare facts, as it were, except why this poem is so good. Why has

---

* I append this elaborate and meticulous footnote not to dazzle but to demonstrate. First, I am concerned to show what others have thought on some points that have exercised me, indeed to show how their ideas have stimulated mine. Second, I am concerned to credit these several authors properly so that readers can pursue these matters as they desire. Third, I am concerned that the student see precisely how one goes about this, and have a very present paradigm for the problems of footnoting that we discuss in Chapter 13, pp. 298; 306–311. I reproduce the text of the first edition as edited by J. Max Patrick, *The Complete Poetry of Robert Herrick*, The Stuart Editions (New York: New York University Press, 1963), p. 344.

Herrick did write a poem "Upon Julia's Breasts," which has nothing of the clothed ambiguity of "brave Vibration," a phrase that has raised much controversy. Elisabeth Schneider argues that the first stanza is Julia dressed; and the second, Julia undressed. Jeremy Bentham, an eighteenth-century English jurist referred to taking a walk as "vibrating," and, in the seventeenth century, vibration was generally connected with the slow swing of a pendulum. Hence, Schneider believes, Herrick pictures "the rhythmical motion back and forth, 'each way free,' of [Julia's] unencumbered naked limbs" (*Explicator*, 13 [March 1955], item 30). Michael J. Preston backs her up, by pointing to Ovid's *Amores* I.5, about his Corinna (a name Herrick used in several distinctive poems), who many think is Augustus's daughter Julia, coming to his apartment one afternoon dressed, and then undressing, and both Herrick and his readers were full of classical knowledge (*Explicator*, 30 [May 1972], item 82). Lewis E. Weeks, Jr., unaware of Schneider's suggestions, also opts for nudity ("Julia Unveiled: A Note on Herrick's 'Upon Julia's Clothes,'" *CEA Critic*, 25 [June, 1963], 8).

But most commentators agree that Julia keeps her clothes on, many, however, preferring the rear view. The poem is, after all, about Julia's clothes, not her limbs. William O. Harris points out the significant distinction between sound in the first stanza and sight in the second, as he answers Schneider's complaint that nothing new would happen in the second stanza, leaving it repetitive and redundant, unless Julia has undressed between stanzas (*Explicator*, 21 [December 1962], item 29). The only other significant point, which I have omitted, is the "submerged metaphor" about fishing — Julia in the liquid element, then *cast*, then something glittering, like both a fish and a fisherman's lure, then *takes*, in which the fisherman finds himself caught, in the typical wiles of love: first pointed out by Louis H. Leiter (*Modern Language Notes* 73 [1958], 331; *Explicator*, 25 [January 1967], item 41); see also J. D. Shuchter (*Explicator* 25 [November 1966], item 27), and Roger B. Rollin, *Robert Herrick* (New York: Twayne, 1966), pp. 86–87. Schneider, however, well states the inescapable point, which all the poem's admirers have registered in one way or another, that the poem's power and charm lie in its "neatness and symmetry." Earl Daniels finds an interesting smoothness in the "Julia" lines (I.1 and 3; II.2) and an excited unevenness in the "observer" lines (I.2 and II.1 and 3) (*Explicator*, 1 [March 1943], item 35).

it stood out, as a favorite, these three centuries, among all the changes of costume and changing customs of frankness and reticence? It says nothing profound. It is a tiny little thing, really. A young man liked to look at the girl he loved ("*my* Julia" tells us that). Men, young and old, still can hardly keep their eyes off shapely women, loved or not. So what is so great about it? Well, my own explication would start with the audacious thesis that no other piece of literature conveys so beautifully, vividly, and succinctly a young man's pleasure in looking at the woman he loves, making this particular moment of emotional intensity both explicit and universal. Can you find six lines anywhere that do as much on this most central human emotion? I know I cannot. But this is probably farther than you will want to go. Your own explication would feature one salient point—the *liquefaction–brave Vibration* bit, perhaps. The point about explication is to find some thesis that justifies all its searching-out of detail and local meaning, and then simply to ask yourself questions and find answers wherever they are, in dictionaries, mythologies, histories, portraits, the author's other works, or whatever—anywhere that will yield answers and illumination.

EXERCISE

1 Explicate the following poem by Emily Dickinson, considering the following questions. What is the *it* the poem talks about? What advantage is there, if any, in setting the poem up as a riddle? Why not come right out and say what the answer to the riddle is, what the *it* represents? What are the metaphors—what is being compared to what? What is the main metaphor? What words convey it? Are there other metaphors?

Consider *lap*. What are the possible metaphors that *lap* implies? Which one, if any, is most appropriate to the subject being described? Likewise consider *lick, peer, pare, crawl, stanza, chase itself, star*. Explain *Boanerges* (you will need a dictionary for this one). Is this an effective allusion? What do meter and rhyme contribute to this poem? Is there a pattern in stanzas? If so, how does it vary? Does this patterning or lack of it contribute anything to what the poem is saying? What is

notable about the rhyming, or lack of it? Is this a good poem? Why?
(Incidentally, what do you think of that *it's* in the last line?)

I Like To See It Lap the Miles

I like to see it lap the Miles—
And lick the Valleys up—
And stop to feed itself at Tanks—
And then—prodigious step

Around a Pile of Mountains—
And supercilious peer
In Shanties—by the sides of Roads—
And then a Quarry pare

To fit its sides
And crawl between
Complaining all the while
In horrid—hooting stanza—
Then chase itself down Hill—

And neigh like Boanerges—
Then—prompter than a Star
Stop—docile and omnipotent
At it's own stable door—

STEPS AND QUESTIONS

Each work stirs its own interest, and, as with Julia and her
clothes, presents us with questions, and more questions, as we become more interested. These questions are what you write about.
We want ultimately to possess what the author wanted us to possess,
since each literary work is, after all, a communication from author
to reader. A writer may wish only to express himself, yes, but he
expects us to understand and value that self-expression as he does.
So, as with Herrick, the questions will arise, almost of themselves,
from each different work. But in writing, and explaining, a questioning mind will help. Why does the author do this? Why that?
What does he intend that vase on the mantle to signify?

This first natural onrush of questions can perhaps be controlled so as to provide us with a kind of system for our explication. How can we formulate questions whose answers will indeed help our reader's understanding? What particularities of a work will most likely provoke the questions you will want to answer in your essay?

To summarize, paraphrase.

The simplest way to start the questions and find the answers is to summarize, letting the process of writing do its fundamental job of discovering our ideas for us. A paraphrase is the closest kind of summary. Paraphrasing a poem — translating it into clear English prose in your own words — is an excellent way to come to grips, in your own mind, with exactly what it says, raising the primary questions as to which of the possible meanings the author seems to intend. Shakespeare writes (Sonnet 116):

> O, no; [love] is an ever-fixed mark
> That looks on tempests and is never shaken;
> It is a star to every wandering bark,
> Whose worth's unknown, although his height be taken.

One student paraphrases like this:

> O, no; love is an object that always needs fixing, that looks on storms and is never shaken; it is a moon barked at by every wandering dog, who is probably worthless and homeless, although his height is taken into account.

In class, he defends his paraphrase by saying that the moon is a kind of star, and Shakespeare is saying that love is like the moon, which wears away and fixes itself up each month. Love is also always in need of repair. The moon looks down on storms untouched; dogs always bark at the moon. Other students argue that *bark* means a ship, and that love is like an actual star, fixed and stationary above storms, which a wandering ship would use in navigating, taking its height with a sextant but never knowing its actual physical nature or worth. The first student says, "Well, I guess *bark* threw me off." The practice of paraphrasing has pin-pointed the ambiguous words, and has made them yield the meaning the author probably intended, since it fits better, as we put aside the less probable meanings.

A summary of a poem, a novel, or a play will yield much the same kind of clarification: "Shakespeare compares love to a star . . . ." Or:

> **The story opens with an unnamed "he" alone in a dingy room. One door of a cabinet is hanging from a single hinge. A spring and some stuffing stick up through a sofa cushion. We soon learn that his wife has just left him. He is angry and bitter. Piece by piece, from his thoughts, we learn what has happened—their high-school romance, their fashionable wedding, his "bad luck," as he calls it, losing one job after another only because he likes "to have a little fun." In the end, he finishes wrecking the cabinet, his wife's special treasure, and stamps off to the local bar, never learning what a hopeless fool he is, and will continue to be.**

Such a summary has crystallized the story clearly and whole. Use it in your own essay, to help your readers see the story as you see it. Some thesis about the story in general, or particular, a little more detail and illustration, and you would have a complete essay.

To search out style, imitate with parody.

Parody is a kind of burlesque paraphrase that alerts one especially to style, though it will also get well into what the author is saying. It is most effective with short passages, since a joke can go on too long. If you imitate a paragraph of James Joyce, or Faulkner, let us say, you will learn something about his style that may open the way to an essay about how it works, what patterns are characteristic, what words and kinds of phrasing are favorites. This is only an exercise to strengthen your own style as you discover possibilities in his—as you discover what, in his, needs explaining to your readers. The game is to match the sentences exactly, borrowing especially characteristic words, but with a totally different subject. Here is a brief passage from Faulkner's *Sanctuary*, followed by a parody:

> He dozed. The train clicked on, stopped, jolted. He waked and dozed again. Someone shook him out of sleep into a primrose dawn. Among unshaven puffy faces washed lightly over as though with the paling ultimate stain of holocaust, blinking at one another with dead eyes into which personality returned in secret opaque waves.*

> She hosed. The shower poured on, stopped, squirted. She scrubbed and hosed again. Someone beckoned her out of the shower into the primrose dressing room. Among sagging puffy faces washed lightly over then smeared with face cream as though with the paling ultimate frost of the final freeze, blinking in the mirror at dead eyes into which she hoped some personality would return before her secret opaque class.

With poems, parody is a pleasant way to find out how meter works, as again you attend to what the poet is saying. Shakespeare's Sonnet 30 begins:

> When to the sessions of sweet silent thought
> I summon up remembrance of things past,
> I sigh the lack of many a thing I sought,
> And with old woes new wail my dear time's waste:
> Then can I drown an eye, unused to flow,
> For precious friends hid in death's dateless night
> And weep afresh love's long since cancel'd woe,
> And moan the expense of many a vanished sight . . . .

An anonymous parody:

> When to the sessions of sweet midnight talk
> I summon up my roommate, Mildred Bod,
> I sigh the lack of many a moonlight walk
> And with old beaus new wail my present clod:
> Then can I drown an eye, unused to flow,
> For Charlie, and another dateless night,
> And weep afresh love's never cancel'd woe,
> And moan the expense of everything in sight . . . .

* New York: The Modern Library (Random House, Inc.), 1932, pp. 201-202.

VERSIFICATION

Find the sound in poetry.

Poetry heightens the sounds of language in six major ways, each depending on some kind of repetition-with-variation.

1. *Meter* — the regular measure, as varied by the language flowing over it. See *Meter, below.*

2. *Rhyme* — line-ends the same, with a necessary difference: *bird/third.*

3. *Repetition* — the same word repeated, but with different force: "Of hammered *gold* and *gold* enameling" (Yeats).

4. *Alliteration* — first letters of words or first accented syllables the same: "a *l*ittle *l*ost a*ll*iteration."

5. *Assonance* — middle letters (vowels) the same: s*oa*ked c*oa*t, gl*a*d r*a*g, h*o*t r*o*d.

6. *Consonance* — end letters the same, but vowels different (also called "slant rhyme"): *bored/third,* the *supple/apple, cried/bleed.*

METER. English has one dominant meter — iambic — and three others that lend iambic an occasional foot, for variety, and produce a few poems. (Modern verse is predominantly "free," with no regular pattern.)

RISING METERS

Iambic: ◡ —
Anapestic: ◡◡ —

FALLING METERS

Trochaic: — ◡
Dactylic: — ◡◡

The number of these metrical units, or feet, in a line also gives the verse a name:

1 foot: monometer
2 feet: dimeter
3 feet: trimeter
4 feet: tetrameter
5 feet: pentameter

6 feet: hexameter

7 feet: heptameter (rare)

All meters will show some variations, and substitutions of other kinds of feet, but three variations in iambic writing are virtually standard:

Inverted foot: — ‿ (a trochee)

Spondee: — —

Ionic double-foot: ‿ ‿ | — —

Examples of scansion:

IAMBIC TETRAMETER

‿ — | ‿ — | ‿ — | ‿ — |
An-ni -hil-a -ting all that's made

‿ ‿ | — — | ‿ ‿ | — — |
To a green thought in a green shade.

Andrew Marvell, "The Garden"

IAMBIC PENTAMETER

— — | — — | ‿ — | ‿ — | ‿ — |
Love's not Time's fool, though ros -y lips and cheeks

‿ — | ‿ — | ‿ — | ‿ — | ‿ — |
Within his bend -ing sick -le's com -pass come

Shakespeare, Sonnet 116

— ‿ | ‿ — | ‿ — | ‿ — | ‿ — |
When to the ses -sions of sweet si -lent thought

or

— ‿ | ‿ — | ‿ ‿ | — — | ‿ — |
When to the ses -sions of sweet si -lent thought

Shakespeare, Sonnet 30

ANAPESTIC TETRAMETER

‿ — | ‿ ‿ — | ‿ — | ‿ ‿ — |
The pop -lars are felled; farewell to the shade

‿ ‿ — | ‿ ‿ — | ‿ ‿ — | ‿ ‿ — |
And the whis -pering sound of the cool colonnade

William Cowper, "The Popular Field"

TROCHAIC TETRAMETER

— ‿ | — ‿ | — ‿ | — ‿ |
Tell me not in mournful numbers

Longfellow, "A Psalm of Life"

DACTYLIC HEXAMETER

— ‿ ‿| — ‿   ‿ | — ‿   ‿| —   ‿ ‿| —   ‿ ‿| —   ‿ |
This is the forest prim -eval. The murmuring pines and the hemlocks

— ‿   ‿ | —
Bearded with moss . . . .

Longfellow, "Evangeline"

A *caesura* ("seZHURa") is a frequent and attractive variation, in which punctuation suspends the meter for a moment as a clause ends. A *masculine caesura* suspends the meter at the end of a foot, as after *felled* in Cowper's lines above. A *feminine caesura* suspends the meter mid-foot, as after Longfellow's *primeval* in the last example.

These are the major sounds of poetry, which you can appreciate, and can describe for your readers, as they contribute to the poem's pleasures and emphasize its meanings.

Determine the genre.

A sonnet is a sonnet. It belongs to the *genre,* or class, we recognize as "sonnet" — fourteen lines of iambic pentameter rhymed in certain ways (see next exercises). Recognizing the genre and its conventions will help you understand how well a writer exploits or varies the conventional pattern, especially with such unconventional sonnets as Gerard Manley Hopkins's "The Windhover" (see p. 268), or a number of E. E. Cummings's fourteen-liners, which he seems to carve from the conventional sonnet-block. So — if you write about a sonnet, explain how well it employs the conventional form to express its thought, or how it varies the conventional form to express its freedom (and its thought).

Tragedy and comedy are the largest genres. Recognizing to which one a story, novel, or play belongs, or where it lies between, will help you to describe it. Romance is a special genre on the comic side, ending happily, like comedy, but without the laughs and comic foolery and with a high coloration of the wishful and the far away in time and place. Satire, again on the comic side, though more cruel, pokes fun at some social absurdity, allegedly to cure it by laughing it out of countenance. Fantasy is unreality made real, with perhaps a touch of comic fear, as when *Alice in Wonderland* engages our psychic misgivings, or of grim humor, as when Vonnegut's *The Cat's Cradle* freezes to death man's scientific irresponsibility. Fantasy, indeed, may be the predominant characteristic of contemporary literature, as writer after writer projects our overreachings and shortcomings into some horrifying future. Placing any work in its genre will help your reader to understand it.

EXERCISES

2 Here is Shakespeare's Sonnet 18, built on the pattern he and others derived from the Italians: fourteen lines of iambic pentameter (five beats, ten syllables, alternating light-heavy), organized by alternate rhymes into three groups of four lines (quatrains) with a concluding couplet (two lines rhymed). His rhyme scheme is a,b,a,b, c,d,c,d, e,f,e,f, g,g. The Italian is a,b,b,a, a,b,b,a, c,d,e,c,d,e, with the last six lines often arranged c,d,d,c, e,e, or otherwise varied. Shakespeare, like the Italians, also organized his rhetoric into an octave (eight lines), which states the problem, or poses the question, and a sestet (six lines), which concludes the problem, or answers the question.

> Shall I compare thee to a summer's day?
> Thou art more lovely and more temperate:
> Rough winds do shake the darling buds of May,
> And summer's lease hath all too short a date:
> Sometime too hot the eye of heaven shines,
> And often is his gold complexion dimm'd;
> And every fair from fair sometime declines,
> By chance or nature's changing course untrimm'd;
> But thy eternal summer shall not fade,
> Nor lose possession of that fair thou owest;
> Nor shall Death brag thou wander'st in his shade,
> When in eternal lines to time thou grow'st:
> So long as men can breathe, or eyes can see,
> So long lives this, and this gives life to thee.

First, scan the poem into its iambic feet and stresses, as follows:

— ᴗ ᴗ — ᴗ — ᴗ — ᴗ —
Shall I / compare / thee to / a sum / -mer's day? /

Does the poem seem mostly regular or irregular?

Are there any, or many, inverted feet ($-\smile$)? Are there any, or many, spondees ($--$)?

Does Shakespeare use the sonnet's conventional structure to organize his statements?

Do his sentences and phrases end with the line-end or run on?

What effect does this have?

Now, consider meaning: Why will the person's "eternal summer" never fade?

What does *this* in the last line refer to?

What significance have *breathe* and *eyes?*

What is the essential metaphor, or comparison?

What metaphor do *lease* and *date* suggest?

What is wrong with the metaphor concerning *the eye of heaven* and *his gold complexion?*

Explain *fair from fair.*

What is the metaphor in *nature's changing course untrimm'd?*

Explain *When in eternal lines to time thou grow'st.*

Write a brief essay of explication, using your findings and organized by some thesis *about* the poem, perhaps that it has remained a favorite because many readers probably do not understand what it says.

3 Here is a famous and difficult poem by Gerard Manley Hopkins. First, using your dictionary (and not omitting the title), write out as full a prose translation of it as you can, beginning something like this: "This morning, I caught sight of . . . ."

Next, explain whatever metaphors your translation has not made clear, including those that remain ambiguous. Is a *skate* an ice-skate or a sting-ray, for instance, a *heel,* the heel of a foot or the tilting of a stingray, a *bow-bend* the bending of an archer's bow or the bend of a ship's bow? Is *buckle* to clasp together or to collapse under pressure?

How does Hopkins use the sonnet form?

Finally, from this analysis and these notes, write an essay in which your thesis is what the poem means.

THE WINDHOVER

To Christ Our Lord

I caught this morning morning's minion, king-
    dom of daylight's dauphin, dapple-dawn-drawn Falcon, in his
      riding
  Of the rolling level underneath him steady air, and striding
High there, how he rung upon the rein of a wimpling wing

In his ecstasy! then off, off forth on swing,
 As a skate's heel sweeps smooth on a bow-bend: the hurl and gliding
 Rebuffed the big wind. My heart in hiding
Stirred for a bird,—the achieve of, the mastery of the thing!

Brute beauty and valour and act, oh, air, pride, plume, here
 Buckle! AND the fire that breaks from thee then, a billion
Times told lovelier, more dangerous, O my chevalier!

 No wonder of it: shéer plód makes plough down sillion
Shine, and blue-bleak embers, ah my dear,
 Fall, gall themselves, and gas gold-vermilion.

THE NOVEL AND THE DRAMA

Analyze titles, names, allusions.

A book's title or its characters' names can carry part of the message. Look here for clues to explain to your reader. The "cat's cradle" of Vonnegut's title simultaneously informs us and raises a question. We see in our minds the loops of string interlaced between two hands; we know it is some kind of game, or pastime. In the end, we see it as a symbol of man's aimless and dangerous scientific ingenuity, and its meaninglessness: "See, no cat, no cradle," as one character says. Browning's "My Last Duchess" tells us, by his title alone, that a duke is speaking, and that he has had several duchesses (a servant could be speaking, of course, but the poem itself soon puts that possibility aside). Look out for these details—and explain them to your reader.

An author may deliberately look for neutral and natural names for his characters, and this in itself tells us that he aims toward realism. If his names seem somehow merely contrived, as in a story that begins "Stephanie Marsh had spoken to Stephen Blair only once," we suspect the slick and shallow. But an author may also name his characters to tell us what kinds of people they are, or what he wishes them to represent. Fielding's Mr. Allworthy is clearly the ideal worthy man; his Tom Jones, in the very commonness of his name, represents the common human lot. Dickens is a genius at making his names suggestive without labeling his people directly: Podsnap, Gradgrind, Murdstone, Steerforth, Uriah Heep. Introduce your reader to these possibilities. Show how they support your author's meanings.

Names may also be allusions. Look up *Uriah* in your dictionary, and you will discover Uriah the Hittite, an officer in King David's army, whom David ordered deserted and left to the enemy in the forefront of battle, so that David could marry Uriah's wife, Bathsheba. A good dictionary will also tell you that *Uriah* means "Yahweh [God] is my light." Explain this, and apply it to the story at hand. The creepy Uriah Heep is certainly the ironic opposite of his namesake: *he* is the treacherous one, as he heaps up swindles that he hopes will finally include the boss's daughter. Dickens has alluded, ironically, to one of the Bible's most famous stories. Similarly, almost any garden may prompt an author to allude to the Garden of Eden, strengthening his meaning from an even more famous biblical source. Shakespeare also is a frequent source. When Faulkner names his novel *The Sound and the Fury*, he wants us to remember, or discover, Macbeth's eloquent despair, which ends: "[Life] is a tale / Told by an idiot, full of sound and fury / Signifying nothing" (V.v.26–28). Faulkner's first section is literally "told by an idiot," the thirty-three-year-old Benjy, whose impressions and memories flow in sometimes incoherent sounds and frustrated furies, and the whole novel is a somber comment on life's fruitless struggles, which seem to signify nothing. Allusions are myriad in their variety, of course, but keeping alert for them will turn them up, and will help you explain to your reader what this is all about. Look up every biblical name—Timothy, Tobias, even Elizabeth—to see if the author may have had something allusive in mind. Catching an allusion will expand understanding both for you and your reader.

Look for symbols.

Symbols are a kind of concrete allusion—a physical object that calls to mind, or acquires, a cluster of meanings—asking you for explanation. In *The Sound and the Fury*, for instance, clocks and watches recurringly symbolize the passage and the waste of time, and sometimes the elegance of good times past as against the tawdry present, sometimes the measure of time as against the fluid and insubstantial life of memory and thought. Similarly, a soiled wedding slipper symbolizes spoiled aspirations, empty institutions, and the failures and hopeless yearnings of love.

When a metaphor produces or reinforces a symbol, the effect is unusually rich and the analysis illuminating. If you discover one, you can almost write a book, and you can surely write an essay. Hopkins's "The Windhover," for instance, has the subtitle "To Christ Our Lord." We soon see that the bird Hopkins describes, the windhover, has reminded him of certain qualities of Christ, and that he is making the bird, hovering in air with wings outstretched like a cross, a symbol for Christ. Then immediately his metaphor, that the bird is like a knightly prince riding the air, reinforces the symbol, since, in the days of chivalry, Christ was often thought of as a knight and prince, the heir of heaven. But unless the author brings his object into sufficient prominence to become a symbol, be cautious: it may be just one more of several objects that together suggest wealth, good taste, bad taste, acquisitiveness, carelessness, or the like. These are not symbols but merely parts of the setting, which you describe as a total impression.

Identify the written voice: point of view.

Every word speaks. In literature, every word is dramatic, since it conveys a human personality, its speaker's, whether that speaker is the author or a character, whether that word speaks from an essay, a poem, a story, or a play. Locate the speaker, assemble in your mind the personality speaking, and then describe it for your reader. The first question any text poses is: "Who is speaking?" The author? A dramatized voice of authority? A character? With Herrick's poem on Julia's clothes, the question of whether the speaker is actually Robert Herrick or some imagined lover is not immediately significant. But in poems or stories where the speaker seems markedly different from the author, the question becomes significant. We know instantly, for example, that Faulkner and Browning are dramatizing an idiot and a duke distinct from themselves. But frequently we must wait some time for certainty as to whose voice utters the enchanting words from the first sentence onward: "She looked around. The world was all white velvet, with nothing beyond. Where were the walls? . . ." The voice may represent one of three speakers:

1. The omniscient narrator;
2. A character observing;
3. A character participating.

THE OMNISCIENT NARRATOR. The "all-knowing" narrator speaks in the third person: "she thought; he went; they arrived." The omniscient narrator speaks in a godlike voice, knowing all that has happened, recounting the story, quoting the characters ("she said"), summarizing their thoughts: *Where were the walls?* This third-person narrator—who may be very different from the actual author who is putting him on paper—tells us exactly what he wants us to know, taking us into one character's thoughts, describing another only from the outside, giving us a third only as another character sees him. The voice thus gives us the station—the point—from which we view everything. The narrator seems to locate himself, and us, just behind the shoulder of one character, or perhaps several, like a TV camera that can also transcribe thought. But the narrator and his omniscient voice can also move off, again like the camera and its commentator, to survey the large scene or to probe a small detail somewhere else. His reportage is godlike, and our interpretation must include both the reportage and the godlike reporter.

FIRST-PERSON OBSERVER. A character observes the action. His first-person "I" tells us the tale. This "I" is close enough to the principal characters to know the details, but not so close as to be badly caught in their troubles. Dramatic irony—in which the speaker does not understand the full implications of what he reports—carries much of the impact. The barber who tells the story in Ring Lardner's "Haircut" is a classic example. You, as the explicator, explain these implications.

FIRST-PERSON PARTICIPANT. Defoe's Crusoe tells us all that happened to him, with some touches of verbal irony at his former mistakes and limitations. But the first-person participant is most effective, again, as the voice of dramatic irony: he does not understand the full import of what he does and tells and explains. The speaker, like Browning's duke, or Henry James's literary thief in *The Aspern Papers,* or Iris Murdoch's Bradley Pearson in *The Black Prince,* unknowingly reveals his meanness or other shortcomings in the very act of explaining or excusing himself. This inadvertent revelation, this dramatic irony, may be grim, as with Browning, or comic, as with James and Murdoch.

Your analytical question, then, is simply *Who is speaking?* From there you unfold for your reader what the point of view is— whether third-person-omniscient or one of the two first-persons— and what that implies for the reportage. How limited is the view? How reliable the report? How deep the dramatic irony, if any?

Identify the written voice: tone and style.

Tone and style come through together, of course, from the first sentence onward, giving us the author's, or speaker's, tone of voice and the attitude toward his story that this tone conveys. Hemingway's is like a sad bell that strikes a note and floats on in the same mellow resonance from first word to last. Joyce's is immediately ironic, as he looks down on his Leopold Bloom with amused detachment and a touch of scorn. Jane Austen's tone is also that of irony, as she describes her Emma, but warmer and more affectionate. Virginia Woolf's is the yearning inner voice of sensitive perception responding to the wonder and evanescence of life as it passes before us and we pass through it. Their various styles convey these various tones. Look for the typical sentence, the favorite words, and describe them, giving examples, if they are unusual and meaningful enough. You may not need, or want, to describe this for your reader, but you should ask yourself if it is distinctive enough to warrant description.

Determine the setting.

Where are we? As the voice implies its person, it also conjures up a place, even if only some lost mist of nonbeing. Frequently the setting is as dense as a sitting room, and it conveys the stuffiness of the people who sit in it. Sometimes the setting is so vaguely implied that we must fill it in only with the utmost tentativeness, as with the courtly surroundings that Julia's silks suggest. The setting may signify little or nothing, but you should at least ask yourself *where* and *when* it is, and what, if anything, it does signify—or you will miss a point your reader should know.

Describe the plot.

What happens? Nothing? That, too, is a significant happening. Describe it. Probably the happening is all in the past, put together by recollections—"flashbacks"—like flashes of lightning vivifying a moment along the trail of the past. Or the story may be highly plotted, one move causing another, invariably different from what the mover intended or we expected, though it may fulfill our general fears or expectations. Describe this too, trying to see how much the author emphasizes chance as against human intention and error. Whether the story is static and open-ended or active and conclusive, something is in conflict. Find out exactly what *is* in conflict. What motives, wishes, beliefs, assumptions collide? Who are the good guys and the bad guys, and what do they represent? Then locate those crucial events, mistakes, moments, that determine the outcome, and ask what the people might have done differently— what and where the crucial mistakes are. These may be the very center of your essay.

In plot, irony of circumstance rides high, since what seems to intrigue us about life is its contrariness. When things go as expected, we hardly notice, and we have little of interest to report. But buy a new car and have it dented, buy a watch for a lifetime and have it stolen the first hour, and you have a tale to tell. Plots are usually a chain of intentions ironically backfiring, or veering off, to the worst, or funniest, consequences. Romeo intends to stop a fight and end a feud, but his intervention kills his friend and seals his own doom. In describing any plot, comic or tragic, or in between, note the force and turn of these circumstantial ironies.

Distinguish plot and plotting.*

An author rations his material. The *plot* is everything that happened—what we would summarize in straight chronological order after we learned the full story—and the storyteller knows its entirety before he begins. The *plotting* is his strategy of letting us discover, eventually, everything that happened, and probably not in the sequence of happening. He must keep us in suspense, in the dark, letting in the light only a bit at a time until the final illumination. What side-trips does he take? How does he delay even as he informs? What red herrings does he drag across the trail to draw us from the scent? Keeping the plot and the plotting distinct will help you to describe the story's effect as it unfolds, and finally achieves its end.

Look especially for those things the author lets us misinterpret. In Austen's *Emma*, Frank Churchill goes all the way to London for a haircut. Everyone, including us, takes this as a sign of his frivolity. He (and Jane Austen) lightheartedly lets everyone cultivate this impression. In the end, we surmise the truth the author never tells us directly: he got his haircut, of course, but he really went to London to buy the slightly mysterious piano everyone has explained in another way. This is plot, after we have assembled all the details. The plotting is in dissociating the two significant details so that we miss their connection, and infer it only after we have learned all the facts of the plot. The author has indulged in, and enjoyed at our expense, the necessary deception of plotting, allowing room to deepen her characterization of Churchill as well. And we, too, enjoy the deception, as we take in the full light at the end, admiring her deftness and economy, and her accuracy in depicting human personality and human misperceptions. This is the charm of storytelling, the excitement in not knowing, in waiting to learn, in trying to guess and being surprised, until the master storyteller finally lets us fully into the secret. This is the strength of plotting. Your

---

*This distinction between plot and plotting originated in my "Bridget Allworthy: The Creative Pressures of Fielding's Plot," *Papers of the Michigan Academy of Science, Arts, and Letters,* 52 (1967), 345–356, reprinted in *Tom Jones,* Norton Critical Edition, ed. Sheridan Baker (New York: W. W. Norton & Co., 1973), pp. 906–916.

readers will appreciate your pointing it out to them, if it is notably good, as it certainly is in *Emma*.

Characters: individuals or stereotypes?

"Begin with an individual," writes F. Scott Fitzgerald, "and before you know it you find that you have created a type; begin with a type, and you find that you have created—nothing."* The writer has not *created*, in other words; he has merely borrowed a stereotype, a figure so thin and conventional as to be uninteresting or, worse, irritating, because the author thinks he has offered something new when he has given us only the fixed outline of the rich man, the poor man, the merchant, the chief, the Negro, the Jew, the Scotsman, the Irishman—all reflecting the haughty prejudices that produced them. An effective character does seem an individual, a real person, however fanciful the setting, on whatever mission impossible.

But a character must also seem typical of something in the human spectrum, or he will mean nothing. Actually, Fitzgerald is wrong about starting with a type. Probably all good writers often start precisely there—the young lover, the worried parent—and individualize the type as they go, as with Chaucer's marvelous array of types, each vividly individual. The greater the character, the more individualized, the more complex in motives and traits, and yet the more universally typical too, perhaps even *archetypical*, becoming a universal model forevermore, like Don Quixote or Falstaff or Hamlet or Huckleberry Finn.

In analyzing and describing characters, then, look first for their type. Labeling them may help you describe them for your readers— their names may tell something: *Flora* (the goddess of flowers), *Pinchpenny* (the ultimate tightwad). So try to find a label: the budding adolescent, the ineffectual old man, the pushy matron, the wily lawyer. Now you can present them a little more clearly, and show more clearly what energies in this fictional drama are in conflict. Then ask if the author individualizes them or leaves them

---

* Opening sentence, "The Rich Boy," first published in two parts, *Redbook Magazine*, January and February, 1926, and now widely anthologized.

merely typical. E. M. Forster divided characters into "round" and "flat," and the contrast has remained highly useful.* The round character has complexities, contradictions, depths, which make him seem fully rounded into life. The flat character we see only from the outside and from one side, knowing only a few of his typical traits, which remain the same, since his purpose is only to represent something typical. So tell your reader if your character is round or flat, and whether we learn something of his inner life or see him solely in one dimension.

Finally, try to say what individualizes this person, who is, of necessity, also a type. In *Ulysses,* for example, Joyce's Bloom is the typical alienated modern man. He is also Ulysses, tossed on strange shores and seeking home. He is also an Irishman, and also the Wandering Jew. He is a sensualist, who loves scented soap, and eats "with relish the inner organs of beasts and fowls," each sensuality putting a slight but different mark on the negative side of Bloom's ledger. Bloom is also a father seeking the son he has lost, and a jolly good fellow in the pub. In Bloom, we see surprisingly that individuals are bundles of typical traits, the naming of which helps us to define the individual. We apparently individualize the typical by mixing in more typicalities. Any detail of dress, any mannerism that particularizes, any "human touch," as we say, engages our attention because it is typically human. Pinpoint these details for your reader.

Types may also operate powerfully in stylized contexts, as in Japanese No plays, or in those several modern satirical fantasies with characters named Boy, Girl, Stenographer, Machine, and so forth. Describe the odd punch of these machined abstractions. Conversely, one sign of the great writer is to vitalize some insignificant and momentary character who would usually remain no more than a shadowy type. A highwayman in *Tom Jones* will pay an old woman a saucy compliment as he robs her, and will live forever in her memory, and ours. Shakespeare will let us glimpse an apothecary in Mantua so poor he will sell a deadly poison against his better will, or a soldier in Denmark who knows a piece of farmland when he sees one. These glimpses of vitalized types at the

---

* *Aspects of the Novel* (New York: Harcourt Brace Jovanovich, Inc., 1927), p. 103.

story's edges make the life it portrays broader and more solid. Describe them.

Analyze characterization.

We should therefore explain *how* the author presents his characters. He may tell us about them directly. D. H. Lawrence, for instance, frequently begins with a brilliant, almost breathtaking, summary of his protagonist's situation and personality. But watch out for irony in the author's tone, as when Joyce says "inner organs" instead of liver. The first question, then, and perhaps the last, is the author's attitude toward his character. Then tell whether he sketches out his portrait gradually, or fills in and colors an initial outline. For your description of an author's method, ask how we come to know his main characters, whether by one or several of the following: (1) how they look, (2) what they do, (3) what they say, (4) what others say of them, or (5) how others react to them. Note especially how your author introduces his characters. Description followed by speech and action? Other characters talking about them first? Dialogue? Inner monologue? These questions will help you explain how your author works, how he puts his portraits together.

Describe the author's blend of narration and scene.

The author tells us what he wants us to know, describes what he wants us to see, and gives us "scenes" of dialogue, in which his story seems much like a play. Each author's proportion of narration to scene, of "telling" to "showing," is different.* So explain how your storyteller handles his scenes. Do they proceed mostly in the

---

* This popular and useful distinction originates with Percy Lubbock, *The Craft of Fiction* (London: Jonathan Cape, 1921), p. 62: ". . . the art of fiction does not begin until the novelist thinks of his story as a matter to be *shown,* to be so exhibited that it will tell itself." But Joseph Warren Beach, also writing on Henry James and acknowledging his debt to Lubbock in general, probably popularized the terms: "I like to distinguish between novelists that *tell* and those that *show*" ("Introduction: 1954," *The Method of Henry James* [Philadelphia: Albert Saifor, 1954], pp. xxix–xxx).

author's voice, with astute pinpoints of dialogue? Or are they briefly set, with dialogue carrying almost everything thereafter? In Fielding's *Joseph Andrews,* Lady Booby asks Joseph, her footman, to bring up her teakettle. Notice how Fielding's first sentence moves from description to dialogue with an indirect quotation in italics; his second places it within quotation marks. Then the dialogue becomes direct, with only an occasional descriptive touch, as with Joseph's "Confusion" (Fielding's capitals and italics are typical of the eighteenth century):

> The Lady being in Bed, called *Joseph* to her, bad him sit down, and having accidently laid her hand on his, she asked him, *if he had never been in Love? Joseph* answered, with some Confusion, 'it was time enough for one so young as himself to think on such things.' 'As young as you are,' replied the Lady . . . .
> (*From* Joseph Andrews, *Wesleyan ed., I.v.29*)

Each author moves into his scenes in a slightly different way. So try to describe these transitions especially, and then notice how much, or how little, the author's descriptive comments are present as he sets his dialogue before us.

Consider the structure.

Simply step back from the work for a moment and see how it is built. What follows what? What are the high points, what the transitions? Since all temporal works must begin somewhere, must arch through, or sag through, some middle ground, and then must end somewhere, consider Beginning, Middle, and End. You may find a work neatly proportioned and architectural, constructed in three equal parts, with the center of complexity almost at the exact mathematical center, as in *Tom Jones* or *Emma,* or in the central scene in the central third act as in Shakespeare's five-act plays. Or you may find a work that flows, breaks off, and resumes, to be structured around some physical point, like Virginia Woolf's *To the Lighthouse* or Faulkner's *Light in August.* However it may be, consider the physical construction, and how it contributes to our comprehension of the work. Structure, in itself, may stir you to an essay — it really is, fundamentally, fascinating.

Note the similarities and differences of drama and fiction.

As our terms — plot, character, scene — suggest, fiction and the drama (and film, a vividly pictorial form of drama) share the same stuff of life and its mimesis. The drama tells a story, and the story-teller dramatizes his tale. Our impressions of both, especially if we *read* a play, are so similar that we hardly notice the differences of presentation. But two differences are essential:

1. Drama unfolds in the immediate present; fiction reports something already past.
2. The drama presents directly what fiction can only describe.

Drama is present tense; fiction is past tense. Drama is first person ("I"); fiction is, most frequently, third ("he, she"). The play is before us, minute by minute. The story tells us things that have happened. Even the narrator's dramatic scenes, which seem to unfold directly before us, as if on a stage, are actually reports from the past (he *said,* she *said*), with the storyteller mimicking the speakers' voices superbly well. But characters in plays (and films) speak *now*. "Now *I am* alone," says Hamlet. "Now *he was* alone," writes the storyteller.

As the narrator's scenes borrow "presentness" from the drama, so the dramatist must fill in some of the past. How he manages this exposition of past events is an index of his skill. A professional bore called a *nuntius* may come puffing in from Marathon to report triumph or disaster, or Shakespeare's repetitious Nurse may fix Juliet's birthday and age so amusingly in our minds that we do not notice the exposition. Or stark secrets may emerge from the past in intensely dramatic moments, as they do from the lips of Strindberg's Miss Julie, almost at the play's, and her own, tragic end. So look for background from the past (or from across the street a few moments before), and explain how well the playwright disguises its essentially undramatic exposition.

Finally, the drama's "presentness" is physical, it is visual and aural. Music, the dance, gesture, spectacle — royal processions with crowns bestowed or torn asunder — have added meaning to the spoken words ever since the Greeks evolved their drama from pagan ritual. And modern theater, with lighting and sights and sounds at its fingertips, has evoked effects that earlier theaters could approximate only in words, if they could imagine them at all. Your estimate of any play must ponder these wordless effects, or must visualize them from stage directions, estimating what they add to the spoken drama.

EXERCISE

4 (a) Here is a scene that has proved widely effective on the stage, yet it is´ almost entirely narrative. It comes from Edward Albee's one-act play *The American Dream*, which he describes as "an examination of the American scene." The curtain rises on Mommy and Daddy sitting on opposite sides of a very dismal living room. From the exposition, as they talk, we gather that, years ago, they bought a child who proved "unsatisfactory" and eventually died. Now they want their money back, and are waiting for satisfaction.

Write a brief explanation of what Albee is saying about "the American scene" through this stylized "examination" of it. Note especially what he implies by his setting and his brief stage directions. Why "Mommy" and "Daddy" rather than names? How would you have them look and act? What is their relationship like? What is Mommy's relationship with "the chairman of our woman's club"? Why is her husband "adorable"? Why the indistinguishable colors? Why the repeated "lovely"? What is the point about buying and selling? What is the satisfaction Daddy says you can't get today, and what is Mommy's satisfaction? Finally, what does Albee gain or lose by having Mommy narrate the hassle of the hat rather than staging it directly?

From THE AMERICAN DREAM*

Edward Albee

MOMMY (*giggles at the thought; then*): All right, now. I went to buy a new hat yesterday and I said, "I'd like a new hat, please." And so, they showed me a few hats, green ones and blue ones, and I didn't like any of them, not one bit. What did I say? What did I just say?

DADDY: You didn't like any of them, not one bit.

MOMMY: That's right; you just keep paying attention. And then they showed me one that I did like. It was a lovely little hat, and I said, "Oh, this is a lovely little hat; I'll take this hat; oh my, it's lovely. What color is it?" And they said, "Why, this is beige; isn't it a lovely little beige hat?" And I said, "Oh, it's just lovely." And so, I bought it. (*Stops, looks at* DADDY)

DADDY (*to show he is paying attention*): And so you bought it.

MOMMY: And so I bought it, and I walked out of the store with the hat right on my head, and I ran spang into the chairman of our woman's club, and she said, "Oh, my dear, isn't that a lovely little hat? Where did you get that lovely little hat? It's the loveliest little hat; I've always wanted a wheat-colored hat *myself*." And, I said, "Why, no, my dear; this hat is beige; beige." And she laughed and said, "Why no, my dear, that's a wheat-colored hat . . . wheat. I know beige from wheat." And I said, "Well, my dear, I know beige from wheat, too." What did I say? What did I just say?

DADDY (*tonelessly*): Well, my dear, I know beige from wheat, too.

MOMMY: That's right. And she laughed, and she said, "Well, my dear, they certainly put one over on you. That's wheat if I ever saw wheat. But it's lovely, just the same." And then she walked off. She's a dreadful woman, you don't know her; she has dreadful taste, two dreadful children, a dreadful house, and an absolutely adorable husband who sits in a wheel chair all the time. You don't know him. You don't know anybody, do you? She's just a dreadful woman, but she *is* chairman of our woman's club, so naturally I'm terribly fond of her. So, I went right back into the hat shop, and I said, "Look here; what do you mean selling me a hat that you say is beige, when it's wheat all the time . . . wheat! I can tell beige from wheat any day in the week, but not in this artificial light of yours." They have artificial light, Daddy.

DADDY: Have they!

MOMMY: And I said, "The minute I got outside I could tell that it wasn't a beige hat at all; it was a wheat hat." And they said to me, "How could you tell that when you had the hat on the top of your head?" Well, that made me angry, and so I made a scene right there; I screamed as hard as I could; I took my hat off and I threw it down on the counter, and oh, I made a terrible scene. I said, I made a terrible scene.

DADDY (*snapping to*): Yes . . . yes . . . good for you!

MOMMY: And I made an absolutely terrible scene; and they became frightened, and they said, "Oh, madam; oh, madam." But I kept right on, and finally they admitted that they might have made a mistake; so they took my hat into the back, and then they came out again with a hat that looked exactly like it. I took one look at it, and I said, "This hat is wheat-colored; wheat." Well, of course, they said, "Oh, no, madam, this hat is beige; you go outside and see." So, I went outside, and lo and behold, it *was* beige. So I bought it.

DADDY (*clearing his throat*): I would imagine that it was the same hat they tried to sell you before.

MOMMY (*with a little laugh*): Well, of course it was!

DADDY: That's the way things are today; you just can't get satisfaction; you just try.

MOMMY: Well, *I* got satisfaction.

4 (b) Here is a scene, "Block Eight," from Tennessee Williams's *Camino Real,* a theatrical fantasy about some vaguely Spanish and timeless seaport that is the "terminal stretch of the road that used to be royal," as one character says in "Block Ten." A note tells us to Anglicize the title: *CAMino REal.* The play opens with Don Quixote, dressed like an old desert prospector, advancing down the aisle from the back of the theater, exhausted but dauntless. Sancho stumbles after, swearing, carrying the Don's rusty armor. Sancho doesn't like this place. His chart indicates that it is the end of the CaMINo ReAL and the beginning of the CAMino REal. "Halt there," it says, "and turn back, Traveler, for the spring of humanity has gone dry in this place and . . . there are no birds in the country except wild birds that are tamed and kept in . . . *Cages!*" He departs, but Don Quixote lies down to dream throughout the play, before pressing on at the end with Kilroy.

> More than any other work that I have done [says Williams in his "Foreword"], this play has seemed to me like the construction of another world, a separate existence. Of course, it is nothing more nor less than my conception of the time and world I live in, and its people are mostly archetypes of certain basic attitudes and qualities with those mutations that would occur if they continued along the road to this hypothetical terminal point in it.

Gutman, "a lordly fat man wearing a linen suit and a pith helmet," in the stage directions, is proprietor of the Siete Mares hotel and the play's master of ceremonies. The fountain in the plaza has gone dry, but there is plenty to drink in the Siete Mares. Abdullah, dressed in Arabian burnoose, acts as errand boy. Marguerite is the passionate tubercular heroine of *La Dame aux Camélias* ("The Camellia Lady") by Alexandre Dumas *fils* (1852). She has died for love. Jacques is Giacomo Casanova (1725–98), the great lover. The Dreamer drifts around, playing softly on a guitar. The details of Shelley's cremation match pretty well with

Byron's and Trelawney's reports of it. Byron himself, however, was not later cremated ("a crepe suzette — burned in brandy"): his embalmed body was shipped from Greece to England in a keg of "spirits," which may well have been brandy. Kilroy is the mythical figure who emerged on the walls of latrines and captured villages, from Atlantic to Pacific, in World War II: "Kilroy was here." Gutman has forced him to wear a clown's suit, with "the red fright wig, the big crimson nose that lights up and has horn rimmed glasses attached, a pair of clown pants that have a huge footprint on the seat." The Alleyway Out and the arch lead to Terra Incognita, "a wasteland between the walled town and the distant perimeter of snow-topped mountains," over which the desert wind rises and falls throughout the play, "accompanied by distant, measured reverberations like pounding surf or distant shellfire."

Now, explain what Byron seems to be affirming, and then describe how all the theatrical, nonverbal effects qualify that message. Begin with the desert wind. Consider the Hunchback and the Dreamer, the other characters' reactions, Byron's gestures, his limp, his bird cages, and Kilroy's closing activity. Consider, too, the pictorial effects we get in Byron's account of the cremation.

From CAMINO REAL*
Block Eight: "The Departure of Lord Byron"
TENNESSEE WILLIAMS

[*There is the sound of loud desert wind and a flamenco cry followed by a dramatic phrase of music.*

A flickering diamond blue radiance floods the hotel entrance. The crouching, grimacing Hunchback shakes his hoop of bells which is the convention for the appearance of each legendary figure.

Lord Byron appears in the doorway readied for departure. Gutman raises his hand for silence.]

GUTMAN: You're leaving us, Lord Byron?

BYRON: Yes, I'm leaving you, Mr. Gutman.

GUTMAN: What a pity! But this is a port of entry and departure. There are no permanent guests. Possibly you are getting a little restless?

BYRON: The luxuries of this place have made me soft. The metal point's gone from my pen, there's nothing left but the feather.

---

* Copyright 1948, 1953 by Tennessee Williams. Reprinted by permission of New Directions Publishing Corporation.

GUTMAN: That may be true. But what can you do about it?

BYRON: Make a departure!

GUTMAN: From yourself?

BYRON: From my present self to myself as I used to be!

GUTMAN: *That's* the *furthest* departure a man could make. I guess you're sailing to Athens? There's another war there and like all wars since the beginning of time it can be interpreted as a — struggle for *what?*

BYRON: For *freedom!* You may laugh at it, but it still means something to *me!*

GUTMAN: Of course it does! I'm not laughing a bit, I'm beaming with admiration.

BYRON: I've allowed myself many distractions.

GUTMAN: Yes, indeed!

BYRON: But I've never altogether forgotten my old devotion to the —

GUTMAN: To the *what*, Lord Byron?

[*Byron passes nervous fingers through his hair.*]

You can't remember the object of your one-time devotion?

[*There is a pause. Byron limps away from the terrace and goes toward the fountain.*]

BYRON: When Shelley's corpse was recovered from the sea . . .

[*Gutman beckons the Dreamer who approaches and accompanies Byron's speech.*]

— It was burned on the beach at Viareggio. — I watched the spectacle from my carriage because the stench was revolting . . . Then it — fascinated me! I got out of my carriage. Went nearer, holding a handkerchief to my nostrils! — I saw that the front of the skull had broken away in the flames, and there —

[*He advances out upon the stage apron, followed by Abdullah with the pine torch or lantern.*]

And there was the brain of Shelley, indistinguishable from a cooking stew! — *boiling, bubbling, hissing!* — in the *blackening — cracked — pot* — of his skull!

[*Marguerite rises abruptly. Jacques supports her.*]

— Trelawney, his friend, Trelawney, threw salt and oil and frankincense in the flames and finally the almost intolerable stench —

[*Abdullah giggles. Gutman slaps him.*]

—was *gone* and the burning was *pure!*—as a man's burning should be . . .

A man's burning *ought* to be pure!—*not* like mine—(a crepe suzette—burned in brandy . . .)

Shelley's burning was finally very *pure!*

But the body, the corpse, split open like a grilled pig!

[*Abdullah giggles irrepressibly again. Gutman grips the back of his neck and he stands up stiff and assumes an expression of exaggerated solemnity.*]

—And then Trelawney—as the ribs of the corpse unlocked—reached into them as a baker reaches quickly into an oven!

[*Abdullah almost goes into another convulsion.*]

—And snatched out—as a baker would a biscuit!—the *heart* of Shelley! Snatched the heart of Shelley out of the blistering corpse!—Out of the purifying—blue-flame . . .

[*Marguerite resumes her seat; Jacques his.*]

—And it was *over!*—I thought—

[*He turns slightly from the audience and crosses upstage from the apron. He faces Jacques and Marguerite.*]

—I thought it was a disgusting thing to do, to snatch a man's heart from his body! What can one man do with another man's heart?

[*Jacques rises and strikes the stage with his cane.*]

JACQUES [*passionately*]: He can do this with it!

[*He seizes a loaf of bread on his table, and descends from the terrace.*]

He can twist it like this!

[*He twists the loaf.*]

He can tear it like this!

[*He tears the loaf in two.*]

He can crush it under his foot!

[*He drops the bread and stamps on it.*]

—*And kick it away—like this!*

[*He kicks the bread off the terrace. Lord Byron turns away from him and limps again out upon the stage apron and speaks to the audience.*]

BYRON: That's very true, Señor. But a poet's vocation, which used to be my vocation, is to influence the heart in a gentler fashion than you have made your mark on that loaf of bread. He ought to purify it and lift it above its ordinary level. For what is the heart but a sort of —

[He makes a high, groping gesture in the air.]

— A sort of — *instrument!* — that translates *noise* into *music,* chaos into — *order* . . .

[Abdullah ducks almost to the earth in an effort to stifle his mirth, Gutman coughs to cover his own amusement.]

— *a mysterious order!*

[He raises his voice till it fills the plaza.]

— That was my vocation once upon a time, before it was obscured by vulgar plaudits! — Little by little it was lost among gondolas and palazzos! — masked balls, glittering salons, huge shadowy courts and torch-lit entrances! Baroque façades, canopies and carpets, candelabra and gold plate among snowy damask, ladies with throats as slender as flower-stems, bending and breathing toward me their fragrant breath —
— Exposing their breasts to me!
Whispering, half-smiling! — And everywhere marble, the visible grandeur of marble, pink and gray marble, veined and tinted as flayed corrupting flesh, — all these provided agreeable distractions from the rather frightening solitude of a poet. Oh, I wrote many cantos in Venice and Constantinople and in Ravenna and Rome, on all of those Latin and Levantine excursions that my twisted foot led me into — but I wonder about them a little. They seem to improve as the wine in the bottle — dwindles . . . *There is a passion for declivity in this world!* And lately I've found myself listening to hired musicians behind a row of artificial palm trees — instead of the single — pure-stringed instrument of my heart . . .
Well, then, it's time to leave here!

[He turns back to the stage.]

— There is a time for departure even when there's no certain place to go!
I'm going to look for one, now. I'm sailing to Athens. At least I can look up at the Acropolis, I can stand at the foot of it and look up at broken columns on the crest of a hill — if not purity, at least its recollection . . .

I can sit quietly looking for a long, long time in absolute silence, and possibly, yes, *still* possibly —

The old pure music will come to me again. Of course on the other hand I may hear only the little noise of insects in the grass . . .

But I am sailing to Athens! *Make voyages! — Attempt them! —* there's nothing else . . .

MARGUERITE [*excitedly*]: *Watch where he goes!*

[*Lord Byron limps across the plaza with his head bowed, making slight, apologetic gestures to the wheedling Beggars who shuffle about him. There is music. He crosses toward the steep Alleyway Out. The following is played with a quiet intensity so it will be in a lower key than the later Fugitivo Scene.*]

Watch him, watch him, see which way he goes. Maybe he knows of a way that we haven't found out.

JACQUES: Yes, I'm watching him, Cara.

[*Lord and Lady Mulligan half rise, staring anxiously through monocle and lorgnon.*]

MARGUERITE: Oh, my God, I believe he's going up that alley.

JACQUES: Yes, he is. He has.

LORD and LADY MULLIGAN: Oh, the fool, the idiot, he's going under the arch!

MARGUERITE: Jacques, run after him, warn him, tell him about the desert he has to cross.

JACQUES: I think he knows what he's doing.

MARGUERITE: I can't look!

[*She turns to the audience, throwing back her head and closing her eyes. The desert wind sings loudly as Byron climbs to the top of the steps.*]

BYRON [*to several porters carrying luggage — which is mainly caged birds*]: THIS WAY!

[*He exits.*]

[*Kilroy starts to follow. He stops at the steps, cringing and looking at Gutman. Gutman motions him to go ahead. Kilroy rushes up the stairs. He looks out, loses his nerve and sits — blinking his nose. Gutman laughs as he announces —*]

GUTMAN: Block Nine on the Camino Real!

[*He goes into the hotel.*]

EVALUATION

Evaluation sums up the questions we have been asking. Ultimately, all writing about literature—all criticism, in fact—entails
evaluation. Merely selecting a story or poem to write about is an
act of evaluation, since you are distinguishing it from others of its
kind as exceptional, good or bad, outstanding in some ways, faulty
in others. I would not have selected "Upon Julia's Clothes," for
instance, had I not thought it great, and wanted to find out and explain exactly why. You may wish to explain a novel's point, making
your thesis an assertion of what the novel's implied thesis is, and
this would seem a perfectly neutral kind of exposition. But your
selection has already made the initial evaluation, and your essay
will assume that treating this particular novel, whether good or bad,
will produce more illumination than would treating another. Or
you may wish explicitly to take the final step and make your thesis
openly evaluative: "This novel is unusually significant because . . . ."
    To discover the thesis of your novel (or poem, play, or film),
you may ask yourself the four essential critical questions:

> What?
> How?
> How well?
> So what?

The first two take you into the area of description, the last two into
evaluation. As you make notes toward answering these questions,
you will develop not only your thesis, but also all the evidence you
need to illustrate it. The many ways of addressing the *What?* and
How? questions, the many elements of a novel, play, or poem to
which you direct these questions, we have just surveyed. Now,
most important of all—what does it add up to? What is the thesis?
    The first of your two evaluative questions—*How well?*—is
perhaps a lesser one, of technique and aesthetic effect, of means
rather than ends. You may in fact not need to answer it, unless the
means—the style, organization, and general management of the book
—contribute noticeably to the end, to the book's final power and
meaning. Most books are reasonably well written, and you may
need little beyond a sentence observing the fact. The *How well?*
becomes important only when technique makes an unusual contribu-

tion, or when it is noticeably at odds with content, as with a book that is skillfully written but empty, like a clever advertisement. On the other hand, you will occasionally find a book whose lack of art is forgivable because it has something to say. Although Defoe's *Moll Flanders*, for example, is an awkward and cluttered book, its moral vitality has enabled it to endure these two centuries and a half. If you know *Moll Flanders* at all, you understand that by *moral vitality* I do not mean simply "goodness," but any instructive and vital display of the various heavens and hells of existence.

The ultimate evaluative question, *So what?*, is one we like to ask but hate to answer. Evaluation is extremely hard, and it is dangerous. When it applies inappropriate standards to something new, it may go badly wrong, as when critics decried Beethoven's dissonance. But warmth of judgment, even though wrong, is better than an eternal freeze of indecision. A mind gathered firmly around a reasoned conviction is better than no mind at all. Try to reach a judgment. Is it a good book (or movie) or a poor one? What does it amount to? What do its particulars tell you about life in general?

Here is a film that takes place in three hours in Hoboken, as two characters search for a lost train and relive their lives, seem to fall in love, but then move off on different tracks, both richer for the experience. It is ably done, perfectly believable, and the characters look and speak like real people. It seems to say that we are all on trains that pass in the night. Well—so what? You know it is good. But to explain to your readers *why* it is good, you must go beyond the movie to what man seems to value in life itself—love over hate, compassion over vindictiveness, sympathy over selfishness, understanding over ignorance—to some perception of the whole agony and wonder of being human.

Here is a book. It has held your attention and moved you, and you feel that it is good. But what has it said, what has it amounted to? What, in short, is its thesis and the worth of its thesis? The story is about a boy in prep school who has run away to the city because everything at school has suddenly turned to ashes in his mouth. Everyone and everything—the whole system—seems false, as if they would turn to dust when touched. He finds the same in the city's more devious ways. But he also comes to see that life, at its center, can sustain its false surfaces if one can give something of himself to others equally lost, if one can find some mutual support in the family. He may not have a stable center himself, but he sees that life does have this center, whereas he formerly saw only a void.

You have been describing, of course, Salinger's amusing and moving *The Catcher in the Rye*. You have summarized *what is there* until you have come to a statement of the novel's thesis. Although working unseen among the details, the thesis also has been *there* for you to find and state, if you are to grasp the novel as anything more than a series of serio-comic episodes. Now you can write your first paragraph:

> J. D. Salinger's *The Catcher in the Rye* at first seems no more than a humorous, slangy tale about an adolescent boy in a hunting cap, which he wears turned backward for some obscure adolescent reason. We follow Holden Caulfield's escapades in New York City with amusement, and we listen to his wild, earnest slang with delight. How can anyone resist such good entertainment? But as we read on, we discover that that the story is not simply funny; it is also pathetic. For all his distraught immaturity, Holden is a very decent person. We soon find ourselves believing he is right and the world is wrong, until finally we discover, with him, that the wrong, empty world can have a center after all, that the center consists in helping the still more helpless, in an act of protective love much like a parent's for a child. In short, at the center of the sham and chaos is a simple affection and understanding that begins at home, in the family.

In criticism, write in the present tense.

You will notice that that paragraph describes *The Catcher in the Rye* in the present tense. You should continue in the present throughout the rest of your paper. The custom and the rule is this: in describing events in plays or novels, or in writing about a poem, *write in the present tense.* Write "Holden *goes* to New York" not "Holden *went* to New York." Likewise you would write "Herrick *repeats* the rhyme" not "Herrick *repeated* the rhyme." The past tense unveils you, as a student and amateur, experiencing the book last night, now in your own past. The present tense testifies to the timeless present in which literature lives, and it also exhibits your own sophistication as critic in recognizing that timeless present. Herrick will still repeat, and Holden will still go, tomorrow and tomorrow and tomorrow (when you and I can no longer do either), and at the same place in the poem or book. And be careful not to drift into the past without noticing, as you recall reading by the midnight lamp, or think of Herrick himself as long since dead. Now, in the present tense, we can continue with Holden.

Describe and explain.

The middle of your "Holden" paper may now well begin by summarizing the *What*, describing the story and the people, in more detail.

> **The story beings at Holden's prep school, on a Saturday night, when ends are especially loose . . . .**

You tell just enough to establish the book for your reader without telling him everything. But do not assume that he has read the book, or you will not explain the action fully and clearly enough.

Next you will probably want to say something about the *How*, since the book's language is not only striking but important. Holden's improper idiom carries us to the truth, which the proper world has apparently lost. Proper speech seems a sham, and the only true language left is Holden's yearning, vivid, inaccurate slang. So you give an example or two of this. Another important *How* about the book, one that immediately moves into the question of *How well*, arises at the end. There we discover that Holden's entire story has been a monologue addressed to his psychiatrist. His telling of his story has presumably straightened out his perspectives. You would certainly point out this unusual technical feature to your reader, and comment on whether it works. Salinger gives some clues in the first chapter, but are they sufficient to forestall the reader's surprise at the end? Perhaps you think the end a bit too much the gimmick to come off with complete conviction. Nonetheless, you think the book stands up under the sudden strain of its ending. Explaining the strain and the survival will lead you to the heart of the book's value. You will have come from describing contents and technique to answering the question *So what?*, to which your thesis addressed itself, though briefly, at the start.

Here you are, then, at the last section of your middle and just before your conclusion, ready to answer the question that will give your thesis its fullest explanation: how, exactly, does the book assert its thesis that familial affection triumphs over social chaos? Here you explain the title: Holden's hunting cap symbolizes his role as "catcher" in the rye; he wears it backward, like a baseball catcher's cap, though he does not know why he likes it that way. You explain his curious misunderstanding of the song "Coming Through the Rye"; his seeing the little boy on a Sunday stroll with his father and mother, happily walking the gutter's edge; his imagining himself waiting in the rye, the savior of little children, ready to catch them just before they fall over cliffs. Then, of course, you describe his little sister, "old Phoebe," and tell how he gives her his hunting cap, and how *she* saves *him*.

Notice that you have not needed to answer directly the devastating final question of value. You have implied its answer. From the very first, everything you have said has implied, "This book is valuable." You have asserted the grounds for its value: its thesis that love, and family love, can hold the world together. Few would think to dispute that assertion very strenuously. Furthermore, your paper has shown, without directly saying so, that this valid thesis is convincingly acted out, in Salinger's superb mimesis.

Now we have sketched out the various ways you may write about literature, and the questions to ask to get started. Don't feel that you must answer all of them, all at once, for any one paper. I have tried to cover the possibilities, to make them available if, and when, you may need them. Actually, you write in much the same terms whatever you choose to discuss: the importance of a minor character, let us say, or of a particular speech or scene, the prominence of a particular metaphor, the balance and emphasis of form, the force of a style, the difference between two similar stories or poems. You simply assert that something is significant, then explain how this is so, describing what you see and quoting for specific illustration. And you shape your essay in the usual way, following the essential psychology of how we take things in, through time: a thesis to guide and organize, a beginning, middle, and end.

EXERCISES

5 Write an essay evaluating the following short story, including as much
explication as you need.

EVANGELIST*
JOYCE CARY

John Pratt, fifty-five, on holiday at the sea, gets up one sunny
morning, looks from the window, says, "It won't last," and picks
from his seven suits the only dark one. He dresses himself with care,
and eats for breakfast one piece of dry toast.

"A touch of liver," he says to himself, takes his umbrella and a
bowler, and goes for his morning walk along the Parade.

"Why the bowler?" he asks himself. "I'm not going back to
town." And suddenly it strikes him that he is bored. "Impossible,"
he says; "I've only been here a week and my regular time is always a
fortnight."

He looks about him to discover some usual source of pleasure
in this charming old place; and immediately he is seized, possessed,
overwhelmed with boredom, with the most malignant and hopeless
of all boredoms, holiday boredom. It rises from his stomach, it falls
from the lukewarm air. Everything in sight is instantly perceived as
squalid, mercenary, debased by mean use and vulgar motives. The
Regency façades whose delicate taste he has so much admired, which
bring him year after year to a place neither smart nor quiet, seem to
leer at him with the sly, false primness of old kept women on the look-
out for some city lecher, willing to set off cracked plaster against lewd
dexterity.

He looks at the sea for freshness. But it appears thick, greasy:
he murmurs with horror, "The cesspool of the whole earth." He sees
the drains discharging from a million towns, the rubbish unbucketed
from ten thousand years of ships, wrecks full of corpses; the splash
of glitter beyond the pier is like the explosion of some hidden corrup-
tion. The ozone comes to his nose like a stench.

* "Evangelist" in *Spring Song and Other Stories* (New York: Harper & Row,
Publishers). Copyright 1952 by Arthur Lucius Michael Cary and David Alexander
Ogilvie, Executors of the Estate of Joyce Cary. Reprinted by permission of Harper
& Row, Publishers, Inc. and Curtis Brown Ltd. on behalf of the Estate of Joyce Cary.

He sees from the distance a friend, the Colonel in his light gray suit, stepping briskly. He is whirling his stick—it is plain that he is in his usual high spirits.

Pratt crosses the road to avoid him. A taxi hoots in an angry and distracted manner, but he does not hurry, he would rather be killed than betray the dignity of his despair. The taxi's brakes squawk like Donald Duck—it comes to a stop at his elbow—a furious young man with upstanding black hair and red-rimmed eyes, thrusts out his neck and bawls insults. Bystanders laugh and stare. Pratt does not turn his head or quicken his walk. He accepts these humiliations as appropriate to such a morning in such a world.

The shopping housewives with their predatory eyes and anxious wrinkled foreheads fill him with a lofty and scornful pity, as for insects generated by a conspiracy of gases and instinct to toil in blind necessity for the production of more insects.

Yes, he thinks, humanity is like the maggots on a perishing carcass. Its history is the history of maggots; the fly, the buzz, the coupling of flies, the dropping of their poison on every clean thing, the hunt for some ordure, some corpse, the laying of eggs, and another generation of maggots. Foulness upon foulness. Tides of disgust and scorn rise in his soul; he stalks more grandly; he has become a giant for whom all history is meaner than the dust on his boot soles.

Suddenly he is accosted by a red-faced man, an hotel acquaintance, who starts out of a shop and seizes him by the hand—impossible to avoid this person. The red-faced man is in a fluster. Has Mr. Pratt seen the news? Is there going to be a war, is this it? Should he sell out his investments and pay his debts; should he fetch back his family from abroad?

Pratt draws himself up and out of mere wrath at this intrusion, utters in severe tones such banalities as amaze his own ears. If war comes, he says, it will come, and if not, then not. There are good arguments on both sides of the question. If we believe our freedom is worth defending, then we should be ready to defend it at all costs. For faith is not faith, not what we truly believe, unless we are prepared to die for it. And in a conflict of faith those alone who are prepared to die for what they believe deserve to win. As for bombs, one can die but once. One will die anyhow and possibly much worse than by a bomb.

And all these panic-mongers, are they not more than foolish? Panic is not only useless, it is a treachery—a defeat—an invitation to the enemy within as well as without.

The red-faced man is taken aback by this rigmarole of eloquence. He listens with surprised attention in his green eyes—then with respect. Pratt's unmoved solemnity, his severe tone born of scornful indifference, impress him. He ejaculates murmurs of approval. He says that this is just what he himself has always thought. And this is probably true. He could scarcely have escaped such reflections.

At last he is greatly moved. He turns even redder, his gooseberry eyes shine. He grasps Pratt's hand with fervor and a glance that means, "This is an important, a solemn occasion. You are a bigger man than I took you for. Men of sense and courage, like ourselves, should be better acquainted." He departs exalted.

Pratt walks on alone, his step is still majestic but full of spring. He is exhilarated; he looks at the sea and it appears to him noble in its vastness, transcendent in its unconcern, venerable in its intimation of glorious deeds. The houses are like veteran soldiers in line, meeting with stoic pride the injuries of time. The housewives, striving, saving for their families, wear the brows of angels; the battered angels roughly carved on some primitive church. He salutes with heroic elation a world made for heroes. He perceives with joy that it is going to be a fine day, that he is hungry. He whirls his umbrella.

6 Pick two of Shakespeare's sonnets and demonstrate that one is better than the other.

7 Pick two stories from James Joyce's *Dubliners,* or from any similar collection of stories by another author, and demonstrate that one is better than the other.

8 Write an essay on a novel you have read recently, or a movie you have seen, checking your analysis against the four critical questions: What? How? How well? So what?

9 Following the same procedure, write an essay on a work of nonfiction — a book of ideas, political, sociological, philosophical, an autobiography, a biography, a history.

Thirteen
Research

Now to consolidate and advance. Instead of one thousand words, you will write three thousand. Instead of a self-propelled debate or independent literary analysis, you will write a scholarly argument. You will also learn to use the library, and to take notes and give footnotes. You will learn the ways of scholarship. You will learn to acknowledge your predecessors as you distinguish yourself, to make not only a bibliography, but a contribution.

The research paper is very likely not what you think it is. *Research* is searching again. You are looking, usually, where others have looked before; but you hope to see something they have not. Research is not combining a paragraph from *The Encyclopaedia Britannica* and a paragraph from *The Book of Knowledge* with a slick pinch from *Time*. That's robbery. Nor is it research even if you carefully change each phrase and acknowledge the source. That's drudgery. Even in some high circles, I am afraid, such scavenging is called research. It is not. It is simply a cloudier condensation of what you have done in school as a "report" — sanctioned plagiarism to teach something about ants or Ankara, a tedious compiling of what is already known. That such material is new to you is not the issue: it is already in the public stock.

Take care against plagiarism.

Plagiarism is presenting someone else's work as your own. Since in research you will be dealing with what others have written, and with a number of ideas already stated and shared, plagiarism, inadvertent or intentional, may seem hard to avoid. But simple honesty will guide you, and care in your note-taking will protect you. Actually, care against plagiarizing will make your research self-evidently more solid and thorough. If you borrow an idea, footnote your source. If you have an idea of your own and then discover that someone has beaten you to it, swallow your disappointment and footnote your predecessor, seeing what more you can add to get back some of your own. Or you can keep even more of your own by saying, in footnote, "I discover that James Smith agrees with me on this point," explaining, if possible, what Smith has overlooked, or his differing emphasis, and again giving a full citation of Smith's article for all future reference.

In taking notes, copy out possible quotations accurately, with full details of source and page, and mark them clearly so that you will know they are quotations later. Quote them directly in your paper, and footnote your source:

> According to Freud, establishing the ego is a kind
>
> of "reclamation work, like the draining of the
>
> Zuyder Zee."[1]
>
> [1] New Introductory Lectures on Psycho-Analysis,
> trans. W. J. H. Sprott (New York: W. W. Norton & Co.,
> 1933), p. 112.

The author's name does not appear in the footnote because I have already named him in my text, which is the best place. Notice also that I have quoted the shortest possible segment of Freud's sentence to get the sharpest focus, and that I have run it into my own sentence within quotation marks. You would indent and single-space a long quotation, and omit the quotation marks: for further details see, pp. 57; 432–434.

Or you may quote indirectly, rephrasing unmistakably in your own words:

```
Freud likens psychotherapy to reclaiming territory

from the sea.¹
```

The danger lies in copying out phrases from your source as you summarize what it says, and then incorporating them in your essay, with or without realizing that those phrases are not yours. The solution is, again, to take down and mark quotations accurately in your notes, or to summarize succinctly in your own words, words as far away from the original as possible, keeping the two as distinct as you can, so that nothing from your source will leak through your notes, unmarked, into your paper, arousing your reader's suspicions. Remember that the word *plagiarism* comes from the Latin word for kidnapping (from *plaga*, "net"), and that it is indeed a crime—one that can bring lawsuits and expulsions from college. Remember, too, that your instructor can almost invariably detect changes in your vocabulary and style that indicate a kidnapping of someone else's brainchild. Be honest, and your papers and prose will reflect that honesty.

CHOOSING YOUR SUBJECT

Find a thesis.

Well, then, with facts in the public stock and ideas with other people's names on them, what can you do? You move from facts and old ideas to new ideas. Here the range is infinite. Every old idea needs new assertion. Every new assertion needs judgment. Here you are in the area of values, where everyone is in favor of virtue but in doubt about what is virtuous. Your best area for research is in some controversial issue, where you can add, and document, a new judgment of "right" or "wrong."

I have put it bluntly to save you from drowning in slips of paper. Remember that an opinion is not a private fancy; it is an opinion *about* what the right is, what the truth is, what the facts mean. It is a judgment of what *is*—out there somewhere, not merely in somebody's head. An opinion, when careful and informed, is usually as close as you will get to truth: a statement of what the truth of the matter seems to be. Your opinion may be just as accurate as anybody's, and the major task of the research paper is to sift opinions.

Your sifter, as always, is your thesis, right there at the neck of your beginning paragraph. Your thesis, as always, is your essay in miniature. Make your thesis first, *before you begin research.* Call it a hypothesis (a "subthesis") if that will make you comfortable. It does seem unscientific. But it is nearer the scientific method than it looks. The scientist, too, plays his hunches. James Watt saw the steam condenser in the lid of his aunt's teakettle; Donald Glaser saw the tracks of atomic particles in the bubbles of his beer. As with scientific experiment and the simple essay, if the hypothesis proves wrong, the testing will have furnished means to make it more nearly right. With the research paper, if you do not have a thesis to lead you through the twists and turns of print, you will never come out the other end. Unless you have a working hypothesis to keep your purpose alive as you collect, or at least a clear question to be answered, you may collect forever, forever hoping for a purpose. If you have a thesis, you will learn—and then overcome— the temptations of collecting only the supporting evidence and ignoring the obverse facts and whispers of conscience. If further facts and good arguments persuade you to the other side, so much the better. You will be the stronger for it.

Persuade your reader you are right.

You do not search primarily for facts. You do not aim to summarize everything ever said on the subject. You aim to persuade your reader that the thesis you believe in is right. You persuade him by: (1) letting him see that you have been thoroughly around the subject and that you know what is known of it and thought of it,

(2) showing him where the wrongs are wrong, and (3) citing the rights as right. *Your* opinion, *your* thesis, is what you are showing; all your quotations from all the authorities in the world are subservient to *your* demonstration. You are the reigning authority. You have, for the moment, the longest perspective and the last word.

Pick an argument.

The tactics of the research paper, then, are exactly those of any argumentative essay. Any straight exposition can take a helpful argumentative edge: not "House Cats" but "House cats are more intelligent than most people realize." You can find something to prove even in straight description: "See," you say, "this has been overlooked; this has not been appreciated; this has been misunderstood." But you will be stronger yet in dealing with a controversial topic. Therefore: (1) pick a subject in which much is to be said on both sides; (2) take the side where your heart is; (3) write a thesis-sentence with a *because* in it; (4) gather your material around and about the *pro* and the *con;* (5) write an essay with beginning, middle, and end, and with a *pro-and-con* structure like one of those described on pages 42–43.

Pick something that interests you.

You need not shake the world. Such subjects as "Subsidized College Football," "Small College versus Big University," or the worth of "A Best-Selling Novel" well suit the research paper—a threefold elaboration of the simple essay involving: (1) the handling of your argument, (2) the citation of others' facts and arguments *as part of your own,* and (3) the managing of footnotes and bibliography. Bigger subjects, of course, will try your mettle: subjects like "The Rights of Slaveholders in the Old South," "Euthanasia," "Legal Abortion." The whole question of governmental versus private endeavors affords many lively issues for research and decision—the ills and virtues of commercial television, governmental control of the environment, regulation of big industries, and the like.

THE JOB OF RESEARCH

Now you are ready to dig in. You have decided on your subject and your tentative thesis. You will have scouted the library's possibilities, taking as your detailed guide Section F, "How to Use the Library," in THE HANDBOOK.

Make your bibliography as you go.

But even before you start toward the library, get some 3 × 5 cards for your bibliography. Plan on some ten or fifteen sources for your three thousand words of text. As you pick up an author or two, and some titles, start a bibliographical card for each: *one card for each title*. Leave space to the left to put in the call number later, and space at the top for a label of your own, if needed. Put the author (last name first) on one line, and the title of his work on the next, leaving space to fill in the details of publication when you get to the work itself—for books, place of publication, publisher, and date; for magazine articles, volume number, date, and pages. Italicize (that is, underscore) titles of books and magazines; put titles of articles *within* books and magazines in quotation marks. The card catalog will supply the call numbers, and much of the other publishing data you need; but check and complete all your publishing data when you finally get the book or magazine in your hands, putting a light ✔ in pencil to assure yourself that your card is authoritative, that quotations are word for word and all your publishing data accurate, safe to check your finished paper against. Get the author's name as he signed it, adding details in brackets, if helpful: Smith, D[elmar] P[rince]. Get all the information, to save repeated trips to the library. The completed cards and bibliography with our sample paper (pp. 322, 324, 335–336) will show you what you need.

Take few notes.

Some people abhor putting notes on bibliographical cards. But the economy is well worth the slight clutter. Limiting yourself to what you can put on the front and back of one bibliographical card will restrain your notes to the sharp and manageable. You can always add another note card, or a 3 × 5 slip of paper, if you must. If you find one source offering a number of irresistible quotations, put each one separately on a 3 × 5 slip (with author's name on each), so you can rearrange them later for writing.

However you do it, keep your notes brief. Read quickly, with an eye for the general idea and the telling point. Holding a clear thesis in mind will guide and limit your note taking. Some of your sources will need no more than the briefest summary: "Violently opposed, recommends complete abolition." This violent and undistinguished author will appear in your paper only among several others in a single footnote to one of your sentences: "Opposition, of course, has been long and emphatic.²"

Suppose you are writing a paper to show (as the student-author of our sample paper actually did) that Hawthorne's *The Scarlet Letter* is historically inaccurate. You find an article (Baughman's — see the first card and first footnote, Chapter 14, pp. 322–323) that asserts Hawthorne's historicity. Here is a perfect piece of opposition, a *con*, to set your thesis against. But don't copy down too much. Summarize the author's points briefly in your own words, and copy down directly, within distinct quotation marks, only the most quotable phrases: "was on sure historical grounds at all times." Add the page number in parentheses. Then verify your copying against the text, word for word, comma for comma, and give it a penciled check when you know it is accurate.

Take care with page numbers. When your passage runs from one page to the next — from 29 over onto 30, for instance — put "(29–30)" after it, *but also mark the exact point where the page changed.* You might want to use only part of the passage and then be uncertain as to which of the two pages contained it. An inverted L-bracket and the number "30" after the last word of page 29, will do nicely: see the bottom card on page 324. Do the same even when the page changes in mid-word with a hyphen: "having con- ⌐30 vinced no one."

In a research paper on a piece of literature, like our Hawthorne paper, you would also make a bibliographical card for the edition you are using, and would probably need a number of note slips for summaries and quotations from the work itself — one slip for each item, for convenience in sorting. Here again, check for accuracy of quotation and page number, probably identified in the lower right corner as "Hawthorne 213," or "SL 213," for page 213 in *The Scarlet Letter*. Our sample bibliographical card (p. 324, top) does not need a call number because *The Portable Hawthorne* was the student's textbook.

YOUR FIRST DRAFT

Plot your course.

Formal outlines, especially those made too early in the game, can take more time than they are worth, but a long paper with notes demands some planning. First, draft a beginning paragraph, incorporating your thesis. Then read through your notes, arranging them roughly in the order you think you will use them, getting the opposition off the street first. If your thesis is strongly argumentative, you can sort into three piles: *pro's, con's,* and *in-between's* (often simple facts). Now, by way of outline, you can simply make three or four general headings on a sheet of paper, with ample space between, in which you can jot down your sources in the order, *pro* and *con,* that is best for your argument. Our Hawthorne paper would block out something like this:

```
I. Hawthorne's historical
   claims

                    PRO                 CON

                                   Custom House
                                   Text
                                   Early refs to
                                   scarlet A

II. The critics
                                   Baughman
    But—Green
        Trollope
                                   H's own belief
    But—Schwartz
        Waggoner
        Kaul
```

```
III. Actual historical content
                              H's "religion
                              and law"
                              Smith—confession
 IV. Unhistorical details

     But—courts and church later
          H's dating—before 1650
          Hester's treatment
           (Lawrence, Nettels, Morgan, Winthrop's
            journal, Smith)
          Dimmesdale
           (Smith)
          Chillingworth
```

Outline more fully, if you wish.

You can easily refine this rough blocking (probably more nearly complete here than yours would actually be) into a full topic outline, one that displays your points logically, not necessarily in the actual sequence of your writing (see p. 235). The principle of outlining is to rank equivalent headings — keeping your headings all as nouns, or noun phrases, to make the ranks apparent. For further details, see Chapter 11 on "Outlines," especially pages 235–240.

Begin to write soon.

You have already begun to write, of course, in getting your thesis down on paper, and then drafting a first paragraph to hold it. Now that you have blocked out your argument, however roughly, plunge into your first draft. Your ideas will have been well warmed. Don't let them cool too long. Settle down to the keyboard, and begin your second paragraph.

Put in your references as you go.

Your first draft should have all your footnotes, abbreviated, right in the text. Otherwise you will lose your place, and go mad with numbers. Put the notes at the *end* of the last pertinent sentence, with as many of your references as possible grouped in one note. Make your quotations in full, all distinctly set within quotation marks, and include the author's surname and the page number with each citation. You will change these in your final draft, of course, filling in the names or leaving them out of the note altogether if they appear in the text. But it will help you in checking against your cards to have an author's name and a page number for each citation. *Don't number your footnotes yet.* When your draft is finished, add the numbers in pencil, so you can change them; circle them in red pencil, so you can see them. As you type along, mark your notes with triple parentheses: (((. . .)))—the easiest distinction you can make. See page 326 for a sample first-draft page, with its accompanying transformation into smooth and final copy.

YOUR FINAL DRAFT

Reset your long quotations.

Your final draft will change in many ways, as the rewriting polishes up your phrases and turns up new and better ideas. But some changes are merely presentational. The triple parentheses of your first draft will disappear, along with the quotation marks around the *long* quotations, since you will single-space and indent, *without quotation marks,* all quotations of more than fifty words, to simulate the appearance of a printed page. You will do the same with shorter quotations, if you want to give them special emphasis, and also with passages of poetry. If your quotation begins as a paragraph, indent its first line further, to reproduce the paragraphing. Again, pages 326–327 show how a first-draft quotation is transformed in the final draft. Check the rules about quotation marks on pages 56–57 and 432–435.

Allow space for notes at the foot of the page.

Some instructors like footnotes gathered all together in a section at the end, as they would be in a manuscript prepared for the printer. But most prefer them at the foot, where you can see them, as if on a printed page. From your preliminary draft, you can see about how many footnotes will fall on your page, and about how much space to allow at the bottom. Allow plenty. You will begin your notes three spaces below your text (you have been double-spacing your text). Do *not* type a solid line between text and notes: this indicates a footnote continued from the preceding page. Single-space each note, but double-space between notes. Indent as for a paragraph. To type the number, use the variable line-spacer and roll down about half the height of a capital letter. After typing the number, return to your normal typing line:

> [16] Smith, p. 62.

After the first line, notes return to the left margin, as in paragraphs.

Footnotes carry only information not mentioned in the text. At first mention in text or note, give your author's full name, in normal order—"Ernest W. Baughman"—and use only his last name thereafter. (Your alphabetized bibliography will give last name first.) If your text names the author, the note carries only the title of his work, the publishing data, and the page number. If your text names the author and his work, the note carries only the publishing data and the page number. Once you have cited a source, you can put the page numbers of further citations directly in your text, within parentheses. Note where the periods and the quotation marks go:

> Baughman states that Hawthorne was familiar with John Winthrop's journals and other Puritan docu-ments (p. 539).
>
> . . . what Kaul refers to as "the interpretative Puritan myth" (p. 9).

At the end of a long indented, single-spaced quotation from a work already cited, the page number in parentheses *follows* the period (see example on p. 333):

> . . . God's forgiveness as inexhaustible. (p. 63)

Make and punctuate your footnotes meticulously.

The three principal kinds of references produce three forms of footnotes:

BOOK
¹ Malcolm Cowley, <u>The Portable Hawthorne</u> (New York: Viking Press, 1948), p. 269.

QUARTERLY MAGAZINE
² Ernest W. Baughman, "Public Confession and <u>The Scarlet Letter</u>," <u>New England Quarterly</u>, 40 (1967), 548-549.

When giving the volume number, "40," you omit the "p." or "pp." before page numbers, which I prefer in full. If you choose to abbreviate them, do it thus: "548–49," not "548–9"; "27–29," not "27–9"; but "107–8," not "107–08." Convert all roman volume numbers into arabic: "XL" becomes "40." (Also see "Capitalization," p. 455.)

POPULAR MAGAZINE
³ J. J. Uptight, "Swinging Puritans," <u>Saturday Night Journal</u>, Sept. 30, 1984, p. 5.

Ignore volume number, if any. As in this last example, give the full date for a popular magazine, instead of volume number and year, and *use no parentheses.* Newspaper articles follow the same pattern:

⁴ "The Trouble with Puritans" (editorial), <u>New York Times</u>, April 10, 1984, Sec. 4, p. 8.

Notice the comma here: omitted after "Puritans" and inserted after the parenthesis. Do the same with any parenthetical explanation of a title. With this newspaper, you need to give the section number because each section begins numbering anew.

Here are some further complications:

⁵ Abraham B. Caldwell, "The Case for a Puritan Revival," <u>American Questioner</u>, June 20, 1979, p. 37, quoted in Albert N. Mendenhall, <u>The Time Is Now</u> (Princeton: Little House, 1979), p. 308.

You have found the quotation in Mendenhall's book.

⁶ D. C. Hill, "Who Is Communicating What?" in <u>Essays for Study</u>, ed. James L. McDonald and Leonard P. Doan (New York: Appleton Hall, 1973), p. 214; reprinted from <u>Era</u>, 12 (1972).

McDonald and Doan have edited the collection, or casebook. A title ending in a question mark should not take a comma.

⁷ David R. Small, "The Telephone and Urbanization," in <u>Annals of American Communication</u>, ed. Walter Beinholt (Boston: Large, Green and Co., 1969), III, 401.

The *Annals of American Communication* is a series of bound books, not a magazine: the volume number is in roman numerals, and it *follows* the parenthesis. Had this been a magazine, the entry would have omitted the "in," the editor, and the place of publication, and would have read ". . . *Annals of American Communication,* 3 (1969), 401."

⁸ Arnold Peters, "Medicine," <u>Encyc. Brit.</u>, 11th ed.

Abbreviate familiar titles, so long as they remain clear. You need neither volume nor page numbers in alphabetized encyclopedias; and only the number (*or* the year of publication) of the edition you are citing, without parentheses. Here the article was initialed "A. P.," and you have looked up the author's name in the contributors' list.

9 "Prunes," <u>Encyc. Brit.</u>, 11th ed.

Here the article was not initialed.

10 George L. Gillies, "Robert Herrick's 'Corinna,'" <u>Speculation</u>, 2 (1881), 490.

This shows where to put the comma when the title of a magazine article ends in a quotation, and you have to use both single and double quotation marks. Gillies's original title would have looked like this: Robert Herrick's "Corinna."

11 <u>Romeo and Juliet</u> II.iii.94, in <u>An Essential Shakespeare</u>, ed. Russell Fraser (New York: Prentice-Hall, 1972).

Note the absence of the comma after the play's title, and the periods and close spacing between Act.scene.line. Subsequent references would go directly in your text within parentheses: "(IV.iii.11–12)." Or, if you are quoting several of Shakespeare's plays: "(*Romeo* IV.iii.11–12)." See further instructions on page 315.

12 P[aul] F[riedrich] Schwartz, <u>A Quartet of Thoughts</u> (New York: Appleton Hall, 1943), p. 7.

13 [Lewes, George H.], "Percy Bysshe Shelley," <u>Westminster Review</u>, 35 (April 1841), 303-344.

These two footnotes show how to use brackets to add details not actually appearing in the published work. Of course, famous initials are kept as initials, as with T. S. Eliot, H. G. Wells, or D. H. Lawrence.

14 "The Reading Problem," mimeographed pamphlet, Concerned Parents Committee, Center City, Arkansas, Dec. 25, 1975, p. 8.

15 U. S. Congress, House Committee on Health, Education, and Welfare, <u>Racial Integration</u>, 101st Cong., 2nd sess., 1969, H. Rep. 391 to accompany H. R. 6128.

These represent the infinite variety of pamphlets, and other oddities, that may contain just the information you want. These you must play by instinct, including all the details, as briefly as possible, that would help someone else hunt them down. These examples, together with the footnotes in our sample research paper, should cover most footnoting problems, or suggest how you can meet them.

EXERCISES

1 Assume that you are quoting the following passage in its entirety, and that you have not mentioned it, or its author, earlier in your paper. Devise a sentence to introduce the passage, quote the passage and give it a footnote-number, then write a footnote covering the necessary bibliographical data. The author is Gilbert K. Chesterton. The book, *Heretics,* was published in 1905 by John Lane, in London. The passage is on page thirty-eight:

When Byron divided humanity into the bores and bored, he omitted to notice that the higher qualities exist entirely in the bores, the lower qualities in the bored, among whom he counted himself. The bore, by his starry enthusiasm, his solemn happiness, may, in some sense, have proved himself poetical. The bored has certainly proved himself prosaic.

2 Now write a sentence referring to Chesterton's point that a bore may be poetical, quoting directly only the phrase *his starry enthusiasm.* Assume that you have already fully cited Chesterton, and give your reader whatever bibliographical information this new quotation demands.

3 Write four footnotes illustrating the four different kinds of sources, described below, for the same hypothetical fact: *300 dropouts annually.*

1. You found this in an article with these characteristics:

Quarterly magazine entitled: Schools and Scholars
Volume number: Forty-nine
Author: Gladys P. Spencer
Page: One hundred three
Date: January 1976
Title: Our Local Schools

2. Write the same footnote as if the magazine were a popular weekly dated January 10, 1976.

3. Write the same footnote to your statistic as if you had found it, together with a full citation of this article in the popular monthly, on page 460 of a book entitled *Education for Educators* by Featherbush Brown published in Philadelphia in 1980 by the P. J. Slacks Company, incorporated.

4. Write the same footnote assuming that you found Spencer's statistic on page forty-nine in a collection of essays entitled *Readings for Reading,* which Beatrice Long and Bernard Short edited, and which the Grimm Publishing Company produced in 1980, in New York City.

4 W. L. Cranberry has written the following two studies, both of which you want to cite:

Book: The Dying Locomotive
Article: Transportation No Problem

First, write a footnote for the book — Verity and Company published it in Miami in 1981 — in which you inform your reader that the author's full name is Walter Lightfoot Cranberry. You have quoted from page one.

Next, assume that you have already given the first full citation for both the book and the article. Now write footnotes 3 and 4, footnote 3 for the book, footnote 4 for the article, making up and providing suitable page numbers.

Abbreviate your references after the first full citation.

Two old favorite abbreviations are now mercifully out of style. Do NOT USE:

ibid. — *ibidem* ("in the same place"), meaning the title cited in the note directly before. Instead, USE THE AUTHOR'S LAST NAME, AND GIVE THE PAGE.

op. cit. — *opere citato* ("in the work cited"), meaning a title referred to again after other notes have intervened. Again, USE THE AUTHOR'S LAST NAME INSTEAD, AND GIVE THE PAGE: "Smith, p. 62." If you have two Smiths, simply include their initials. If Smith has two articles or books on the Puritans, devise two convenient short titles for subsequent references:

²Smith, <u>City</u>, p. 62.

³Smith, "Puritan Souls," p. 301.

Three are still used and especially useful (do *not* italicize them):

cf. — *confer* ("bring together," or "compare"); do not use for "see."

et al. — *et alii* ("and others"); does not mean "and all"; use after the first author in multiple authorships: "Ronald Elkins et al."

loc. cit. — *loco citato* ("in the place cited"); use without page number, when you cite a page previously noted. Best in parentheses *in the text.* See page 323, toward the bottom.

Two more Latin terms, also not italicized, are equally handy:

passim — (not an abbreviation, but a Latin word meaning "throughout the work; here and there") use when a writer makes the same point in many places within a single work; use also for statistics you have compiled from observations and tables scattered throughout his work.

sic — a Latin word meaning "so"; "this is so"; always in brackets — [sic] — because used only within quotations following some misspelling or other surprising detail to show that it really was there, was "so" in the original and that the mistake is not yours.

Other useful abbreviations for footnotes are:

c. or **ca.**	*circa,* "about" (c. 1709)
ch., chs.	chapter, chapters
ed.	edited by, edition, editor
f., ff.	and the following page, pages
l., ll.	line, lines
MS., MSS.	manuscript, manuscripts
n.d.	no date given
n.p.	no place of publication given
p., pp.	page, pages
rev.	revised
tr., trans.	translated by
vol., vols.	volume, volumes

A footnote using some of these might go like this (you have already fully cited Weiss and Dillon):

[16]See Donald Allenberg et al., <u>Population in Early New England</u> (Boston: Large, Green and Co., 1974), pp. 308 ff.; cf. Weiss, p. 60. Dillon, passim, takes a position even more conservative than Weiss's. See also A. H. Hawkins, ed., <u>Statistical Surveys</u> (Chicago: Nonesuch Press, 1960; rev. 1973), pp. 71-83 and ch. 10. Records sufficient for broad comparisons begin only ca. 1850.

EXERCISE

5 Write a summarizing footnote, including the following phrases and abbreviations: *c., see, ed., see also, ch., ff., rev., et al., passim,* and dealing with the following supposed items:

1. An essay entitled Too Many Cars by L. A. Crump, in an anthology called Traffic edited by Arlene Pringle and several others, which the Willing Company published in New York in 1978 and then revised in 1983 — you wish to refer your reader to an extended account beginning on page ten.

2. Certain statistics have become available only from about 1920.

3. Wilma May Smithers, whom you have already cited in full, says something on her page four that the reader should compare with Crump; the reader should also look at her sixth chapter.

4. Griffin, another writer you have already cited, takes a generally hostile view of Crump's work.

5. You want the reader to consult also the entry about automobiles in The Encyclopaedia Britannica, volume dated 1987.

Abbreviate books of the Bible, even the first time.

The Bible and its books, though capitalized as ordinary titles, are never italicized. Biblical references go directly into your text, within parentheses — no footnote, no commas, *lowercase* roman numerals for chapter, arabic for verse: "Mark xvi.6"; "Jer. vi.24"; "II Sam. xviii.33." No comma—only a space—separates name from numbers; periods separate the numbers, *with no spacing.* The dictionary gives the accepted abbreviations: Gen., Exod., Lev., Deut. Make biblical references like this:

```
There is still nothing new under the sun (Eccl.

i.9); man still does not live by bread alone

(Matt. iv. 4).


As Ecclesiastes tells us, "there is no new thing

under the sun" (i.9).
```

Abbreviate plays and long poems after the first time.

Handle plays and long poems like biblical citations, after an initial footnote that identifies the edition (see page 310). Italicize the title (underscore the title with your typewriter): "*Merch.* II iv.72–75" (this is *The Merchant of Venice,* Act II, Scene iv, lines 72–75); "*Caesar* V.iii.6," "*Ham.* I.i.23," "*Iliad* IX.93," "*P.L.* IV.918" (*Paradise Lost,* Book IV, line 918). Use the numbers alone if you have already mentioned the title, or have clearly implied it, as in repeated quotations from the same work.

Match your bibliography to your footnotes.

When your paper is finally typed, arrange the cards of the works cited in your footnotes in alphabetical order (by authors' last names or, with anonymous works, by first words of titles—ignoring initial *The, A,* or *An*). You will not have used all your notes, nor all the articles you have carded. In typing your bibliography, pass over them in decent silence. *Include no work not specifically cited.* Your bibliographical entries will be just like your footnotes except that: (1) you will put the author's last name first; (2) you will give the total span of pages for magazine articles—none at all for books; (3) you will reverse indentation so that the author's name will stand out; (4) you will punctuate differently—putting one period after the alphabetized name or title, and another (no parentheses) after a book's place and date of publication; and (5) you will double-space, triple-spacing between entries. Your single-spacing of footnotes has been the typewriter's approximation of passages set in small print. Your research paper's bibliography should look like the one with our sample paper (pp. 335–336). Here are some special cases:

> Hill, D. C. "Who Is Communicating What?" in *Essays for Study*, ed. James L. McDonald and Leonard P. Doan. New York: Appleton Hall, 1973. Pp. 211-219. Reprinted from *Era*, 12 (1972), 9-18.

Notice the capitalized "Pp. 211–219." Since this article is in a book, the publishing data have required a period after "1973."

> Jones, Bingham. *The Kinescopic Arts and Sciences*. Princeton: Little House, 1970.
>
> ————. "Television and Vision: The Case for Governmental Control," *Independent Review*, 7 (1969), 18-31.

When listing other works by the same author, use a solid line (your underscorer) and a period.

> Small, David R. "The Telephone and Urbanization," in *Annals of American Communication*, ed. Walter Beinholt. Boston: Large, Green and Co., 1969. III, 398-407.
>
> "*The Trouble with Puritans*," Anon. editorial, *New York Times*, April 10, 1984, Sec. 4, p. 8.

I have based these instructions on *The MLA Style Sheet* (compiled by the Modern Language Association of America) and Kate L. Turabian, *A Manual for Writers of Term Papers, Theses, and Dissertations*, following the customs for work in literature and the humanities.

The sciences use slightly different conventions. Bingham Jones's article would look like this in a botanical bibliography (no quotation marks, no parentheses, fewer capitals):

> Jones, B. 1969. Television and vision: the case for governmental control. <u>Independent Review</u>, <u>7</u>:8-31.

For some advanced courses, you may also want to consult:

> McCrum, Blanche, and Helen Jones. *Bibliographical Procedures & Styles: A Manual for Bibliographers in the Library of Congress.* Washington, D.C.: Superintendent of Documents, 1954.
> *Publication Manual of the American Psychological Association.* Washington, D.C., 1957.
> *Style Manual.* U.S. Government Printing Office. Rev. ed. Washington, D.C., 1959.
> *Style Manual for Biological Journals.* Washington, D.C., 1960.
> Wood, George McLane. *Suggestions to Authors . . . , United States Geological Survey.* 4th ed. rev. by Bernard H. Lane, Washington, D.C., 1935.

EXERCISE

6 Make a bibliography, listing one entry each from *Exercises 1, 3, 4, and 5,* adding hypothetical page numbers, if necessary.

Follow the conventional format.

Since the full-dress research paper usually has four parts, here is a checklist for your convenience:

I. Title Page (not numbered)*
   A. In the upper half, centered on the page, type your title in capitals, and beneath it, your name.
   B. In the lower third, designate on separate lines, also centered, the course and section, your instructor's name, and the date.
II. Outline (page not numbered, but if it needs more pages, number them in lower case roman numerals: ii, iii, iv)
   A. Head the page with your title.
   B. State your thesis in a sentence.
   C. Present your outline — topic or sentence as your instructor specifies. (Remember that the headings of a sentence outline — like your thesis, which is always a complete sentence — end in a period, but those of a topic outline do not.) It will serve as your paper's table of contents.
III. Text with Footnotes (pages numbered in arabic numerals, 2, 3, 4, but first page not numbered)
   A. After heading the first page with your title, type your text double-spaced — except for long quotations, which you indent and single-space, without quotation marks, to simulate smaller print.
   B. Type your footnotes at the bottom of your text pages, each single-spaced, but with a space between notes, and in proper form (see pp. 307–311; 325). Or your instructor may ask you to group all your footnotes together following the text, beginning on a new page headed "Footnotes," and continuing the page numbering of the text.
IV. Bibliography (pages numbered in continuation of text paging)
   A. Head the first page "Bibliography" or "Works Cited."
   B. Arrange the works in one of two ways: (1) alphabetized, by author's last name (Eliot, T. S.), and by title when the author is unknown ("Medicine," *Encyclopaedia Britannica*); or (2) grouped by kind of source, the entries within each group arranged alphabetically: "Primary Sources" (works of literature, historical documents, letters, and the like) and "Secondary Sources" (works *about* your subject)

---

* Some instructors do not require a separate title page. Our sample research paper (p. 321) will show you how to set up your first page to combine the title and the outline. Either way, the page is not numbered unless the outline runs to more than one page (see "Outline" section of this checklist).

—and you may further divide these groups, if your bibliography is long enough to justify it, into "Books" and "Articles."

Suggested Subjects for Research Papers

A Famous Trial (Alger Hiss, Angela Davis, Daniel Ellsberg)

A Famous Scandal (The Watergate, The Teapot Dome)

Abortion Laws: The Moral and Legal Issues

Symbolism in Faulkner's *The Bear* (Beckett's *Waiting for Godot,* Fellini's *8½*)

The Environment (Air or Water Pollution, Nuclear Power, Preservation of Species)

Drug Control: Pro or Con

An Issue in Women's Rights

Malcolm X

Ethnic Liberation Movements (Black, Chicano, American Indian)

Symbolism in Three Poems by Robert Frost (Robert Lowell, James Dickey)

The Urban Crisis

Censorship

Legislation to Control Guns

Why Johnny Can't Read

Pacifism and Violence

The Spiritual Revival (Zen, Jesus People, Buddhists, Fundamentalists)

Our Disappearing Whales (Wild Mustangs, Eagles)

New Life in Art (Happenings, Neorealism, Environmental Art)

In the final chapter of THE RHETORIC, we will see how one reader of this book put the rest of it to use in writing her research paper.

Fourteen
The Full Research Paper

Here is a sample, a complete research paper (an exceptionally good one, from one of my classes), to show what the final product can look like. This paper started from our reading and discussing Nathaniel Hawthorne's novel *The Scarlet Letter.* As you can see, the student-author, a history major, brought her personal interests nicely to bear on a literary subject. You can follow this sample paper throughout for customs of typing and spacing. To convey an idea of the whole process, the backs of the first three pages show bibliographical cards with notes corresponding to the first four footnotes, and a page of the first draft, which matches the text it faces at the line (mid-page) beginning "about the difficulty of writing . . . ."

320

Marilyn Ferris
English 269
Mr. Baker
April 16, 1977

HAWTHORNE'S PURITANS

Thesis: Despite its moral power and claims to authenticity,

The Scarlet Letter is historically untrue.

I. Hawthorne's claims of historical accuracy   *Topic*
    A. The "Custom House" introduction   *Outline*
    B. Phrases in the text implying historical accuracy
    C. Hawthorne's prior references to a scarlet "A"
        1. "Endicott and the Red Cross"
        2. Entry in notebook

II. The critical estimate
    A. Baughman's assertion "sure of historical grounds"
    B. Green's attack
    C. Trollope's view as "romance"
    D. Hawthorne's own belief
        1. Entry in notebook: "old colony law"
        2. Schwartz's evidence
        3. Waggoner's analysis
        4. Kaul's comment on archaism
    E. Hawthorne's "Puritan myth"

III. Hawthorne's actual use of history
    A. Union of religion and law
    B. The Puritan's idea of community
    C. Isolation by sin
    D. Reunion by confession and repentence

IV. Hawthorne's unique characters
    A. Hester
        1. Hester's alienation
            a. Resistance to community
            b. Impenitence
        2. Hester's independent solution
    B. Dimmesdale
    C. Chillingworth

V. Hawthorne's projecting unique cases from general Puritan
    practices, and making them universal

F
1
N4 Baughman, Ernest W.
    "Public Confession and _The Scarlet Letter_,"
    New England Quarterly, 40 (1967),
    532-550. ✓

Public confession, an English custom—required by
church and state in Mass. Bay Colony from
its founding on, in Plymouth from 1624, in Va.
at least 30 years before _SL_ takes place. (533)

  H. familiar with John Winthrop's _Journals_,

FRONT

1630-1650. W. records 16 pub. confessions, 4
for adultery. (539)

Hester not reunited w. community because she refuses
to repent and name her partner. (544)

Hawthorne "was on sure historical grounds at all
times." (548) He uses custom of confession of sins
that isolate "from the fellowship of the church."
(544) Characterization consistent w. Puritan thought
"though, until the end, much of their conduct
is at odds w. the tradition." (549)

BACK

---

813   Levin, David
S 816   "Nathaniel Hawthorne, _The Scarlet Letter_,"
        in _The American Novel from James
        Fenimore Cooper to Wm Faulkner_, ed.
        Wallace Stegner (New York: Basic
        Books, 1965), pp. 13-24. ✓

"... he studied Puritan history w. a persistence
that some scholars (along with H. himself)
have considered obsessive." (13)

SINGLE ENTRY

HAWTHORNE'S PURITANS

In The Scarlet Letter, Hawthorne presents the system of

Beginning

ethics, law, and punishment in a Puritan New England town. He

introduces his story of adultery and expiation with an elaborate

account of finding a faded red-cloth "A" twisted around a roll of

papers, among other documents in the Salem Custom House, which he   *(Funneling to)*

intends to give to the Essex Historical Society. The roll of

papers contains, in "Surveyor Pue's" handwriting, the story of

Hester Prynne. In the narrative itself, Hawthorne makes numerous

other assertions of historical fact. But all of this is fiction.

Actually, The Scarlet Letter, though generally acknowledged as a   *Thesis*

great moral novel, is historically untrue.

Ernest W. Baughman, however, claims that Hawthorne "was on   *Opposing
Views*

sure historical grounds at all times," because he employs the

Puritan idea that public confession reunites the sinner with the

community.[1] Baughman concedes that "until the end, much of [the]   *Footnote
Number*

conduct is at odds with the tradition," but he insists that the

essential characterization and the underlying idea are histori-

cally faithful (loc. cit.). Baughman states that Hawthorne was

familiar with John Winthrop's journals and other Puritan docu-

ments (p. 539). According to David Levin, Hawthorne "studied

---

[1]"Public Confession and The Scarlet Letter," New England   *Footnote at
Quarterly, 40 (1967), 548-549.   Bottom*

14. THE FULL RESEARCH PAPER
323

Cowley, Malcolm
   The Portable Hawthorne, ed., with Introduction
   and Notes, by Malcolm Cowley (New York:
   Viking Press, 1948). ✓

Character wearing "the letter A on the breast of
her gown" appears in 1 sentence, "Endicott
and the Red Cross." pub. 1837 – first hint
of SL. (269)
Seven yrs. later, in one of H.'s note books is

FRONT

BACK

" plot of a new story he planned to write:
  'The life of a woman who, by the old colony
  law, was condemned always to wear the
  letter A, sewed on her garment, in token
  of her having committed adultery.' " (269)

820.6   Green, Martin
E58l   "The Hawthorne Myth: A Protest," Essays and
        Studies by Members of The English Association,
        16 (1963), 16-36. ✓

"T.S. Eliot has said that H.'s is a true criticism of
the Puritan morality, true because it has the
fidelity of the artist & not a mere conviction of the
man, but there is very little that is Puritan in The SL.
The thoughts and emotions expressed all belong to $|^{30}$ the
nineteenth century" (29-30) Claims "to be historical
are so insistent and so unacceptable..." (29)

ALL ON
ONE SIDE

Puritan history with a persistence that some scholars (along with Hawthorne himself) have considered obsessive."[2]

But the evidence undermines Hawthorne's claims of factuality. First, a character wearing a "letter A on [her] breast" appears briefly in an early Hawthorne story ("Endicott and the Red Cross," 1837); then seven years later and six years before he started The Scarlet Letter, Hawthorne records in his notebook plans to write: "The life of a woman, who, by the old colony law, was condemned always to wear the letter A, sewed on her garment, in token of her having committed adultery."[3] Hawthorne mentions discovering no manuscript and faded letter, and such a discovery would certainly have been exciting news, to be recorded in his notebook and in letters to his friends. He records no such discovery. Clearly, his "document," and his claims of finding it, are fictitious, if not fraudulent.

Martin Green is the severest of Hawthorne's critics. He sets aside T. S. Eliot's claim that Hawthorne's picture of Puritan morality is true "because it has the fidelity of the artist." The book's claims to historicity, says Green, are "so insistent and so unacceptable": ". . . there is very little that is Puritan in The Scarlet Letter. The thoughts and emotions all belong to

Topic Sentence

Underline for Italics

Supporting Views

[2]"Nathaniel Hawthorne, The Scarlet Letter," in The American Novel from James Fenimore Cooper to William Faulkner, ed. Wallace Stegner (New York: Basic Books, 1965), p. 13.

[3]Malcolm Cowley, The Portable Hawthorne (New York: Viking Press, 1948), p. 269.

Cutting Words

First Draft Reference

Complete Reference

Reference Style

Improving Tone

Becomes Footnote

Cutting Words

of writing ~~entertaining and~~ lively children's stories ~~for children~~ using with

"such unmaleable material as the somber, stern, and rigid

Puritans," ((("Three Aspects of Hawthorne's Puritanism," The New England Quarterly, 36 (1936), 202.))) ~~He also~~ noting that Hawthorne consistently ~~looked upon~~ viewed his Puritan ancestors as

"gloomy, joyless, and rigid." (((Schwartz, loc. cit.))) Apparently Hawthorne's view of the Puritans distorted his picture of the past ~~was distorted.~~ As Hyatt H. Waggoner puts it: "Despite his long absorption in Puritan writings, it is pretty clear that Hawthorne had a typical nineteenth-century view of his ancestors. He exaggerated their gloominess and their intolerance and probably attributed their persecution of sexual offenses to ideas other than those they actually held." (((Hawthorne, A Critical Study (Cambridge: Harvard University Press, 1963), p. 14))) As A. N. Kaul says, "This archaism appears to have been a necessary condition for the richest engagement of his imagination, and also, paradoxically, for his deepest intuitions of the modern spirit." ((("Introduction," Hawthorne: A Collection of Critical Essays (Englewood Cliffs: Prentice-Hall, 1966), p. 2.)))

But we must concede that ~~Of course,~~ Hawthorne ~~does~~ follows ~~history~~ historical facts at least part of the way ~~time.~~ As he states in Chapter 2, the Puritans were in fact "a people amongst whom ~~and~~ religion and law were almost identical." Page Smith, ~~in his book As a City Upon a Hill, tells about how~~ reports that the early Puritans were forced to confess their sins before the entire congregation, which consisted of almost the entire population of the town. The penitent sinner ~~who was penitent~~ was then ~~taken~~ accepted back into the congregation, but the impenitent sinner ~~who was~~ ~~not~~ was excommunicated regardless of the relative mildness of ~~how mild~~ his sin ~~was.~~

the nineteenth century."[4] Of course, Hawthorne called his book

"A Romance" on the title page. Anthony Trollope, writing in 1879,

is probably typical of Hawthorne's readers in accepting the his-

torical pretense as a usual part of fiction: "His is a mixture

of romance and austerity, quite as far removed from the realities

of Puritanism as it is from the sentimentalism of poetry."[5]

    Nevertheless, in spite of the fictional deceit of the Custom *Reasoned*

House introduction, Hawthorne himself probably thought he was *Concession*

more historically accurate than Trollope allows. His statement

in his notebook about "the old colony law" shows his belief in

its authenticity. Joseph Schwartz quotes Hawthorne's complaint

about the difficulty of writing lively children's stories with

"such unmalleable material as the somber, stern, and rigid Puri-

tans," noting that Hawthorne consistently viewed his Puritan an-

cestors as "gloomy, joyless, and rigid."[6] Apparently, Hawthorne's

view of the Puritans distorted his picture of the past. As Hyatt

H. Waggoner puts it:

> Despite his long absorption in Puritan writings, it is   *Extended*
> pretty clear that Hawthorne had a typical nineteenth-   *Quotation*
> century view of his ancestors. He exaggerated their   *Set Off*
> gloominess and their intolerance and probably attributed
> their persecution of sexual offenses to ideas other than
> those they actually held.[7]

[4]"The Hawthorne Myth: A Protest," *Essays and Studies by Mem-*   *Magazines*
bers of the English Association, 16 (1963), 29-30.   *Footnoted*

[5]"The Genius of Nathaniel Hawthorne," *North American Review*,   *Rare Source:*
129, No. 274 (Sept. 1879), 206.   *Extra Detail*

[6]"Three Aspects of Hawthorne's Puritanism," *New England*
Quarterly, 36 (1963), 202.

[7]*Hawthorne, A Critical Study* (Cambridge: Harvard University   *Book*
Press, 1963), p. 14.   *Footnoted*

As A. N. Kaul says, "This archaism appears to have been a necessary condition for the richest engagement of his imagination, and
also, paradoxically, for his deepest intuitions of the modern
spirit."[8]

Concession   But we must concede that Hawthorne follows historical facts
at least part of the way. As he states in Chapter 2, the Puritans
were "a people amongst whom religion and law were almost identical." Page Smith reports that the early Puritans were forced to
confess their sins to the congregation, which consisted of almost
the entire population of the town. The penitent sinner was then
accepted back into the congregation, but the impenitent sinner
was excommunicated, regardless of the relative mildness of his

Reference for Indirect Quotation   sin.[9] Hester, as Baughman points out, refuses to repent, and to
name her partner, and is thus isolated from the community (p. 544).

This tradition of public confession was continued later in
larger Puritan towns. Cases involving morals and religious beliefs were tried in civil courts and also punished by the church.[10]
The Scarlet Letter takes place in Boston, and apparently at such
a later date, with civil and religious authority collaborating,
and yet Hawthorne clearly dates his events in very early Puritan

Brief Quotation and Reference   times. The action occurs, he says, "not less than two centuries
ago" (Ch.2), that is, at some time before 1650, since The Scarlet

[8]Introduction, Hawthorne: A Collection of Critical Essays
(Englewood Cliffs: Prentice-Hall, 1966), p. 2.

First Reference   [9]As a City upon a Hill (New York: Alfred A. Knopf, 1966),
pp. 60-61.

Second Reference   [10]Smith, pp. 129-130.

14. THE FULL RESEARCH PAPER
328

Letter was published in 1850. Hawthorne mentions that Hester has been sentenced by the magistrates. But when she is forced to stand on the scaffold, a civil punishment, the church, in the persons of the clergymen Wilson and Dimmesdale, urges her to reveal the name of her partner in sin. Years later, when Hester and Pearl visit the governor, he discusses the case with the Reverend Mr. Dimmesdale.

Not only civil and religious authorities were involved in the punishment of sin, but the people themselves. The townspeople are present at Hester's punishment. They avoid her when they meet her in public, and they tell their children stories about her. The punishments of standing on the scaffold and wearing the scarlet letter are effective only because they make Hester aware of the way the townspeople feel about her. Facing the stares of the people, on the scaffold and for years afterward, is her real punishment.

Beyond this union of church authority, state authority, and public opinion in the punishment of sin, Hester's treatment is not characteristic of Puritan justice and mercy. The scaffold itself, and Hester's being forced to stand on it for public scorn, are probably not historically accurate. In the early Puritan community, the sinner was usually punished only mildly, if at all, and was forgiven and reunited with the community after a public confession. Later, sinners were punished more severely, but the punishment was usually brief, such as an afternoon in the stocks or a whipping. Long-term punishments, such as jail sen-

*Restatement
of Thesis*

tences, were almost nonexistent.[11]   Some cases are recorded of
women being branded or forced to wear the letter "A," but such
cases were rare, and, according to Curtis P. Nettels, concerned
only habitual offenses:

> In seventeenth-century New England, women guilty of repeated
> moral lapses were whipped or occasionally forced to wear the
> scarlet letter; after 1720, whipping was resorted to only
> for serious offenders.[12]

Hester's offense is clearly not habitual: Hawthorne presents her
only arrest, and she has offended with one man only. Hawthorne's
townswomen who call for branding, and even death, are evidently

Ellipses   not authentic, as Hawthorne claims them to be: ". . . there was
a coarser fiber in those wives and maidens of old English birth
and breeding, than in their fair descendants . . ." (Ch. 2).

Puritan religious and civil law covered such a wide range of
sins that everyone must have committed some sin at one time or
another, and, in fact, in some towns, nearly every citizen was
brought before the court during the course of a few years. Court
records are full of cases in which a man and a woman were forbid-
den to see each other or a woman was awarded payment from the
father of an illegitimate child.[13] Since these cases were public
knowledge, the sinner knew that he was not alone.

[11]Henry W. Lawrence, The Not-Quite Puritans (Boston: Little,
Brown, and Co., 1928), p. 171.

[12]The Roots of American Civilization: A History of American
Colonial Life, 2nd ed. (New York: Appleton-Century-Crofts, 1963),
p. 463.

[13]Edmund S. Morgan, "The Puritans and Sex," in Pivotal Inter-
pretations of American History, ed. Carl N. Degler (New York:
Harper and Row, 1966), I, 11, 14.

14. THE FULL RESEARCH PAPER

The members of the early Puritan community were bound to forgive the penitent sinner and restore him to their community. Even when a member was excommunicated, he automatically became a member again if he confessed his guilt.[14] Baughman points out that the English Puritan societies practiced public confession, and naturally imported it to America when they came. Public confessions were required by the church and state in the Massachusetts Bay Colony from its beginning, and in Plymouth from 1624. John Winthrop's journal, with which Hawthorne was familiar, describes sixteen cases of public confession between 1630 and 1650, four of them for adultery.[15] In Groton, Massachusetts, sixty-six of the two hundred persons who were members of the town by baptismal covenant between 1761 and 1775 confessed to fornication before marriage. Nine of the sixteen couples admitted to full communion between 1789 and 1791 had confessed to fornication.[16]

The Puritans felt that the entire community was united in a covenant with God. The sins of one person could bring God's judgment on all. Therefore, for the common good, the community tried to redeem all sinners as quickly as possible and reunite them with the community.[17] Confession and punishment were forms of cleansing after which the sinner could rejoin the community,

[14]Smith, pp. 60-61.

[15]Baughman, pp. 533, 539.

[16]Smith, p. 62.

[17]Smith, pp. 7-8.

Book Titles Cited Earlier

14. THE FULL RESEARCH PAPER
331

both religiously and socially, on an equal level with everyone
else and with no stigma. When one member of the community was
purged of sin and forgiven, the community was reunited, as a
child is reunited with his parents after being spanked.

*Author's
Contribution*

Hester's permanent alienation from the community, though
partially self-imposed, is not characteristic of the Puritans.
Her punishment must be seen not as an example of the way the Puritans dealt with sinners, but as an example of an individual's
failure to accept the moral and legal system designed to reunite
him with the community, and of the community's failure to forgive
a sinner and restore him to full fellowship, under God's covenant. Hawthorne has freely interpreted Puritan beliefs about the
community, and about sin as isolating the individual and harming
the community.

Hester's public admission of her act, whether or not she
considered it sinful, and her punishment cleanse her of guilt,
just as they would have in historical times, but only if she had
fully confessed and repented. But Hester does not name her partner, and she remains impenitent and even, at first, defiant. She
refuses to accept the moral and legal system for reuniting the
sinner with the community; then she works out her own way,
through her needlecraft and care of the sick, to rejoin the community while still remaining isolated and independent.

*End
Section*

Hawthorne does not present Hester as a case of Puritan injustice, as the beginning of his story suggests. Hester's story
presents not the injustice of the Puritan code, but a specific
instance wherein the code fails to preserve justice. Hawthorne

imagines a unique personality and a unique experience within the general context of Puritan beliefs. He creates not Puritan history, but what Kaul refers to as "the interpretative Puritan myth" (p. 9).

Dimmesdale and Chillingworth are similarly interpretative projections of Puritan beliefs, rather than authentic types. When one person broke the community's covenant with God by sinning, and was cast out for not repenting, the community was not whole. The sin spread throughout the community, as its members were tempted to hate or ignore the outcast, to gossip and act hypocritically. Smith gives the historical context:

> The congregations were doubtless on occasion cruel, and the system itself put fearful strains on the delinquent saints as well as their judges. But the records are impressive evidence of the fidelity with which most congregations observed scriptural injunctions to charity. Within a harsh system, they frequently showed great patience and forbearance with the sinners who appeared before them. If their church was a community of justice, it was also a community of mercy, surrogate for a Christ who had spoken of God's forgiveness as inexhaustible. (p. 63)

Extended Quotation from Work Already Cited, with Reference in Parentheses at End

Smith further reports that the Puritans had "a country realism about sex that is in sharp contrast to late nineteenth-century sexual attitudes," which have pictured the Puritans inaccurately "as full of inhibitions, prudery, and repressions" (loc. cit.). The small Puritan town contained a great deal of illicit sex, most of it eventually confessed in public, repented, and accepted by the community as the usual human weakness. The Puritan community aimed chiefly to bring the lost soul back into fellowship with the community and with God, and to repair the break in their communal covenant.

14. THE FULL RESEARCH PAPER

Chillingworth is, of course, not a Puritan. But Hawthorne presents him as a kind of obsessive Puritan, in nineteenth-century terms, ruined by his inability to forgive sin, as an actual Puritan would have done. His psychological torture of Hester and Dimmesdale leads not to their reunion with society but to their further alienation. Dimmesdale lives a tortured life, unable to experience the purging from sin by confession and punishment that would reunite him psychologically with the community. His inhibitions and conscience, which shut him off from the Puritan system, probably belong, as Green would claim, to the nineteenth century rather than the seventeenth.

Thesis Restated

Hawthorne, in fact, has not created a historically accurate story. From the general Puritan beliefs about the wholeness of the community and the isolation of sin, he has projected three

Summary

unique and atypical individuals. Through them, he works out his universal themes of alienation and social community, of sin, guilt, confession, punishment, and redemption. He has combined aspects of Puritan America with aspects of nineteenth-century America to create a story that is universal and symbolic, rather

Final Statement

than historical. The story's only flaw lies in Hawthorne's misleading his readers to believe that his Puritans are historically authentic, as perhaps he himself mistakenly believed them to be.

BIBLIOGRAPHY

Baughman, Ernest W. "Public Confession and The Scarlet Letter," *Journal Article*
   New England Quarterly, 40 (1967), 532-550.

Cowley, Malcolm. The Portable Hawthorne, ed., with Introduction *Edited Book*
   and Notes. New York: Viking Press, 1948.

Green, Martin. "The Hawthorne Myth: A Protest," Essays and *Journal Article*
   Studies by Members of the English Association, 16 (1963),
   16-36.

Kaul, A. N. Introduction, Hawthorne: A Collection of Critical *Introduction to Book of Essays*
   Essays. Englewood Cliffs: Prentice-Hall, 1966.

Lawrence, Henry W. The Not-Quite Puritans. Boston: Little, *Book*
   Brown, and Co., 1928.

Levin, David. "Nathaniel Hawthorne, The Scarlet Letter," in The *Article in Book*
   American Novel from James Fenimore Cooper to William Faulkner,
   ed. Wallace Stegner. New York: Basic Books, 1965.
   Pp. 13-24.

Morgan, Edmund S. "The Puritans and Sex," in Pivotal Interpre- *Essay in Annual Series of Volumes*
   tations of American History, ed. Carl N. Degler. New York:
   Harper and Row, 1966. I, 4-16.

Nettels, Curtis P. The Roots of American Civilization: A History *Revised Book*
   of American Colonial Life. Second ed. New York: Appleton-
   Century-Crofts, 1963.

14. THE FULL RESEARCH PAPER

Smith, Page. <u>As a City upon a Hill</u>. New York: Alfred A. Knopf,

    1966.

Schwartz, Joseph. "Three Aspects of Hawthorne's Puritanism,"

    <u>New England Quarterly</u>, 36 (1963), 192-208.

Extra Detail: Trollope, Anthony. "The Genius of Nathaniel Hawthorne,"
Rare Magazine

    <u>North American Review</u>, 129, No. 274 (Sept. 1879), 203-223.

Waggoner, Hyatt H. <u>Hawthorne: A Critical Study</u>. Cambridge: Har-

    vard University Press, 1963.

14. THE FULL RESEARCH PAPER

THE
HANDBOOK

Section A
The English Language

In your writing course, as in the rest of your life, you deal with and through an extraordinary language. The speech you are born to is rich and supple because of the many historic threads that constitute its weave. For a century or so it has been, and for at least the near future it will continue to be, a worldwide language, constantly absorbing greater variety of expression and enlarging its communicative power. THE HANDBOOK, therefore, begins with a long look at the past, the peoples and the tongues, from which our current speech developed and is developing. Fascinating in itself, this story can help you to understand your medium, and to use it more effectively.*

* For this survey, I am basically indebted to a splendid course in philology with Professor Arthur Brodeur, University of California, 1947–48, and, in addition to Murray, Pyles, and Dillard, as cited, to Albert H. Marckwardt, *American English* (New York: Oxford University Press, 1958), Richard Middlewood Wilson, "English Language," *Encyc. Brit.* (1967), from whom I have selected a number of word-lists, James R. Hulbert, *Bright's Anglo-Saxon Reader,* revised and enlarged (New York: Henry Holt and Co., 1936), and Calvert Watkins, "Indo-European and the Indo-Europeans," *The American Heritage Dictionary* (1969), pp. 1496–1502. I am also grateful to Professor John H. Fisher of the University of Tennessee and Professor William Labov of the University of Pennsylvania for informed and helpful comments.

THE INDO-EUROPEANS

The story of English begins about 5000 B.C. with a late Stone Age people in the Eurasian grasslands of what is now western Russia, where man first domesticated the horse. Words surviving in many of the eight big groups of languages descending from their speech show that they were an inland people, living among rivers and lakes, among waterfowl and grazing animals, knowing wolves, bears, deer, and beavers, in open country with deciduous trees, and snow — all suggesting a Eurasian terrain, perhaps near modern Lithuania, rather than the deserts and jungles of the countries farther east and south where their language also eventually thrived.

They were hunters and herdsmen. They had horses, and were acquiring bronze and gold. They were also warriors, as the dominance and spread of their language suggest, since they had no writing. Their language spread very slowly, over thousands of years and many generations, as one segment or another moved to new grass and hunting grounds, displacing and absorbing other peoples before them, slowly separating into divers races and derivative languages. Their general movement to new territories was probably underway by 3500 B.C., when the Egyptians had already begun to write and to build the world's first great civilization. The modern world has named these people *Aryans,* or, better, *Indo-Europeans,* a name indicating the ultimate span of their language from Europe to India.

Derivatives of Indo-European speech and people eventually covered Europe, and Russia, flowing gradually down the peninsulas and subcontinents of Spain, Italy, Greece, Asia, and India, and northward into Scandinavia, and westward into the British Isles — possibly dry-soled over ridges not yet sunken under the North Sea, or not broken at the Straits of Dover. The English language itself arrived several thousand years later, a very late comer, a division of a small subdivision that had evolved in Germany to become, today, the most widespread of any of the Indo-European languages — virtually an international language. And, oddly, most of the basic Indo-European words modern scholars can reconstruct are still represented in modern English, through inheritance or borrowing from other Indo-European languages — words like *father, mother, east,* for instance, and *name, bear,* and their combination *number.*

Here is a table of the Indo-European languages, to help you

visualize this astonishing linguistic dispersal that eventually produced English:

Indo-European Languages

I. "SATEM" LANGUAGES*

  A. Indo-Iranian

    1. **Indic:** Sanskrit, Pakrit, Pali, Hindi, Urdu, Hindustani, Bengali, Gujarati, Marathi, Punjabi, Singhalese, Romany

    2. **Iranian:** Avestan (the oldest of the Indo-Iranian group), Old Persian, Pahlavi (Middle Persian), Sogdian (ancient Central Asia), Scythian (ancient southeastern Europe and Asia), Baluchi (modern Baluchistan, India), Pashtu (Afghanistan), Persian, Kurdesh, Ossetic (Russia, between the Black and Caspian seas)

  B. **Armenian:** Classical Armenian, Eastern, and Western Armenian

  C. **Albanian:** Thracian, Illyrian (ancient coastal Yugoslavia), Albanian

  D. Balto-Slavic

    1. **Slavic:** Old Bulgarian, Bulgarian, Serbo-Croatian, Slovenian, Czech, Slovak, Polish, Wendish (ancient German area), Great Russian, White Russian, Ukrainian

    2. **Baltic:** Old Prussian, Lithuanian, Latvian

* Linguists divide the Indo-European languages into two groups according to whether they have kept the Indo-European *k*-sound or changed it to *s*. Linguists arbitrarily chose the word for "hundred," *satem* in Avestan, *centum* in Latin, to designate the two groups. As you probably know, the Latin *c* is "hard," pronounced as *k*.

Sir William Jones, a learned orientalist and lawyer appointed to the British supreme court in Calcutta, took the first step toward uncovering the Indo-European languages. He put forward, for the first time with sufficient evidence and force (1786), the theory that Sanskrit had derived from the same source as Greek and Latin. Nineteenth-century German scholars—notably Jacob Grimm, who, with brother Wilhelm, wrote the famous fairy tales, and Karl Verner, whose law explains some changes beyond Grimm's Law—completed the basic analysis, identifying the related languages and the principles by which they had changed the sounds of the consonants in the parent tongue.

Modern scholars identify two other small groups, separate from the Satems and Centums: (1) ancient Hittite and related Anatolian languages in Turkey about 2000 B.C. (the oldest), and (2) two Tocharian languages in Chinese Turkestan about 1000 B.C.

II. "CENTUM" LANGUAGES

A. Hellenic: Mycenean Greek, Attic, Ionic (ancient Greeks of western Asia Minor), Doric (ancient central Greece), Aeolic (ancient eastern Greece), Cyprian, Modern Greek

B. Italic

1. Oscan (ancient southern Italy)

2. Umbrian (ancient central Italy)

3. Latin: Faliscan (around prehistoric Rome), Latin, Italian, Provençal, French, Spanish, Catalan, Portuguese, Rumanian

C. Celtic: Gaulish, Welsh, Cornish, Breton, Irish, Manx, Gaelic

D. Germanic

1. East Germanic (Gothic)

2. North Germanic
   a. East Norse: Swedish, Danish, Gutnish
   b. West Norse: Norwegian, Faroese, Icelandic

3. West Germanic
   a. High German: Alemannic, Bavarian, Yiddish
   b. Low Germanic (*Plattdeutsch*)
      i. Franconian: Flemish, Dutch
      ii. Frisian
      iii. English

THE ANGLO-SAXONS (449)

Before "English" came to Britain (named by the Romans for some of its inhabitants, the Brythonic Celts, a western Indo-European branch), the Roman Empire had risen, flourished, and begun to totter. Caesar invaded Britain in 55 B.C., though serious conquest and colonization began almost a century later. Nevertheless, by the time that Angles, Saxons, and Jutes landed in southern England in A.D. 449, bringing the language that was to become "Old English," Romans had lived and died in Britain, representing the dominant culture, for almost five hundred years—a century longer than Americans have been in America. Latin (a southern Indo-European branch) was the language of England. "English," under some other name, might well have become another Romance language, like Italian, Spanish, and French.

But the Roman Empire slipped. Alaric the Goth, after sieges in 408 and 409, finally sacked Rome in 410. Other Gothic tribes were raiding into Roman Gaul (modern France). Britain was the empire's farthest outpost. Emperor Honorius wrote the British cities in 409 that they must fend for themselves. The legions withdrew, and many citizens with them. The elegant resort city of Bath, abandoned, sank back into the sulphur marsh, totally lost and forgotten for another two hundred years. Native chieftains began to gather strength, and to squabble. One, Vortigern, invited two "Saxon" lords and their men to help him fend off raiding Picts and Irish. Hengist and Horsa, two brothers (the first means "stallion," the second, "horse's"), of the Jutes, landed at Ebbsfleet, Kent, on the coast south of the Thames, in 449. They continued to dominate Kent; and other Angles and Saxons — all closely related in race and language — landed, first, on the southern coast, and later, on the eastern coast to the north. The invaders' power as well as their language prevailed over the scattered Celtish fragments left behind by the Romans.

Anglo-Saxon borrowings

The Anglo-Saxons picked up very few Celtic words, and even fewer from British Latin, probably because the Celts had mostly stayed clear of the Romans, and because the new invaders from Europe had the dominant culture. But many place-names in England survived from Roman-Celtic times, notably *ceaster* (from Roman *castrum,* fortified camp), which still remains in names like *Winchester, Westchester,* and *Worcester* (pronounced "Wooster" now, for more than four hundred years). Shakespeare's river Avon is a Celtish name for "river," as are others like Usk, Ouse, Stour, and Wye. London and York are Celtish names (the Romans had called the great city *Londinium,* from the Celtish *Londos,* for "wild"). Of the few other Celtish words the Anglo-Saxons adopted, even fewer remain today, among them *binn,* for "manger," now our flourbins and coalbins, and *cursian,* "to curse."

The Anglo-Saxons had already acquired a stock of Latin words from fighting and trading with the Romans in continental Europe, many still in the language. *Copor,* "copper," from Latin *cuprum/ coprum,* comes in very early, before the Latin in Gaul had shifted pronunciation to *covrum.* Similarly, *wīn* ("wine," pronounced "ween") came in when classical Latin *vinum* was still pronounced "weenum." Our word *vine,* which grows the grapes for the wine, comes from the same Latin word, but six or seven centuries later, after the Norman Conquest, as the English borrowed the French word for the *vines* in the *vinyards* of Bordeaux, which were producing their *wines.* From the Romans, the continental Anglo-Saxons, with the other Germanic peoples, had also borrowed *naep,* now "turnip," *peose* "pea," *culter* "colter" (plowblade), *weall* "wall," *cēap* "to bargain" (hence "cheap"), *pund* "pound," and *mynet* "money" (hence "mint"). They also took the *flasce* for the *wīn* they poured in their *cuppe* to put under their *belt,* and they bought from the Romans *cyse* "cheese," *pipor* "pepper," and *butere* for the *cycene* "kitchen." Roman *cealc* "chalk," *pic* "pitch," and *tigele* "tile" went into buildings. The early continental Germans also borrowed "street" from Roman *via strata* and "mile" from *mil* — a thousand paces of the marching Roman legions. *Segl* "sail" from Latin *sagulum* is the same in almost every Germanic language, as the northerners, especially the Vikings, saw how much it improved the Roman galley. A ruler became *cāsere,* after Caesar, which also produced the German *Kaiser* and the Russian *Czar* or *Tsar.* The last day of the week became *Saeternesdaeg,* "Saturn's day" — the only Roman among a week of Germanic sun, moon, and gods. Christianity, in 597, brought a new flood of Latin words into Anglo-Saxon England.

The Old English period (450–1100)

The Anglo-Saxons referred to themselves and their language as *Anglisc* or *Englisc,* probably because the Angles in Northumbria, in northern England, developed the first literature, centuries earlier than any literature in any of the other Germanic languages. Their language was nearer modern German than English. It was a "synthetic," or inflected language, signaling its grammar by word-endings, as in German or Latin. Here are the opening lines of the *Beowulf,* the greatest remaining Old English epic (pronounce the *ae* like *hat,* but the other vowels separately, with the qualities of Span-

ish or Italian; the *y* pronounces like the *u* in French *lune*; þ and ð are
"th"):

> Hwaet, wē gār-Dena   in gēardagum,
> þēodcyninga,   þrym gefrūnon,
> hū ðā aepelingas   ellen fremedon!

Literally:

> **What! we, of spear-Danes',   in yore-days,**
> **People-kings',   power have heard,**
> **how the noblings   valor performed!**

Only the simple words—*what, we, in, how, the*—remain in English
today, pretty much as they were. Notice that we still pronounce
the beginning of *what* in the Anglo-Saxon way, *hw*, although the
Middle-English scribes changed it to *wh*, for some obscure reason.
Here the Anglo-Saxon harper uses it as a call for the audience's
attention: it is usually translated "Lo" or "Behold." The blocky
half-lines, incidentally, pausing in the middle and alliterated across
the gap, probably coordinated with the harper-reciter's sweeps
across the strings, one sweep for each half-line. We can also recognize the outlines of modern *Dane, yore, day,* and *king,* but all the rest
are entirely foreign to us, lost from the language along with the
seemingly backward word-order, and the inflectional grammatical
endings that support it. In its fifteen hundred years of history,
English has changed from a "synthetic," inflected language to an
"analytic," almost uninflected one, where position in the sentence
(subject-verb-object), together with such indicators as *with, in, to,
by,* expresses meaning, the former function of the vanished word-
endings. And it has traded off a major portion of its old vocabulary
for new.

THE NORSEMEN (789)

Because the Germanic languages characteristically accent the
beginnings of words, Anglo-Saxon had already begun to slur and
to lose older and more complicated inflectional endings before the
Norsemen came. But invading Norsemen, in two waves three hun-

dred years apart, accelerated the change from synthetic to analytic. The Norsemen, or Vikings, began their raids on England in 789, when, as *The Anglo-Saxon Chronicle* tells us, three ships, "the first ships of Danish men," raided a seaport on the southern coast. Raids continued on eastern and northern coasts, Scotland, and Ireland, until the Danes had settled the whole of central England as their territory, known as the "Danelaw." Alfred, the West Saxon king, who had held the Danes out of southern England and had established the last great period of Anglo-Saxon literature and culture, signed the Peace of Wedmore with them in 878. Since the Old Norse of the Danes and the Old English of the Anglo-Saxons were similar Germanic languages but with differing word-endings, people went for the word and forgot the endings, smoothing out the grammar. Nevertheless, only about forty Norse words appear in the written language, still classically Anglo-Saxon under Alfred—notably *lagu* "law," *hūsbonda* "householder," and *þræl* "thrall" (slave, now in *enthrall*)—until after the next and very different Norse invasion, that of the Norman French.

THE NORMAN CONQUEST (1066)

The raids and settlement of Norsemen southward—the Age of the Vikings—lasted from the first appearance of Danish ships off southern England (789) until the treaty of St. Clair-sur-Epte (912), which established the Norsemen in Normandy, France. Some social upheaval, perhaps overpopulation, had turned the Nordic custom of sea-raiding ("Viking" means "sea-raider") into conquest. By land, the Norsemen pushed into western Russia, and southward into the Burgundy of modern France, which bears the tribal name of its Norse invaders and settlers. By sea, they raided the coasts of France and Spain, and pushed into the Mediterranean to settle in Sicily (where, at Monreale, near Palermo, you can still see a magnificent Norman cathedral built by their Christianized descendants).

But the most significant of the Norse settlements was in Normandy, which, like Burgundy, bears the invaders' name. While Alfred was fighting the Vikings in England, other Norsemen sailed up the Seine to Rouen, devastating the countryside and eventually repopulating it with a Nordic-Gallic admixture. But France (or French women) prevailed after all, for the conquerors lost their language, ultimately adopting both Christianity and French. When the Norman William, the Conqueror, landed at Hastings, in England, in 1066, about the only Norse remaining was his battle cry, *Tur ai!*, "Thor, aid!" The rest of the swearing was in French.

MIDDLE ENGLISH (1100–1500)

The language of English upper-class culture was now Norman French. Anglo-Saxon went underground, the speech of peasants. All the riches of Anglo-Saxon poetry, like *hron-rād,* "whale-road," for "sea," and *eard-stapa,* "earth-stepper," for a wandering outcast, never found in common prose, disappeared from the language. But all the Old Norse words acquired in common parlance in Anglo-Saxon days now begin to appear in writing, many of them eventually replacing their Old English synonyms with such central words as *sky, die, take, fellow, leg, low, egg, awe.* Some Old English words acquired an Old Norse synonym of slightly differing meaning: *rear/raise, from/fro, craft/skill, hide/skin, to/til, sick/ill,* and *shirt/skirt,* which became the female version of the belted Anglo-Saxon smock, or "shirt," worn by both sexes. Any *sk* word in modern English is very likely from Old Norse. Old Norse also endowed us with the pronoun *she,* a clearer distinction than the Old English *hēo,* and with the other pronouns *they, their, them,* for the same reason. Other important Old Norse words still with us, surfacing after the Norman Conquest, are *though, aloft, athwart,* and *seemly.*

But the Norseman's most significant imprint on English was not of Norse but of his more recent Norman French, which cut Anglo-Saxon off from writing and accelerated its incipient change from synthetic to analytic grammar, offering as reinforcement a language already analytic in structure. Many new words came in directly from Latin, still the language of learning and science, and many more French words derived directly from their ancestral Latin. English and French words, surviving side by side, give us some interesting opportunities for one-upmanship: *hearty/cordial, ask/demand, answer/reply, house/mansion, ghost/spirit, room/chamber, shun/avoid, seethe/boil, yearly/annual.* In most of these pairs, the French half, the second one, still carries an air of social superiority— *house/mansion,* for instance. While the Anglo-Saxon peasantry herded, in their own language, the *calves, steers, swine,* and *sheep,* and refrained from killing the *deer,* the French lords and ladies ate in French: *veal, beef, pork, mutton, venison.* Since Anglo-Saxon *lamb* is our word for both the animal and the meat, we may assume that the French lords liked their *mutton* mature, and that roast leg of lamb came into favor only after the lordly descendants of the Normans had shifted to English. Synonyms also borrowed later from both Norman and Parisian French give us some other interesting pairs: *catch/chase, canal/channel, real/royal, wage/gage, warden/ guardian, warrant/guarantee.*

But although the Norman Conquest deposed and then largely rebuilt much of our vocabulary, English, as evolving from Anglo-Saxon, continued to work itself upward. By the reign of Edward III (1327–1377), the nobility were speaking English. About 1350, "John Cornwal, a maystere of gramere," changed the language of teaching in grammar school from "Freynsch into Englysch."* A statute of Edward's in 1362–1363 made English the language for pleadings in the lawcourts. And Chaucer's great works, beginning in 1359 and culminating in the *Canterbury Tales* (1387), though heavily influenced by French, are, of course, in Middle English. French is again a foreign language.

The opening lines of Chaucer's *Canterbury Tales* well show what has happened to the Old English inflectional endings, which had signaled subjects, objects, indirect objects, and so forth: they have all rounded down to a meaningless final *e,* pronounced "uh," or not pronounced at all when the meter (or the rush of conversation) crowds it against the vowel of a word following. *Aprille* is pronounced "Ah-prill-uh," and *shoures soote* is pronounced "shoor-uhs soht-uh"; but *veyne* is pronounced exactly like modern *vein* because the *i* of the following *in* absorbs the final *e,* or at least most

* John de Trevisa, translation of Ranulf Rigden's *Polychronicon,* 1387, quoted in Sir James A. H. Murray, "English Language," *Encyc. Brit.,* 11th ed. (1910), p. 594.

of it. *Drought* sounded about like modern "looked" with a guttural *gh* for the *k*, like a clearing of the throat. I have scanned the lines into their iambic pentameter (which allows for an extra light syllable at the end of its usual ten-syllable line), so you can see how the word-endings work, and how Middle English sounded at its very best. Pronounce the *a*'s as in *ah,* long *e*'s as in "swayt-uh brayth," long *i* like the double *ee* in "peer," and long *u* and *o* as in "shoor-uhs soht-uh."

˘ — | ˘–˘ — | ˘ — | ˘ —|˘
Whan that Aprille with his shoures soote

˘ — | ˘ — | ˘ — | ˘ —| ˘ — |˘
The drought of March hath perced to the roote,

˘ — | ˘ —| ˘ — | ˘ — | ˘ — |
And bathed every veyne in swich licour

˘ — | ˘ —| ˘ — | ˘ —| ˘ — |
Of which vertu engendred is the flour;

˘ — | ˘ —| ˘ — | ˘ — | ˘ — |
Whan Zephirus eek with his sweete breeth

˘ —| ˘ — | ˘ —| ˘ — | ˘ — |
Inspired hath in every holt and heeth

˘ — | ˘ — | ˘
The tendre croppes, . . .

(When April, with his sweet showers, has pierced the drought of March to the root, and bathed every vein in that certain liquor of whose potency the flower is engendered, when Zephyr, moreover, with his sweet breath has inspired the tender crops in every field and heath, . . .)

This opening sentence of Chaucer's runs on for another four-and-a-half lines before reaching its main clause (*Thanne longen folk to goon on pilgrimages,* "Then folk long to go on pilgrimages"), and for another six lines beyond that before the period. His sentence is 128 words long. English has loosened, and flexed, and sophisticated considerably since the hardy, blocky phrases of the *Beowulf.*

To illustrate further the change from Old English to Middle English to Modern English, here are three translations of the same passage from the Latin Bible — New Testament, St. Mark iv. 2–9:

Old English
West-Saxon Gospels (c. 1000)

(2) And hē hi fela on bigspellum lǣrde, and him tō cwæð on his lāre, (3) Gehȳrað: Ūt ēode sē sǣdere his sǣd tō sāwenne. (4) And þā hē sēow, sum fēoll wið þone weg, and fugelas cōmon and hit frǣton. (5) Sum fēoll ofer stānscyligean, þār hit næfde mycele eorðan, and sōna ūp ēode; and for þām hit næfde eorðan þiccnesse, (6) þā hit ūp ēode, sēo sunne hit forswǣlde, and hit forscranc, for þām hit wyrtruman næfde. (7) And sum fēoll on þornas; þā stigon ðā þornas and forðrysmodon þæt, and hit wæstm ne bær. (8) And sum fēoll on gōd land, and hit sealde ūppstīgendne and wexendne wæstm; and an brōhte þrītig-fealdne, sum syxtifealdne, sum hundfealdne. (9) And hē cwæð, Gehȳre, sē ðe ēaran hæbbe tō gehȳranne.

Middle English
John Wycliffe's Bible (1382)

(ȝ = the Old English gutteral *gh*-sound; v = u, and u sometimes = v, as in *heuene,* vp, and *ȝaue*)

And he tauȝte hem in parablis many thingis. And he seide to hem in his techynge. Heere ȝee. Loo! a man sowynge goth out for to sowe. And the while he sowith, an other seed felde aboute the wey, and briddis of heuene, or of the eire, camen, and eeten it. Forsothe an other felde doun on stony placis, wher it had nat myche erthe; and anoon it sprong vp, for it hadde nat depnesse of erthe. And whenne the sunne rose vp, it welwide for heete, and it dried vp, for it hadde not roote. And an other felde doun into thornes, and thornes stieden vp, and strangliden it, and it ȝaue not fruyt. And an other felde doun in to good lond, and ȝaue fruyt, styinge vp, and wexinge; and oon brouȝte 'thritty fold, and oon sixtyfold, and oon an hundridfold. And he seide, He that hath eris of heeryng, heere.

Modern English
King James Version (1611)

(2) And he taught them many things by parables, and he said unto them in his doctrine, (3) Hearken; Behold, there went out a sower to sow: (4) and it came to pass, as he sowed, some fell by the wayside, and the fowls of the air came and devoured it up. (5) And some fell on stony ground, where it had not much earth; and immediately it sprang up, because it had no depth of earth: (6) but when the sun was up, it was scorched; and because it had no root, it withered away. (7) And some fell among thorns, and the thorns grew up, and choked it, and it yielded no fruit. (8) And other fell on good ground, and did yield fruit that sprang up and increased, and brought forth, some thirty, some sixty, and some a hundred. (9) And he said unto them, He that hath ears to hear, let him hear.

After English had firmly reestablished itself by the middle 1300's, a new tide of Latin borrowings came in, alongside the French words, which also derived from Latin. From the days of the Roman Empire onward, steadily through the Dark Ages, the Middle Ages, the Renaissance, and well into modern times, the international language of learning and science was Latin. All discourse at the universities was in Latin. Today, ceremonial lectures at Oxford and Cambridge continue to be delivered in Latin. The new tide of Latin brought into Middle English such familiar words as *client, psalm, equivalent, allegory, formal, library, dissolve, ascension, impediment, alienate,* and *dissent.* But it reached its height in the fifteenth century with a number of self-conscious poetic inventions, like *dispone,* and *equipolent,* known as "aureate [that is, gilded] diction." Most of these faded away, but some became permanent, like *laureate, mediation, oriental,* and *prolixity.* From the early 1500's, as the Modern period opened, and up through the days of Queen Elizabeth and Shakespeare, similar immense borrowings from Latin came into English, many literary and self-conscious, which were soon called, in reaction, "inkhorn terms." But most came in naturally as the Renaissance moved into England, as interest in the Greek and Roman classics revived under the stimulus of humanists like John Colet, William Lyly, and Erasmus, and as scientists and voyagers expanded their discoveries.

MODERN ENGLISH (1500 onward)

The Modern period of the English language really begins when William Caxton brought the printing press to England, and London, in 1476. On the continent, where he learned the trade, he had already issued, probably in 1474 and 1475, the first two books printed in English: his translation of a French romance concerning the Trojan War, *Recuyell of the Histories of Troy,* and *The Game and Play of Chesse,* also translated from the French. Setting up at Westminster, he issued almost eighty books, many his own translations, in his remaining fourteen years of life. His books confirmed the English of London as the national standard, though great variety in dialect and usage persisted as perfectly acceptable well into the seventeenth century. Throughout the sixteenth century, the language "seems to be in a plastic, unformed state, and its writers, as it were, experiment with it, bending it to constructions which now seem indefensible," writes Sir James A. H. Murray.* Nevertheless, Caxton did a great deal toward stabilizing a language even more fluid and diversified, worrying about what words to use so the largest number could understand him, whether to write *eggs* as *egges* (from Old Norse), which a country woman could not understand, or as *eyren* (from Old English), which presumably would puzzle others.†

By Shakespeare's day, English had somewhat settled down, but was still exploring its riches, with a sense of freedom. The civil war that tore England apart in the middle 1600's also shook the language into further transition, but with the Restoration of 1660 and the general reaching out for postwar stability, the language settled into a recognizably modern form, with the Bloodless Revolution of 1688 usually taken as the final watershed into modernity, as the language attained a new smoothness and fluency under the pen of John Dryden.

Samuel Johnson's *Dictionary* of 1755 helped to stabilize English spelling, and Bishop Robert Lowth's *A Short Introduction to English Grammar* (1762) did much the same for grammar, setting the pattern

---

* p. 601.
† In his Preface to his translation of Virgil's *Aeneid,* 1490; see below, p. 362.

for school texts almost down to our own time. Johnson and Lowth shared the age's wish for stability, definition, and clarity. Both looked at the classical languages, particularly Latin, as fountainheads, at which modern languages ought again to refresh themselves. Their works, and others following, answered the urge of a new mercantile society moving upward to affluence and literacy, and wanting to know what was deemed correct in cultivated circles. Nineteenth-century America, sprawling rapidly to new and newer frontiers, pursued correctness in pronunciation and usage even more persistently than England, toward which America continued to feel secretly and chronically inferior.

The influence of Latin on English has been, from the first, considerable. Some 60 percent of our modern vocabulary comes, one way or another, from Latin, and many influential writers from the sixteenth through the nineteenth centuries have had Latin in their heads as they wrote their English. Schooling of every boy in England from Shakespeare through Fielding and on to about 1866, consisted basically of studying the classics and memorizing Lyly's *Latin Grammar* (c. 1513), used in all schools in England, and later in America, with almost no change for three and a half centuries. This classical cast of mind helped frame the Declaration of Independence and the U.S. Constitution—note the "Senate" straight from ancient Rome—and shaped the linguistic habits of those who wrote and spoke English well into the twentieth century. A certain learned eloquence persisted in correspondence and conversation, as men and women read George Eliot and Dickens aloud, quoted poetry to each other, and attended to the ornate oratory of the pulpit and the popular lecture platform. Before World War I, most American universities still required a proficiency in Latin for admission.

AMERICAN ENGLISH

The language the people of Jamestown and Plymouth first brought to America was not only ample in heritage and potential, but was in the especially fluid and fluent state of the late Renaissance. The most significant shift in pronunciation since 449, though almost completed, was still in progress. The English long vowels — *ah, a, ee, oh, oo* — shifted from the "continental" quality they shared with their sister languages to the diphthongs of modern English, the double vowels all of us say, though we hear them as single letters: we think *a*, but pronounce it to rhyme with something like "May-ee." Beginning in the fifteenth century, *a* shifted from *ah* to the "May-ee" of *make*. Long *e*, which had sounded like modern *make*, shifted to *ee*; *i* became *ai*; *o* became *oh-oo*; *u* changed from *oo* to the *au* in *ouch*. In Virginia to this day, people retain something of the older *u*, because their ancestors came over before the *u* had fully shifted, calling a *house* a "huh-oos" and a *mouse* a "muh-oos," after the Old English *hūs* ("hoos") and *mūs* ("moos"). English-speaking Canadians, whose ancestors came largely from Scotland two centuries later, say these words very much like Virginians, because in Scotland the Old English *u* never fully shifted to *au*.

British and American pronunciations now differ considerably, with New England and the South being somewhat nearer to British in their dropping of final *r*, but differing from educated British and from each other in many other ways. These areas were settled mostly by people from the old East-Anglian region — southeastern England, including London. The middle area — New Jersey, Delaware, Maryland, Pennsylvania, which now stretches to the west coast and northwest — came mostly from more northern English regions where the *r* remained hard, or even trilled. Consequently, most Americans say *water* not *watah*.

Aside from "New England" and "Southern," the vast majority of Americans can hardly detect regional differences among themselves, though these exist both in qualities of pronunciation and in vocabulary. Radio, TV, and the movies have evened out American pronunciation considerably. Although levels of education and affluence still produce marked differences, as do the many minority dialects, particularly Black English, the lines between regional and social groups in America are not so explicitly drawn in pronunciation and vocabulary as they are between upper class and working class in England, or among the numerous regional and rural dialects of Britain, which retain many differing traces from old Anglo-Saxon-Nordic times — dialects that many Americans and some Britishers have great difficulty in understanding.

These Old English traces remain in American regional usages also. America keeps the Anglo-Saxon *dune,* but limits it to a sand-hill; England uses the later vowel-shifted version, *down,* for its hills (which mixes Americans up). American English frequently retains these older forms that British has long since lost: *gotten,* for instance, as against British (and American) *got.* The British say "his attitude *to* sports"; Americans, "his attitude *toward* sports," keeping the more elaborate and less frequent of the two Anglo-Saxon alternatives. The Old Germanic habit of accenting beginnings and swallowing endings is stronger in England, producing what Americans call the "clipped" British way of speaking, with "Thank you" sounding like "kyup!" and *extraordinary* like *strórdnr,* and even *got* and *that* now swallowed back in the throat, in common parlance, to the briefest *ga'* and *tha',* so that the modern Londoner sounds like the traditional Scot with his "Will y' na' come back again." Americans have followed the printed word more closely than have the British, tending to pronounce syllables and letters slurred over by Britishers — evidently, as we have seen, from the early feeling of cultural inferiority and the drive to be educated. Nevertheless, in rural American speech, some words the city-dweller thinks mere country ignorance actually reflect the oldest forms, as they do also in rural England: *lookee,* for instance, from the archaic *look ye* that goes straight back to Anglo-Saxon, and *ax,* for "ask," which still seems to reflect the dominant Anglo-Saxon verb, *ācsian* or *āxian,* of which *āscian* was then only a minor variant.

Many such differences in American speechways reflect the region of England (and sometimes the historical period) from which a particular group of settlers came. But since most groups included people widely assorted from different old Anglo-Saxon dialectical areas, the reasons for one American region's saying, for instance, *pail* and another's saying *bucket* are obscure. *Pail* goes back to Anglo-Saxon; *bucket,* to the Normans. But why one should prevail in Maine and the other in Pennsylvania eludes certainty. The different choices in America simply demonstrate how language will develop independently in any region not consistently communicating with another. So an American's car has a *hood;* a Britisher's, a *bonnet.* One buys *gas;* the other *petrol. Two-lane traffic* is a *dual carriageway;* an *overpass,* a *flyover;* a *drugstore,* a *chemist's shop.*

Corn, in England, is wheat, or any grain; in America it's on the cob, or in something generally rural or *corny.* And an American's *crotch* is a Britisher's *crutch.*

American English has always been inventive, and highly absorptive, and many Americanisms have gone back to England and around the world. *O.K.* may be the world's most universal word.* Our Thomas Jefferson invented the ever-popular *belittle. Cocktail, jackpot, know-how, fizzle, bingo, honk* are all American innovations as are most of our terms of racial contempt, like *honky,* first applied (in the form *Bohunk,* "Bohemian-Hungarian") to Hungarian immigrants of the steel mills and coal mines by established whites, now applied to all whites by blacks. *Honkytonk,* which seems to have come from a tinking-tonking piano, and *jazz,* which arose, with the music, from the black culture of New Orleans, both with an African origin (Pyles, p. 47), have become international English words. Another is *Yankee,* perhaps from *Janke,* the diminutive of *Jan* (Dutch for "John"), as a nickname for New York's early Dutch settlers.

But the most curious thing about American English is the great difference in pronunciation between New England and the South—areas both settled mostly from southeast England in the same span of history. New Englanders apparently tended to nasalize, especially the Puritans, whom an Englishman in 1770 reported as having a "whining cadence" in their speech (Pyles, p. 241). On the other hand, Southern speech seems to have mellowed.

However one may attempt to explain this distinction—the

---

* Allen Walker Read traces it to the O.K. Club, supporting Martin Van Buren against William Henry Harrison in the presidential campaign of 1840. "O.K." stood for "Old Kinderhook," Van Buren's nickname, from his birthplace, Kinderhook, New York. "The O.K. Club" first appeared in print on March 23, 1840. But the opposition decided to smudge the Democrats by an article "explaining" O.K. as an illiterate abbreviation of "All Correct" by the incumbent President, Andrew Jackson, Van Buren's sponsor ("The Evidence on O.K.," *The Saturday Review of Literature,* July 19, 1941, summarized and discussed by Thomas Pyles, *Words and Ways of American English* [New York: Random House, Inc., 1952], pp. 158–165). But O.K. had already appeared in fashionable slang in the 1830's *(The American College Dictionary; The American Heritage Dictionary).* The O.K. Club was apparently exploiting a coincidence with popular slang. A later theory, that *O.K.* derived from American Choctaw Indian *hoke* ("it is so"), a theory much liked by President Woodrow Wilson, who wrote it *okeh,* gave the term a certain respectable boost.

languid climate and slower pace in life, for instance — the greatest single distinction between North and South was, almost from the first, a considerable population of African slaves. Black slaves, often deliberately assorted from different tribes to minimize revolts on shipboard and ashore, had no common language.* The slave's greatest need was to talk with his fellow captives. The white master had little to say to him. A *git*, a *wuk*, a *come*, a *go*, and a whip, would probably suffice. For communication among themselves, slaves used whatever lingua franca they could acquire from their captors and each other. In the fourteenth century, Sabir, the French-Italian-Spanish pidgin of the Arab slavers, the oldest in the business, was current. When the Portuguese began to dominate world trade in the fifteenth and sixteenth centuries, the West African slaving areas began to acquire Pidgin Portuguese. *Pickaninny, savvy,* and *Negro* (reinforcing the earlier Sabir-Spanish) testify to their Portuguese origin. The simplified grammar of Pidgin Portuguese probably copied that of Sabir, and the simplified grammar of Pidgin English probably followed that of both.†

But African intonations and words were shaping whatever pidgin or creole a slave community acquired. In Louisiana, a French pidgin evolved into an indigenous French Creole. Slaves who escaped to islands offshore of South Carolina, Georgia, and Florida evolved from the pidgins of Portuguese and English, and their native African, an independent creole language known as Gullah, a language which in turn put many Africanisms first into Black English, then into general American usage: *jazz*, most notably, and *tote, gumbo, buckaroo, banjo, okra, juke, bozo, voodoo,* and probably other special usages like *hip, hep,* and *cat* (Dillard, pp. 118–119). *Mon*, or "man," almost universal for address and exclamation in black dialects around the Caribbean, has now become almost equally universal in young American speech.

Thus, even as blacks were acquiring English, something of their intonations and idioms was tempering the English of their white masters. The white pidgin-speaker, when giving orders, would

---

* For this point and a number of others following, I am indebted to J. L. Dillard, *Black English* (New York: Random House, Inc., 1972), pp. 73 ff.

† Keith Whinnon, "The Origin of the European-based Creoles and Pidgins," *Orbis* (1968), pp. 509–526, cited Dillard, p. 21.

naturally imitate the black to make himself understood, and some of that imitation would eventually remain. Even more significant was the black mammy, and her children, with whom the white child spent much of his time from infancy onward. William Faulkner's short story "That Evening Sun" illustrates the process still at work in relatively modern times. Conversely, Southern vowels were changing in ways wholly unrelated to West African, Caribbean, or Gullah,* and blacks were acquiring them as they learned the white community's speech. From the first, the early pidgins and Plantation Creole moved steadily over toward the evolving Standard English,† and moved outward to virtually every state in the nation. The dual process continues from coast to coast, as whites acquire black idioms and intonations, and blacks acquire the shared standard usages.

Writing makes the ultimate selection, and is perhaps the ultimate educator. Like Caxton in 1490, the modern writer ponders which words will reach the widest audience, which will connect him with the largest sharing of culture, which will persuade, which may lose him the credit he needs to be convincing. His choices, and their social nuances, are richly varied, since English has gathered and kept synonyms not only from its Germanic-Latin-Norse-French mainstream but from most of the other languages one can name. English probably has the largest living vocabulary in the world, because its literature — the written language — keeps alive, in great works, those words that speech alone would have long since lost.

Literature continually breathes new life into the inevitable decay of daily usage as metaphors and precisions fade into gobbledegook, and prominent people can utter with satisfaction such densities as *fuel economy program success.* A word like *sanction,* for instance, which means "a blessing," comes in official jargon to mean also its opposite, a "penalty," its precision impaired, until some poet comes along to remind us again of what it means, at the root, in the holy sanctions of the heart. The spoken word dies on our breath. The written word endures — *litera scripta manet* — because the writer

---

* William Labov, commenting on my earlier draft of this section.

† Dillard notes that runaway slaves — people of nerve and ability — "were likely to be just those slaves who did attain a relative mastery of Standard English " (p. 86): a runaway would need to communicate with a wide diversity of people who would not understand Plantation Creole, and reading and writing Standard English was frequently to their advantage.

makes words say what they mean, and renews their durable life. As Auden reminds us, Time, who is

> **. . . indifferent in a week**
> **To a beautiful physique,**
>
> **Worships language and forgives**
> **Everyone by whom it lives.***

To join that timeless crowd by whom language lives is the writer's secret obsession, as he searches the clutter of everyday usage for the real riches of the world's most extended language.

The process of writing, then, brings these riches into our personal usage, and our speech acquires the breadth and span of the written language, moving into the mainstream from whatever regional or dialectical point we may have started. This mainstream, this Standard English, is constantly gathering new vitalities from its edges and dropping others no longer of use. To use it well is to share a living entity, perhaps with some wonder at the strange energy in Indo-European that slowly flowed outward over Europe and Asia, and then, in a much changed and minor dialect, reached southern England in 449 to carry itself on around the world.

EXERCISES

1 Pick five common words now in slang or dialectical usage — *joint,* or *roach,* for marijuana cigarette, for instance. Write a clear definition of each in Standard English anyone could understand, then look up the word's origin in the dictionary. Put this origin, together with a brief speculation on how the slang term may have derived, in parentheses after your definition.

EXAMPLE: *joint:* a cigarette made from dried flower clusters and leaves

---

*W. H. Auden, from "In Memory of W. B. Yeats," in *Collected Shorter Poems 1927–1957* (New York: Random House, 1966). Copyright 1940, renewed 1968 by W. H. Auden. Reprinted by permission of Random House, Inc.

of the hemp plant, *cannabis sativa,* usually rolled loosely in paper by the user. (Middle English, from Old French, from the past participle of *joindre,* "to join," possibly because the user "joins" the materials.)

   If your term is not in the dictionary, try another that is. If you can see no connection between its origin and its slang usage, say "slang origin obscure."

2 Translate the following passage of standard prose into your own local or regional dialect of English, or into contemporary college slang. You will need to keep some of the author's words and phrases, of course, but make the transformation as thorough as possible. Would Schlesinger's article be more effective, or less, if it moved some of the way toward your version? All the way?

   What more astonishing adventure could there have been than that of the settlement of America? Anonymous men and women, renouncing a familiar and traditional existence, abandoning places where their families had lived for centuries, embarked on frail ships, crossed perilous seas and put down roots in an unknown and alien continent. It requires a violent thrust of the contemporary imagination to comprehend the courage—the courage and the despair and the hope—that lay behind countless individual decisions in quiet European villages. And so they came, laid their lives on the line, endured hardship and vicissitude. Many gave up or starved or were killed by disease or Indians. The survivors gradually came to terms with the new land.

   Roanoke Island, 1585: the lost colony, the settlers mysteriously vanished, only the word CROATOAN carved on a post to mark the fact that Englishmen had tried to live there, the enigma of their disappearance unsolved to this day. Jamestown, 1607: two-thirds of the first settlers dying from famine and sickness. "There were never Englishmen left in a forreigne Country in such miseries as we," wrote one of them. "So lamentable was our scarcity," wrote another, "that we were constrained to eat dogs, cats, rats, snakes, toadstools, horsehides and what not; one man out of the misery that he endured, killing his wife, powdered her up to eat her, for which he was burned." Plymouth, 1620: half the colonists dying in the first year.

   But the survivors hung on. "It is not with us as with other men," the Pilgrims said, "whom small things can discourage, or small discontentments cause to wish themselves at home again." They built their dwellings, organized their governments, enacted their laws, cleared their forests, discovered new crops and new ways to farm, heard the call of the dark and silent wilderness beyond. Nor was the invasion of America an English monopoly. The Dutch settled on

A. THE ENGLISH LANGUAGE

Manhattan Island, Swedes along the Delaware, Scotch-Irish and Germans in Pennsylvania, French and Spanish in Florida. Whether sustained by relish of adventure or by the search for gold or by the desire to worship God as they saw fit, they were men and women beyond the reach of small discontentments.*

* From Arthur Schlesinger, Jr., "The Birth of a Nation — A Journey into America's Past," *Travel & Leisure* (American Express Publishing Corp.), July 1974. Copyright © 1974 American Express Publishing Corporation.

3 Translate into clear contemporary English the following famous passage from William Caxton's Prologue to his translation (from the French) of Virgil's *Aeneid,* which he spelled *Eneydos* (1490). Remember that printed *u* frequently stood for *v,* as in *ouer,* and that printed *v* frequently stood for *u,* as in *vnderstande.* In his *yᵗ,* he is using *y* for the Old English thorn, þ, the *th*-sound, which, combined with the little superscript *t* was an abbreviation for *that.* (The *ye* of Middle English and the sixteenth century, incidentally, similarly stood for the sound *the,* when used as an article, as in *ye booke,* not *ye,* as we now read it; but *ye,* meaning "you" was pronounced "yee.") His *tamyse* is the river Thames; *zelande* is Zeeland (southern Holland); *forlond* is Foreland, the farthest tip of land on the southern shore of the Thames estuary, just north of where the Jutes landed in 449.

. . . I delybered and concluded to translate it in-to englysshe, And forthwyth toke a penne & ynke, and wrote a leef or tweyne whyche I ouersawe agayn to corecte it. And whan I sawe the fayr & straunge termes therin I doubted that it sholde not please some gentylmen whiche late blamed me, sayeng, yᵗ in my translacyons I had ouer curyous termes whiche coude not be vnderstande of comyn peple and desired me to vse olde and homely termes in my translacyons. and fayn wolde I satysfye euery man and so to doo, toke an olde boke and redde therin and certaynly the englysshe was so rude and brood that I coude not wele vnderstande it. And also my lorde abbot of west-mynster ded do shewe to me late, certayn euydences wryton in olde englysshe, for to reduce it in-to our englysshe now vsid. And certaynly it was wreton in suche wyse that it was more lyke to dutche than englysshe; I coude not reduce ne brynge it to be vnderstonden. And certaynly our langage now vsed varyeth ferre from that whiche was vsed and spoken whan I was borne. For we englysshe men ben borne vnder the domynacyon of the mone, whiche is neuer stedfaste but euer wauerynge, wexynge one season and waneth & dyscreaseth another season. And that comyn englysshe that is spoken in one shyre varyeth from a nother. In so moche that in my dayes happened that certayn marchauntes were in a shippe in tamyse, for to haue sayled ouer the see into zelande and for lacke of wynde, thei taryed atte forlond, and wente to lande for to refreshe them; And one of theym named sheffelde, a mercer, cam in-to an hows and axed for mete; and specyally he axyd after eggys; And the goode wyf answerde, that she coude speke no frenshe. And the marchaunt was angry, for he also coude speke no frenshe, but wolde haue hadde egges and she vnderstode hym not. And thenne at laste a nother sayd that he wolde haue eyren. then the good wyf sayd that she vnderstod hym wel. Loo, what sholde a man in thyse dayes now wryte, egges or eyren. certaynly it is harde to playse euery man by cause of dyuersite & chaunge of langage. For in these dayes euery man that is in ony reputacyon in his countre, wyll vtter his commynycacyon and maters in suche maners & termes that fewe men shall vnderstonde theym. And som honest and grete clerkes haue ben wyth me, and desired me to wryte the moste curyous termes that I coude fynde. And thus bytwene playn rude & curyous, I stande abasshed. but in my Iudgemente the comyn termes that be dayli vsed, ben lyghter to be vnderstonde than the olde and auncyent englysshe

4 Translate into clear contemporary English the following passage from Herman Melville's *Typee* (1846, Chapter 17). Melville (1819–1891) was a young New Yorker, who, after trying schoolteaching, shipped out as a sailor before the mast at nineteen. With a companion, he jumped ship at Nuku Hiva, Marquesas Islands, in 1842. They crossed the mountainous island, and dropped into the steeply enclosed valley, opening seaward, that was the territory of the Typees, a tribe of cannibals. The chiefs and warrior-elite ate enemies slain in battle, at ritualized feasts from which all commoners were excluded, but Melville had no way of knowing how far their dietary habits might extend. His friend escaped in two weeks, and he, eventually, in four. He had caught a fever, accompanied by a painfully swollen leg, in crossing the mountains. Kory-Kory was the man assigned to serve and guard him. The "Happy Valley" is the blissfully utopian mountain-valley in Samuel Johnson's *Rasselas* (1759), from which no one who enters can escape.

   After you have made your translation, list ten of Melville's words (or short phrases) that sound odd in modern English, and for which you found modern synonyms. Look up their derivations in your dictionary, and record them in parentheses. Then put down your words and derivations beneath each of Melville's. What can you say about the differences in vocabulary between Melville's American English of the 1840's and yours of the 1970's? What other differences can you see between his passage and yours? What things have remained fairly stable?

Day after day wore on, and still there was no perceptible change in the conduct of the islanders towards me. Gradually I lost all knowledge of the regular occurrence of the days of the week, and sunk insensibly into that kind of apathy which ensues after some violent outbreak of despair. My limb suddenly healed, the swelling went down, the pain subsided, and I had every reason to suppose I should soon completely recover from the affliction that had so long tormented me.

As soon as I was enabled to ramble about the valley in company with the natives, troops of whom followed me whenever I sallied out of the house, I began to experience an elasticity of mind which placed me beyond the reach of those dismal forebodings to which I had so lately been a prey. Received wherever I went with the most deferential kindness; regaled perpetually with the most delightful fruits; ministered to by dark-eyed nymphs; and enjoying besides all the services of the devoted Kory-Kory, I thought that for a sojourn among cannibals, no man could have well made a more agreeable one.

To be sure there were limits set to my wanderings. Toward the sea my progress was barred by an express prohibition of the savages; and after having made two or three ineffectual attempts to reach it, as much to gratify my curiosity as anything else, I gave up the idea. It was in vain to think of reaching it by stealth, since the natives escorted me in numbers wherever I went, and not for one single moment that I can recall to mind was I ever permitted to be alone.

The green and precipitous elevations that stood ranged around the head of the vale where Marheyo's habitation was situated effectually precluded all hope of escape in that quarter, even if I could have stolen away from the thousand eyes of the savages.

But these reflections now seldom obtruded upon me; I gave myself up to the passing hour, and if ever disagreeable thoughts arose in my mind, I drove them away. When I looked around the verdant recess in which I was buried, and gazed up to the summits of the lofty eminence that hemmed me in, I was well disposed to think that I was in the "Happy Valley," and that beyond those heights there was nought but a world of care and anxiety.

As I extended my wanderings in the valley and grew more familiar with the habits of its inmates, I was fain to confess that, despite the disadvantages of his condition, the Polynesian savage, surrounded by all the luxurious provisions of nature, enjoyed an infinitely happier, though certainly a less intellectual existence, than the self-complacent European.

GRAMMAR AS THERAPY

You have already seen, in THE RHETORIC, many of the ills of writing—the ailing thesis that weakens the whole system, the *of*-and-*which* disease, the recurring rashes of wordiness. But many a sentence suffers from ailments more deeply genetic. You can probably tell when a sentence feels bad, especially after your instructor has marked it up. You can, in other words, detect the symptoms, but to work an efficient cure you need also to find the causes and to treat them directly. You need some skill in the old household remedies of grammar.

Learn to trace symptoms back to causes.

Here are fifteen ailing sentences, each with a different kink, or quinsy, which a knowledge of grammar can help you cure. You will see the specific treatments in a moment, but for a first lesson in home therapy, look over these fifteen different symptoms, noting the affected parts (italicized):

The *professor,* as well as the students, *were* glad the course was over.
AILMENT: *Were* does not agree with *professor.*

They study hard, but *you* do not have to work all the time.
AILMENT: *You* does not agree with *They.*

Holden *goes* to New York and *learned* about life.
AILMENT: *Learned* does not agree in tense with *goes.*

As *he looked up,* a *light could be seen* in the window.
AILMENT: The subject has shited awkwardly from *he* to *light,* and the verbal construction from active to passive.

A *citizen* should support the government, but *they* should also be free to criticize it.
AILMENT: *They* does not agree with *citizen.*

Now we knew: *it* was *him.*
AILMENT: *Him* does not agree in case with the subject, *it.*

Let's keep this *between* you and *I.*
AILMENT: *I* cannot be the object of *between.*

The students always elect *whomever is* popular.
AILMENT: *Whomever* cannot be the subject of the verb *is.*

She hated *me leaving* so early.
AILMENT: She hated not *me* but the *leaving.*

Bill told *Fred* that *he* failed the exam.
AILMENT: *He* can mean either *Bill* or *Fred.*

Father felt *badly.*
AILMENT: *Badly* describes *Father's* competence, not his condition.

They *walked leisurely.*
AILMENT: The verb requires an adverb, like *slowly.*

She said *on Tuesday* she *would call.*
AILMENT: The position of *on Tuesday* confuses the times of *saying* and *calling.*

Walking to class, her *book* slipped from her grasp.
AILMENT; *Walking* refers illogically to *book.*

While *playing* the piano, the *dog* sat by me and howled.
AILMENT: Dogs don't play pianos.

With each of these, you sense that something is wrong. And by applying a little common logic you can usually find the dislocated parts. But that each ailment requires a different diagnosis and a different kind of grammatical cure may not be so readily apparent. We first need to understand something of the basic physiology of grammar.

Know the basic parts of speech.

The parts of speech are the elements of the sentence. A grasp of the basic eight—nouns, pronouns, verbs, adjectives, adverbs, prepositions, conjunctions, and interjections—will give you a sense of the whole.

NOUNS. Nouns name something. A *proper noun* names a particular person, place, or thing. A *common noun* names a general class of things; a common noun naming a group as a single unit is a *collective noun*. A phrase or clause functioning as a noun is a *noun phrase* or a *noun clause*. Here are some examples:

> COMMON: **stone, tree, house, girl, artist, nation, democracy**
> PROPER: **George, Cincinnati, Texas, Europe, Declaration of Independence**
> COLLECTIVE: **committee, family, quartet, herd, navy, clergy, kind**
> NOUN PHRASE: *Riding the surf* **takes stamina.**
> NOUN CLAUSE: *What you say* **may depend on** *how you say it.*

PRONOUNS. As their name indicates, pronouns stand "for nouns." The noun a pronoun represents is called its *antecedent*. Pronouns may be classified as follows:

> PERSONAL *(standing for persons):* **I, you, he, she, we, they; me, him, her, us, them; my, his, our, and so on**
> REFLEXIVE *(turning the action back on the doer):* **I hurt** *myself.* **They enjoy** *themselves.*
> INTENSIVE *(emphasizing the doer):* **He** *himself* **said so.**
> RELATIVE *(linking subordinate clauses):* **who, which, that, whose, whomever, whichever, and so on**
> INTERROGATIVE *(beginning a question):* **who, which, what**
> DEMONSTRATIVE *(pointing to things):* **this, that, these, those, such**

INDEFINITE *(standing for indefinite numbers of persons or things):*
  **any, each, few, some, anyone, no one, everyone, somebody,
  and so on**
RECIPROCAL *(plural reflexives):* **each other, one another**

VERBS.   Verbs express actions or states of being.   A verb may
be *transitive,* requiring an object to complete the thought, or *intransitive,* requiring no object for completeness.   Some verbs can function
either transitively or intransitively.   *Linking verbs* link the subject to
a state of being.

TRANSITIVE: **He** *put* **his feet on the chair.   She** *hit* **the ceiling.
  They** *sang* **a sad old song.**
INTRANSITIVE: **He** *smiled.*   **She** *cried.*   **They** *sang* **like birds.**
LINKING: **He** *is* **happy.   She** *feels* **angry.   This** *looks* **bad.**

ADJECTIVES.   Adjectives describe nouns or pronouns.   An *adjectival phrase* or *adjectival clause* functions in a sentence as a single adjective would.

ADJECTIVES: **The** *red* **house faces west.   He was a** *handsome* **devil.
  The** *old haunted* **house was** *empty.*
ADJECTIVAL PHRASE: **He had reached the end** *of the book.*
ADJECTIVAL CLAUSE: **Here is the key** *that unlocks the barn.*

ADVERBS.   Adverbs describe verbs, adjectives, or other adverbs, completing the ideas of *how, how much, when,* and *where.*   An
adverbial phrase or *adverbial clause* functions as a single adverb
would.

ADVERBS: **Though** *slightly* **fat, he runs** *quickly* **and plays** *extremely*
  well.
ADVERBIAL PHRASE: **He left** *after the others.*
ADVERBIAL CLAUSE: **She lost the gloves** *after she left the store.*

PREPOSITIONS.   A preposition links a noun or pronoun to another word in the sentence.   A preposition and its object form a
prepositional phrase.

By **late afternoon, Williams was exhausted.**
He walked *to* **his car and drove** *from* **the field.**

CONJUNCTIONS.   Conjunctions join words, phrases, and clauses. *Coordinating* conjunctions — *and, but, or, yet* — join equals:

> Mary *and* I won easily.
> Near the shore *but* far from home, the bottle floated.
> He was talented, *yet* he failed.

Subordinating conjunctions join minor thoughts to main ones:

> *Since* it was late, they left.
> He worked hard *because* he needed an A.
> They stopped *after* they reached the spring.

INTERJECTIONS.   Interjections interrupt the usual flow of the sentence to emphasize feelings:

> But, *oh,* the difference to me.
> Mr. Dowd, *alas,* has ignored the evidence.
> The consumer will suddenly discover that, *ouch,* his dollar is cut in half.

SENTENCES

Learn to identify the simple subject and its verb.

Grammar conveniently classifies the words in your sentences into parts of speech.   With the natural and logical joining of parts, thought begins.   And the very beginning is the subject and its verb. A noun expresses a meaning, which, when expressed, gathers other meanings to it.   The mere idea of *tree* moves on to include some idea of a verb: *tree is.*   And other subject-verb thoughts are probably not far behind: *tree sways; it drops its leaves.*   With *The poplar tree sways in the wind, dropping yellow leaves on the lawn,* you have a full-grown sentence.   At its heart are *tree* — the simple subject (the subject shorn of all modifiers) — and *sways,* the verb.   All the rest is a filling out, or explaining, of the simple subject and its verb.   You should accustom yourself to locating these two parts in an ailing sentence.   They will help you see how its other parts are behaving — or ought to be behaving. First, find the verb, since that names the action: *sways*. Then ask *who* or *what*. The answer gives you your subject, which, with modifiers cut away, is the simple subject. Having found the heart — *simple subject* plus *verb* — you are well on the way to understanding the rest of your sentence's anatomy.

Know the structure — and modifications — of the simple sentence.

The simple English sentence can take one of three essential forms:

    I. Subject-Verb
   II. Subject-Verb-Object
  III. Subject-Is-Something

These three incorporate the three major kinds of verbs (indicated in brackets):

    I. Subject-Verb *[intransitive]*

        She *smiles.*
        He *laughs* **like a perfect idiot.**
        The tree *sways* **in the wind.**

   II. Subject-Verb *[transitive]*-Object

        Boy *meets* **girl.**
        He *liked* **her minibus.**
        They *cashed* **the check.**

  III. Subject-Is *[linking]*-Something

        The temperature *is* **up.**
        They *are* **here.**
        This *tastes* **salty.**
        The pie *smells* **good.**

Is is the most common link in the last form's equation; but, as you see, a number of other verbs may serve: *taste, smell, feel, look, seem, appear, act, get, grow, turn, become.*

Simple Sentence   Although the structure is simple, the simple sentence may exhibit considerable variation.   It may contain compounds in subject or predicate:

> The *boy and* the *girl,* the *aunt, and* the whole hypocritical *family* smile. [compound subject]
> He *hit* the right note with her *and struck* a full sympathetic chord with her parents. [compound predicate]
> The *president* of the company *and* the *chairman* of the board *stormed and raged.* [compounds in subject and predicate]

Or it may attach modifiers to subject and verb:

> Beautiful beyond imagination, glowing with health, *she* won the contest. [*She* is the subject.]
> He *swam,* unaware of sharks, indifferent to snipers' bullets, as if he were merely racing again in the varsity pool. [*Swam* is the verb.]

Or put the verb before the subject:

> Near the window *stood* a folding *screen.*
> Behind it *was* the *murderer.*
> There *is* your *problem.* [The expletive *there* can never be a subject.]
> It *was* too bad *that he quit.* [*That he quit,* a noun clause, is the subject. Like *There, It* is an expletive introducing the sentence.]

Or use a verbal form for subject:

> *To see* it will be enough.
> *Seeing* it will convince you.

Or omit the subject (*you* implied) in a command or request—an *imperative* sentence:

> Get smart.
> If it is not too much trouble, please punctuate accurately.
> Take, oh take, those lips away.

Two or more simple sentences can combine into a *compound* sentence: *Compound Sentence*

> He drove the car, and she did the talking.
> He liked the scenery, she liked the maps, and they both enjoyed the motels.
> The food was good; the prices were reasonable.
> Either the plan was bad, or the instructions failed.

A simple sentence with one or more subordinate clauses added becomes a *complex* sentence: *Complex Sentence*

> When the weather cleared, they started their vacation.
> Although the weather was fine, although the timing was perfect, although expenses were no problem, their vacation was miserable.
> They returned home as soon as they could.

Two or more simple sentences combined with one or more subordinate clauses become a *compound-complex* sentence: *Compound-Complex Sentence*

> When the weather cleared, they started their vacation; but they returned home as soon as they could.

EXERCISE

1 Treat these ailing sentences. In your cured versions, underline the simple subject of each clause once, and the subject's verb twice. Underline any other changes, and put brackets around subordinate clauses where you find them.

SIMPLE SENTENCES

1. The old and the young, the feeble and the sprightly, joins the dance.
2. John Stevenson liked everything about the old town, her relatives, and she most of all.
3. There is one or two things left to do.

4. Solving several specific problems are good exercise.

5. Ann, as well as her mother, like to sew.

COMPOUND SENTENCES

6. He drives the car, and she, a friendly girl, do the talking.

7. Jim drove the car, and her friends think him crazy.

8. They liked the dinner, but they forget to thank Gertrude and I.

9. Either the bed was too hard, or it is too expensive for one night.

COMPLEX SENTENCES

10. While leaving the stadium, the game was over.

11. Whenever he comes, a party could be expected to begin.

12. Them who gets there first gets the best seats.

13. After all these years, they still envied him succeeding in everything he tried.

14. The old and the young, the feeble and the sprightly, comes when the drum begins to beat.

15. All the people, whoever happened to be in the village, was welcome.

SUBJECTS

Avoid awkward changes of subject in midsentence.

Unnecessary shifts in structure can confuse a sentence's vision and its sense of direction. A needless change in subject may make a sentence appear unsure whether it is coming or going.

FAULTY: As *I* entered the room, *voices* could be heard.
REVISED: As *I* entered the room, *I* could hear voices.

FAULTY: The *audience* was pleased by his performance, and *he* earned a standing ovation.
REVISED: His performance pleased the audience and earned him a standing ovation.

FAULTY: The first *problem* is political, but there are *questions* of economics that are almost entirely involved in the second problem.

REVISED: **The first** *problem* **is political; the second, principally economic.**

FAULTY: *Jim* **rolled up his sleeves, the** *axe* **was raised, and the** *sapling* **came down with four powerful strokes.**

REVISED: *Jim* **rolled up his sleeves, raised the axe, and cut the sapling down with four powerful strokes.**

Avoid illogical shifts in person and number.

Person refers to the form a pronoun and verb take to indicate who is speaking, who is being spoken to, and who is being spoken about:

I am — **first person**
You are — **second person**
He is, they are — **third person**

Person

Number refers to the form a noun or pronoun and verb take to indicate one *(singular)* or more than one *(plural)*. A sentence that shifts illogically in person or number is almost completely unhinged: it cannot distinguish between persons, or it has forgotten how to count.

FAULTY: *They* **have reached an age when** *you* **should know better.**

Number

REVISED: *They* **have reached an age when** *they* **should know better.**

FAULTY: *The reader has* **difficulty in following the argument.** *You get* **lost in qualifications.**

REVISED: *The reader has* **difficulty in following the argument.** *He gets* **lost in qualifications.**

FAULTY: **If** *someone asks* **her a question,** *they get* **a straight answer.**

REVISED: **If** *someone asks* **her a question,** *he gets* **a straight answer.**

FAULTY: **A motion** *picture can improve* **upon a book, but** *they* **usually** *do* **not.**

REVISED: **A motion** *picture can improve* **upon a book, but** *it* **usually** *does* **not.**

EXERCISE

2 Revise the following sentences, correcting the awkward shifts of subject, person, and number.

1. A stitch was dropped, and Barbara sighed.
2. Whenever a stitch was dropped, Barbara would sigh.
3. First he investigated the practical implications, and then the moral implications that were involved were examined.
4. Sam sat down at the counter, catsup was poured on the hamburger, and there was hunger in his face as he ate it.
5. These statistics are impressive, but error is evident in them.
6. The United Nations is not so firmly established that they can enforce international law.
7. One should never assume that they have no faults.
8. A person is overwhelmed by the gardens. Everywhere you look is beauty.
9. The buffalo is far from extinct. Their numbers are actually increasing.
10. People distrust his glibness. One feels they are being taken in by him.

VERBS

Keep your verb and its subject in agreement.

Match singulars with singulars, plurals with plurals. You will have little trouble except when subject and verb are far apart, or when the number of the subject itself is doubtful. (Is *family* singular or plural? What about *none?* —about *neither he nor she?*)

Sidestep the plural constructions that fall between your singular subject and its verb:

FAULTY: The *attention* of the students *wander* out the window.
REVISED: The *attention* of the students *wanders* out the window.

FAULTY: *Revision* **of their views about markets and averages** *are* **mandatory.**

REVISED: *Revision* **of their views about markets and averages** *is* **mandatory.**

FAULTY: **The** *plaster,* **as well as the floors,** *need* **repair.**

REVISED: **The** *plaster,* **as well as the floors,** *needs* **repair.**

Collective nouns *(committee, jury, herd, group, family, kind, quartet)* are single units; give them singular verbs, or plural members:

FAULTY: **Her** *family were* **ready.**

REVISED: **Her** *family was* **ready.**

Collective Nouns

FAULTY: **The** *jury have disagreed* **among themselves.**

REVISED: **The** *members* **of the jury** *have disagreed* **among themselves.**

FAULTY: *These kind* **of muffins** *are* **delicious.**

REVISED: *This kind* **of muffin** *is* **delicious.**

Remember that in clauses introduced by expletive *there* (which can never be a subject though it may look like one), the subject follows the verb and governs its number:

There *is* **only one good** *choice.*

There *are* **several good** *choices.*

"There"   ·

But expletive *it* always takes a singular verb:

It *is* [*was*] **the** *child.*

It *is* [*was*] **the** *children.*

"It"

Watch out for the indefinite pronouns *each, either, neither, anyone, everyone, no one, none, everybody, nobody.* Each of these is (not *are*) singular in idea, yet each flirts with the crowd from which it singles out its idea: each of *these,* either of *them,* none of *them.* They all take singular verbs.

Indefinite Pronouns

FAULTY: *None* **of these men** *are* **failures.**

REVISED: *None* **of these men** *is* **a failure.**

FAULTY: *None* of the class, even those best prepared, *want* the test.

REVISED: *None* of the class, even those best prepared, *wants* the test.

FAULTY: *Everybody* on the committee *are* present.

REVISED: *Everybody* on the committee *is* present.

FAULTY: *Neither* the right nor the left *support* the issue.

REVISED: *Neither* the right nor the left *supports* the issue.

Exception: when one side, or both, of the *either-or* contrast is plural, the verb is plural:

Either the players or the coach *are* bad.
Neither the rights of man nor the needs of the commonwealth *are* relevant to the question.

None of them are is very common. From Shakespeare's time to ours, it has persisted alongside the more precise *none of them is,* which seems to have the edge in careful prose.

When a relative pronoun *(who, which, that)* is the subject of a clause , it takes a singular verb if its antecedent is singular, a plural verb if its antecedent is plural:

Relative Pronouns

The *person* who *tries* cannot fail.
The *people* who *try* cannot fail.

FAULTY: **Phil is one of the best *swimmers* who *has* ever been on the team.**

REVISED: **Phil is one of the best *swimmers* who *have* ever been on the team.**

FAULTY: **Phil is the only *one* of our swimmers who *have* won three gold medals.**

REVISED: **Phil is the only *one* of our swimmers who *has* won three gold medals.**

Don't let a plural noun in the predicate lure you into a plural verb:

FAULTY: **His most faithful rooting *section are* his girl and his family.**

REVISED: **His most faithful rooting *section is* his girl and his family.**

Use the tense that best expresses your idea.

Tense means time (from Latin *tempus*). Using verbs of the right tense means placing the action in the right period of time. Usually, you have no trouble choosing the forms to express simple past, present, and future; but you may have trouble expressing "perfected" forms of past, present, and future—especially when they must appear in the same sentence or paragraph with the simpler forms.

Here, with active and passive examples, are the six principal tenses found in English:

TENSE	ACTIVE VOICE	PASSIVE VOICE
Present	He asks	He is asked
Past	He asked	He was asked
Future	He will ask	He will be asked
Present Perfect	He has asked	He has been asked
Past Perfect	He had asked	He had been asked
Future Perfect	He will have asked	He will have been asked

Each tense has its own virtues for expressing what you want your sentences to say.

Use the *present tense* to express present action:

Present Tense

> **Now she** *knows.* **She** *is leaving.*

Use the present also for habitual action:

> **He** *sees* **her every day.**

or for future action:

> **Classes** *begin* **next Monday.**

or for describing literary events:

> **Hamlet** *finds* **the king praying, but he** *is* **unable to act; he** *lets* **the opportunity slip.**

or for expressing timeless facts:

> **The Greeks knew the world *is* round.**

or for the "historical present":

> **King Alfred *watches* as the spider *mends* her web. He *determines* to rebuild his kingdom.**

But reserve the historical present for such deliberate literary effect. In ordinary narration or exposition, *avoid* this kind of thing:

> **One day I *am watching* television when the phone *rings;* it *is* the police.**

Past Tense   Use the *past tense* for all action before the present:

> **He just *left.***
> **One day I *was watching* television when the phone *rang;* it *was* the police.**

Use the *future tense* for action expected after the present:

Future Tense
> **He *will finish* it next year.**
> **When he *finishes* next year, ... [The present functioning as future]**
> **He *is going to finish* it next year. [The "present progressive" is *going* plus an infinitive, like *to finish,* commonly expresses the future.]**

Present Perfect Tense   Use the *present perfect tense* for action completed ("perfected") but relevant to the present moment:

> **I *have gone* there before.**
> **He *has sung* forty concerts.**
> **She *has driven* there every day.**

Past Perfect Tense   Use the *past perfect tense* to express "the past of the past":

> **When we *arrived* [past], they *had finished* [past perfect].**

Notice that the present perfect (*have* plus past participle) becomes the past perfect (*had* plus past participle) when you step from present to past. Everything moves back one step:

> The flare *signals* that he *has started.*
> The flare *signaled* that he *had started.*

Use the *perfect tense* or the *future perfect tense* to express "the past of the future": *Future Perfect Tense*

> When we *arrive* **[future],** they *will have finished* **[future perfect].**
> You **will have worked** thirty hours by Christmas.
> The flare *will signal* **[future]** that he *has started* **[perfect].**

Avoid unnecessary shifts in tense, voice, and mood.

Inconsistencies in verbal forms will bother your reader, and usually muddle your ideas as well. Choose your tense and stay with it, stepping away only when the thought demands some other tense to make a distinction of time.

> FAULTY: Then Antony *looked up* from the body and *begins* to speak. *Agreement of Tenses*
> REVISED: Then Antony *looked up* from the body and *began* to speak.

> FAULTY: King Alfred *thanks* the peasant, and *went* his way. He *gathered* his men. They *are* overjoyed.
> REVISED: King Alfred *thanks* the peasant, and *goes* his way. He *gathers* his men. They *are* overjoyed.

> FAULTY: While the executives *stayed* in the plant, the strikers *picket* outside.
> REVISED: While the executives *stayed* in the plant, the strikers *picketed* outside.

> FAULTY: Although the government *has stated* its policy **[present perfect],** the people *have* still *been* confused **[present perfect].**
> REVISED: Although the government *has stated* its policy **[present perfect],** the people *are* still confused **[present].**

AWKWARD: We *will have left* [future perfect] by the time they *will have arrived* [future perfect].

REVISED: We *will have left* [future perfect] by the time they *arrive* [present functioning to express future action].

English has only two "voices"—the active and the passive (I *see,* I *am seen*)—of which, as we have seen, the active is by far the more efficient. But whether using active or passive, avoid awkward shifts, especially if they also bring awkward shifts of subject.

Active and Passive

FAULTY: This plan *reduces* taxes and *has been proved* workable in three other cities.

REVISED: This plan *reduces* taxes and *has proved* workable in three other cities.

FAULTY: He *had paid* for the new tires and the new upholstery; and now even the car *was paid for.*

REVISED: He *had paid* for the new tires and new upholstery; and now he *had* even *paid* for the car.

FAULTY: After they *laid out* the pattern, electrical shears *were used* to cut around it.

REVISED: After they *laid out* the pattern, they *cut* around it with electrical shears.

Mood (also called *mode:* "manner") is the attitude of the speaker toward the action his verb names. English has three moods. The *indicative mood* declares a fact or asks a question:

Indicative Mood

This pie *is* good. Susan *baked* it.
Susan *baked* it? *Is* there any left?

The *imperative mood* expresses a command or request:

Imperative Mood

Get out. Please *be* careful. *Take* two aspirin.

The *subjunctive mood* expresses an action or condition not asserted as actual fact. Such conditional, provisional, wishful, suppositional ideas are usually subjoined (*subjunctus,* "yoked under") in subordinate clauses. The form of the verb is often plural, and often in a past-tense form, even though the subject is singular, and the condition is present or future.

> **He looked as if he** *were* **confident.**
> **If I** *were* **you, Miles, I would ask her myself.**
> **If this** *be* **error, and upon me [***be***] proved . . .**
> *Had* **he** *been* **sure, he would have said so.**
> **I demand that he** *make* **restitution.**
> **I move that the nominations** *be closed,* **and that the secretary** *cast* **a unanimous ballot.**

Subjunctive Mood

Avoid awkward or faulty shifts of mood:

> FAULTY: **If I** *was* **you, John, I would speak for myself.**
> REVISED: **If I** *were* **you, John, I would speak for myself.**
>
> FAULTY: **If he** *would have known,* **he never would have said that.**
> REVISED: **If he** *had known,* **he never would have said that.**
> REVISED: *Had* **he** *known,* **he never would have said that.**
>
> FAULTY: **He moved that the club buy the picture, and that the secretary** *shall bill* **the members.**
> REVISED: **He moved that the club buy the picture, and that the secretary** *bill* **the members.**
>
> FAULTY: **You** *should read* **carefully and** *don't miss* **his irony.**
> REVISED: **You** *should read* **carefully** *to avoid missing* **his irony.**
> REVISED: *Read* **carefully, and** *don't miss* **his irony.**

Change in Mood

Master the tenses of the troublesome verbs.

Six short verbs are among the most troublesome in English: *lie, lay; sit, set; rise, raise.* These are six separate verbs, with six separate meanings. Master their meanings and their "principal parts" (present tense, past tense, and past participle—the form used with *has* or *had* in compound verbs), and your sentences will comport themselves comfortably and healthily. Indeed, three of the six suggest the convalescing patient: *lie, sit, rise.* These three are intransitive: they never take an object. The other three function more aggressively, always transitively, always taking an object: *lay, set, raise.*

Now for the meanings, principal parts, and uses of them all.

First, the intransitive verbs, *lie, sit, rise.*

Lie, lay, lain (present, past, past participle) means to recline, or to be at rest.

Intransitive

PRESENT: **The patient** *lies* **quietly asleep.**
The patient *is lying* **quietly asleep.**
PAST: **After the visitors left, the patient** *lay* **quietly asleep.**
The purse *lay* **unnoticed on the chair.**
PAST PARTICIPLE: **He has** *lain,* **quiet and asleep, all afternoon.**

Sit, sat, sat means to assume, or remain in, a sitting position.

PRESENT: **I** *sit* **by the bed.**
A clock *sits* **on the table near the bed.**
PAST: **The patient** *sat* **in the sun today.**
PAST PARTICIPLE: **He had** *sat* **by the window yesterday.**

Rise, rose, risen means to stand up, or to move upward.

PRESENT: **When supply is short, prices** *rise.*
PAST: **To my surprise, he** *rose* **to greet me.**
PAST PARTICIPLE: **To my surprise, he had** *risen* **to greet me.**

Here are the transitive verbs, *lay, set, raise.*

Lay, laid, laid means to place or put something.

Transitive

PRESENT: **He** *lays* **the suitcase on the bed.**
He *is* **already** *laying* **plans for a new life.**
PAST: **Yesterday he** *laid* **new tile in the playroom.**
PAST PARTICIPLE: **By now he has** *laid* **the cornerstone of the new city hall.**

Set, set, set means to place something in position.

PRESENT: **I** *set* **the chair near the window.**
He *sets* **the checkerboard on the table.**
PAST: **He** *set* **the chair near the window.**
PAST PARTICIPLE: **He has** *set* **the checkerboard on the table.**

Don't confuse it with *sit* or *sit down:*

> FAULTY: He *sat* the chair near the window.
> REVISED: He *set* the chair near the window.

> FAULTY: He *set* himself *down* by the entrance.
> REVISED: He *sat* himself *down* by the entrance.

Finally, *raise, raised, raised* usually means to make something move up or grow.

> PRESENT: When supply is short, businessmen *raise* prices.
> PAST: He *raised* his hand in greeting.
> PAST PARTICIPLE: She has *raised* three beautiful children.

Part of the difficulty is that the first five of these six trouble-makers are *irregular verbs* — verbs not forming the past and the past participle by adding the usual *-ed.* Here are some more to watch; learn to control their past and past-participial forms:

arise, arose, arisen
awake, awoke, awaked [but *was awakened*]
bear, bore, borne [But: "She was *born* in 1960."]
beat, beat, beaten
begin, began, begun
bid ("order"), *bade* [pronounced "bad"], *bidden*
burst, burst, burst
drag, dragged, dragged [Not *drag, drug, drug*]
draw, drew, drawn
drink, drank, drunk
fit, fitted [or *fit,* especially intransitively], *fitted*
fling, flung, flung
get, got, got (gotten)
hang ("suspend"), *hung, hung* [But: *hang* ("execute"), *hanged, hanged*]
lead, led, led [Don't let the *lead* in *lead* pencil trick your spelling.]
lend, lent, lent
light, lit (lighted), lit (lighted)
ride, rode, ridden
ring, rang, rung

sew, sewed, sewn (sewed)
shine ("glow"), shone, shone **[Distinct from "polish"** —*shine, shined, shined***]**
show, showed, shown (showed)
shrink, shrank (shrunk), shrunk (shrunken)
sing, sang, sung
sink, sank, sunk
sow, sowed, sown (sowed)
slink, slunk, slunk
spring, sprang, sprung
swim, swam, swum
swing, swung, swung
wake, woke (waked), waked

EXERCISES

3 Treat these troubles, mostly verbal:

1. Conservatism, as well as liberalism, are summonses for change in American life as we now know it.
2. These kind of questions are sheer absurdities.
3. The committee were miles apart.
4. None of these proposals are unworkable.
5. Neither the tweed of his jacket nor the silk of his tie impress us.
6. Neither the question nor the answers seems pertinent to the issue.
7. None of us are perfect.
8. John was the second one of the fifty boys who has volunteered.
9. Each who have come this far have shown real determination.
10. His idea of fine foods are hamburgers and French fries.
11. Doug is the only one of the tall boys who always stand straight.
12. Last year we are warned of higher taxes and getting lower taxes. This year we are promised lower taxes and getting higher taxes. What next year is holding, we can only guess. But sooner or later we are being promised and taxed into disbelief.

4 Clinch your mastery of *lie, lay, sit, set, rise,* and *raise* by writing for each a set of three active sentences: the first using the present tense, the second using the past tense, the third using the past participle.

5 Straighten out the inconsistencies of tense, voice, and mood in this cripple:

> A third principle that industry should recognize was the need for constant appraisal by management of an employee's progress. Management would determine what a person, when he or she would of been hired, were expected by it to achieve; and it then judges whether it now had had that person poorly assigned. They probably know their own limitations, and jobs beyond their capacity are poorly handled by them. But it is not enough that a manager sit down periodically with employees and reviews their performance. The important thing is that the manager understands a person well enough and be articulate enough to make sure the person has become conscious of needs for further development. If the manager will have been sufficiently observant, he might have helped his employees to an accurate evaluation of their own potential.

PRONOUNS AS SUBJECTS AND OBJECTS

Match a pronoun's form to its function.

Unlike nouns, pronouns change form when they change from subject to object. *John* remains *John,* whether on the giving or receiving end of the verb: *John* hits Joe; Joe hits *John.* But the pronoun changes from subjective to objective form: *He* hits Joe; Joe hits *him.* We all know the difference between *who* (subject) and *whom* (object), if only because we are so often uncertain about them. We tend to say, "*Who* did you see," because *who,* though really the object of the verb *see,* comes first—in the slot usually reserved for subjects. "*Whom* did you see" is historically correct. Though *who,* as object, is displacing *whom* in some uses, knowing the distinction will help your writing in tricky constructions. We are also sometimes skittish about "between you and me," which is solidly correct, *me* being the object of the preposition *between.* Pronouns can cause considerable uncertainty—but they need not if you merely remember which forms are subjective and which objective. Here are the pronouns that give trouble:

SUBJECTIVE	OBJECTIVE
I	me
he	him
she	her
we	us
they	them
who	whom
whoever	whomever

Use subjective pronouns for subjective functions.

Compound subjects, like "Bill and I," are a common source of trouble. For an easy way to check whether *I* or *me* (*he* or *him*) is right, drop the "Bill" and see how well the pronoun alone stands as subject of the verb. You would not, for instance, say "Me reported the incident."

Compound
Subject

FAULTY: Bill and *me* signed the petition.
REVISED: Bill and *I* signed the petition.

FAULTY: Sally and *her* rode up front.
REVISED: Sally and *she* rode up front.

FAULTY: *Us* and *them* should have cooperated on this.
REVISED: *We* and *they* should have cooperated on this.

FAULTY: Pierce, Finch, and *myself* have resigned.
REVISED: Pierce, Finch, and *I* have resigned. [Keep *myself* where it belongs, as an intensive (I *myself*) or reflexive (I hurt *myself*), and be unashamed of *me* where it properly fits.]

A *complement* is a word that "complements" or completes the meaning of a verb. *Subjective complements* are words that complete the meaning of a linking verb, like *is,* while referring back to the subject ("Tom is *chairman*"). Pronouns serving as subjective complements must, of course, be subjective in form:

> FAULTY: **This is** *him.*
> REVISED: **This is** *he.*

> FAULTY: **He discovered that it was** *me.*
> REVISED: **He discovered that it was** *I.*

> FAULTY: **It was** *them* **who signed the treaty.**
> REVISED: **It was** *they* **who signed the treaty.**

A pronoun *in apposition* with the subject (that is, positioned near, and meaning the same thing as, the subject), or in apposition with a subjective complement, must also take the subjective form:

> FAULTY: *Us* **students would rather talk then sleep.**
> REVISED: *We* **students would rather talk than sleep.**

> FAULTY: **Both of us—Mike and** *me*—**should have gotten the credit.**
> REVISED: **Both of us—Mike and** *I*—**should have gotten the credit.** [*Mike and I* **are in apposition with the subject,** *Both,* **not with the object of the preposition,** *us.*]

> FAULTY: **They were both to blame—Lord Hervey and** *him.*
> REVISED: **They were both to blame—Lord Hervey and** *he.*

When a pronoun follows *than* or *as,* it must be subjective if it is the subject of an implied verb:

> FAULTY: **She is taller than** *me* **[am].**
> REVISED: **She is taller than** *I* **[am].**

> FAULTY: **You are as bright as** *him* **[is].**
> REVISED: **You are as bright as** *he* **[is].**

> FAULTY: **She loves you as much as** *me* **[love you].**
> REVISED: **She loves you as much as** *I* **[love you].**

> FAULTY: **She loves you better than [she loves]** *he.*
> REVISED: **She loves you better than [she loves]** *him.* [**Here the pronoun is objective, since it is the object of the implied verb.**]

Use objective pronouns for objective functions.

A pronoun functioning as a *direct object, indirect object,* or *object of a preposition* must be objective in form. Compound objects give most of the trouble (again, see if the pronoun would stand by itself):

Compound Object

FAULTY: The mayor complimented Bill and *I.*
REVISED: The mayor complimented Bill and *me.*

FAULTY: She typed the letter for Stuart and *he.*
REVISED: She typed the letter for Stuart and *him.*

FAULTY: Will you have dinner with Mary and *I?*
REVISED: Will you have dinner with Mary and *me?*

FAULTY: Between her and *I,* an understanding grew.
REVISED: Between her and *me,* an understanding grew.

FAULTY: Everyone but Mildred and *she* contributed.
REVISED: Everyone but Mildred and *her* contributed. [*But* is used here as a preposition with the meaning "except."]

FAULTY: The petition was drafted by Nielsen, Wright, and *my-self.*
REVISED: The petition was drafted by Nielsen, Wright, and *me.*

Pronouns in apposition with objects must themselves be objective:

Apposition with Object

FAULTY: The mayor complimented us both—Bill and *I.*
REVISED: The mayor complimented us both—Bill and *me.*

FAULTY: She gave the advice specifically to us—Helen and *I.*
REVISED: She gave the advice specifically to us—Helen and *me.*

FAULTY: Between us—Elaine and *I*—an understanding grew.
REVISED: Between us—Elaine and *me*—an understanding grew.

FAULTY: He would not think of letting *we* girls help him.
REVISED: He would not think of letting *us* girls help him.

Use a subjective pronoun for the subject of a noun clause.

This is one of the trickiest of pronominal problems. When a pronoun is the subject of a noun clause, it will often follow a verb or preposition, and therefore look like an object. But it is the subject, after all, and it must take a subjective form:

FAULTY: **The sergeant asked** *whomever* **did it to step forward.**

REVISED: **The sergeant asked** *whoever* **did it to step forward.**
[*Whoever did it* **is a noun clause functioning as direct object of the verb** *asked.* **But** *whoever* **is the subject of the clause.]**

After Verb

FAULTY: **They promised the medal to** *whomever* **would go.**

REVISED: **They promised the medal to** *whoever* **would go.**
[*Whoever would go* **is a noun clause functioning as object of the preposition** *to.* **But** *whoever* **is the subject of the clause.]**

After Preposition

Similarly, parenthetical remarks like *I think, he says,* and *we believe* often make pronouns seem objects when they are actually subjects:

FAULTY: **Ellen is the girl** *whom* **I think will succeed.**

REVISED: **Ellen is the girl** *who* **I think will succeed.**

Parenthetical Remark

FAULTY: **Jim will vote for** *whomever* **they say is a winner.**

REVISED: **Jim will vote for** *whoever* **they say is a winner.**

The *who* pronouns also match form to function in relative adjectival clauses:

FAULTY: **The man** *whom* **had lied to her came in.**

REVISED: **The man** *who* **had lied to her came in. [***Who* **is the subject of the clause** *who had lied to her.***]**

In Relative Clause

FAULTY: **The man** *who* **she hated came in.**

REVISED: **The man** *whom* **she hated came in. [***Whom* **is the direct object of the verb in the clause** *whom she hated.***]**

BETTER: **The man she hated came in.**

But the *subject of an infinitive — and its complements —* is objective in form:

With Infinitive

FAULTY: **They guessed the author to be** *I.*

REVISED: **They guessed the author to be** *me.*

FAULTY: They will pay *whoever* they find the artist to be.
REVISED: They will pay *whomever* they find the artist to be.

Use the possessive pronoun before a gerund.

Gerunds are verbal forms used as nouns (*hunting, skating, reading, sleeping*). *Participles* look exactly the same, but serve as adjectives.

GERUND: *Hunting* is good exercise.
PARTICIPLE: *Hunting* the southern hills, he came upon an old cabin.

A gerund accompanied by a pronoun often runs into trouble:

FAULTY: She disliked *him* hunting.
REVISED: She disliked *his* hunting.

The object of her dislike is not *him* but *hunting;* hence the possessive pronoun merely modifies the true object, the gerund. Sometimes, however, the choice is not so clear:

They caught *him* cheating on the first exam.
They caught *his* cheating on the first exam.

Here the difference is not one of correctness, since both examples are correct, but of meaning as expressed through grammatical structure. In the first sentence, the object of *caught* is *him,* which is modified by the participle *cheating.* In the second sentence, the object is the gerund *cheating,* which is modified by *his.*

FAULTY: Her father disapproved of *me* dating her.
REVISED: Her father disapproved of *my* dating her.

FAULTY: I am bothered by *him* not asking me out.
REVISED: I am bothered by *his* not asking me out.

FAULTY: He consented to *them* making the trip.
REVISED: He consented to *their* making the trip.

EXERCISE

6 Cure the disabled pronouns:

1. It was him all right.
2. She disliked him whistling the same old tune.
3. They cheered both of us—Andy and I.
4. I admit it was me to whom they first confided.
5. We all three like it—Helen, Ann, and myself.
6. Us sophomores should all sign the petition.
7. Both her and me were elected.
8. He told her and I to leave.
9. They always elect whomever is popular.
10. They choose whoever they like.
11. My mother insists on me buying my own clothes.
12. Everybody thinks us girls should go.
13. Little love is lost between him and I.
14. In the end, it was them who succeeded.
15. The child who he adored finally broke his heart.

PRONOUNS AND THEIR ANTECEDENTS

Keep your antecedents specific, unambiguous, and close at hand.

The antecedent states your pronoun's meaning. If an antecedent is missing, ambiguous, vague, or too far away, the pronoun will suffer from "faulty reference" and throw your sentence into disarray. Here is the malady in its various forms:

FAULTY: **In Texas *they* produce a lot of oil.**   *Missing*
REVISED: ***Texas* produces a lot of oil.**

FAULTY: **My father is a doctor, and *this* is the work I want to do too.**
REVISED: **My father is a doctor, and *medicine* is the profession I want to follow too.**

Ambiguous

FAULTY: Peter told Sam that *he* had played terribly. [Is *he* Pete or Sam?]

REVISED: Pete said that *Sam* had played terribly.

REVISED: To Sam, Pete admitted having played terribly.

FAULTY: Adams told Andrews that *he* could send *him* to London.

REVISED: Adams threatened Andrews with being sent to London.

FAULTY: Paul smashed into a girl's car *who* was visiting his sister.

REVISED: Paul smashed into the car of a *girl* visiting his sister.

FAULTY: He aimed at the tiger's eye, but *it* ran away.

REVISED: He aimed at the eye, but *the tiger* ran away.

FAULTY: Jane Austen saw Emma as a projection of *her* personality.

REVISED: Jane Austen saw Emma as a projection of *her (Jane Austen's)* personality. [Improved, but awkward.]

BETTER: Jane Austen saw *her Emma* as a projection of *her own* personality.

Vague

FAULTY: He is an excellent guitarist. *This* is because he began studying *it* as a child.

REVISED: He is an excellent guitarist because he began taking lessons when a child.

FAULTY: Because Ann had never spoken before an audience, she was afraid of *it.*

REVISED: Because Ann had never spoken before an audience, she was afraid.

FAULTY: He shouted outside the window and pounded on the frame, *which* finally broke the glass.

REVISED: He shouted outside the window and pounded on the frame till he finally broke the glass.

Remote

FAULTY: The mayor's committee reported on the remaining problems of polluted air, poor traffic control, inadequate schools, and rat-infested slums. The mayor was proud of *it.*

REVISED: The mayor's committee reported on the remaining problems of polluted air, congested traffic, inadequate schools, and rat-infested slums. The mayor was proud of *the report.*

FAULTY: The castle was built in 1337. The rooms and furnishings are carefully kept up for the eyes of tourists, and at the entrance stands a coin-fed turnstile. *It* still belongs to the Earl.

REVISED: The castle, which still belongs to the Earl, was built in 1337. The rooms and furnishings are carefully kept up for the eyes of tourists, and at the entrance stands a coin-fed turnstile.

With an indefinite antecedent, use a singular pronoun.

Prominent among the indefinite antecedents are *anybody, anyone, each, either (neither), everybody, everyone, no one, nobody.* Also included are generic nouns like *kind, sort, man, woman,* and *person,* and the collective nouns like *family, jury,* and *clergy.* All of these, collecting plural items under one head, retain a certain misleading plural feeling, which may wrongly tempt you to plural pronouns of reference.

FAULTY: Modern woman is frequently unable to pursue *their* true goals.

REVISED: Modern woman is frequently unable to pursue *her* true goal.

FAULTY: *Everybody* paid for *their* ice cream.

REVISED: *Everybody* paid for *his* ice cream.

FAULTY: *Each* of the students hoped to follow *their* teacher's footsteps.

REVISED: Each of the students hoped to follow *the* teacher's footsteps.

FAULTY: After *everybody* in the crowd had contributed, Stan thanked *him.* [The grammar is correct, but the meaning is wrong.]

REVISED: After *all* the crowd had contributed, Stan thanked *them.*

FAULTY: If the *clergy* dares to face the new philosophy, *they* should declare *themselves.*

REVISED: If the *clergy* dares to face the new philosophy, the *clergy* should declare *itself.*

EXERCISE

7 Strengthen the faulty references:

1. He sent him his high-school pictures.

2. He kicked the child's toy by accident who was visiting.

3. Everyone knows their own best interest.

4. He missed several classes, which in the end defeated him.

5. When industries fail to make plans far enough into the future decades, they often underestimate them.

6. She ended her performance, but it was too late.

7. He opened the bird's cage, and it flew away.

8. My family is always throwing their weight around.

9. Shakespeare has Edgar portray his essential position.

10. These sort of snakes are very deceptive in their coloring.

11. The roofers finished early, after last touches to the trim and shingles, and they had really made it sparkle.

12. She loves swimming especially in the surf, thinking it the best exercise in the world.

13. His article was accepted by *Sport* magazine, for which he acknowledged his gratitude.

14. People should insure themselves against death and accident. These provide for the welfare of their loved ones.

15. There is a sandwich shop by the police station, and we phone them when we get hungry.

16. Coaches sometimes ignore the best interests of their players for the sake of winning games, and they are angry if they lose them because of bad grades, after working them too hard.

17. When he had his last heart attack, it almost stopped beating.

18. A governor should know a little about law and a lot about people, and apply them diplomatically.

MODIFIERS MISUSED AND MISPLACED

Learn the difference between adjectives and adverbs.

Adjectives describe nouns; adverbs describe verbs, adjectives, or other adverbs ("He *very shrewdly* played a *really* conservative game"). But the adjective sometimes wrongly crowds out the adverb ("He played *real* well"). And the adverb sometimes steals the adjective's place, especially when the linking verb looks transitive but isn't *(feels, looks, tastes, smells)*, making the sense wrong. "He feels *badly*" means incompetence, not misery. "It tastes *wonderfully*" means skill in the taster. And certain adjectives ending in -*ly* (*lonely, lovely, leisurely*) tend to masquerade as adverbs:

> WRONG: She swam lovely.
> DOUBTFUL: They walked leisurely.
> WRONG: He brooded lonely.

But notice how quickly you can restore the adjective if you press your words for their meanings:

> She swam, lovely as a swan.
> They walked, leisurely and thoughtful.
> I wandered lonely as a cloud.

Or you can simply assert the adverbial:

> She swam beautifully.
> They strolled slowly.
> He brooded solitarily.

Some words serve both as adjectives and adverbs: *early, late, near, far, only, little, right, wrong, straight, well, better, best, fast,* for example.

> He waited *late* for the *late* train.
> Think *little* of *little* things.
> Go *straight* up the *straight* and narrow path.

Near is both an adverb of place (*near to it, near the barn*) and an adjective *(the near hill, the near future)*; and *near*, the adverb of place, is often confused with *nearly*, the adverb of degree, which means "almost."

> RIGHT: It was *near* Toledo. [adverb of place]
> RIGHT: It was *nearly* perfect. [adverb of degree]

To avoid confusing the two, substitute *almost* or *nearly* for the *near* of degree that tends to slip wrongly into your prose, or convert it into a proper *near* of place, actual or figurative:

> FAULTY: He was near exhausted.
> REVISED: He was nearly exhausted.
> REVISED: He was near exhaustion.
>
> FAULTY: It was a near treasonous statement.
> REVISED: It was a nearly treasonous statement.
>
> FAULTY: We are nowhere near knowledgeable enough.
> REVISED: We are not nearly knowledgeable enough.
>
> FAULTY: With Dodge, he has a tie of near-filial rapport.
> REVISED: With Dodge, he has a nearly filial rapport.
> REVISED: With Dodge, he has an almost filial rapport.

Slow has a long history as an adverb, encouraged by its crisp antithesis to *fast* (and its convenience for street-signs), but *slowly* keeps the upper hand in print. Notice that adverbs usually go after and adjectives before:

> The *slow* freight went *slowly*.

Put your modifiers where their meaning is clear.

Some modifiers seem to look in two directions at once—the so-called "squinting" modifiers. Put them in their proper places. Make clear which way you want them to face.

> AMBIGUOUS: She said on Friday to phone him.
> REVISED: On Friday, she said to phone him.
> REVISED: She said to phone him on Friday.

AMBIGUOUS: They agreed when both sides ceased fire to open negotiations.

REVISED: They agreed to open negotiations when both sides ceased fire.

REVISED: When both sides ceased fire, they agreed to open negotiations.

AMBIGUOUS: Several delegations we know have failed.

REVISED: We know that several delegations have failed.

AMBIGUOUS: They hoped to try thoroughly to understand.

REVISED: They hoped to try to understand thoroughly.

AMBIGUOUS: He resolved to dependably develop plans.

REVISED: He resolved to develop dependable plans. [See "Split infinitives," in "A Glossary of Usage," Section D.]

AMBIGUOUS: Prices moved upward sufficiently to virtually wipe out the loss.

REVISED: Prices rose almost enough to wipe out the loss.

Make your comparisons complete.

Both adjectives and adverbs have "comparative" and "superlative" forms:

ADJECTIVE: green, green*er,* green*est*
ADVERB: smoothly, *more* smoothly, *most* smoothly

All comparatives demand some completion of thought, some answer to the question *than what?* — "Greener than what?"; "More smoothly than what?"

FAULTY: The western plains are flatter.
REVISED: The western plains are flatter than those east of the Mississippi.

FAULTY: He plays more skillfully.
REVISED: He plays more skillfully than most boys his age.

FAULTY: He was as tall if not taller than his sister.
REVISED: He was as tall as his sister, if not taller.

FAULTY: Jane told her more than Ellen.
REVISED: Jane told her more than she told Ellen.

FAULTY: His income is lower than a busboy.
REVISED: His income is lower than a busboy's.

FAULTY: The pack of a paratrooper is lighter than a soldier.
REVISED: A paratrooper's pack is lighter than a soldier's.

Superlatives also need completion:

FAULTY: This is the best painting.
REVISED: This is the best painting in the exhibit.

FAULTY: Here was the prettiest if not the fastest car in the show.
REVISED: Here was the prettiest car in the show, if not the fastest.

EXERCISE

8 Cure the faulty modifiers:

1. They asked after ten days to be notified.
2. We wanted to win enough to cry.
3. Everyone feels badly about it.
4. She sang melancholy.
5. The bidding began quietly and leisurely.
6. The work of a student is more intense than his parents.
7. It was a near perfect shot.
8. Some girls have expectations beyond a husband.
9. The party planned to completely attempt reform.
10. Industry is as strong if not stronger than before the depression.

DANGLING CONSTRUCTIONS

Connect a modifier clearly to what it modifies.

Verbals are those *-ing* words, the gerunds (verbal nouns) and participles (verbal adjectives): *laughing, cooking, concentrating.* The phrases and clauses growing out of these words have a tendency to slip loose from the main sentence and dangle. "Going home, the walk was slippery" indicates that the *walk* was going home. The writer has actually compressed two sentences:

I was going home.
I found the walk slippery.

But the compression has accidentally omitted the true subject altogether, which we can put back, to keep that *Going* from dangling:

Going home, *I found* **the walk slippery.**

Make sure your modifying verbal connects with its true subject:

FAULTY: **When getting out of bed, his toe hit the dresser.**
REVISED: **When getting out of bed, he hit his toe on the dresser.**

Infinitive phrases also can dangle badly:

FAULTY: **To work well, keep your scooter oiled.**
REVISED: **To work well, your scooter needs frequent oiling.**

FAULTY: **To think clearly, some logic is important.**
REVISED: **To think clearly, you should learn some logic.**

Any clause or phrase may dangle:

FAULTY: **When only a freshman, Jim's history teacher inspired him.**
REVISED: **When Jim was only a freshman, his history teacher inspired him.**

FAULTY: **After he had lectured thirty years, the average student still seemed average.**
REVISED: **After he had lectured thirty years, he found the average student still average.**

EXERCISE

9 Mend these dangling constructions:

1. What we need is a file of engineers broken down by their specialties.
2. Following the games on television, the batting average of every player was at his fingertips.
3. When entering the door, the lamp fell over.
4. To study well, a quiet room helps.
5. After he arrived at the dorm, the dean phoned.

THE HEALTHY ENGLISH SENTENCE

If you have been actively speaking and reading and writing these many years since your first step, your prose is probably in good grammatical health. But you do need to exercise to keep it vigorous. Slips in grammar can only distract your reader from what you are saying, and start him thinking, unflatteringly, about you. Keep your mind and your language alert, and you will retain his attention and respect. Keep the parts of your sentence well fitted, your prose active and spare, your meanings clearly working together. Keep trimly to the essential structure of the simple active sentence. Rid yourself of all inconsistencies in tense, voice, and mood. Above all, make your thoughts complete, with every noun and pronoun and verb in proper form, with nothing dangling, and with your meaning unmistakable. Good grammatical prose takes exercise, but nothing can make you feel so thoroughly on top of the world.

EXERCISE

10 Bring these sentences to full health:

1. The only light coming from machine-gun fire and explosions, it is hard for the audience to see whom is hit.

2. The audience, as well as the cast, were glad when they were finished.

3. In 1965, blacks numbered only 14 out of 863 students at the Bronx High School of Science, 23 out of 629 students at Stuyvesant High School, 45 in 368 at the High School of Music and Art, and out of 907 at Brooklyn Technical School you could only find 22.

4. If the Republicans would have checked into the activities that were being done by the Democrats in an honest manner, they would have avoided the mess of Watergate.

5. Either the report is incomplete or deliberately lying to both the public and he personally.

6. Not only did he delight in youth, but he had an almost pathological fear that it was already too late to enjoy it.

7. They study hard here, but you do not have to work all the time.

8. The contest between Louise and I was decided by only the absentee ballots, and they totaled them inaccurately.

9. Walking to the game, it was decided to give the team their due, whether or not it was going to bring us the championship.

10. Speaking before the committee, everything he said damaged his case.

11. Every member of the committee had tried to keep their minds open.

12. He sat his briefcase carefully on the desk, hoping it would not be too late to use the evidence in it, and left it laying there when he answered the phone.

13. She was awakened by a loud knocking, which turned out to be across the hall where they were installing a new floor.

Section C
Punctuation, Spelling, Capitalization

Punctuation gives the silent page some of the breath of life. It marks the pauses and emphases with which a speaker points his meaning. Loose punctuators forget what every good writer knows: that even silent reading produces an articulate murmur in our heads, that language springs from the breathing human voice, that the beauty and meaning of language depend on what the written word makes us *hear*, on the sentence's tuning of emphasis and pause. Commas and semicolons and periods do what they can to transcribe our meaningful pauses to the printed page.

THE PERIOD: SENTENCES AND FRAGMENTS

Learn what a sentence is.

Having used sentences all our lives, we all think we know what one is. But commas still appear where periods should be, and the reader blunders ahead when he should have stopped. Think of a *sentence* as a subject completed in its verb and tacked home with a period.   We rarely mistake a *phrase* for a sentence, since, having no verb, it cries for completion.   But a *clause,* which does have subject and verb, is indeed a complete sentence—unless it looks to the main sentence for fulfillment:

> *After the ball,* **the sweepers come.** [phrase]
> *After the ball is over,* **the sweepers come.** [clause]

Your sentence is complete if the first part clearly looks ahead toward the period, and if the end feels fully completed.

Suppose you wrote a sentence like this:

> **Trying to write well in all his classes.**

It just seems to hang in air, not tied to anything.   Your voice and your meaning do not come down with a sense of completion at the period.   The *Trying* seems to be looking ahead for something to complete its half-formed idea, something like:

> **Trying to write well in all his classes, he made straight A's.**

Or it may be looking back for something it itself is making complete:

> **He made straight A's, trying to write well in all his classes.**

If you find the first part of your sentence looking back, or looking ahead in vain, you have no sentence: you have a fragment that should be hooked, with a comma, to its governing sentence:

> **He dropped his teeth.**   *Which had cost two hundred dollars.*
> **A good example is Hawthorne.**   *A writer who could dramatize abstract moral theories.*
> **Cleopatra is the stronger.**   *Trying to create Antony in her own Egyptian image.*

The accidental fragment is usually found *after* its governing sentence.

But try an occasional rhetorical fragment.

Nothing so firmly demonstrates your command over the sentence as a judicious fragment, as I have already suggested (p. 100).

Make it stand alone, and no mistake. Fragments are safest and most effective, exerting all their transitional force, at the head of a paragraph. Such fragments are especially dramatic, economical, and close to speech:

> **First, a word to the wise.**
> **Another point.**
> **Of course.**
> **Not at all.**
> **Expert within limits, that is.**

Notice that all these fragments — condensations, afterthoughts, answers, quiet exclamations — usually omit some hypothetical form of *is,* with its subject:

> **First, [here is] a word to the wise.**
> **Of course [it is** *or* **he did].**
> **[It is] not at all [so].**

This kind of dramatic fragment, in other words, is talking about existences, about what *is,* letting the words assert their own being — exactly the kind of streamlining the Latin writers liked, and still swift and racy. But be careful.

Beware the comma splice.

This is the beginner's most common error, the exact opposite of the fragment — putting a comma where we need a period, splicing two sentences together with a comma:

> **The comma splice is a common error, it is the exact opposite of**
> **a fragment.**

You can see that you really have two sentences, to be restored as such:

> **The comma splice is a common error. It is the exact opposite**
> **of a fragment.**

Or to be coordinated by adding a conjunction after the comma:

> **The comma splice is a common error, and it is . . . .**

Or to be subordinated by making the second sentence a phrase:

> **The comma splice is a common error, the exact opposite . . . .**

You will accidentally splice with a comma most frequently when adding a thought (a complete short sentence) to a longer sentence:

> **The book describes human evolution in wholly believable terms, comparing the social habits of gorillas and chimpanzees to human behavior, it is very convincing.**

But your reader will be confused by your drift. Which way is that *comparing*–phrase supposed to go? You must help him by repairing your splice with a period, either like this:

> **The book describes human evolution in wholly believable terms, comparing the social habits of gorillas and chimpanzees to human behavior. It is very convincing.**

Or like this:

> **The book describes human evolution in wholly believable terms. Comparing the social habits of gorillas and chimpanzees to human behavior, it is very convincing.**

In short, be sure to attach all accidental fragments–that *comparing* phrase, by itself, would be a fragment–to your main sentence. But be sure each complete sentence–*It is very convincing*–stands clear and alone with its own capital and period.

EXERCISES

1 Write five "sentences," each with a floating, comma-spliced clause in the middle, like the "book" sentence above. Follow each "sentence" with your solution, correcting the splice.

2 Write three groups of three or four sentences, each group containing a *rhetorical* fragment that cannot be mistaken for a mistake.

Use a period after a declarative sentence.

This, of course, is the everyday period, the one ending the sentences and fragments we have been discussing. It ends a declaration and makes it independent. It concludes each thought you complete with subject, verb, and other attachments, even when you only imply both subject and verb, as in the fragment *Of course.* Notice that you may change your declarations to questions and exclamations merely by switching from the declarative period to a question mark or exclamation point: *Of course? Of course!*

Use a period after an indirect question.

The following are not really questions, but declarations of what the question was; hence the period.

> **She asked me when I was going to finish college.**
> **I wonder if you could come tomorrow.**
> **He wanted to know how I found it and why I hadn't told him.**

Use a period after a polite command or request.
Use exclamations sparingly.

The exclamation point shouts a little, and the question mark can grow a little shrill. My page would startle you had I written: "Use a period after a polite command or request!" Similarly, the question mark may seem too insistent: "Will you kindly remit?"

> **But be careful.**
> **Come when you can.**
> **Will you kindly give this matter your earliest attention.**
> **May the council please have your comments at your convenience.**

Use a period in abbreviations.

Use periods after standard abbreviations (Colo., Ave.), and after initials used as abbreviations (A.D., D.C., U.S.A.). This is the rule, but exceptions are many. Use your dictionary to determine accepted forms. Alphabetical titles and acronyms ("tip-names" made from the initials or "tips" of longer titles, as in FCC, NOW, or UNESCO) usually go without periods. Radio and television stations (WQXR-FM, NBC-TV) and tuberculosis (TB) are other common exceptions. MS. and MSS. (manuscript, manuscripts) are curious hybrids. Here are some special problems:

1. An abbreviation at the end of a declarative sentence. End the sentence with the final abbreviating period.

He asked her to mail it C.O.D. [not C.O.D..]

2. An abbreviation at the end of a question or exclamation. Add the question mark or exclamation point after the abbreviating period.

C.O.D.? Yes—but not to Washington, D.C.!

3. An abbreviation inside a sentence. Let the abbreviating period stand as it comes, and add other punctuation as necessary.

All prices are F.O.B. at our nearest warehouse.
I hope my MS., which I mailed Tuesday, reached you in time.
The joy of his life, i.e., his mother-in-law, arrived.

Note that common abbreviations like *i.e., etc., viz.,* and the like, are enclosed in commas, since they are parenthetical remarks. But, except for heavy irony, as with the *i.e.* before *mother-in-law,* your phrase will be smoother if you omit these abbreviations completely, or use *that is, and so on,* and *namely.*

4. Abbreviations like *Mr., Mrs., Ms., Mlle., Mme., Dr., St.* (Saint), *Co.,* and *Ltd.* occur without the period in some British papers and books. Follow U.S. usage, which requires the period. Note that the abbreviation *U.S.* should be used only as an adjective: "U.S. Postal Service," but not "life in the U.S." This should read "life in the United States."

Use periods in designating parts of literary works.

Separate act, scene, and line (or book, chapter, and page, and the like) by intervening periods and *no intervening spaces:* II.iii.22; Sam. xviii.33; *Iliad* IX.93; *Julius Caesar* III.ii.187.

EXERCISES

3 Write five sentences containing indirect questions, ending them properly with periods.

4 Some of the following sentences have correct periods; some run together without punctuation; some fumble the period in various ways. Insert the proper punctuation in the faulty sentences.

1. I have only a faint recollection of the place of my childhood at times, I can close my eyes and call up vague images, but most of the time I just can't remember.

2. Killens's short story deals with Joe, a soldier on his way to Korea.

3. Sitting down in front of the TV set, I kicked off my shoes and loosened my belt, still, I felt very nervous and tense.

4. Two of these packages are headed for Washington, D.C., the third is going to Baltimore.

5. Please climb down you'll hurt yourself.

6. The COD order arrived just after lunch on Thursday afternoon, but since Jim didn't have any money, the driver wouldn't leave the package.

7. The International Brigades, which were formed by Comintern to fight in Spain, were a combination of displaced and dissatisfied people from all over the world, many of the first to join were people forced by Fascist governments to leave Germany and Italy.

8. During the Depression, Wright held a number of jobs he was a hospital orderly, a counselor in a boys club, a newspaper correspondent.

9. In studying the similarities in the courtroom strategies of Boris

Max and Clarence Darrow, one can also find parallels between the characters themselves, their lives, their attitudes.

10. Thank you for your answers to my questionnaire I will be able to use much of your response in my report.

11. Sunday, May 23, at 4:00 PM, there will be a symposium on drug abuse.   Interested students should contact Mr Leach at 764-1425.

12. The law school has reached an all-time high in applications. With 13 applicants for each of its 370 openings.

13. About 1,000 scientists from 25 foreign countries are expected to attend the workshop.   Where 180 papers will be presented.

14. In order to gain a full understanding of any book.   One ought to know something of the life and intellectual background of its author.

15. Shortly after 9 PM, Mrs AK Moore was attacked from behind by a purse-snatcher.

16. People seldom form their own judgment about politics they let others form it for them.

17. Although the lawyer knew that his client was guilty.   He defended him vigorously so that he could gain a reputation for victory, if not for justice.

18. I awoke at midnight, my bones were aching and my back felt as if it were being pricked with electric needles.

19. Modern society is built on the automobile every child looks forward to the time when he can drive.

20. Like space, time is a natural organizer.   Ancient.   And simple.

THE COMMA

You need only four rules to use the comma expertly, and the last two share a single principle.   Use a comma:

  I. Before the coordinator—*and-but-or-nor-yet-still-for*—when joining independent clauses.
 II. Between all terms in a series, *including the last two.*
III. To set off parenthetical openers and afterthoughts.
 IV. Before and after parenthetical insertions (use a *pair* of commas).

RULE I
Use a comma before conjunctions like *and*, *but*, and *for*
when joining independent clauses.

You will often see the comma omitted when your two clauses are short: "He hunted and she fished." But nothing is wrong with "He hunted, and she fished." The comma, in fact, shows the slight pause you make when you say it. If you accustom yourself to this fundamental comma, you will also keep control of your lesser pauses as your phrases grow longer. You will guide your reader clearly. Stick to the rule, and you can't go wrong. And you will improve your sense of control.

Think of the "comma-and" **(, and)** as a unit equivalent to the period. The period, the semicolon, and the "comma-and" **(, and)** all designate independent clauses, but with different emphases:

And

.	**He was tired. He went home.**
;	**He was tired; he went home.**
, and	**He was tired, and he went home.**

If you can just think of the **, and** or the **, but** as a unit, perfectly equivalent to the **.** and the **;** as a buffer between independent clauses, you will have mastered the basic problem in punctuation, the cause of most trouble.

What you need is a firm rule to follow. You may find exceptions — or what seem exceptions until you see the underlying reasons, since good punctuation is based on reason and meaning. Look again at E. B. White's *when* sentence (p. 140):

> **Next morning when the first light came into the sky and the sparrows stirred in the trees, when the cows rattled their chains and the rooster crowed and the early automobiles went whispering along the road, Wilbur awoke . . . .**

White omits several commas before *and*, but the reason is dazzlingly clear. He is regimenting short coordinate clauses under one subordinator, *when*. A comma after *sky*, for instance, would block the *when* from the *sparrows* and throw the clauses out of rank. For reasons of rank, he also omits the "introductory" comma after *Next morning*.

A comma here, since only two other commas control the whole long sentence, would have thrown *Next morning* into sudden prominence, into unjustified equality with the long *when* elements.

Your punctuation, or lack of it, signals your meaning as it comes in, word by word. The "comma-and" **(, and)** tells your reader that a whole new predication is coming; just-plain-**and** tells him to expect only a smaller unit:

He hunted the hills and . . . .

brings an entirely different expectation from:

He hunted the hills, and . . . .

In the first you expect something like *dales,* something parallel to *hills.* In the second you expect another subject and predicate: "and he found . . . ," or "and they were . . . ."

Omitting the comma between independent clauses joined by *and* really makes a false parallel, and the silence of print often encourages the error. When you *say* "hills and dales," you do not pause. When you say ". . . hills, and he found . . . ," you do pause. English invariably expresses this difference in meaning by pausing or not. Modern linguists, who call this pause a "double-bar juncture," have reminded us that commas signify meaning.

The same may be seen with *but, or,* and *yet:*

She was naughty but nice.   *But, or, Yet*
She was naughty, but that is not our business.
Wear your jacket or coat.
Wear your jacket, or you will catch cold.
It was strong yet sweet.
It was strong, yet it was not unpleasant.

Of course, you may use a comma in *all* the examples above if your sense demands it. The contrast set by *but, or,* and *yet* often urges a comma, whether or not full predication follows: "It was strong, yet sweet." Notice that the commas always signal where you would pause in speaking.

The meaningful pause also urges an occasional comma in compound predicates, usually not separated by comma:

He granted the usual permission and walked away.
He granted the usual permission, and walked away.

Both are correct. In the first sentence, however, the granting and walking are perfectly routine, and the temper unruffled. In the second, some kind of emotion has forced a pause, and a comma, after *permission*. Similarly, meaning itself may demand a comma between the two verbs:

He turned and dropped the ball.
He turned, and dropped the ball.

In the first sentence, he turned the ball; in the second, himself. Your **, and** in compound predicates suggests some touch of drama, some meaningful distinction, or afterthought.

You need a comma before *for* and *still* even more urgently. Without the comma, their conjunctive meaning changes; they assume their ordinary roles, *for* as a preposition, *still* as an adjective or adverb:

For. Still

She liked him still . . . . [that is, either *yet* or *quiet!*]
She liked him, still she could not marry him.
She liked him for his money.
She liked him, for a good man is hard to find.

An observation: *for* is the weakest of all the coordinators. Almost a subordinator, it is perilously close to *because*. *For* can seem moronic if cause and effect are fairly obvious: "She liked him, for he was kind." Either make a point of the cause by full subordination—"She liked him *because* he was kind"—or flatter the reader with a semicolon: "She liked him; he was kind." *For* is effective only when the cause is somewhat hard to find: "Blessed are the meek, for they shall inherit the earth."

To summarize the basic point (RULE I): put a comma before the coordinator (*and-but-or-nor-yet-still-for*) when joining independent clauses, and add others necessary for emphasis or clarity.

EXERCISES

5 Write six pairs of sentences, using the six conjunctions *and, but, for, or, yet, still,* on the pattern:

He hunted the hills and . . . .
He hunted the hills, and . . . .

6 Write three pairs of sentences with compound predicates showing how a comma changes verbal meaning, briefly explaining the difference in meaning after each:

He turned and dropped the ball.
He turned, and dropped the ball.

RULE II
Use commas between all terms in a series,
including the last two.

Again, the meaningful pause demands a comma. Items in series are equal, and they silently wait for equal treatment:

words, phrases, or clauses in a series
to hunt, to fish, and to hike
He went home, he went upstairs, and he could remember nothing.
He liked oysters, soup, roast beef, wine, and song.

The linguists' recordings will show a pause between the last two items of a series as well as between any other two: not *wine-and-song,* but *wine,* and *song.* The good punctuator would drop the last comma only if he meant *wine and song* as a unit equivalent to *oysters.* Since the last element will always have some climactic or anticlimactic effect, solemn or humorous, don't blur it into the one preceding. Keep *wine* and *song* separate.

By carefully separating all elements in a series, you keep alive a final distinction long ago lost in the daily press, the distinction Virginia Woolf makes (see page 161): "urbane, polished, brilliant, imploring and commanding him . . . ." *Imploring and commanding* is syntactically equal to each one of the other modifiers in the series. If Woolf customarily omitted the last comma, as she does not, she could not have reached for that double apposition. The muscle would have been dead. These other examples of double apposition will give you an idea of its effectiveness:

Double
Appositive
> They cut out his idea, root and branch.
> He lost all his holdings, houses and lands.
> He loved to tramp the woods, to fish and to hunt.

A comma makes a great deal of difference, of sense and distinction.

But adjectives in series, as distinct from nouns in series, change the game a bit. Notice the difference between the following two strings of adjectives:

Adjectives in
Series
> a good, unexpected, natural rhyme
> a good old battered hat

With adjectives in series, only your sense can guide you. If each seems to modify the noun directly, as in the first example above, use commas. If each seems to modify the total accumulation of adjectives and noun, as with *good* and *old* in the second phrase, do not use commas. Say your phrases aloud, and put your commas in the pauses that distinguish your meaning.

Finally, a special case. Dramatic intensity sometimes allows you to join clauses with commas instead of conjunctions:

Intensity
> She sighed, she cried, she almost died.
> I couldn't do it, I tried, I let them all get away.
> He was great, the tackles had him, the pass was perfect.
> It passed, it triumphed, it was a good bill.
> I came, I saw, I conquered.

The rhetorical intensity of this construction—the Greeks called it *asyndeton*—is obvious. The language is breathless, or grandly emphatic. As Aristotle once said, it is a person trying to say many things at once. The subjects repeat themselves, the verbs overlap, the idea accumulates a climax. By some psychological magic, the clauses of this construction usually come in three's. The comma is its sign. But unless you have a stylistic reason for such a flurry of clauses, go back to the normal comma and conjunction, the semi-colon, or the period.

EXERCISE

7 Write five sentences with concluding double appositives which might look like parts of a simple series but which are not: "He loved to tramp the woods, to hunt and to fish."

RULE III
Set off parenthetical openers and afterthoughts with a comma.

Again, note the preliminary pause that expresses your meaning:

Besides, she hated it.
However, she liked him.
Inside, everything was snug.

Stunned, he opened the telegram.
Thoroughly disgruntled, he left.
Green with envy, she smiled weakly.

For several reasons, they stayed home.
Being of stout heart, he dieted.
A good man at poker, he still failed at bridge.

Although his listeners looked bored, he kept on talking.
Because it never gets cold, they wear few clothes.
If it is not too much trouble, punctuate accurately.

FIRST OBSERVATION. A comma often makes considerable differ-ence in meaning:

Meaning
Affected
> **However she tried, she could not do it.**
> **However, she tried.**
> **However she tried. [??]**

You can usually avoid the danger of forgetting the comma and spoiling the sense by substituting *but* for your initial *however*'s: "But she tried." Put your *however*'s within the sentence between commas: "She tried, however, a little longer."

With afterthoughts, the rule still holds: ordinarily you should set them off with a comma. But close sequences of cause and effect (even in openers) often make the comma optional with *for, because,* and *if,* and occasionally with others.

> **They stayed home for several reasons.**
> **For several reasons they stayed home.**
> **Everything was snug inside.**
> **They wear few clothes because it never gets cold.**
> **Punctuate accurately if you can.**

Emphasis makes the difference. A comma would have damaged none of them (when in doubt, follow the rule); it would merely have changed their rhetoric.

SECOND OBSERVATION. What looks like an introductory phrase or clause may actually be the subject of the sentence *and should take no comma.* A comma can break up a good marriage of subject and verb. The comma in each of these is an interloper, and should be removed:

Clause as
Subject
> **That handsome man in the ascot tie, is the groom.**
> **The idea that you should report every observation, is wrong.**
> **The realization that we must be slightly dishonest to be truly kind, comes to all of us sooner or later.**

If your clause-as-subject is unusually long, or confusing, you may relieve the pressure by inserting some qualifying remark after it, between two commas:

> **The idea that you should report every observation,** *however insignificant,* **is wrong.**

> **The realization that we must be slightly dishonest to be truly kind,** *which is obviously the higher motive,* **comes to all of us sooner or later.**

THIRD OBSERVATION.   Our Rule III will comfortably manage the following kinds of preliminaries, afterthoughts, and additions.

1. When adding a contrasting phrase or clause:

> **Use a fork, not a knife.**
> **He is ten, not eleven.**
> **The more he earns, the less he has.**
> **Take your subject seriously, yourself with a grain of salt.**

2. When streamlining parallel clauses by omitting the repeated idea:

> **Jack would eat no fat; his wife, no lean; the dog, only soup.**
> **The Romans lived in marble halls; the British, in mud huts.**
> **On this side of town you will find green suburbs; on that, nothing but salt flats.**

3. In place of the usual colon or dash, when adding informal explanations:

> **He found what he expected, nothing.**
> **His aim was simple, to win a Volkswagen.**

4. For direct address:

> **Goodbye, Mr. Chips.**
> **John, please come here.**
> **Really, Mary, you should have known.**

5. When adding a conversational question:

> **He really can't win, can he?**
> **You're a fine one, aren't you.**

In the second example, since the voice neither rises nor shouts in this kind of question-as-exclamation, you use a period.

6. When reporting inner thought:

How do they know, he wondered.
She never could leave, she thought.

Notice that these last are the way an author suggests the swiftness and quietness of thought only halfway verbalized. Compare:

"I never could leave," she thought.

Now our heroine is thinking explicitly in words, as if imagining herself speaking aloud.

7. When identifying the speaker in dialogue:

"You never could leave," she said.
He said, "I want to go home," and began to cry.

Note that in dialogue the question and exclamation marks replace the comma:

"What have I done now?" she said.
"Nothing!" he said.

EXERCISES

8 Master *however* by writing two groups of three sentences on the following pattern:

However she tried, she could not do it.
She tried, however, a very long time.
She tried; however, she could not do it.

9 Write three sentences with long clauses as subjects, avoiding the temptation of putting a comma after the clause. Then repeat each of these sentences, but after each subject-clause insert a qualifying remark, between commas, thus setting the subject apart from its verb for clearer distinction.

EXAMPLE: The idea that you should report every observation is wrong.
The idea that you should report every observation, *however insignificant,* is wrong.

RULE IV
Enclose parenthetical insertions — nonrestrictives
— with a pair of commas.

When you cut a sentence in two to insert something necessary, you need to tie off both ends, or your sentence will die on the table:

> **When he packs his bag, however he goes.   [, however,]**
> **The car, an ancient Packard is still running.   [, an ancient Packard,]**
> **April 10, 1980 is agreeable as a date for final payment.   [, 1980,]**
> **John Jones, Jr. is wrong.   [, Jr.,]**

You do not mean that 1980 is agreeable, nor are you telling John Jones that Junior is wrong. As the rule indicates, parenthetical insertions need a *pair* of commas:

> **The case,** *nevertheless,* **was closed.**
> **She will see,** *if she has any sense at all,* **that he is right.**
> **Sam,** *on the other hand,* **may be wrong.**
> **Note,** *for example,* **the excellent brushwork.**
> **John Jones,** *M.D.,* **and Bill Jones,** *Ph.D.,* **doctored the punch to perfection.**
> **He stopped at Kansas City,** *Missouri,* **for two hours.**

The same rule applies, of course, to *nonrestrictive* remarks, phrases, and clauses — all elements simply additive, explanatory, and hence parenthetical:

> **John,** *my friend,* **will do what he can.**   *Nonrestrictive*
> **Andy,** *his project sunk, his hopes shattered,* **was speechless.**
> **The taxes,** *which are reasonable,* **will be paid.**
> **That man,** *who knows,* **is not talking.**

Think of *nonrestrictive* as "nonessential" to your meaning, hence set off by commas. Think of *restrictive* as essential and "restricting" your meaning, hence not set off at all (use *which* for nonrestrictives, *that* for restrictives; see pp. 170–171):

Restrictive

The taxes that are reasonable will be paid.
Southpaws who are superstitious will not pitch on Friday nights.
The man who knows is not talking.

The differences between restrictives and nonrestrictives is one of meaning, and the comma pair signals that meaning. How many grandmothers do I have in the first sentence below (restrictive)? How many in the second (nonrestrictive)?

My grandmother who smokes pot is ninety.
My grandmother, who smokes pot, is ninety.

In the first sentence, I still have two grandmothers, since I am distinguishing one from the other by my restrictive phrase (no commas) as the one with the unconventional habit. In the second sentence, I have but one grandmother about whom I am adding an interesting though nonessential, nonrestrictive detail, within a pair of commas. Read the two aloud, and you will hear the difference in meaning, and how the pauses at the commas signal that difference. Commas are often optional, of course. The difference between a restrictive and a nonrestrictive meaning may sometimes be very slight. For example, you may take our recent bridegroom either way (but not halfway):

That handsome man, in the ascot tie, is the groom. [nonrestrictive]
That handsome man in the ascot tie is the groom. [restrictive]

Your meaning will dictate your choice. But use *pairs* of commas or none at all. Never separate subject and verb, or verb and object, with just one comma.

Some finer points. One comma of a pair enclosing an inserted remark may coincide with, and, in a sense, overlay, a comma "already there":

> **In each box, a bottle was broken.**
> **In each box, however, a bottle was broken.**

> **The team lost, and the school was sick.**
> **The team lost, in spite of all, and the school was sick.**

> **The program will work, but the cost is high.**
> **The program will work, of course, but the cost is high.**

Between the coordinate clauses, however, a semicolon might have been clearer:

> **The team lost, in spite of all; and the school was sick.**
> **The program will work, of course; but the cost is high.**

Beware: *however,* between commas, cannot substitute for *but,* as in the perfectly good sentence: "He wore a hat, *but* it looked terrible." You would be using a comma where a full stop (period or semicolon) should be:

> WRONG:
> **He wore a hat, however, it looked terrible.**   *However*

> RIGHT *(notice the two meanings):*
> **He wore a hat; however, it looked terrible.**
> **He wore a hat, however; it looked terrible.**

But a simple **, but** avoids both the ambiguity of the floating *however* and the ponderosity of anchoring it with a semicolon, fore or aft: "He wore a hat, but it looked terrible."

Another point.   *But* may absorb the first comma of a pair enclosing an introductory remark (although it need not do so):

> **At any rate, he went.**   *But*
> **But, at any rate, he went.**
> **But at any rate, he went.**
> **But [,] if we want another party, we had better clean up.**
> **The party was a success, but [,] if we want another one, we had**
> **better clean up.**

Treat the "he said" and "she said" of dialogue as a regular parenthetical insertion, within commas, and without capitalizing, unless a
new sentence begins.

Dialogue   **"I'm going," he said, "whenever I get up enough nerve."**
            "I'm going," he said. "Whenever I get up enough nerve, I'm
            really going."

And of course you should put the comma *inside* ALL quotation marks:

"He is a nut," she said.
She called him a "nut," and walked away.

EXERCISES

10 Write five pairs of sentences showing the difference between nonrestrictive
and restrictive clauses on the pattern:

The taxes, which are reasonable, will be paid.
The taxes that are reasonable will be paid.

11 Correct the following sentences, inserting commas where needed, re-
moving them where not (and, in a few cases, inserting periods). Some of
the sentences are correct as they stand.

1. This report will discuss the equipment to be used, the procedure
to be followed the data to be obtained and the format for presenting the results.

2. We find however that the greatest expense in renovation will be
for labor not for materials.

3. This book, even after seventy-five years, is still one of the finest
examples of sociological scholarship available and it ought to be
required reading in any elementary sociology course.

4. The French Revolution of 1789 sparked a similar revolution led by
Toussaint L'Ouverture, in Haiti in 1791, and shortly thereafter
the French recognized the freedom of the slaves.

5. Remote sensing devices exploit parts of the electromagnetic spectrum invisible to the eye.

6. Will Sexton a long-time member of the department will become sales manager on July 1, 1977 but until that time he will remain on convalescent leave.

7. Tight money and a scarcity of jobs have given a boost to graduate school applications.

8. He depended for his quotations upon the Bible Shakespeare and Emerson.

9. A faithful sincere friend he remained loyal to his roommate even after the unexpected turn of events.

10. We were delayed by the heavy snow, and therefore did not arrive in time for the lecture.

11. Although few readers of *The Adventures of Huckleberry Finn* recognize it at first the book is really a somber story of treachery murder and brutality.

12. Robert E. Lee was born at Stratford Virginia on January 19 1807.

13. In America said the Chinese lecturer people sing "Home Sweet Home." In China they stay there.

14. Should the estimate be too high I will seek other bids.

15. Printed in London bound in New York and first released in Chicago the book cost so much its sales were very limited.

16. The jobs of these machine operators largely assembly-line workers have become as simple repetitive and mechanical as the functions of the machines themselves.

17. Readers of Joseph Heller's book *Catch-22* a comic novel about World War II seem to react in one of two ways. Either they love the book or they can't stand it, in either case the book seems to arouse their passions.

18. Depressed refusing to face the reality of his situation he killed himself, it was as simple as that.

19. Writing in a popular magazine the critic said that Rex Harrison as Henry Higgins and Wilfrid Hyde-White as Colonel Pickering stole the show.

20. Jill Crabtree, in her article, "Foreign Relations at Home" says that American students are not interested in the foreign students on this campus despite the campaign by the International Center to promote their interest.

THE SEMICOLON

Use the semicolon only where you could also use a period, unless desperate.

The dogmatic formula that heads this section, which I shall loosen up in a moment, has saved many a punctuator from both despair and a reckless fling of semicolons. Confusion comes from the belief that the semicolon is either a weak colon or a strong comma. It is most effective as neither. It is best, as we have seen (p. 138), in pulling together and contrasting two independent clauses that could stand alone as sentences:

> **The dress accents the feminine. The pants suit speaks for freedom.**
> **The dress accents the feminine; the pants suit speaks for freedom.**

This compression and contrast by semicolon can go even farther, allowing us to drop a repeated verb in the second element (note also how the comma marks the omission):

> **Golf demands the best of time and space; tennis demands the best of personal energy.**
> **Golf demands the best ot time and space; tennis, the best of personal energy.**

Used sparingly, the semicolon emphasizes your crucial contrasts; used recklessly, it merely clutters your page. *Never* use it as a colon: its effect is exactly opposite. A colon, as in the preceding sentence, signals the meaning to go ahead; a semicolon, as in this sentence, stops it. The colon is a green light; the semicolon is a stop sign.

Of course, you may occasionally need to unscramble a long line of phrases and clauses, especially those in series and containing internal commas:

> **You should see that the thought is full, the words well cleaned, the points adjusted; and then your sentence will be ready to go.** *Note that the period rule would still guide you here: " . . . adjusted.   And then . . . ."*

> Composition is hard because we often must discover our ideas by writing them out, clarifying them on paper; because we must also find a clear and reasonable order for ideas the mind presents simultaneously; and because we must find, by trial and error, exactly the right words to convey our ideas and our feelings about them.

But the semicolon is better when it pulls related sentences together, replacing the period (or the comma-plus-conjunction) for some unusual emphasis:

> They worked hard; they never thought of failure; they were wholly self-sufficient.

And better still when it pivots a contrast:

> Work when you work; play when you play.
> The semicolon is a stop sign; the colon, a green light.

Notice that the semicolon (like the colon) goes *outside* quotation marks:

> This was no "stitch in time"; it was complete reconstruction.

EXERCISES

12 Write five compound sentences, using a semicolon between two contrasting independent clauses.

13 Write five sentences on the pattern:

The semicolon is a stop sign; the colon, a green light.

14 The following selections include examples of both correct and incorrect semicolons. Insert them where needed; remove them where not. Adjust commas and periods as necessary.

1. The book deals with the folly of war, its stupidity, its cruelty, however, in doing this, the author brings in too many characters, repeats episodes over and over again, and spoils his comedy by pressing too hard.

2. Despite these shortcomings; however the book has remained popular because it is fresh and wacky in its approach.

3. Most men smoked either cigars or pipes, for a long time cigarettes were regarded as unmanly.

4. Most men smokers used either cigars or pipes; most women smokers used cigarettes.

5. Steinbeck's fictional strike in *In Dubious Battle* is not unique, in the 1930's, such strikes were very real indeed.

6. The endowment provides stipends for periods of from six months to a year. The scope of support includes; language, both modern and classical, literature, jurisprudence, philosophy, ancient, historical, and modern, archaeology, history (of Western Europe only) and sociology.

7. Your comments should be specific, pointed, and candid, you should not hold back anything.

8. We need to create a new kind of academic community, one with a spirit of openness, the student must be able to find meaning, coherence, and significance behind the jumble of experiences he gets.

9. Many graduating students are scared to death. The job market hasn't been so tight since the 1930's.

10. The law library will be open from 8 A.M. to 1 A.M., now through December 21; from 8 A.M. to 6 P.M., from December 24 to January 4, and closed Christmas Day and New Year's Day.

11. To let him go unpunished was unthinkable, to punish him, unbearable.

12. In McKay's novel, *Home to Harlem,* Jake's character remains rather constant, however, his friend Ray undergoes a fairly substantial change.

13. Although the story was written in 1933; it shows few of the characteristic marks of the period's popular literature.

14. On the one hand, it is obvious that Mr. Bisko disagrees with the company policy, on the other hand, if he wants to keep his job, he has to put up with it.

15. Probably only 5 percent of the potential jobs for naval architects and marine engineers are actually held by people who are trained for them, in fact, probably 50 percent of these jobs are held by people who aren't college educated or technically trained at all.

THE COLON

Use a colon as a green light, or arrow.

The semicolon, as we have seen, makes a full stop; the colon waves the traffic on through the intersection: "Go right ahead," it says, "and you will find what you are looking for." The colon is like one of those huge arrows that say HERE IT IS after you have been following the signs for half a continent. It emphatically and precisely introduces the clarifying detail, the illustrative example, the itemized series, the formal quotation:

> Pierpont lived for only one thing: money.
> In the end, it was useless: Adams really was too green.
> Now he speaks in the romantic mode: "Hasten, O damsel" (I.ii.24).
> The Lord helps those who help themselves: Jasper helped himself.
> Several things were missing: the silver service, his gold watch, Beth's pearls, and the moonstone.
> The committee considered three things: (1) how to reduce expenditures, (2) how to raise more money, and (3) how to handle Smith's unfortunate laxity.
> The point is precisely this: no one can win.
> He thought not only of home: he thought of grandmother's oatmeal cookies.

Use the colon to introduce quotations.

You naturally introduce long quotations with a colon, indenting them and setting them apart from your own words. Do the same with short quotations within your running text, when they need your sentence but are not part of its grammar:

> We remember Sherman's words: "War is hell."

You may use a comma informally:

> We remember Sherman's words, "War is hell."

When a quotation is an integral part of your sentence, punctuate as necessary, but do not use a colon:

> As Sherman implied, "war is hell" for all concerned.
> We remember, as Sherman said, that "war is hell."

Notice that here you do not capitalize "war," although you would capitalize in the most careful scholarly writing, to preserve exactly all the details of your quotation.

Do not use a colon immediately after a verb, a preposition, or the conjunction *that*, where it would break up grammatical connections:

> WRONG:
> The trouble was: he never listened.
> The trouble was that: he never listened.
> She liked the simple things, like: swimming pools, diamonds, and unadorned mink.
> She was fond of: swimming pools, diamonds, and unadorned mink.

Do not capitalize after a colon, unless what follows is normally capitalized, as with a proper name, a quotation beginning with a capital, a title of a work, or, occasionally, a sequence of several sentences.

> RIGHT:
> All effort is painful: pleasure comes with achievement.
> Again we may say with Churchill: "Never have so many owed so much to so few."
> Rhetorical Devices: The Classical Heritage
> But several major considerations remain: Unending leisure is no blessing for the ordinary mortal. We must be occupied, and yet we cannot forever occupy ourselves. Furthermore,....

I still prefer a period after *remain,* since the colon tends to tie the first two sentences too closely.

EXERCISES

15 Write five sentences using the colon to introduce a complete clarifying "sentence" — that is, write your sentence so that the colon is clearly more meaningful than a period and new capitalization would have been:

In the end, it was useless: he really was too green.
The point is precisely this: no one can win.

16 In the following selections, some colons are right, some wrong, some missing: correct all errors, including misused periods, commas, and semicolons.

1. The music is generally excellent; the tunes are quite good and the singing clear and bright.
2. Ralph Ellison, describing in *Shadow and Act* how he switched his interest from music to literature says; "Writing provided me a growing satisfaction and required, unlike music, no formal study. . . ."
3. There's only one thing we need right now — more time.
4. Remote sensing devices exploit the following parts of the electro-magnetic spectrum; infrared radiation, ultraviolet radiation, gamma rays, and microwaves.
5. We're out here for one reason only, to work with Dr. Ravelli.
6. The semicolon, as we have seen, makes a full stop; the colon waves the traffic on through the intersection, "Go right ahead," it says, "and you will find what you are looking for."
7. For assistance call any of the following staff members, Mr. Beatty, 714-1425; Mr. Greenway, 714-2829; Mr. Brooks, 714-4432.
8. A project may be given a national security classification to pro-vide researchers access to classified information, to facilitate visit-ing classified activities, counseling, and participating in advisory functions; or to allow freer exchange of ideas.
9. There's one thing you can say: the plot is timely.
10. This attitude is caused by two things; first, students in a large university tend to think of themselves as being lost in the crowd: and, second, students tend to view administrators — as adminis-trators sometimes view themselves — as substitute parents.

PARENTHESIS AND DASH

The dash says aloud what the parenthesis whispers. Both enclose interruptions too extravagant for a pair of commas to hold. The dash is the more useful—since whispering tends to annoy—and will remain useful only if not overused. It can serve as a conversational colon. It can set off a concluding phrase—for emphasis. It can bring long introductory matters to focus, as in Freud's sentence on page 156. It can insert a full sentence—a clause is really an incorporated sentence—directly next to a key word. The dash allows you to insert—with a kind of shout!—an occasional exclamation. You may even insert—and who would blame you?—an occasional question. The dash affords a structural complexity with all the tone and alacrity of talk.

With care, you can get much the same power from a parenthesis:

> **Many philosophers have despaired (somewhat unphilosophically) of discovering any certainties whatsoever.**
> **Thus did Innocent III (I shall return to him shortly) inaugurate an age of horrors.**
> **But in such circumstances (see page 34), be cautious.**
> **Delay had doubled the costs (a stitch in time!), so the plans were shelved.**

But dashes seem more generally useful, and here are some special points. When one of a pair of dashes falls where a comma would be, it absorbs the comma:

> **If one wanted to go, he certainly could.**
> **If one wanted to go—whether invited or not—he certainly could.**

Not so with the semicolon:

> **He wanted to go—whether he was invited or not; she had more sense.**

To indicate the dash, type two hyphens (--) flush against the words they separate—not one hyphen between two spaces, nor a hyphen spaced to look exactly like a hyphen.

Put commas and periods *outside* a parenthetical group of words (like this one). (But if you make an entire sentence parenthetical, put the period inside.)

EXERCISE

17 Write four sentences, two containing a phrase or clause within dashes, two containing a phrase or clause within parentheses. Try to make your sentences more elaborate than the following simple models—as different from them as possible, and more interesting.

He wrote a sentence containing a phrase—he could have used a clause—inserted between dashes.

He wrote hastily (he pretended to concentrate) as the boss looked over his shoulder.

BRACKETS

Brackets indicate your own words inserted or substituted within a quotation from someone else: "Byron had already suggested that [they] had killed John Keats." You have substituted "they" for "the gentlemen of the *Quarterly Review*" to suit your own context; you do the same when you interpolate a word of explanation: "Byron had already suggested that the gentlemen of the *Quarterly Review* [especially Croker] had killed John Keats." *Do not use parentheses:* they mark the enclosed words as part of the original quotation. Don't claim innocence because your typewriter lacks brackets. Just leave spaces and draw them in later, or type slant lines and tip them with pencil or with the underscore key:

$$[\cdot \cdot \cdot]$$

In the example below, you are pointing out with a *sic* (Latin for "so" or "thus"), which you should not italicize, that you are reproducing an error exactly as it appears in the text you are quoting:

"On no occassion [sic] could we trust them."

Similarly you may give a correction after reproducing the error:

"On the twenty-fourth [twenty-third] we broke camp."
"In not one instance [actually, Baldwin reports several instances] did our men run under fire."

Use brackets when you need a parenthesis within a parenthesis:

(see Donald Allenberg, *The Future of Television* [New York, 1973], pp. 15–16)

Your instructor will probably put brackets around the wordy parts of your sentences, indicating what you should cut:

In fact, [the reason] he liked it [was] because it was different.

QUOTATION MARKS AND ITALICS

Put quotation marks around quotations that "run directly into your text" (like this), but *not* around quotations set off from the text and indented.   You normally inset poetry, as it stands, without quotation marks:

An aged man is but a paltry thing,
A tattered coat upon a stick, unless
Soul clap its hands and sing . . . .

But if you run it into your text, use quotation marks, with virgules (slants) showing the line-ends: "An aged man is but a paltry thing, / A tattered coat . . . ." (See "Indentation," p. 56–57.) Put periods and commas *inside* quotation marks; put semicolons and colons *outside*:

> Now we understand the full meaning of "give me liberty, or give me death."
> "This strange disease of modern life," in Arnold's words, remains uncured.
> In Greece it was "know thyself"; in America it is "know thy neighbor."
> He left after "Hail to the Chief": he could do nothing more.

Although logic often seems to demand the period or comma outside the quotation marks, convention has put them inside for the sake of appearance, even when the sentence ends in a single quoted word or letter:

> Clara Bow was said to have "It."
> Mark it with "T."

If you have seen the periods and commas outside, you were reading a British book or a freshman's paper (or some of America's little magazines).

If you are quoting a phrase that already contains quotation marks, reduce the original double marks (") to single ones ('):

ORIGINAL	YOUR QUOTATION
Hamlet's "are you honest?" is easily explained.	He writes that "Hamlet's 'are you honest?' is easily explained."

Notice what happens when the quotation within your quotation falls at the end:

A majority of the informants thought *infer* meant "imply."	Kirk reports that "a majority of the informants thought *infer* meant 'imply.'"

And notice that a question mark or exclamation point falls between the single and the double quotation marks at the end of a quotation containing a quotation:

> "Why do they call it 'the Hippocratic oath'?" she asked.
> "Everything can't be 'cool'!" he said.

But heed the following exception:

> "I heard someone say, 'Is anyone home?'" she declared.

Do not use *single* quotation marks for your own stylistic flourishes; use *double* quotation marks or, preferably, none:

> It was indeed an "affair," but the passion was hardly "grand."
> It was indeed an affair, but the passion was hardly grand.
>
> Some "cool" pianists use the twelve-tone scale.

Once you have thus established this slang meaning of *cool,* you may repeat the word without quotation marks. In general, of course, you should favor that slang your style can absorb without quotation marks.

Italics   Do not use quotation marks for calling attention to words as words.   Use italics (an underscore when typing) for the words, quotation marks for their meanings.

> This is taking *tergiversation* too literally.
> The word *struthious* means "like an ostrich."

Similarly, use italics for numbers as numbers and letters as letters:

> He writes a *5* like an *s*.

Titles   Use quotation marks for titles *within* books and magazines: titles of chapters, articles, short stories, songs, and poems; use them also for titles of statues and paintings.   But use italics for titles of books, newspapers, magazines, plays, movies, long poems, ships, trains, and airplanes.

> Poe's description of how he wrote "The Raven" was attacked in the *Atlantic Monthly* [or: the *Atlantic*].
> We saw Michelangelo's "Pietà," a remarkable statue in white marble.
> We took the Santa Fe *Chief* from Chicago to Los Angeles.
> He read all of Frazer's *The Golden Bough.*
> His great-grandfather went down with the *Titanic.*
> She read it in *The New York Times.*

Italicize foreign words and phrases, unless they have been as- *Foreign Words*
similated into English through usage (your dictionary should have a
method for noting the distinction; if not, consult one that has):

> **The statement contained two clichés and one** *non sequitur.*
> **The author of this naïve exposé suffers from an** *idée fixe.*

Use neither quotation marks nor italics for the Bible, for its books or *Sacred Books*
parts (Genesis, Old Testament), for other sacred books (Koran, Tal-
mud, Upanishad), nor for famous documents like the Magna Carta,
the Declaration of Independence, the Communist Manifesto, and the *Documents*
Gettysburg Address.

EXERCISE

18 Give the following sentences the necessary quotation marks and italics
(underlining to indicate italics):

1. Like the farmer in Frost's Mending Wall, some people believe that
   Good fences make good neighbors.
2. Germaine Greer's The Female Eunuch is a book to be remembered, especially in phrases like I'm sick of peering at the world
   through false eyelashes and I'm a woman, not a castrate.
3. Some groovy singers seem stuck in one groove.
4. Cleopatra's Husband, I come! seems out of character.
5. Butterfield finds that Cleopatra's Husband, I come! seems out of
   character.
6. The San Francisco Chronicle called it a goof.
7. For him, the most important letter is I.
8. Their favorite books were Huckleberry Finn, the Bible, especially
   Ecclesiastes, and Henry David Thoreau's Walden.
9. Why does the raven keep crying Nevermore! he asked.
10. She hated what she called excess baggage; she loved the world
    from A to Z.
11. Here see means understand.

ELLIPSIS

1. Use three spaced periods . . . (the ellipsis mark) when you omit something from a quotation. Do *not* use them in your own text in place of a dash, or in mere insouciance.

2. If you omit the end of a sentence, add the period . . . .✔

3. If your omission falls after a completed sentence, add the three ellipsis marks to the period already there.✔ . . .

I have put a check over the periods. Notice the difference in spacing. Note that each placement of the ellipsis means something different.

Here is an uncut passage, followed by a shortened version that shows in succession the three kinds of ellipsis, with the third appearing in two variations.

> To learn a language, learn as thoroughly as possible a few everyday sentences. This will educate your ear for all future pronunciations. It will give you a fundamental grasp of structure. Some of the details of grammar will begin to appear. It will give you confidence. If you go abroad, you can buy a newspaper and find your way back to the hotel.
>
> (1)
>
> To learn a language, learn . . . a few everyday sentences. This
>
> (2)
>
> will educate your ear . . . . It will give you a fundamental grasp
>
> (3)   (3)
>
> of structure. . . . It will give you confidence. . . . you can buy a newspaper and find your way back to the hotel.

The three spaced dots of the ellipsis may fall on either side of other punctuation, to indicate exactly where you have omitted something from the text you are quoting:

With Other Punctuation

> In many instances . . . , our careful words are superfluous.
> In many instances of human crisis, . . . words are superfluous.
> We have the bombs . . . ; it looks as if they have the troops.
> Eighteenth-century prisons were vicious: . . . the people no less than the rats and the fevers.
> Alas, poor Yorick! . . . a fellow of infinite jest.
> In this sonnet, Shakespeare is well aware of the foolishness of self-pity: "And trouble deaf heaven with my bootless cries,/ . . . and curse my fate, ..."

If you omit a line or more of poetry, or a paragraph or more of prose, and *if the omission is significant,* use a whole line of elliptical dots:

> When in disgrace with Fortune and men's eyes,
> I all alone beweep my outcast state,
> And trouble deaf heaven with my bootless cries,
> . . . .
> Yet in these thoughts myself almost despising,
> Haply I think on thee, ...

In Poetry

If the omission had not been significant, the ellipsis would have followed *cries:*

> And trouble deaf heaven with my bootless cries, . . .
> Yet in these thoughts . . . .

Be sure that your omissions do not distort your author's meaning. And remember this: *the shorter your quotation, the better.* A short quotation puts your purpose into sharpest focus for your reader's attention. A long quotation may require you to requote or paraphrase to make your point.

If you begin to quote in the middle of a sentence, place three elliptical dots before the first quoted word:

Mid-Sentence

> . . . whether this august republican Union, founded by some of the wisest statesmen that ever lived, cemented with the blood of some of the purest patriots that ever died, should perish or endure. . . .

But if you quote a full sentence that falls in the middle of a paragraph, omit the initial elliptical dots:

Mid-Paragraph

> We have come to dedicate a portion of that field as a final resting place for those who here gave their lives that that nation might live. It is altogether fitting and proper that we should do this.
> But, in a larger sense . . . .

When you use a short partial quotation within a sentence, you can omit the beginning and ending ellipses:

> Lincoln was determined that the Union, "cemented with the blood of . . . the purest patriots," would not fail.

Use the ellipsis in quoted material only. If you use it in your own text, you will seem to drift which is precisely what it means in a novel: the passage of time, or the drifting of thought. Only most rarely can you work it into expository prose, as in Katherine Anne Porter's description of Sylvia Beach. The ellipsis following the first sentence is a part of the passage (see p. 105):

> . . . her modest entirely incidental vanities, face powder, beauty cream, lipstick. . . .
>   Oh, no. She was not there. And someone had taken away the tiger skin from her bed—narrow as an army cot.

It is dramatic, and risky. You risk seeming affected. I have used it only once in this entire book (p. 7), and I do not recall ever having used it before:

> Even the dog-lovers will be uninterested, convinced they know better than you. But the cat . . . .
>   So it is with any unpopular idea. The more unpopular the viewpoint and the stronger the push against convention, the stronger the thesis and the more energetic the essay.

As I threw the cat in after the dogs to emphasize a point already made, the ellipsis seemed right. But the exception does not overturn the rule: use ellipsis marks in quoted material only.

APOSTROPHE

Add apostrophe-*s* to form the singular possessive:

dog's life	man's world
hour's work	day's end
horse's mouth	Marx's ideas

Even to words already ending in *s:*

Yeats's poems	Charles's crown

Leavis's error	Moses's law
Pericles's Athens	Vassilikos's work

A few plurals also form the possessive by adding *'s:*

children's hour	people's attitudes
women's rights	mice's feet
sheep's bellwether	fish's habits

But most plurals take the apostrophe after the *s* (or *s*-sound) already there:

witches' sabbath	ten cents' worth
citizens' rights	the Joneses' possessions
The Beaux' Stratagem	doctors' fees

I repeat, the rule for making singulars possessive is to add *s*, regardless of length and previous ending. Of course, many people will merely add the apostrophe to names already ending in *s (Dickens' novels, Adams' horse)*. Indeed, we can make possessives of some French names in no other way: *Camus' works, Marivaux' life, Berlioz' Requiem*. And certainly there is colloquial and auditory cause for so handling the longest names, as with *Themistocles' death* and *Aristophanes' wit.*

But *Sis' plans* and *the boss' daughter* are not what we say. With single-syllable names like *Keats* and *Yeats,* we likewise probably say *Keatsus death* and *Yeatsus tower,* justifying *Keats's* and *Yeats's,* though many will prefer *Keats'* and *Yeats'.* Even with long words, I myself find the added *s* an improvement in euphony as well as in sense: *ThemIStoCLESes DEATH, ArisTOPHanESes WIT.* The same is true for *Horace's satires, Catullus's villa, Cummings's style, Dickens's Pip.* The extra *s* makes no mistake, and you may prefer to distinguish Dickens from Dicken and Adams from Adam. If your page grows too thick with doube *s*'s, substitute a few pronouns for the proper names, or rephrase: *the death of Themistocles, the Dickens character, Pip.* *Singular Ending in s*

The apostrophe can help to clarify clusters of nouns: These I have actually seen: *Alistair Jones Renown Combo, the church barbecue chicken sale, the uniform policeman training program, the members charter plane.* And of course, *teachers meeting* and *veterans insurance* *String of Nouns* are so common as to seem almost normal. But an apostrophe chips one more noun out of the block. It makes your meaning one word clearer, marking *teachers'* as a modifier, and distinguishing *teacher* from *teachers*. Inflections are helpful, and the written word needs all the help it can get: *Jones's Renowned, church's barbecued, uniformed policeman's, members' chartered.* Distinguish your modifiers, and keep your possessions.

Don't forget the *'s* in the possessive before a gerund:

> **She objected to Bill's smoking.**
> **The teacher's leaving upset our plans.**
> **He didn't like anyone's working overtime.**

Your *'s* makes clear that she is not objecting to Bill and that "He" is not disliking anyone: the smoking and the working are being disliked.

Compounds   Compound words take the *'s* on the last word only: *mother-in-law's hat, the brothers-in-law's attitude* (all the brothers-in-law have the same attitude), *somebody else's problem, Governor Cass of Michigan's proposal.* Joint ownerships may similarly take the *'s* only on the last word *(Bill and Mary's house),* but *Bill's and Mary's* house is more precise, and preferable.

Pronouns   Possessive pronouns have no apostrophe: *hers, its, theirs, yours, whose, oneself* (but *one's self,* if you are emphasizing the self). Note that *it's* means *it is,* and that *who's* means *who is;* for possession, use *its* and *whose.*

Double   The double possessive uses both an *of* and an *'s: a friend of my*
Possessive   *mother's, a book of the teacher's, a son of the Joneses', an old hat of Mary's.* Note that the double possessive indicates one possession among several of the same kind: mother has several friends; the teacher, several books.

Omissions   Use the apostrophe to indicate omissions: *the Spirit of '76, the Class of '02, can't, won't, don't.* Finally, use the apostrophe when adding a grammatical ending to a number, letter, sign, or abbreviation: *1920's; his 3's look like 8's; p's and q's; he got four A's; too many of's and and's; she X'd each box; K.O.'d in the first round.*

EXERCISES

19 Think up, or collect from observation, five strings of nouns an apostrophe-*s* would help clarify; then clarify each string:

the church barbecue chicken sale
the church's barbecued chicken sale
[They were not cooking the church.]

the sophomore cheesecake rally
the sophomores' cheesecake rally
[The cheesecake was no sophomore.]

20 To strengthen your perception of the possessive before a gerund, write five pairs of sentences on the following pattern, explaining after each pair the difference in meaning:

He didn't like anyone working overtime.
He didn't like anyone's working overtime.

HYPHEN

"*Time* abhors the hyphen," someone once said, and, ever since James Joyce's *hooſirons* and *steelyringing*, modern print has tended to compound the work of time and *Time* by squeezing the hyphens out of compounds. But the unfamiliar compound is hard on the eye, and the hyphens come back in—until another burst of editorial housekeeping.

The oldest and most useful compounds have coalesced from their original two words, first through hyphenation, then into one solid compound. *Housekeeping,* with the *housekeeper,* has scrubbed out the hyphen entirely. But many very common compounds live happily separated: *horse racing, Adam's apple, all right, blood pressure, stock market, girl friend.* And many very common compounds go steadily hyphenated, and go no further: *blue-pencil, clear-cut, deep-freeze, good-bye, mother-in-law.* Check your dictionary.

But one rule remains solid: hyphenate two or more words serving together as an adjective. Unhyphenated words acquire hyphens when moved to an adjectival position:

She teaches in high school.
She is a high-school teacher.

He was sick of olive drab.
He was sick of his olive-drab uniform.

He was well known.
He was a well-known drifter.

His serve is red hot.
He has a red-hot serve.

It was never to be forgotten.
It was a never-to-be-forgotten gesture.

You will have to check the hyphenation of prefixes and suffixes in your dictionary, but you can be sure of hyphenating prefixes to proper names:

anti-Semitism	trans-Russian
post-Crimean War	un-American

Similarly, hyphenate suffixes to single capital initials:

F-sharp	U-turn
I-beam	V-neck
T-shirt	X-ray

Hyphenate *ex-*, meaning former, and *self-* (except *selfhood, selfish, selfless,* and *selfsame* where *self* is the root):

ex-champion	self-reliance
ex-president	self-respect

Hyphenate to distinguish meanings:

co-op from coop	re-collect from recollect
re-cover from recover	re-creation from recreation

Hyphenate to avoid doubling *i*'s and tripling consonants:

anti-intellectual	bell-like
semi-invalid	wall-less

Hyphenate compound words expressing numbers:

twenty-one	**three-fourths**
ninety-nine	**one ten-thousandth**
three hundred twenty-four	**twenty-one forty-fourths**

Use the "suspensive," or hanging, hyphen for hyphenated words in series:

We have ten-, twenty-five-, and fifty-pound sizes.
He still prefers the six- to the eight-cylinder job.

Or, with only two items, you can avoid the truncated look by using a few more words:

He still prefers the six-cylinder job to the eight-cylinder one.

EXERCISE

21 Write five pairs of sentences to show your control of the hyphen:

She teaches in high school.
She is a high-school teacher.

It was never to be forgotten.
It was a never-to-be-forgotten gesture.

NUMBERS

In general, spell out numbers that take no more than two words: *two, twelve, thirty-one, one hundred, five hundred, forty thousand, six billion.* You also spell out numbers with fractions: *sixty-three and two-thirds.* Use numerals for the rest: 101; 1976; 200,000. When a two-word number, like *five hundred,* for example, contrasts with a numeral, make them both numerals: *Even with a short assignment of 500 words, you still have 490 to go.*

Similarly, use numerals in any statistical comparison: *14 as against 19; only 2 in 96; 30% as compared to 28.5%* (with only one figure you spell out "percent": *7½ percent*).

Also use numerals, not words, in dates, times, measurements, money, percentages, and so forth: *April 1, 1984; 6:30* A.M. (but *half-past six*); *3 × 5 cards; 240 by 100 feet; 6'3"* (but *six feet tall*); *$4.99; $2 a ticket* (but *16 cents a bunch*), *20 percent*.

Rephrase sentences beginning with numerals, to give your sentence a clear capital: not "*2305 students enrolled*," but "*About 2305 students enrolled.*" See "Numbers" in the Glossary, p. 494, for a table of Roman numerals.

DIACRITICAL MARKS

Many foreign words, though very common in English, retain their native markings, as in *naïveté*. Diacritical marks occasionally appear on native words, as when a writer wishes to distinguish the *learnèd man* from what he has learned. Here are some specifics:

ö   DIAERESIS (*coöperation, coördinate, naïve, Chloë, Danaë*). Let your dictionary be your guide. Newspapers tend to omit the diaeresis, and some very common doubles go unmarked in the most meticulous print, as with *coordination* in this book, and with *cooperation* and *zoology*. But *coördination, coöperation,* and *zoölogy* are perfectly acceptable. You also use the diaeresis to indicate the umlaut in German words: *über, Fräulein, Götterdämmerung.*

é   ACUTE ACCENT. For certain words borrowed from French. The *é* sounds like the *a* in *hay:*

attaché	fiancé, fiancée
blasé	habitué
café	naïveté
cliché	outré
communiqué	passé
décor	précis
décolleté	protégé, protégée
éclat	résumé
exposé	séance

GRAVE ACCENT. For words from French. The *à* sounds like *è*
a in *ah;* the *è* like the *e* in *bet.*

à la carte	*mise en scène*
à la mode	**Molière**
crème de la crème	*pièce de résistance*

CIRCUMFLEX ACCENT. Also for words from French. The *â* *ô*
sounds like *ah;* the *ê* like the *e* in *bet;* the *ô,* like the *o* in *holes:*

bête noire	*raison d'être*
coup de grâce	**table d'hôte**
papier-mâché	**tête-á-tête**

CEDILLA. For words from French, the *ç* being pronounced *s:* *ç*

aperçu	*garçon*
façade	**Provençal**
français	**soupçon**

TILDE. For Spanish words pronouncing *n* like the *ny* in *canyon:* *ñ*
doña, mañana, señor, vicuña.

VIRGULE

Spare this "little rod" (/), and don't spoil your work with the
legalistic *and/or.* Don't write "bacon and/or eggs"; write "bacon
or eggs, or both." Likewise, don't use it for a hyphen: not "male/
female conflict" but "male-female conflict." Use the virgule when
quoting poetry in your running text: "That time of year thou mayst
in me behold / When yellow leaves, . . ."

SPELLING

The dictionary is your best friend as you face the inevitable
anxieties of spelling, but three underlying principles and some
tricks of the trade can help immeasurably:

PRINCIPLE I. Letters represent sounds: proNUNciation can
help you spell. No one proNOUNcing his words correctly would

make the familiar errors of "similiar" and "enviorment." You can even improve your social standing by learning to say *envIRONment* and *goverNment* and *FebRUary* and *intRAmural*. Simply sound out the letters. Of course, you will need to be wary of some words *not* pronounced as spelled: *Wednesday*, pronounced "Wensday," for instance. But sounding the letters can help your spellings. You can even say "convert*i*ble" and "indel*i*ble" and "plaus*i*ble" without sounding like a fool, and you can silently stress the *able* in words like "prob*able*" and "immov*able*" to remember the difficult distinction between words ending in -*ible*, and -*able*.

Consonants   Consonants reliably represent their sounds. Remember that *c* and *g* go soft before *i* and *e*. Consequently you must add a *k* when extending words like *picnic* and *mimic*—*picnicKing, mimicKing*—to keep them from rhyming with *slicing* or *dicing*. Conversely, you just keep the *e* (where you would normally drop it) when making *peace* into *peacEable* and *change* into *changEable*, to keep the *c* and *g* soft.

Single *s* is pronounced *zh* in words like *vision, occasion, pleasure*. Knowing that *ss* hushes ("sh-h-h") will keep you from errors like *occassion*, which would sound like *passion*.

Vowels   Vowels sound short and light before single consonants: *hat, pet, mit(t), hop, mut(t)*. When you add any vowel (including *y*) the first vowel will say its name: *hate, Pete, mite, hoping, mutable*. Notice how the *a* in -*able* keeps the main vowel saying its name in words like *unmistakable, likable*, and *notable*. Therefore, to keep a vowel short, protect it with a double consonant: *petting, hopping*. This explains the troublesome *rr* in *occuRRence*: a single *r* would make it say *cure* in the middle. *Putting* a golf ball and *putting* something on paper must both use *tt* to keep from being pronounced *pewting*. Compare *stony* with *sonny* and *bony* with *bonny*. The *y* is replacing the *e* in *stone* and *bone*, and the rule is working perfectly. It works in any syllable that is accented: compare *forgeTTable* as against *markeTing, begiNNing* as against *buttoNing*, and *compeLLing* as against *traveLing*.

Likewise, when *full* combines and loses its stress, it also loses an *l*. Note the single and double *l* in *fulFILLment*. Similarly, *SOULful, GRATEful, AWful*—even *SPOONful*.

PRINCIPLE II.   This is the old rule of *i* before *e*, and its famous exceptions.

I before *e*
Except after *c,*
Or when sounded like *a*
As in *neighbor* **and** *weigh.*

It works like a charm (*achieve, believe, receive, conceive*). Note that *c* needs an *e* to make it sound like *s*. Remember also that *leisure* was once pronounced "lay-sure," and *foreign*, "forayn." Memorize these exceptions: *protein, seize, weird, either, sheik, forfeit, counterfeit*. Note that all are pronounced "ee" (with a little crowding) and that the *e* comes first. Then note that another small group goes the opposite way, having a long *i* sound as in German "Heil"; *height, sleight, seismograph, kaleidoscope*. *Financier*, another exception, follows its French origin and its original sound.

PRINCIPLE III. Most big words, following the Latin or French from which they came, spell their sounds letter for letter. Look up the derivations of the words you misspell (note that double *s*, and explain it). You will never again have trouble with *desperate* and *separate* once you discover that the first comes from *de-spero*, "without hope," and that se*PAR*ate divides equals, the PAR values in stocks or golf. Nor with *definite* or *definitive*, once you see the kinship of both with *finite* and *finish*. Derivations can also help you a little with the devilment of *-able* and *-ible*, since, except for a few ringers, the *i* remains from Latin, and the *-ables* are either French (*ami-able*) or Anglo-Saxon copies (*workable*). Knowing origins can help at crucial points: resembl*Ance* comes from Latin *simulAre*, "to copy"; exist*Ence* comes from Latin *existEre*, "to stand forth."

Derivations

The biggest help comes from learning the common Latin prefixes, which, by a process of assimilation (*ad-similis*, "like to like"), account for the double consonants at the first sy*LL*abic joint of so many of our words:

AD- **(toward, to):** *abbreviate* **(shorten down),** *accept* **(grasp to).**
CON- **(with):** *collapse* **(fall with),** *commit* **(send with).**
DIS- **(apart):** *dissect* **(cut apart),** *dissolve* **(loosen apart).**
IN- **(into):** *illuminate* **(shine into),** *illusion* **(playing into).**
IN- **(not):** *illegal* **(not lawful),** *immature* **(not ripe).**
INTER- **(between):** *interrupt* **(break between),** *interrogate* **(ask between).**

OB- (**toward, to**): *occupy* (**take in**), *oppose* (**put to**), *offer* (**carry to**).
SUB- (**under**): *suffer* (**bear under**), *suppose* (**put down**).
SYN- (**"together"—this one is Greek**): *symmetry* (**measuring together**), *syllogism* (**logic together**).

Spelling takes a will, an eye, and an ear. And a dictionary. Keep a list of your favorite enemies. Memorize one or two a day. Write them in the air in longhand. Visualize them. Imagine a blinking neon sign, with the wicked letters red and tall — d e f i n I t e — d e f i n I t e. Then print them once, write them twice, and blink them a few times more as you go to sleep. But best of all, make up whatever devices you can — the crazier the better — to remember the tricky parts:

DANCE attenDANCE.
EXISTENCE is TENSE.
There's IRON in this enVIRONment.
The resisTANCE took its STANCE.
There's an ANT on the defendANT.
LOOSE as a goose.

LOSE loses an o.
ALLOT isn't A LOT.
Already isn't ALL RIGHT.
I for gaIety.
The LL in paraLLel gives me *el.*
PURr in PURsuit.

When an unaccented syllable leads to misspelling, you can also get some help by trying to remember a version of the word that accents the troublesome syllable:

academy — acaDEMic
affirmative — affirMAtion
angel — anGELic
apology — apoLOgia
comparable — comPARE
competition — comPETE
definitely — defiNItion
degradation — deGRADE
democracy — demoCRAT
despair — DESperate
dormitory — dorMIR
extravagant — extravaGANza
fantasy — fanTAStic
fertile — ferTILity
hypocrisy — hypoCRItical
imaginative — imagiNAtion

irritable — irriTATE
laboratory — laBORious
liberal — libeRATE
magnet — magNETic
medicine — meDICinal
melody — meLOdious
personal — personALity
preparation — prePARE
prevalent — preVAIL
ridicule — riDICulous
repetition — rePEAT
reservoir — reSERVE
residence — resiDENtial
restoration — reSTORE
Sabbath — sabBATical
vigilance — vigiLANtes

Here are most of the perpetual headaches:*

- **accept, except**—you *accept* criticism, *except* from busybodies.

  accommodate—frequently misspelled *accomodate.*

  acknowledgment, judgment—don't add an extra *e.*

- **advice, advise**—you give *advice* when you *advise.*

  adviser, advisor—used interchangeably, with *adviser* preferred.

- **affect, effect**—you *affect* a British accent, and the *effect* is ridiculous.

- **allusion, illusion, disillusion**—an *allusion* refers to something; an *illusion* is unreal.

  analysis, analyzing, annual—watch the *n*'s and that *z.*

  apologize—frequently misspelled *apollogize, appologize.*

  argument—frequently misspelled *arguement.*

  athlete, athletics—often misspelled *athelete, atheletics.* Athletics is singular.

  balance—frequently misspelled *ballance*: think of that *l* balancing an *a* on each side.

  balloon—frequently misspelled *baloon.*

  beginning—frequently misspelled *begining,* which would rhyme with *shining.*

  businessman, businesswoman—frequently misspelled *businesman, busineswoman.*

- **capital, capitol**—every *capital is –al,* except in Washington, D.C.

  careful—frequently misspelled *carefull,* and even *carfull.*

  challenge—frequently misspelled *challange.* Remember *revenge.*

- **cite, site, sight**—you *cite* an authority and build a house on a *site.*

  committee—frequently misspelled *commitee* or *comittee.* Think of double *m*'s and *t*'s. Perhaps thinking *double m-t empty* will help.

- **complement, compliment**—*complement* completes; *compliment* flatters.

- **council, counsel, consul**—a *council* governs as a group; a *counsel* advises as a person; a *consul* is a foreign diplomat.

  curriculum, career—watch the *r*'s.

---

*The entries marked by ● indicate confusion in meaning as well as spelling, and are treated more fully in the Glossary of Usage, Mechanics, and Common Errors, pages 459–514.

dealt—often misspelled as it sounds: *delt*. Remember *deal*.

decide, divide, devices—watch the *i*'s and *e*'s.

defendant—frequency misspelled *defendent*. A person is usually an *ant*.

definite—frequently misspelled *definate*. Remember *finIte, finIsh, infinIty*.

● **desert, dessert**—the first is sand; the second ice cream.

despair—often misspelled *dispair*, or *despare*.

desperate, separate—one of the most common tangles in spelling. Remember what *desperate* means at the root: *de* (without)-*sperare* (hope). For *separate*, usually misspelled *seperate* on the pattern of *desperate*, remember the *par*, or equal, in golf. You sePARate equals.

detrimental—frequently misspelled *detramental*.

● **dilemma, condemn**—*dilemma* frequently, and wrongly, takes on the ending of *condemn: dilemna*.

disastrous—frequently misspelled *disasterous*, after *disaster*.

disillusion—not *disallusion*. See *allusion*.

dissatisfied—frequently misspelled *disatisfied*. Think of *satisfied* and *dis-satisfied*.

dissolve—not *disolve*, but *dis-solve*, "to loosen apart."

divide—not *devide*. Remember the Latin *dis*, and *di*, for "apart."

embarrassment—commonly misspelled by forgetting one of the *r*'s or *s*'s. Spelling it em*barass*ment is an *embarrassment*.

● **eminent, imminent, immanent**—*eminent* is prominent; *imminent* is soon forthcoming; *immanent* is indwelling.

exaggerate—frequently misspelled *exagerate*.

existence—often misspelled *existance* or *existense*.

explanation—*explain* often induces the misspelling *explaination*.

● **faze, phase**—watch the *s* and the *z*.

● **forward, foreword**—*forward* is a direction; *foreword* is a "word before," a preface.

fulfill, fulfillment—often misspelled *fullfil, fullfilment*, or with double *ll*'s all around.

genius, ingenious—*genius* is supreme talent; *ingenious* is inventive.

harassment—often misspelled *harrasment.*

height—frequently misspelled *heighth.* Think of EIGHT.

hypocrisy—frequently misspelled *hypocracy,* like *democracy.* Remember *hypocrIte, hypocrItical.*

irritable—not *iritable,* nor *irritible.* Remember *irrit*ATE.

lead, led—*led* is often misspelled *lead,* after the *lead* in pencils and pipes.

lonely, loneliness—often misspelled *lonly, lonliness,* which would sound like a *lawn.* Remember *alone* and *loner.*

● **loose, lose**—with a *loose* grip, you *lose* the ball.

misspell—frequently misspelled *mispell.* Think of the meaning: *misspell.*

Negroes, heroes, tomatoes—remember the *e.*

obstacle—frequently misspelled *obsticle.*

occurred, occurring—frequently misspelled by omitting the second *r,* which you need to keep the *u*-syllable from sounding like *cure,* or *your.*

operate (opus, opera)—frequently misspelled *opperate.* Think of OPERA.

possession—frequently misspelled *posession* or *possesion.*

primitive—often misspelled *primative.* That a primate is either an ape or a bishop confuses the issue a bit, since both *primitive* and *primate* derive from Latin *primus,* "first."

● **principal, principle**—the first heads a school; the second is a natural or moral law.

● **proceed, precede, procedure**— the *e*'s are tricky.

pronunciation—frequently misspelled *pro*NOUN*ciation,* after *pronounce.* Remember *e*NUN*ciation,* how one speaks his words.

pursue—frequently misspelled *persue,* aided by the idea of "through" in *per.*

questionnaire—misspelled *questionaire.* Its French form, complete with two *nn*'s and an *e,* shows that it is a recent borrowing.

renown—frequently misspelled *reknown* or *renoun*. Remind yourself that you do not mean "to be *known again*" nor "to replace *nouns*."

resistance—frequently misspelled *resistence*, on the pattern of *existence*. Remember, take a STANCE for resisTANCE.

separate—frequently misspelled *seperate*. Remember PAR, and the idea of sePARating equals. See *desperate*.

similar—frequently misspelled *similiar*, on the pattern of *familiar*. Avoid the LIAR.

successful—frequently misspelled *sucessful*.

suppressed—often misspelled *supressed*.

● **till, until**—watch the *l*'s.

truly—frequently misspelled *truely*.

unnoticed—frequently misspelled *unoticed*. Remember *un-noticed*.

EXERCISE

22 To help you identify your likely errors, here are some sentences with a number of commonly misspelled words. Correct each misspelling you find. Then list the five words that give you the most trouble.

1. Marrage seems to be loosing some of it's traditional signifigance as the devorce rate continues to climb and common-law relationships multiply.
2. Writting is neccessary in almost any proffession.
3. Many women feel there achievements go unrecognized.
4. Offering an explaination is uneccessary unless the personal director asks for one.
5. Certainly one of the most contraversial issues to come along in years, abortion reform has sparked heated arguements in most churches.

6. The proffessor said he would reccomend at least 3 possable sources.

7. I value your opinion.

8. He had a good sence of rythm but a terrible ear for pitch.

9. The preformance last night was embarassing, a suprise considerring the ammount of rehersal time the actors had.

10. Environmental deterioration is probobly the single most disasterous consequence of overcrowding.

11. The wittness was able to supply a good discription.

12. Ammong the words on this page, your likely to find at least a few you commonly mispell.

13. There is really no point in studing the definations of words unless at the same time you make an effort to incorperate them into your speech.

14. Students who have transfered from other schools will recieve credit only for those courses in which their grades were above C.

15. The audiance wasn't conscience that anything unusual had occured, but during the third act the leading man broke his collarbone when he was topled back over the couch in the fight scene.

16. The principle reason for the written examinition is that it allows us to spot canidates who's work isn't likely to meet company standards.

17. The city counsel studied each of the items on the agenda seperately and in it's proper sequence.

18. George gets embarrassed whenever anyone pays him a complement.

19. The committee voted to except the treasurer's annual report, but decided to delay any final judgement on the new buget till after all the members had time to anilize the implications of the previous year's figures.

20. The sucessful businessman usually combines aggressiveness with caution; he is willing to take risks but carefull to minimize those risks as much as possible.

21. There's no point in exagerating the significants of Saturday's loss.

22. Heros are often apologetic about their accomplishments.

23. The curriculum has changed remarkably during the passed 20 years.

24. He may be ingenius but he's certainly no genius.

25. To divide is to seperate.

26. One of the curious side-affects of long contact with DDT seems to be an increased resistance to cancer.

27. Primative versions of the television reciever had tiny screens, barely 4 inches accross.

28. Children often become irratable in the late afternoon.

29. The acknoledgements and the forward precede the table of contents.

30. The Secretery sited the current drop in interest rates as an encouraging sign.

CAPITALIZATION

You know about sentences and names, certainly; but the following points are troublesome.   Capitalize:

1. Names of races, languages, and religions — Negro, Caucasian, Mongolian, Protestant, Jewish, Christian, Roman Catholic, Indian, French, English.   But "blacks and whites in this neighborhood," "black entrepreneurs," "white storekeepers" — especially in phrases that contrast blacks and whites, since *white* is never capitalized.

2. North, south, east, and west *only when they are regions* — the mysterious East, the new Southwest — or parts of proper nouns: the West Side, East Lansing.

3. The *complete* names of churches, rivers, hotels, and the like — the First Baptist Church, the Mark Hopkins Hotel, the Suwannee River (not First Baptist church, Mark Hopkins hotel, Suwannee river).

4. All words in titles, except prepositions, articles, and conjunctions.   But capitalize even these if they come first or last, or if they are longer than five letters — "I'm Through with Love," *Gone with the Wind,* "I'll Stand By," *In Darkest Africa.*   Capitalize nouns, adjectives, and prefixes in hyphenated compounds — *The Eighteenth-Century Background, The Anti-Idealist* (but *The Antislavery Move-*

ment). But the names of numbered streets, and the written-out numbers on your checks are *not* capitalized after the hyphen: *Forty-second Street. Fifty-four . . . Dollars.* When referring to magazines, newspapers, and reference works in sentences, you may drop *The* as part of the title—the *Saturday Evening Post,* the *Kansas City Star,* the *Encyclopaedia Britannica.* (In footnotes and bibliographies, you may either include or omit *The* when citing magazines, newspapers, or reference works; omission is prevalent.)

5. References to a specific section of a work—the Index, his Preface, Chapter 1, Volume IV, Act II, but "scene iii" is usually not capitalized because its numerals are also in lower case.

6. Abstract nouns, when you want emphasis, serious or humorous—". . . the truths contradict, so what is Truth?"; Very Important Person; the Ideal.

Do not capitalize the seasons—spring, winter, midsummer.
Do not capitalize after a colon, unless what follows is normally capitalized (see p. 428).

EXERCISE

23 Capitalize the following, where necessary:

go west, young man.
the east side of town
frost wrote mending wall.
east side, west side
the tall black spoke french.
she loved the spring.
health within seconds (book)
clear through life in time (book)

the methodist episcopal church
the missouri river
my christian name begins with *c.*
the new york public library
the neo-positivistic approach (book)
the st. louis post-dispatch (add italics)
twenty-five dollars (on a check)
33 thirty-third street

Section D
Usage

Speech keeps a daily pressure on writing, and writing returns the compliment, exacting sense from new twists in the spoken language and keeping old senses straight.   Usage, generally, is "the way they say it."   Usage is the current in the living stream of language; it keeps us afloat, it keeps us fresh—as it sweeps us along.   But to distinguish yourself as a writer, you must always battle it, must always swim upstream.   You may say, "Hooja-eatwith?"; but you will write: "With whom did they compare themselves? With the best, with whoever seemed admirable."   Usage is, primarily, talk; and talk year by year gives words differing social approval, and differing meanings.   Words move from the gutter to the penthouse, and back down the elevator shaft.   *Bull,* a four-letter Anglo-Saxon word, was unmentionable in Victorian circles.   One had to use *he-cow,* if at all. Phrases and syntactical patterns also have their fashions, mostly bad. *Like unto me* changes to *like me* to *like I do; this type of thing* becomes *this type thing; -wise,* after centuries of dormancy in only a few words (*likewise, clockwise, otherwise*), suddenly sprouts out the end of everything: *budgetwise, personalitywise, beautywise, prestigewise.*   Suddenly, everyone is saying *hopefully*. As usual, the marketplace changes more than your money.

But the written language has always refined the language of the marketplace. The Attic Greek of Plato and Aristotle (as Aristotle's remarks about local usages show) was distilled from commercial exchange. Cicero and Catullus and Horace polished their currency against the archaic and the Greek. Mallarmé claimed that Poe had given *un sens plus pur aux mots de la tribu*—which Eliot rephrases for himself: "to purify the dialect of the tribe." It is the very nature of writing so to do; it is the writer's illusion that he has done so:

> **I have laboured to refine our language to grammatical purity, and to clear it from colloquial barbarisms, licentious idioms, and irregular combinations. Something, perhaps, I have added to the elegance of its construction, and something to the harmony of its cadence.**

—wrote Samuel Johnson in 1752 as he closed his *Rambler* papers. And he had almost done what he hoped. He was to shape English writing for the next hundred and fifty years, until it was ready for another dip in the stream and another purification. His work, moreover, lasts. We would not imitate it now; but we can read it with pleasure, and imitate its enduring drive for excellence.

Johnson goes on to say that he has "rarely admitted any word not authorized by former writers." Writers provide the second level of usage, the paper money. But even this usage requires principle. If we accept "what the best writers use," we still cannot tell whether it is sound: we may be aping their bad habits. Usage is only a court of first appeal, where we can say little more than "He said it." Beyond that helpless litigation, we can test our writing by reason, and by simple principles: clarity is good, economy is good, ease is good, gracefulness is good, fullness is good, forcefulness is good. As with all predicaments on earth, we judge by appeal to principles, and we often find principles in conflict. Is it economical but unclear? Is it full but cumbersome? Is it clear but too colloquial for grace? Careful judgment will give the ruling.

Which is right, "I feel *bad*" or "I feel *badly*"? "The dress looks *good* on her" or "The dress looks *well* on her"? The man on the street would say, "I feel *bad*" and "The dress looks *good*," and he would be right: because *badly* would indicate shaky fingers and *well* a dress with good eyes. "Tie it tight" means "Tie it so that it is tight." Unfortunately, people trying to be proper follow the pattern of "He writes badly" and fall into the errors of "I feel badly" and "Tie it tightly." But *writes badly* is a verb with an adverb telling how the action is done, and *feel bad* is a verb with a predicate adjective modifying the subject and telling how the subject *is*. The predicate adjective describes existences, as in *ring true* and *come thick*: "they ring, and they are true"; "they come, and they are thick." So it is with other verbs pointing to states of being—*seem, appear, become, grow, sound, smell, taste*—on which "good usage" might rule the wrong way. English simply has an unresolved problem between usage and logic: *he doesn't feel well* says that his feelers are faulty but means that his health is hurting him. Just remember that you don't say "I feel goodly," and let reason be your guide.

Likewise with *the reason . . . is because*. You can find this colloquial redundancy on many a distinguished page. But everything a good writer writes is not necessarily good. The phrase is a collision between two choices, as the mind rushes after its meaning: between (1) *the reason is that . . .* and (2) *it is . . . because*. Delete *the reason . . . is,* the colloquial pump primer, and you save three words, sometimes four (the following eminent sentence, in which I have bracketed the surplus words, also suffers some redundancy of the *be*'s):

> In general it may be said that [the reason why] scholasticism was held to be an obstacle to truth [was] because it seemed to discourage further inquiry along experimental lines.

And so, usage is perhaps where we begin; but if we end there, we may end in wordiness and mediocrity. Clarity and economy are better guides than mere usage. The following prescriptions are just about what the doctor ordered to keep you ticking, and in good company. They summarize the practices of the most careful writers —those who constantly attend to what words mean. They provide tips on avoiding wordiness, and avoiding those slips in diction that sometimes turn your reception a little chilly. I have also included comments on common problems with things like spelling, hyphenation, numerals, and contractions, and on other informational things like "Irony" and "Letter Writing," to supplement discussions in the text.

GLOSSARY OF USAGE, MECHANICS, AND COMMON ERRORS

A, an. Use *a* before *h* sounded in a first syllable: *a hospital, a hamburger.* Use *an* before a silent *h: an honor, an heir, an hour.*

Abbreviations. Use only those conventional abbreviations your reader can easily recognize: *Dr., Mr., Mrs., Ms., Messrs.* (for two or more men, pronounced "messers," as in *Messrs. Adams, Pruitt, and Williams*), *Jr., St., Esq.* (Esquire, following a British gentleman's name, between commas and with *Mr.* omitted), *S.J.* (Society of Jesus, also following a name). All take periods. College degrees are equally recognizable: *A.B., M.A., Ph.D., D. Litt., M.D., LL.D.* Similarly, dates and times: B.C., A.D., A.M., P.M. Though these are conventionally printed as small capitals, regular capitals in your classroom papers are perfectly acceptable. Write them without commas: *2000 B.C. was Smith's estimate.* A number of familiar abbreviations go without periods: *TV, FBI, USSR, USA, YMCA,* though periods are perfectly OK or O.K. *U.N.* and *U.S. delegation* are customary. Note that *U.S.* serves only as an adjective; write out *the United States,* serving as a noun. Certain scientific phrases also go without periods, especially when combined with figures: *55 mph, 300 rpm, 4000 kwh.*

Abbreviations conventional in running prose, unitalicized, are "e.g." (*exempli gratia,* "for example"), "i.e." (*id est,* "that is"), "etc." (*et cetera,* better written out "and so forth") and "viz." (*videlicet,* pronounced "vi-DEL-uh-sit," meaning "that is," "namely"). These are followed by either commas or colons after the period:

The commission discovered three frequent errors in management, i.e., failure to take appropriate inventories, erroneous accounting, and inattention to costs.

> The semester included some outstanding extracurricular pro-
> grams, e.g.: a series of lectures on civil rights, three concerts,
> and a superb performance of *Oedipus Rex.*

The abbreviation *vs.,* usually italicized, is best spelled out,
unitalicized, in your text: "The antagonism of Capulet versus
Montague runs throughout the play." The abbreviation *c.* or
ca., standing for *circa* ("around") and used with approximate
dates in parentheses, is italicized: "Higden wrote *Polychronicon* (*c.* 1350)." For further abbreviations in footnoting, see
Chapter 13, "The Research Paper," pp. 312–315.

Above. For naturalness and effectiveness, avoid such references as
"The above statistics are . . . ," and "The above speaks for itself." Simply use "These" or "This."

Accept, except. Frequently mistaken for each other in writing. *Accept* is to receive willingly; to *except* is to exclude, to make an
exception. As a preposition, except means "other than," "but."

Adapt, adopt. To *adapt* is to modify something to fit a new purpose.
To *adopt* is to take it over as it is.

Advice, advise. Frequently confused. *Advice* is what you get when
advisers *advise* you.

Aesthetic. An adjective: *an aesthetic judgment, his aesthetic viewpoint. Aesthetics* is singular for the science of beauty: "Santayana's *aesthetics* agrees with his metaphysics."

Affect, effect. *Affect* means "to produce an *effect.*" Avoid *affect* as
a noun; just say *feeling* or *emotion. Affective* is a technical term
for *emotional* or *emotive,* which are clearer.

Aggravate. Means to add gravity to something already bad enough.
Avoid using it to mean "irritate."

WRONG	RIGHT
He aggravated his mother.	The rum aggravated his moth-er's fever.

Agreement. A pronoun should agree with its antecedent; a verb,
with its noun; a demonstrative adjective, with its noun. Faulty

agreement is usually between singulars and plurals. Also see text, pp. 374–376; 391–393.

FAULTY	REVISED
Everyone **should roll** *their* **own.**	*Everyone* **should roll** *his* **own.**
It **was** *her.* **[Disagreement in case]**	*It* **was** *she.* **[Both** *It* **and** *she* **are subjective case]**
A politician **should be fair, but** *they* **usually are not.**	*Politicians* **should be fair, but they usually are not.**
Those kind **of sausages** *are* **bad.**	*That kind* **of sausage** *is* **bad.**
Revision **of their views about markets and averages** *are* **mandatory.**	*Revision* **of their views about markets and averages** *is* **mandatory.**

All, all of.   Use *all* without the *of* wherever you can to economize: *all this, all that, all those, all the people, all her lunch.* But some constructions need *of: all of them, all of Faulkner* (but *all Faulkner's novels*).

All ready, already.   Two different meanings. *All ready* means that everything is ready; *already* means "by this time."

All right, alright.   *Alright* is not *all right;* you are confusing it with the spelling of *already.*

Alliteration.   See "Versification," p. 264.

Allusion, illusion, disillusion.   The first two are frequently confused, and *disillusion* is frequently misspelled *disallusion.* An *allusion* is a reference to something; an illusion is a mistaken conception. You disillusion someone by bringing him back to hard reality from his illusions.

Alot.   You mean *a lot,* not *allot.*

Also.   Do not use for *and,* especially to start a sentence; not "*Also,* it failed," but simply "And it failed."

Ambiguous.   If your instructor marks *Amb* in the margin, he means "this has two meanings," one of which you probably have not noticed. Have you said, "Socrates admitted he was wrong"? This could mean that Socrates admitted that he, Socrates, was wrong, or it could mean that Socrates admitted that Crito was wrong. Check your statements to see that they cannot mean something else to the innocent reader.

Among. See *Between.*

Amount of, number of. Use *amount* with general heaps of things; use *number* with amounts that might be counted: *a small amount of interest, a large number of votes.*

And/or. An ungainly hairsplitter and thought stopper. You never *say* it. Don't write "for stage and/or screen"; write "for stage or screen, or both." Or just write "for stage and screen," and skip the finer possibilities.

Ante-, anti-. *Ante-* means "before": *an antebellum house* (a house built before the [Civil] War); *antedate* (to date before). *Anti-* means "against": *antifeminine, antiseptic.* Hyphenate before capitals, and before *i: anti-American, anti-intellectual.*

Anxious. Use to indicate *Angst,* agony, and anxiety. Does not mean cheerful expectation: "He was *anxious* to get started." Use *eager* instead.

Any. Do not overuse as a modifier:

POOR	GOOD
She was the best of any senior in the class.	She was the best senior in the class.
If any people know the answer, they aren't talking.	If anyone knows the answer, he's not talking.

Add *other* when comparing likes: "She was better than *any other* senior in the class." But "This junior was better than any senior."

Anybody. Don't write it as two words — *any body* — unless you mean "any corpse," or other inanimate object (stellar body, body of water).

Any more. Written as two words, except when an adverb in negatives and questions:

She never wins *anymore.*
Does she play *anymore?*

Anyone. Don't write it as two words—*any one*—unless you mean "any one thing."

Anyplace, someplace. Use *anywhere* and *somewhere* (adverbs), unless you mean "any *place*" and "some *place*."

Appear. Badly overworked for *seem*.

Appearing. Don't write "an expensive-appearing house." "An expensive-looking house" is not much better. Write "an expensive house," or "the house looked expensive."

Apostrophe-*s*. It signals possession. Use it as pronounced: *boss's daughter, Kraus's great idea*. Use it to distinguish the possessor's name: *Adams's, Dickens's, Jones's*. Use it to indicate the plurals of letters, dates, and words: *four a's, the 1960's, too many which's*. See also pp. 438–440.

Appreciate. Means "recognize the worth of." Do not use to mean simply "understand."

LOOSE	CAREFUL
I appreciate your position.	I understand your position.
I appreciate that your position is grotesque.	I realize that your position is grotesque.

Area. Drop it. *In the area of finance* means *in finance*. Be specific.

POOR	GOOD
This chart is conclusive in all areas.	This chart is conclusive.
	This chart thoroughly displays all departments.

Around. Do not use for *about:* it will seem to mean "surrounding."

POOR	GOOD
Around thirty people came.	About thirty people came.
He sang at around ten o'clock.	He sang at about ten o'clock.

As. Use where the cigarette people have *like*: "It tastes good, *as* a goody should." (See also *Like*.)

Do not use for *such as:* "Many things, *as* nails, hats, toothpicks . . . ." Write "Many things, *such as* nails . . . ."

Do not use *as* for *because* or *since*; it is ambiguous:

AMBIGUOUS	PRECISE
As I was walking, I had time to think.	Since I was walking, I had time to think.
	Because I was . . . . [even clearer]

Do not use *as* to mean "that" or "whether" (as in "I don't know *as* he would like her").

As . . . as. Use positively, not forgetting the second *as:*

WRONG	RIGHT
as long if not longer than the other.	*as* long *as* the other, if not longer.

Negatively, use *not so . . . as,* it is clearer (but more formal) than *as . . . as:*

It is *not so* long *as the* other.
His argument is *not so* clear *as* it ought to be.
His argument is *neither so* clear *nor so* thorough *as* it ought to be.

As far as. A wordy windup.

WORDY	IMPROVED
As far as winter wraps are concerned, she is well supplied.	She has a good supply of winter wraps.

As if. Takes the subjunctive:

as if he *were* cold

As of, as of now. Avoid, except for humor. Use *at,* or *now,* or delete entirely.

POOR	IMPROVED
He left as of ten o'clock.	He left at ten o'clock.
As of now, I've sworn off.	I've sworn off.
	I've just sworn off.

As to. Use only at the beginning of a sentence: "As to his first allegation, I can only say . . . ." Change it to *about*, or omit it, within a sentence: "He knows nothing *about* the details"; "He is not sure [as to] [whether] they are right."

As well as. You may mean only *and*. Check it out. Avoid such ambiguities as *The Commons voted as well as the Lords.*

Aspect. Overused. See *Jargon*.

Assonance. See "Versification," p. 264.

At. Do not use after *where*. "Where is it at?" means "Where is it?"

Awake, awakes. See *Wake*.

Awhile, a while. You usually want the adverb: *linger awhile, the custom endured awhile longer.* If you want the noun, emphasizing a period of time, make it clear: *the custom lasted for a while.*

Bad, badly. Remember that *bad* is an adjective: *a bad trip, a bad book.* And that *badly* is an adverb: *he traveled badly, he wrote badly.* Confusion arises with the linking verbs. *He is bad* is clear enough. But the logic extends to *he looks bad, he smells bad, he acts bad, the dress looks bad, the air seems bad, I feel bad.* These are right! Don't be tricked into using *badly*.

Back of, in back of. *Behind* says it more smoothly.

Balance, bulk. Make them mean business, as in "He deposited the balance of his allowance" and "The bulk of the crop was ruined." Do not use them for people.

POOR	IMPROVED
The balance of the class went home.	The rest of the class went home.
The bulk of the crowd was indifferent.	Most of the crowd was indifferent.

Basis. Drop it: *on a daily basis* means *daily*.

Be sure and. Write *be sure to*. See *Try and*.

Because of, due to. See *Due to*.

Behalf—in your behalf, on your behalf. A nice distinction. "He did it *in your behalf*" means he did it in your interest. "He did it *on your behalf*" means he was representing you, speaking for you.

Besides. Means "in addition to," not "other than."

POOR	IMPROVED
Something besides smog was the cause [unless smog was also a cause].	Something other than smog was the cause.

Better than. Unless you really mean *better than,* use *more than.*

POOR	IMPROVED
The lake was better than two miles across.	The lake was more than two miles across.

Between, among. *Between* ("by twain") has *two* in mind; *among* has several. *Between,* a preposition, takes an object; *between us, between you and me.* ("Between you and I" is sheer embarrassment; see *me,* p. 491.) But words sometimes fail us. "Between you and me and the gatepost" cannot conform to the rule and become "among you and me and the gatepost." *Between* connotes an intimate sharing *among* all concerned, each to each. *Between* also indicates geographical placing: "It is midway between Chicago, Detroit, and Toledo." "The grenade fell between Jones and me and the gatepost"; but "The grenade fell among the fruit stands." Keep *between* for two and *among* for three or more—unless sense forces a compromise. "Between every building was a plot of petunias" conveys the idea, however nonsensical "between a building" is. "Between all the buildings were plots of petunias" would be better, though still a compromise.

Bimonthly, biweekly. Careless usage has damaged these almost beyond recognition, confusing them with *semimonthly* and *semiweekly.* For clarity, better say "every two months" and "every two weeks."

Boarder, border. The *boarder* eats his meals in a house north of the Mexican *border.*

But, cannot but. "He can but fail" is old but usable. After a negative, however, the natural turn in *but* causes confusion:

POOR	IMPROVED
He cannot *but* fail.	He can only fail.
He could not doubt but that it	He could not doubt that it . . . .
He could not help but take	He could not help taking . . . .

Similarly, *but*'s too close or frequent keep your reader spinning:

POOR	IMPROVED
The campaign was successful *but* costly. *But* the victory was sweet.	The campaign was costly, but victory was sweet.

When *but* means "except," it is a preposition.

WRONG	RIGHT
Everybody laughed but I.	Everybody laughed but me.

But that, but what. Colloquial redundancies.

POOR	IMPROVED
There is no doubt but that John's is the best steer.	There is no doubt that John's is the best steer.
	John's is clearly the best steer.
There is no one but what would enjoy it.	Anyone would enjoy it.

c., ca. Indicates an approximate date, used only in a parenthesis with numerals, always italicized: "(*c.* 1496)." It stands for *circa,* "around."

Can, may (could, might). *Can* means ability; *may* asks permission, and expresses possibility. *Can I go?* means, strictly, "Have I the physical capability to go?" In speech, *can* usually serves for both ability and permission, though the salesgirl will probably say, properly, "May I help you?" In assertions, the distinction is clear: "He can do it." "He may do it." "If he can, he may." Keep these distinctions clear in your writing.

Could and *might* are the past tenses, but when used in the present time they are subjunctive, with shades of possibility, and hence politeness: *"Could* you come next Tuesday?" *"Might* I inquire about your plans?" *Could* may mean ability almost as strongly as *can:* "I'm sure he could do it." But *could* and *might* are usually subjunctives, expressing doubt:

Perhaps he could make it, if he tries.
I might be able to go, but I doubt it.

Cannot, can not. Use either, depending on the rhythm and emphasis you want. *Can not* emphasizes the *not* slightly.

Can't hardly, couldn't hardly. Use *can hardly, could hardly,* since *hardly* carries the negative sense.

Can't help but. A marginal mixture in speech of two clearer and more formal ideas *I can but regret* and *I can't help regretting.* Avoid it in writing.

Capability. Often "scientific" jargon. Say *it does* or *can do,* not *it has a capability for.*

Capital, capitol. Frequently confused. You mean *capital,* the head thing (from Latin *capitalis,* "of the head") whether writing of the head city of a state or national government, the head letter of a sentence, or the top (the "head") of a Greek column. *Capitol,* always capitalized, is the special name of the Temple of Jupiter on the Capitoline Hill in Rome, and also of the Capitol building where Congress sits in Washington, D.C., or the Capitol Hill in Washington on which the Capitol stands (the American founders named their new headquarters, and the hill they stood on, after the Roman ones). Confusion comes especially when you think of Washington:

WRONG	RIGHT
Washington, D.C., is the *capitol* **of the United States.**	**Washington, D.C., is the** *capital* **of the United States.**

Capitalization. Capitalize the first letters of sentences, the names of people, places, books, magazines, organizations, races, nationalities, religions, languages, a Supreme Diety and pronouns referring to Him, the first person pronoun *I.* For further details, see Section C, "Capitalization" (pp. 454–455).

Case. Chop out this deadwood:

POOR	IMPROVED
In many cases, ants survive.	Ants often . . . .
In such a case, surgery is recommended.	Then surgery is recommended.
In case he goes	If he goes . . . .
Everyone enjoyed himself, except in a few scattered cases.	Almost everyone enjoyed himself.

Cause, result. Since *all* events are both causes and results, suspect yourself of wordiness if you write either word.

WORDY	ECONOMICAL
The invasions caused depopulation of the country.	The invasion depopulated the country.
He lost as a result of poor campaigning.	He lost because his campaign was poor.

Cause-and-effect relationship. Verbal adhesive tape. Recast the sentence, with some verb other than the wordy *cause:*

POOR	IMPROVED
Othello's jealousy rises in a cause-and-effect relationship when he sees the handkerchief.	Seeing the handkerchief arouses Othello's jealousy.

Censor, censure. Frequently confused. A *censor* cuts out objectionable passages. *To censor* is to cut out or prohibit. *To censure* is to condemn: "The *censor censored* some parts of the play, and *censured* the author as an irresponsible drunkard."

Center around. A physical impossibility. Make it *centers on,* or *revolves around,* or *concerns,* or *is about.*

Character development. A common cliché, literary jargon. Avoid it. It is ambiguous and cumbersome (noun-on-noun). You mean either *characterization,* the way an author fills out his portraiture, or something like *maturity, evolution, growth in perception or integrity* — the way a literary personality develops. Make clear to your reader which you mean, and avoid the term altogether. See *Jargon.*

Circumstances. *In these circumstances* makes more sense than *under these circumstances,* since the stances are standing around (*circum*), not standing under. Often jargon: *The economy is in trouble* (not *in difficult circumstances*).

Cite. See *Site, sight, cite.*

Clichés. Don't use unwittingly. But they can be effective. There are two kinds: (1) the rhetorical — *tried and true, the not too distant future, sadder but wiser, in the style to which she had become accustomed;* (2) the proverbial — *apple of his eye, skin of your teeth, sharp as a tack, quick as a flash, twinkling of an eye.* The rhetorical ones are clinched by sound alone; the proverbial are metaphors caught in the popular fancy. Proverbial clichés can lighten a dull passage. You may even revitalize them, since they are frequently dead metaphors (see page 188). Avoid the rhetorical clichés unless you turn them to your advantage: *tried and untrue, gladder and wiser, a future not too distant.*

Colloquial, colloquialism. A characteristic of speech, frequently too personal, informal, or unclear for writing.

Come and, try and, go and, be sure and. All colloquial ways of saying *come to, try to, go to, be sure to. Come and see us* means "Come to see us," and so forth.

Comma splice, comma fault. The most common mistake in writing: putting a comma where you need a period. See *Run-on sentence,* and Section C, "Punctuation, Spelling, Capitalization" (pp. 404–405).

COMMA SPLICE	REPAIRED
The car, already ten years old, and looking twenty, collapsed in a heap of oily steam, it had run its last mile.	The car, already ten years old, and looking twenty, collapsed in a heap of oily steam. It had run its last mile.
	. . . oily steam, having run its last mile.

Compare to, compare with. To compare *to* is to show similarities (and differences) between different kinds; to compare *with* is to show differences (and similarities) between like kinds.

Composition has been compared *to* architecture.
He compares favorably *with* Mickey Spillane.
Compare Shakespeare *with* Ben Jonson.

Comparisons. Make them complete; add a *than:*

It is more like a jigsaw *than a rational plan.*
They are more thoughtful *than the others.*
The first is better *than the second.* **(Or "The first is *the* better.")**

Complected. A dialectical variant of *complexioned.* Better avoid the problem altogether by phrasing another way: *Her coloring was light; his complexion was dark.*

Complement, compliment. Frequently confused. *Complement* is a completion; *compliment* is a flattery: "When the regiment reached its full *complement* of recruits, the general gave it a flowery *compliment.*"

Concept. Often jargonish and wordy.

POOR	IMPROVED
The concept of multiprogramming allows	Multiprogramming allows. . . .

Connected with, in connection with. Always wordy. Say *about, with,* or *in.*

POOR	IMPROVED
They discussed several things connected with history.	They discussed several historical questions.
They liked everything in connection with the university.	They liked everything about the university.
He is connected with the Smith Corporation.	He is with the Smith Corporation.

Consensus. A *consensus of opinion* has seemed redundant to many stylists, since consensus means "feeling together," or "an agreed opinion." But you can write "they reached a consensus" and "they reached a consensus of opinion" with equal confidence that your words are saying what they mean. *They agreed* or *Their opinions coincided* would be original and economical, however.

Consider, consider as. The first means "believe to be"; the second, "think about" or "speak about": "I consider him excellent." "I consider him first as a student, then as a man."

Consonance. See "Versification," p. 264.

Contact. Don't *contact* anyone: get in touch with him, call him, write him, find him, tell him. Don't make a good *contact*, make a helpful friend.

Continual, continuous. You can improve your writing by *continual* practice, but the effort cannot be *continuous*. The first means "frequently repeated"; the second, "without interruption."

> **It requires continual practice.**
> **There was a continuous line of clouds.**

Contractions. We use them constantly in conversation: *don't, won't, can't, shouldn't, isn't*. Avoid them in writing, or your prose will seem too chummy. But use one now and then when you want some colloquial emphasis: *You can't go home again.*

Contrast. See *Compare to*.

Could, might. See *Can, may*.

Could care less. You mean *couldn't care less*. Speech has worn off the *n't*, making the words say the opposite of what you mean. A person who cares a great deal could care a great deal less; one who does not care *"couldn't* care less."

Could of, would of. Phonetic misspellings of *could've* ("could have"), and *would've* ("would have"). In writing, spell them all the way out: *could have* and *would have*.

Couldn't hardly. Use *could hardly*.

Council, counsel, consul. *Council* is probably the noun you mean: a group of deliberators. *Counsel* is usually the verb "to advise." But *counsel* is also a noun: an adviser, an attorney, and their advice. Check your dictionary to see that you are writing what you mean. A *counselor* gives you his *counsel* about your courses, which may be submitted to an academic *council*. A *consul* is an official representing your government in a foreign country.

Couple. Use *two, a few,* or *several.* In some breezy moments, you can lighten your prose with *a couple of.*

Credible, creditable. Sometimes confused. *Credible* means "believable." *Creditable* means "worthy of praise" — putting something down to your credit: "His catching the pass at third hand was *credible,* but not really *creditable,* since after Jones's fumble he hardly knew he had the ball."

Curriculum. The plural is *curricula,* though *curriculums* will get by. The adjective is *curricular.*

> **The school offers three separate curricula.**
> **Extracurricular activities also count.**
> **The dean has asked for curricular innovations.**

Dangling modifier. An introductory phrase dangles, with nothing to relate to: "Bowing to the crowd, the bull caught him unawares"; "Driving across country, the prices get higher and higher." You have left out the real subject your modifier modifies: "Bowing to the crowd, the toreador . . . "; "Driving across country, we . . . ." Other mismatches are frequent: "Having broken the dam, the sandbags could not hold the water" ("The water, having broken the dam, rushed through the sand bags"); "Born in Hungary, his knowledge of American folklore was minimal" ("Born in Hungary, he knew little about American folklore"). For further details see pp. 146–147; 399.

Data. A plural, like *curricula, strata, phenomena:*

> **The data are inconclusive.**

Definitely. A high-school favorite, badly overused.

Desert, dessert. Frequently confused. You usually mean *desert,* either the sandy place, running away, or getting what you deserve, your "just deserts." *Dessert* comes after dinner. Remember one *s* for *s*and, two *ss*'s for the *s*weet stuff.

Different from, different than. Avoid *different than,* which confuses the idea of differing. Things differ *from* each other. Only in comparing several differences does *than* make clear sense: "All three of his copies differ from the original, but his last one is *more* different *than* the others." But here *than* is controlled by *more,* not by *different.*

WRONG	RIGHT
It is different *than* I expected.	It is different *from* what I expected.
	It is not what I expected.
This is different *than* all the others.	This is different *from* all the others.

Dilemma. Frequently misspelled *dilemna,* or *dillema.* A *lemma* is a proposition in logic, an argument; a *di-lemma* is a two-pronged proposition of equal choices that leave one puzzled.

Discreet, discrete. Frequently confused. *Discreet* means someone careful and judicious; *discrete* means something separate and distinct: "He was discreet in examining each discrete part of the evidence."

Disinterested. Does not mean "uninterested" nor "indifferent." *Disinterested* means impartial, without private interests in the issue.

WRONG	RIGHT
You seem disinterested in the case.	You seem uninterested in the case.
	The judge was disinterested and perfectly fair.
He was disinterested in it.	He was indifferent to it.

Double negative. A negation that cancels another negation, making it accidentally positive: "He couldn't hardly" indicates that "He could easily," the opposite of its intended meaning. "They can't win nothing" really says that they *must* win something.

The double negative was standard in Middle English, patterned as it was on French, notably the French *ne . . . pas* ("*no . . . not*") that frames the verb. Chaucer's Absolon, the young priest in "The Miller's Tale," for instance, liked the women so well *That of no wyf ne took he noon offrynge* ("that of no wife no took he none offering"). We still double our nega-

tives to intensify: "No, no, not so." And the habit most languages share of putting affirmative questions in the negative—
"Isn't that so?" when we mean it *is* so (*N'est-ce pas? Nicht
wahr?*)—makes some other double negatives also emphatic:
"Don't think he couldn't care" means something like "He cares
a great deal, but you seem to think he doesn't." A doubled
negation carries the same kind of indirect emphasis—a mild
irony, really—in such tentative assertions as "One cannot be
certain that she will not prove to be the century's greatest
poet," or "a not unattractive offer." But make sure your negatives don't cancel each other out, as in *couldn't hardly,* or land
you in some mind–boggling absurdity like *No Trespassing
Without Permission.*

Due to. Never begin a sentence with *"Due* to circumstances beyond
his control, he . . . ." *Due* is an adjective and must always relate
to a noun or pronoun: "The catastrophe *due to* circumstances
beyond his control was unavoidable," or "The catastrophe was
due to circumstances beyond his control" (predicate adjective).
But you are still better off with *because of, through, by,* or *owing
to. Due to* is usually a symptom of wordiness, especially when
it leads to *due to the fact that.*

WRONG	RIGHT
He resigned due to sickness.	He resigned because of sick-ness.
He succeeded due to hard work.	He succeeded through hard work.
He lost his shirt due to leaving it in the locker room.	He lost his shirt by leaving it in the locker room.
The Far East will continue to worry the West, due to a general social upheaval.	The Far East will continue to worry the West, owing to a general social upheaval.

Due to the fact that. A venerable piece of plumbing meaning *because.*

JARGON	IMPROVED
The program failed due to the fact that a recession had set in.	The program failed because a recession had set in.

Effect. As a noun, it means "result"; as a verb, "to bring about" (not to be confused with *to affect,* meaning "to concern, impress, touch, move" — or "to pretend." See *Affect.*

> What was the effect?
> He effected a thorough change.
> How did it affect you?

But note that "He effected a change" is wordy for "He changed."

E.g. "For example" (*exempli gratia*). Not in italics. Preceded by a comma, followed by comma or colon. "They lost through errors, e.g., Wilson's fumble, Mitchell's miscall." See *Abbreviations.*

Either, neither. One of two, taking a singular verb: *Either is a good candidate, but neither speaks well. Either . . . or (neither . . . nor)* are paralleling conjunctions. See *Parallelism.*

Eminent, imminent, immanent. Often confused. *Eminent* is something that stands out; *imminent* is something about to happen. *Immanent,* much less common, is a philosophical term for something spiritual "remaining within, indwelling." You usually mean *eminent.*

Enormity. Means "atrociousness"; does not mean "enormousness."

> the enormity of the crime
> the enormousness of the mountain

Enthuse. Don't use it; it coos and gushes:

WRONG	RIGHT
She *enthused* over her new dress.	She gushed on and on about her new dress.
He was *enthused.*	He was enthusiastic.

Environment. Frequently misspelled *enviorment* or *envirnment.* It is business jargon, unless you mean the world around us.

WORDY	IMPROVED
in an MVT environment	in MVT; with MVT; under MVT
He works in the environment of cost analysis.	He analyzes costs.
We need to improve the landscaping in the environment of the offices.	We must improve the landscaping around the offices.

Equally as good. A redundant mixture of two choices, *as good as* and *equally good.* Use only one of these at a time.

Etc. Substitute something specific for it, or drop it, or use something like "and so forth." See *Abbreviations.*

POOR	IMPROVED
She served fruit, cheese, candies, etc.	She served fruit, cheese, candies, and little sweet pickles.
	She served fruit, cheese, candies, and the like.

Ethic. A mannered rendition of *ethics,* the singular and plural noun meaning a system or science of moral principles. Even poorer as an adjective for *ethical.*

Everyday, every day. You wear your *everyday* clothes *every day.*

Everyone, everybody. Avoid the common mismatching *their:*

"Everyone does *his* [or **her** but not *their*] own thing."

Except. See *Accept, except.*

Exclamation. *Exclaim* often induces the misspelling *exclaimation.* Avoid overusing exclamation marks (!!!).

Exists. Another symptom of wordiness.

POOR	IMPROVED
a system like that which exists at the university	a system like that at the university

Facet. This means "little face," as on a diamond. Use metaphorically or not at all.

POOR	IMPROVED
This problem has several facets.	This problem has five parts.
	Each facet of the problem sparkles with implications.

The fact that. Deadly with *due to,* and usually wordy by itself.

POOR	IMPROVED
The fact that Rome fell due to moral decay is clear.	That Rome fell through moral decay is clear.
This disparity is in part a result of the fact that some of the best indicators make their best showings in an expanding market.	This disparity arises in part because some of the best indicators . . . .
In view of the fact that more core is installed	Because it has more core . . . .

Factor. Avoid it. We've used it to death. Try *element* when you mean "element." Look for an accurate verb when you mean "cause."

POOR	IMPROVED
The increase in female employment is a factor in juvenile delinquency.	The increase in female employment has contributed to juvenile delinquency.
Puritan self-sufficiency was an important factor in the rise of capitalism.	Puritan self-sufficiency favored the rise of capitalism.

Farther, further. The first means distance; the second means time or figurative distance. You look *farther* and consider *further.*

Faze, phase. See *Phase.*

Fewer, less. See *Less, few.*

The field of. Try to omit it—you usually can—or bring the metaphor to life. It is trite and wordy.

POOR	IMPROVED
He is studying in the field of geology.	He is studying geology.

POOR	IMPROVED
He changed from the field of science to fine arts.	He moved from the field of science to the green pasture of fine arts.

Firstly. Archaic. Trim all such terms to *first, second, third,* and so on.

Fit, fitted. A little tricky in the past tense. Since either *fit* or *fitted* is idiomatic English for the main verb in intransitive ideas—*It fit like a glove; It fitted like a glove*—*fit* sometimes slips awkwardly into transitive statements and into the past participle. Sticking to *fitted* all the way will avoid the problem.

AWKWARD	IMPROVED
The tailor fit him carelessly.	The tailor fitted him carelessly.
It has fit him in previous productions.	It has fitted him in previous productions.
The poem fit into his sequence.	The poem fitted into his sequence.

Fix. The word means "to establish in place"; it means "to repair" only in speech or colloquial writing.

Flaunt, flout. *Flaunt* means to parade, to wave impudently; *flout* means to scoff at. The first is metaphorical; the second, not: "She *flaunted* her wickedness and *flouted* the police."

Folks. Use *parents, mother and father,* or *family* instead.

For. Be sure to distinguish the conjunction with a comma, or it will look like a preposition.

MISLEADING	ACCURATE
He went for the time was ripe.	He went, for the time was ripe.

Former, latter. Passable, but they often make the reader look back. Repeating the antecedents is clearer.

POOR	IMPROVED
The Athenians and Spartans were always in conflict. *The former* had a better civiliza-	The Athenians and Spartans were always in conflict. Athens had the better cul-

POOR (cont.)	IMPROVED (cont.)
tion; *the latter* had a better army.	ture; Sparta, the better army.

Forward, foreword.   The first is direction; the second, an introduction to a book, a "fore" word or two.

Fragment.   An incomplete sentence.   A piece of a sentence.   Both those statements are, grammatically, fragments, since they contain no verb.   Complete your sentences by giving each subject its existence, or its action: its verb.   But you can use a *rhetorical* fragment, one that your reader will not mistake as a mistake, most effectively, especially at the beginning of a paragraph: *Not so.   Overwhelmed completely.   Of course.*   These are forceful trimmings from a complete sentence, the rest of which is left understood.   See pp. 160–161; 402–404.

Fun.   *Fun thing, fun time, fun party* — all popular jargon.   Keep *fun* as a noun: "It was fun."   Or try something more vivid and original: "The party was hilarious from start to finish."

Funny.   Avoid it, especially when you must explain "not funny 'ha-ha,' but funny queer."

Further.   See *Farther.*

Gerund.   The verb-form ending in -*ing* when it acts as a noun: "*Swimming* is healthful."   See *Participle for gerund.*

Go and see, come and see, be sure and see, try and see.   All conversational versions of *go to, come to,* and so forth.

Good, well.   *He done real good* — 75 percent wrong for written communication, as a young English instructor in Texas said, turning in his first batch of papers, with his contract, and becoming a librarian.   *Good* is the adjective: *good time.   Well* is the adverb: *well done.*   In verbs of feeling, we are caught in the ambiguities of health.   *I feel good* is more accurate than *I feel well,* because *well* may mean that your feelers are in good order.   But *I feel well* is also an honest statement: "I feel that I am well."   Ask yourself what your readers might misunderstand from your statements, and you will use these two confused terms clearly.

Got, gotten. Both acceptable and equivalent. Your rhythm and emphasis will decide. America prefers the older *gotten* in many phrases; Britain goes exclusively for *got*.

Gray. America prefers *gray;* England, *grey* — matching each country's initials.

Hanged, hung. *Hanged* is the past of *hang* only for the death penalty.

They hung the rope and hanged the man.

Hardly. Watch the negative here. "I can't *hardly*" means "I *can* easily." Write: "One can hardly conceive the vastness."

Healthy, healthful. Swimming is *healthful;* swimmers are *healthy.*

Height. Not *heighth.*

His/her, his (her). Shift to the neutral plural, or otherwise rephrase to avoid this awkwardness. *His* stands for both sexes, if you can stand it.

Historically. A favorite windy throat clearer. Badly overused.

Honorable. See *Reverend.*

Hopefully. An inaccurate dangler, a cliché. "Hopefully, they are at work" does not mean that they are working hopefully. Simply use "I hope": not "They are a symbol of idealism, and, hopefully, are representative," but "They are a symbol of idealism and are, I hope, representative."

However. Bury it between commas, or replace it with *but* or *nevertheless.*

POOR	IMPROVED
However, the day had not been entirely lost.	*But* the day had not been entirely lost.
However, the script that Alcuin invented became the forerunner of modern handwriting.	The script that Alcuin invented, *however,* became the forerunner of modern handwriting.

Initial *however* should be an adverb:

However **long it takes, it will be done.**
However **she did it, she did it well.**

Humanism (mistaken for "human nature" or "humanitarianism"). The intellectual awakening in the late Renaissance when men like Erasmus (1466–1536) rediscovered the culture and literature of ancient Greece and Rome, and began to shift attention from God and eternity to man and his capacities. Since the term has this specific historical meaning, find something else when you want to express, more generally, some focus on human nature.

MISLEADING	CLEARER
This study will be based on *humanism.*	This study will focus on *human nature.*
They pardoned him for *human-istic* reasons.	They pardoned him for *humanitarian* reasons.

Hung. See *Hanged.*

Hyphenation. When you must break a word at the end of a line, put your hyphen where your dictionary marks the syllables with a dot: *syl·lables, syl-lables.* If you must break a hyphenated word, break it after the hyphen: *self-/sufficient.* Don't hyphenate an already hyphenated word: *self-suf-/ficient.* It's hard on the eyes and the printer. When you write for print, underline those line-end hyphens you mean to keep as hyphens, making a little equals sign: self=/sufficient.

For clarity, hyphenate all groups of words acting as one adjective or one adverb: *eighteenth-century-urban attitude, early-blooming-southern crocus.* Distinguish between a *high school,* and a *high-school teacher.*

Hyphenate prefixes to proper names: *ex-Catholic, pro-Napoleon,* and all relatively new combinations like *anti-marriage.* Consult your dictionary.

Hyphenate after prefixes that demand emphasis or clarity: *ex-husband, re-collect* ("to collect again," as against *recollect,* "to remember"), *re-emphasize, pre-existent.*

Use the hanging hyphen for clarity: *All two- or three-time losers.*

Hyphenate those slants: not "psychic/social complex" but "psychic-social complex." See also pp. 441–443.

The idea that.   Like *the fact that*—and the cure is the same.

POOR	IMPROVED
He liked the idea that she was going.	He was pleased she was going.
The idea that space is infinite is difficult to grasp.	That space is infinite is difficult to grasp.

Identify.   Give it an object:

> He *identified the wallet.*
> He *identified himself* **with the hero. ("He identified with the hero" is acceptable but not preferred.)**

I.e.   See *Abbreviations.*

If, whether.   *If* is for uncertainties; *whether,* for alternatives. Usually the distinction is unimportant: *I don't know if it will rain; I don't know whether it will rain [or not].* To be absolutely clear, use *if* unless you express an *or.*

Image.   Resist its popularity, make it mean what it says, and never make it a verb. Do NOT SAY, "The university should *image* the handsome intellectual."

Imminent, Immanent.   See *Eminent.*

Imply, infer.   The author *implies;* you *infer* ("carry in") what you think he means.

> He *implied* **that all women were hypocrites.**
> **From the ending, we** *infer* **that tragedy ennobles as it kills.**

Importantly.   Often an inaccurate (and popular) adverb, like *hopefully.*

INACCURATE	IMPROVED
More importantly, he walked home.	More important, he walked home.

He did not walk home importantly, nor more importantly.

In back of.   Use *behind.*

Includes. Jargonish, as a general verb for specific actions.

POOR	IMPROVED
The report includes rural and urban marketing.	The report analyzes rural and urban marketing.

Indentation. See the discussion in Chapter 4 (pp. 56–57).

Individual. Write *person* unless you really mean someone separate and unique.

Infer. See *Imply, infer.*

Infinitive. The form of the verb with *to — to be, to know, to swim.* It functions as a noun: *To run is fun.* But, being a verb, it also may have an object and take a qualifying adverb: *To run a shop is fun; To run fast is fun.*

Ingenious, ingenuous. Sometimes confused. *Ingenious* means clever; *ingenuous,* naïve.

Inside of, outside of. "They painted the *outside of* the house" is sound usage; but these expressions can be redundant and in-accurate.

POOR	IMPROVED
inside of half an hour	within half an hour
He had nothing for dinner outside of a few potato chips.	He had nothing for dinner but a few potato chips.

Instances. Redundant. *In many instances* means *often, frequently.*

Interesting. Make what you say interesting, but never tell the reader *it is interesting:* he may not believe you. *It is interesting* is merely a lazy preamble.

POOR	IMPROVED
It is interesting to note that nicotine is named for Jean Nicot, who introduced to-bacco into France in 1560.	Nicotine is named for Jean Nicot, who introduced to-bacco into France in 1560.

Intransitive. A verb not taking an object: "She *weeps.*"

Irony. Not the same as *sarcasm* (which see). A clash between appearance and reality. Irony may be either comic or tragic, depending on your view. But, comic or tragic, irony is of three essential kinds:

VERBAL IRONY. You say the opposite of what you mean: "It's a *great* day," appearing to mean "great" but really meaning "terrible."

DRAMATIC IRONY. Someone unwittingly states, or acts upon, a contrariety to the truth. A character in a play, for example, might say "This is my great day," and dance a jig, when the audience has just seen his daughter abducted and the mortgage foreclosed.

IRONY OF CIRCUMSTANCE. The opposite of what ought to happen happens (it rains on the day of the Weather Bureau's picnic; the best man of all is killed); and we are sharply aware of the contrast.

Irregardless. A faulty word. The *ir-* (meaning *not*) is doing what the *-less* already does. You are thinking of *irrespective,* and trying to say *regardless.*

Is when, is where. Avoid these loose attempts.

LOOSE	SPECIFIC
Combustion is when oxidation bursts into flame.	Combustion is oxidation bursting into flame.
"Trivia" is where three roads meet.	"Trivia" is the place where three roads meet.

It. Give it a specific reference, as a pronoun. Avoid the expletive, non-referential *it:* it is wordy and often ambiguous (see also *There is*):

FAULTY	IMPROVED
She quit smoking. *It* is said that it is harmful.	She quit smoking. Some think it harmful.

Italics.   Italicize words as words, letters as letters, numbers as numbers: "He used the word *word* repeatedly; three *l*'s; four 2's." Italicize the names of books, newspapers, magazines, plays, movies, long poems, ships, trains, and airplanes.   Italicize foreign words not fully naturalized (see your dictionary). Italicize, *occasionally*, for emphasis.   Underline to indicate italics.   Do not italicize famous documents: the Bible, Genesis, the Declaration of Independence.   See pp. 434–435.

-ize.   A handy way to make verbs from nouns and adjectives (*patron-ize, civil-ize*).   But handle with care.   Manufacture new *-izes* only with a sense of humor and daring ("they Harvardized the party").   Business overdoes the trick: *finalize*, a relative newcomer, has provoked strong disapproval from writers who are not commercially familiarized.

Jargon.   A technical, wordy phraseology that becomes characteristic of any particular trade, or branch of learning, frequently with nouns modifying nouns, and in the passive voice.   Break out of it by making words mean what they say.

JARGON	CLEAR MEANING
The plot structure of the play provides no objective correlative.	The play fails to act out and exhibit the hero's inner conflicts. The plot is incoherent. The structure is lopsided.
The character development of the heroine is excellent.	The author sketches and deepens the heroine's personality skillfully. The heroine matures convincingly.
Three motivation profile studies were developed in the area of production management.	The company studied its production managers, and discovered three patterns of motivation.

Jingles.   Avoid jingling your sounds together inadvertently.

Use ample *illumination* **for every** *examination.*

A *visionary revision* **of the** *decision.*
A *beautiful* **example of** *dutiful* **bureaucrats.**

Judgment, judgement. Americans have made *judgment* standard; the British prefer *judgement,* along with *labour, colour,* and so forth.

Kind of, sort of. Colloquialisms for *somewhat, rather, something,* and the like. "It is *kind of* odd" will not get by. But "It is a *kind of* academic hippopotamus" will get by nicely, because *a kind of* means *a species of.* Change "a kind of a poor sport" to "a kind of poor sport," and you will seem as knowledgeable as a scientist.

Lay. Don't use *lay* to mean *lie. Lay* means "to put" and needs an object; *lie* means "to recline." Memorize both their present and past tenses, which are frequently confused:

I *lie* down when I can; I *lay* down yesterday; I have *lain* down often. [Intransitive, no object.]
The hen *lays* an egg; she *laid* one yesterday; she has *laid* four this week. [Transitive, *lays* an object.]
Now I *lay* the book on the table; I *laid* it there yesterday; I have *laid* it there many times.

Lend, loan. Don't use *loan* for *lend. Lend* is the verb; *loan,* the noun: "Please *lend* me a five; I need a *loan* badly." Remember the line from the song: "I'll *send* you to a *friend* who'll be willing to *lend.*"

Less, few. Do not use one for the other. *Less* answers "How much?" *Few* answers "How many?"

WRONG	RIGHT
We had *less* people than last time.	We had *fewer* people this time than last.

Letter writing. Except for private correspondence, type your letters, with date, names and titles, addresses, and salutations in full, keeping a copy for reference. Though official correspondence frequently aligns everything flush with the left margin, includ-

ing signature, such styling may seem pretentious from a private
person. The following form and spacing are usual:

```
                                        12345 Elmwood Drive
                                        Tracy, Illinois 50123

                                        July 1, 1976


        Professor Alan P. Kurtz, Chairman
        Department of English
        University of Michigan
        Ann Arbor, Michigan 48104

        Dear Professor Kurtz:

             You may remember me from your class in freshman
        composition, English 123, last spring.  I do not re-
        call the section number.  But perhaps you will remem-
        ber that I did not appear for the final examination.
        My name in class was Kathy Miller.

             I have recently received my grades, indicating a
        C in English.  Since my average had been at least a
        strong B, or even B+, as I remember, I thought this
        was a little severe.

             I am writing to ask if I might make up the final,
        and receive some adjustment in my grade.  I would be
        happy to come to Ann Arbor, at your convenience, or
        to arrange some time early in the fall term.  Please
        let me know what the regulations are, and if I can hope
        for a second chance.  I had some extreme problems
        right at the end of the semester.  I really enjoyed
        the course.

                                    Sincerely yours,

                                    Kathy Miller Albright

                                    (Mrs.) Kathy Miller Albright
```

Space long names of institutions equally in two (or more) lines
in your salutation:

```
        Dr. Robert A. Nordham, President
        Society for Developing
        Countries in Asia and
        the Western Hemisphere
        9876 Central Street
        Clintdale, West Virginia 11213
```

Use "Dear Sir:" or "Dear Sirs:" for salutation to organizations when you do not know a person to address. To women's organizations "Dear Madam:" is customary. "Sincerely" or "Sincerely yours" will meet most situations.

Level. Usually redundant jargon. *High level officials* are *high officials* and *college level courses* are *college courses*.

Lie, lay. See *Lay*.

Lighted, lit. Equally good past tenses for *light* (both "to ignite" and "to descend upon"), with *lit* perhaps more frequent. Rhythm usually determines the choice. *Lighted* seems preferred for adverbs and combinations: *a clean well-lighted place; it could have been lighted better.*

Like, as, as if. Usage blurs them, but the writer should distinguish them before he decides to go colloquial. Otherwise, he may throw his readers off.

> **He looks** *like* **me.**
> **He dresses** *as* **I do.**
> **He acts** *as if* **he were high.**

Note that *like* takes the objective case, and that *as*, being a conjunction, is followed by the nominative:

> **She looks like** *her.*
> **He is as tall as** *I* **[am].**
> **He is tall, like** *me.*

The pattern of the prepositional phrase *(like me, like a house, like a river)* has caused *like* to replace *as* where no verb follows in phrases other than comparisons *(as . . . as):*

> **It works** *like* **a charm.** **(. . .** *as* **a charm** *works.*)
> **It went over** *like* **a lead balloon. (. . .** *as* **a lead balloon** *does.*)
> **They worked** *like* **beavers. (. . .** *as* **beavers** *do.*)

Notice that *as* would give these three statements a meaning of substitution or disguise: "It works as a charm" (but it really isn't a charm); "It went over as a lead balloon" (disguised as a lead balloon).

Literally. Often misused, and overused, as a general emphasizer: "We *literally* wiped them off the field." Since the word means "by the letter," a *literal* meaning is distinct from a *figurative* meaning. *His heart was stone* means, literally, that his blood pump was, somehow, made of stone; it means, figuratively, "He was cruel." Avoid it unless you mean to show exactly what a word, or a statement, means: *To decapitate means literally to take the head off.*

Loan. See *Lend*.

Loose, lose. You will *lose* the game if your defense is *loose*.

Lots, lots of, a lot of. Conversational for *many, much, great, considerable*. Try something else. See *Alot*.

CASUAL	IMPROVED
Henry VIII had *lots of* problems.	Henry VIII had *many* problems.
Latimer showed *lots of* courage.	Latimer showed *considerable* courage.
Their diet included *a lot of* pepper.	Their diet included *much* pepper.

Majority. More than half the votes, sometimes loosely used for a plurality, the highest number of votes but less than half, when more than two are running. Erroneously applied to quantities rather than numbers.

ERRONEOUS	ACCURATE
He ate *the majority* of the watermelon.	He ate *most* of the watermelon.
The majority of the play is comic.	*Most* of the play is comic.

Often wordy, even when applied to numbers:

WORDY	IMPROVED
The majority of the students take composition.	Most students take composition.

Manner. Drop this from your working vocabulary. *In a . . . manner* is a favorite redundancy. Replace it with an adverb: *in a* *clever manner* means "cleverly"; *in an awkward manner* means "awkwardly." *Manner* usually reveals your amateur standing, unless you really mean a mannerism in gesture or speech, or social manners, good and bad. Use *way,* or something else.

AMATEURISH	IMPROVED
In this *manner,* we learn . . .	In this *way,* we learn . . .
The play proceeds in this *manner* for three more acts.	The play goes on *like this* for three more acts.

Maximum (minimum) amount. Drop *amount.* The minimum and the maximum *are* amounts. Don't write *a minimum of* and *as a minimum:* write *at least.*

May. See *Can, may.*

Maybe. Conversational for *perhaps.* Sometimes misused for *may be.* Unless you want an unmistakable colloquial touch, avoid it altogether.

FAULTY	IMPROVED
The book *maybe* popular, but *maybe* it will endure.	The book *may be* popular, but perhaps it will endure.
It has sold *maybe* a million copies.	It has sold *perhaps* a million copies.

Me. Use *me* boldly. It is the proper object of verbs and prepositions. Nothing is sadder than faulty propriety: "between you and *I,*" or "They gave it to John and *I,*" or "They invited my wife and *I.*" Test yourself by dropping the first member: "between I" *(no),* "gave it to I" *(no),* "invited I" *(no).* And do NOT substitute *myself.*

Medium, media. The singular and the plural. Avoid *medias,* and you will distinguish yourself from the masses.

Might. See *Can, may.*

Misplaced modifier. A word or phrase misplaced so that it says something confusing or literally absurd. Frequently marked "DM," or "Dangling Modifier" for convenience. "She said *on Friday* to phone him" could mean "On Friday, she said . . ." or "to phone him on Friday." See *Dangling modifier,* and pp. 146–147; 399.

MISPLACED	CLARIFIED
She *only* loved her mother.	She loved *only* her mother.
They decided when the teams tied to end the game.	When both teams tied, they decided to end the game.
	They decided to end the game when both teams tied.
He liked people in his way.	In his way, he liked people.

Most.   Does not mean *almost.*

WRONG	RIGHT
Most everyone knows.	Almost everyone knows.

Must, a must.   *A must* is popular jargon.   Try something else.

JARGON	IMPROVED
Beatup is really a *must* for every viewer.	Everyone interested in film should see *Beatup.*
This is a *must* course.	Everyone should take this course.

Myself.   Use it only reflexively ("I hurt *myself*"), or intensively ("I *myself* often have trouble").   Fear of *me* leads to the incorrect "They gave it to John and *myself.*"   Do not use *myself, himself, herself, themselves* for *me, him, her, them.*

Nature.   Avoid this padding.   Do not write *moderate in nature, moderate by nature, of a moderate nature;* simply write *moderate.*

Near.   Avoid using it for degree:

POOR	IMPROVED
a near perfect orbit	a nearly perfect orbit
	an almost perfect orbit
We are nowhere near knowledgeable enough.	We are not nearly knowledgeable enough.
It was a near disaster.	It was nearly a disaster [*or* nearly disastrous].

Neither.   See *Either.*

No one.   Two words in America, not *noone,* nor *no-one* (which the British prefer).

None.   This pronoun means "no one" and takes a singular verb, as do *each, every, everyone, nobody,* and other distributives. *None are* has been common and admissible for centuries, but *none is* holds its own, with a certain prestige, even in the daily newspaper. Another pronoun referring back to any of these must also be singular.

POOR	IMPROVED
None of them *are* perfect.	None of them *is* perfect.
Every one of the men *eat* a big breakfast.	Every one of the men *eats* a big breakfast.
None of the discoveries *appear* significant.	None of the discoveries *appears* significant.
Everybody thinks *they have* the worst of it.	Everybody thinks *he has* the worst of it.

Nonrestrictive.   See *Restrictive, nonrestrictive.*

Not . . . as, not . . . so.   See *As . . . as.*

Noun habit, noun-on-noun.   Modifying nouns with nouns. Characteristic of wordy writing and jargon. If you find yourself writing *plot structure* or *character trait* or *production management* or *student survey,* suspect yourself of both. See *Jargon,* and the discussion on pp. 172–175.

NOUN-ON-NOUN	REPAIRED
A lower volume of *product sales*	A lower volume of *sales* . . . .
His *character involvement* is	He *involves* his *characters* . . . .

Nowhere, noplace.   Use *nowhere* (not *nowheres*), and reserve *no place* (not *noplace*) only for literal meanings: "He could find no place that would hold it."

Nowhere near.   Use *not nearly,* or *far from,* unless you really mean *near:* "He was nowhere near the end."   See *Near.*

D. USAGE

AWKWARD	IMPROVED
It was *nowhere near* long enough.	It was *not nearly* long enough.
They had *nowhere near* enough food.	They had *far from* enough food.

Number of.   Usually correct.   See *Amount of.*

Numbers.   Spell out those that take no more than two words *(twelve, twelfth, twenty-four, two hundred)*; use numerals for the rest *(101, 203, 14,510)*.   But use numerals to make contrasts and statistics clearer: *20 as compared to 49; only 1 out of 40; 200 or 300 times as great.*   Change a two-word number to numerals when it matches a numeral: *with 400* [not *four hundred*] *students and 527 parents.*   Numbers are customary with streets: *42nd Street, 5th Avenue,* which may also be spelled out for aesthetic reasons: *Fifth Avenue.*   Use numbers also with dates, times, measurements, and money: *April 1, 1984; 6:30* A.M. (but *half-past six*); *3 x 5 cards; 240 by 100 feet; 6'3"* (but *six feet tall*); *$4.99; $2 a ticket* (but *16 cents a bunch*).

ROMAN NUMERALS
(Subtract a smaller number preceding a larger: IV = 4, XL = 40)

1	I	14	XIV	30	XXX	110	CX
2	II	15	XV	40	XL	199	CIC
3	III	16	XVI	41	XLI	200	CC
4	IV	17	XVII	49	XLIX	400	CD
5	V	18	XVIII	50	L	500	D
6	VI	19	XIX	60	LX	900	CM
7	VII	20	XX	70	LXX	1000	M
8	VIII	21	XXI	90	XC	1500	MD
9	IX	22	XXII	91	XCI	1600	MDC
10	X	23	XXIII	98	XCVIII	1700	MDCC
11	XI	24	XXIV	99	IC	1865	MDCCCLXV
12	XII	25	XXV	100	C	1492	MCDXCII
13	XIII	29	XXIX	101	CI	1976	MCMLXXVI

Use Roman numerals together with Arabic to designate act, scene, and line in plays, and book, chapter, and page in the novels that use them:

> **Romeo lies on the floor and cries like a child (III.iii.69–90).**
> **When Tom Jones finds the banknote (XII.iv.483), ...**

You would have already identified, in a footnote, the edition you are using. For further details see pp. 310; 315; 408.

Off of. Write *from:* "He jumped *from* his horse."

On behalf, in behalf. See *Behalf.*

On the part of. Wordy.

POOR	IMPROVED
There was a great deal of discontent *on the part of* those students who could not enroll.	The students who could not enroll were violently discontented.

One. Avoid this common redundancy.

POOR	IMPROVED
One of the most effective ways of writing is rewriting.	The best writing is rewriting.
The Ambassadors is one of the most interesting of James's books.	*The Ambassadors* is James at his best.
The meeting was obviously a poor one.	The meeting was obviously poor.

In constructions such as "one of the best that . . ." and "one of the worst who . . . ," the relative pronouns often are mistakenly considered singular. The plural noun of the prepositional phrase *(the best, worst),* not *the one,* is the antecedent, and the verb must be plural too:

WRONG	RIGHT
one of the best [*players*] who *has* ever swung a bat	one of the best [*players*] who *have* ever swung a bat

Only. Don't put it in too soon; you will say what you do not mean.

WRONG	RIGHT
He *only liked* **mystery stories.**	**He liked** *only mystery stories.*

Outside of. See *Inside of.*

Overall. Jargonish. Use *general,* or rephrase.

DULL	IMPROVED
The overall quality was good.	**The lectures were generally good.**

Parallelism. Putting similar ideas into the same grammatical construction, for emphasis and clarity, usually in the same sentence. See discussion, pp. 151–157.

Participle. A form of the verb that functions as an adjective: a *going* concern, a *gone* goose; *Liking* candy, he bought two pounds; He is well *liked.* *Going* and *liking* are present participles; *gone* and *liked,* past participles. See pp. 146–147; 399.

Participle for gerund. Avoid this frequent confusion of the *-ing's.* The participle works as an adjective; the gerund, as a noun. You want gerunds in the following constructions, and you can get them by changing the misleading noun or pronoun to the possessive case:

WRONG	RIGHT
Washington commended *him passing* **through the British lines.**	**Washington commended** *his passing* **through the British lines.**
Do you mind *me staying* **late?**	**Do you mind** *my staying* **late?**
She disliked *Bill smoking.*	**She disliked** *Bill's smoking.*
We all enjoyed *them singing* **songs and** *having* **a good time.**	**We all enjoyed** *their singing* **songs and** *having* **a good time.**

You can catch these errors by asking yourself if you mean that "You mind *me,*" or that "She disliked *Bill*" (which you do not).

Per. Use *a:* "He worked ten hours *a* day." *Per* is jargonish, except in conventional Latin phrases: *per diem, per capita* (not italicized in your running prose).

POOR	IMPROVED
This will cost us a manhour *per* machine *per* month a year from now.	A year from now, this will cost us a manhour a machine a month.
As *per* your instructions	According to your instructions

Per cent, percent, percentage. *Percent* (one word) seems preferred, though *percentage,* without numbers, still carries polish: "A large *percentage* of non-voters attended"; "a significant *percentage* of the students." Use the % sign and numerals only when comparing percentages, and in technical reports. Otherwise, spell it out, along with the numbers: *twenty-three percent, ten percent, a hundred percent* (see *Numbers*).

Perfect. Not "more perfect," but "more nearly perfect."

Personal. Change "personal friend" to "good friend," and protect him from seeming too personal.

Personally. Always superfluous.

POOR	IMPROVED
I want to welcome them *personally.*	I want to welcome them [myself].
Personally, I like it.	I like it.

Phase. *Phase* is not *faze* ("daunt"), nor does it mean *aspect* or *part;* it is a stage in a familiar cycle, like that of the moon or the caterpillar. Unless you can carry the specific metaphor, avoid it, along with *facet.*

Phenomena. Frequently misused for the singular *phenomenon:* "This is a striking *phenomenon*" (not *phenomena*).

Phenomenal. Misused for a general intensive: "His popularity was *phenomenal.*" A phenomenon is a fact of nature, in the ordinary nature of things. Find another word for the extraordinary: "His success was *extraordinary*" (*unusual, astounding, stupendous*).

Picket. A pointed fence post, or a person so staked. *To picket* is to deploy people as pickets, or to join with others as a protesting fence against wrongs.

POOR	IMPROVED
They began a picket of	They began to picket . . . .
They began their picket	They began picketing . . . .
Until they withdraw their picket	Until they withdraw their pickets . . . .

Plan on. Use *plan to.*

WRONG	RIGHT
He planned on going.	He planned to go.

Playwrite, playwright. The *playwright* writes plays. Use *playwrite* only as a participle: "his *playwriting* days."

Plot structure. Jargon. See *Noun habit,* and *Jargon.*

Possessives. See *Apostrophe-s.*

Power vacuum. A physical contradiction, since a vacuum is the absence of power. Delete *power,* or put it where it belongs, and your phrase will be accurate. See *Noun habit.*

INACCURATE	IMPROVED
The junta rushed into the *power vacuum* created when the big three withdrew their support.	The junta rushed into the *vacuum* left as the three big *powers* withdrew.

Prejudice. When you write "He was *prejudice,*" your readers may be *puzzle.* Give it a *d*: "He was *prejudiced,*" then they won't be *puzzled.*

Presence, presents. Sometimes confused. "Your *presence* is requested while we distribute the Christmas *presents.*"

Presently. Drop it. Or use *now.* Many readers will take it to mean *soon*: "He will go *presently.*" It is characteristic of official jargon.

POOR	IMPROVED
The committee is meeting *presently.*	The committee is meeting.
	The committee is meeting *soon.*
He is *presently* studying Greek.	He is studying Greek.

Principle, principal. Often confused. *Principle* is a noun only, meaning an essential truth, or rule: "It works on the *principle* that hot air rises." The *pal* is the *a*djective: remember the *a*'s, and the *pal* in the princip*al* person at our schools. The high-school *principal* acts as a noun because usage has dropped the *person* the adjective once modified. Likewise *principal* is the principal amount of your money, which draws interest.

> Our *principal* is a woman of *principle.*
> If you withdraw your *principal* from the bank, you will lose some interest.
> His *principal* motive was greed.
> The committee formulated two basic *principles.*

Proceed, precede, procedure. Continually mixed up in spelling. *Proceed* is to go ahead; *precede* is to go before. *Procedure* is a way of doing. The only solution here is memorizing, after you get the three meanings clearly in mind.

Proof, evidence. *Proof* results from enough *evidence* to establish a point beyond doubt. Be modest about claiming proof:

POOR	IMPROVED
This *proves* that Fielding was in Bath at the time.	Evidently, Fielding was in Bath at the time.

Proved, proven. *Proved* is the past participle, which may serve as an adjective meaning "successfully tested or demonstrated"; *proven* is an adjective only, and means "tested by time":

WRONG	RIGHT
It has proven true. [past part.]	It has proved true.
a proven theory [past part. as adj.]	a proved theory
The theory was proven. [same]	The theory was proved.
a proved remedy [pure adj.]	a proven remedy

Provide. If you *absolutely cannot* use the meaningful verb directly, you may say *provide*, provided you absolutely cannot *give, furnish, allow, supply, enable, authorize, permit, facilitate, force, do, make, effect, help, be, direct, cause, encourage . . . .*

Providing that. Use *provided,* and drop the *that.* *Providing,* with or without *that,* tends to make a misleading modification. See *Dangling modifier.*

POOR	IMPROVED
I will drop, *providing that* I get an incomplete.	I will drop, *provided* I get an incomplete.

In "I will drop, *providing* I get an incomplete," *you* seem to be providing, contrary to what you mean.

Put across. Try something else: *convinced, persuaded, explained, made clear. Put across* is badly overused.

Quality. Keep it as a noun. Too many *professional quality writers* are already producing *poor quality* prose, and *poor in quality* means *poor.* See *Noun habit* and *Jargon.*

Quite. An acceptable but overused emphatic: *quite good, quite expressive, quite a while, quite a person.* Try rephrasing it now and then: *good, very good, for some time, an able person.*

Quote, quotation. Quote your quotations, and put them in quotation marks. Distinguish the verb from the noun. The best solution is to use *quote* only as a verb and to find synonyms for the noun: *passage, remark, assertion.* See "Punctuation," pp. 432–437, for further details.

WRONG	RIGHT
As the following quote from Milton shows:	As the following passage from Milton shows: . . . .

Rarely ever. Drop the *ever:* "Shakespeare *rarely* misses a chance for comedy."

Real. Do not use for *very.* *Real* is an adjective meaning "actual":

WRONG	RIGHT
It was *real* good.	It was *very* good.
	It was *really* good.

Reason . . . is because. Knock out *the reason . . . is,* and *the reason why . . . is,* and you will have a good sentence.

> [The reason] they have difficulty with languages [is] because they have no interest in them.

Regarding, in regard to. Redundant or inaccurate.

POOR	IMPROVED
Regarding the banknote, Jones was perplexed. [Was he *looking* at it?]	Jones was perplexed by the banknote.
He knew nothing *regarding* money.	He knew nothing about money.
She was careful *in regard to* the facts.	She respected the facts.

Regardless. Correct. See *Irregardless* for the confusion.

Repetition. Avoid saying again what you have already said sufficiently. Avoid also inadvertent repetitions:

> Of *course,* the *course* itself was boring.
> *By* this time, people could *buy* some things *by* means of money.
> The banking *interests* were *interested* in peace.

But you may repeat words and phrases for effective emphasis. See "Rhetorical Devices," pp. 528–530. Repeating a necessary word is far better than trying for synonyms that may mislead your reader by making nonexistent distinctions.

POOR	IMPROVED
In London, most *shops* were small. The owner frequently lived above *the establishment.* Some *stores* were large.	In London, most *shops* were small, though some were large. The owner frequently lived above his *shop.*

Respective, respectively. Redundant.

POOR	IMPROVED
The armies retreated to their *respective* trenches.	The armies retreated to their trenches.

POOR	IMPROVED
Smith and Jones won the first and second prize *respectively.*	Smith won the first prize; Jones, the second.

Restrictive, nonrestrictive. A restrictive clause limits and designates what it modifies, *without surrounding commas:* "The book *that was open* was new" (that is, among several other books); "The girl *who sang* was Mildred." Nonrestrictive clauses merely add detail, with *which* and commas: "The book, *which was open,* cost twenty dollars." See pp. 143–144; 170–171; 419–420.

Reverend, Honorable. Titles of clergymen and congressmen. Use both with first names or initials: "Reverend Smith" and "Honorable Jones" should be *Mr. Smith* and *Mr. Jones,* omitting the title altogether. The fully proper forms, as in the heading of a letter (*the* would not be capitalized in your running prose), are:

The Reverend Mr. Claude C. Smith
The Honorable Adam A. Jones [omit *Mr.***]**

In running prose, the Reverend Mr. Smith is most proper; *Rev. Claude Smith* and *Hon. Adam Jones* will get by, but the best procedure is to give the title and name its full form for first mention, then to continue with *Mr. Smith* and *Mr. Jones.*

Rise, raise. Frequently confused. *Rise, rose, risen* means to get up. *Raise, raised, raised* means to lift up. "He *rose* early and *raised* a commotion."

Round. British for *around.*

Run-on sentence. Two or more sentences run together as one, either with no punctuation, or with a comma where a period or semicolon should go. See *Comma splice.*

RUN-ON	REPAIRED
The hero can no longer think he nearly goes insane.	The hero can no longer think. He nearly goes insane.

RUN-ON	REPAIRED
The book is well written, it is full of fascinating information.	The book is well written. It is full of fascinating information.
The novel fails to make Gatsby convincing, the movie brings him to life.	The novel fails to make Gatsby convincing; the movie brings him to life.

Sanction. Beatifically ambiguous, now meaning both "to approve" and "to penalize." But why contribute to confusion? Stick to the root; use it only "to bless," "to sanctify," "to approve," "to permit." Use *penalize* or *prohibit* when you mean just that.

POOR	IMPROVED
They exacted sanctions.	They exacted penalties.

Sarcasm. The student's word for irony. Sarcasm intends personal hurt. It may also be ironic, but need not be. "Well, little man, what now?" is pure sarcasm when a dwarf interrupts the class; it is ironic sarcasm when a seven-footer bursts in. See *Irony*.

Seldom ever. Redundant. Cut the *ever*.

Set, sit. Frequently confused. You *set* something down; you yourself *sit* down. Confine sitting to people (*sit, sat, sat*), and keep it intransitive, taking no object. *Set* is the same in all tenses (*set, set, set*).

CONFUSED	CLARIFIED
The house *sets* too near the street.	The house *stands* too near the street.
The package *sat* where he left it.	The package *lay* where he left it.
He *has set* there all day.	He *has sat* there all day.

Shall, will; should, would. The older distinctions—*shall* and *should* reserved for *I* and *we*—have faded; *will* and *would* are usual: "I will go"; "I would if I could"; "he will try"; "they all would."

Shall in the third person expresses determination: "They shall not pass." *Should,* in formal usage, is actually ambiguous: *We should be happy to comply,* intended to mean "would be happy," seems to say "ought to be happy."

Should of.   See *Could of, would of.*

[sic].   Latin for "so," put in brackets within a quotation, unitalicized, after some error or detail that might puzzle the reader. See "Brackets," pp. 431–432.

Similar to.   Use *like:*

POOR	IMPROVED
This is *similar to* that.	This is *like* that.

Sit.   See *Set, sit.*

Site, sight, cite.   Often confused.   *Site* is a piece of land to put a building on, or holding a building.   You do not see the *sites;* you see the *sights.*   To *cite* is to quote or mention an authority, or other evidence.

Situate.   Usually wordy and inaccurate.   Avoid it unless you mean, literally or figuratively, the act of determining a site, or placing a building.

FAULTY	IMPROVED
Ann Arbor is a town *situated* on the Huron River.	Ann Arbor is a town on the Huron River.
The building is *situated* in the slums.	The building is in the slums.
The control panel is *situated* on the right.	The control panel is on the right.
He is well *situated.*	He is rich.
The company is well *situated* to meet the competition.	The company is well prepared to meet the competition.

Situation.   Usually jargon.   Avoid it.   Say what you mean: *state, market, mess, quandary, conflict, predicament . . .*

Size.   Often redundant.   *A small-sized country* is *a small country. Large in size* is *large.*

Slant-line (/).   See *Virgule,* and p. 445.

Slow.   GO SLOW is what the street signs and the men on the street all say, but write "Go slowly."

So.   Should be followed by *that* in describing extent: "It was *so* foggy *that* traffic almost stopped."   Avoid its incomplete form, the schoolgirl's intensive — *so nice, so wonderful, so pretty* — though occasionally this is effective.

So . . . as.   See *As . . . as.*

Someplace, somewhere.   See *Anyplace.*

Sort of.   See *Kind of, sort of.*

Split infinitives.   Improve them.   They are cliché traps: *to really know, to really like, to better understand.*   They are misleaders: *to better . . . , to further . . . , to well . . . , to even . . . ,* all look and sound like complete infinitives: *to further investigate* starts out like *to further our investigation,* throwing the reader momentarily off the track.   *To better know* is to make *know* better, *to even like* is to make *like* even, all of which is nonsense.   Indeed, in perverse moments *to eventually go* seems to say that *go* is being "eventualied."   They are one of the signs of a wordy writer; they are usually redundant: *to really understand* is *to understand.*   The quickest cure for split infinitives is to drop the adverb.

   Even the splitters do not recommend splitting as a rule. The rule remains DON'T SPLIT; and if you must, learn what you are doing — a little deviltry is better for the soul than ignorance. But I am convinced that you can always mend the split for a gain in grace, and often for a saving of words.   You can sometimes change the adverb to an adjective, gaining force; saving letters and words:

POOR	IMPROVED
to adequately think out solutions	to think out adequate solutions
to enable us to effectively plan our advertising	to enable us to plan effective advertising

Or you can drop the adverb — often exuberant — or bring it forward, or move it along:

POOR	IMPROVED
I cannot bring myself to really like the fellow.	I cannot bring myself to like the fellow. I cannot bring myself really to like the fellow. I really cannot bring myself to like the fellow.

George O. Curme gives the following examples from eminent splitters, arguing that usage makes them right.* But each of them can be improved:

POOR	IMPROVED
I wish the reader to clearly understand this. (Ruskin)	I wish the reader to understand this. I wish the reader to understand this clearly.
It would have overburdened the text to there incorporate many details. (Hempl, *Mod. Lang. Notes*)	Details there would have overburdened the text.
. . . without permitting himself to actually mention the name. (Arnold)	. . . without permitting himself to mention the name.
. . . of a kind to directly stimulate curiosity. (Pater)	. . . of a kind to stimulate curiosity.
. . . things which few except parents can be expected to really understand. (Oliver Wendell Holmes)	. . . things only parents can understand.
. . . to bravely disbelieve (Browning, *The Ring and the Book*, Cambridge ed., p. 570)	. . . bravely to disbelieve

Browning's full line, in fact, would have thumped somewhat less if he had dared bravely to vary his meter and mend his infinitive:

Whence need bravely to disbelieve report.

* *English Grammar* (New York: Barnes and Noble, 1947), p. 269.

Stationary, stationery. Sometimes confused. Remember that you get your station*e*ry from a station*er*.

Structure. A darling of the jargoneer, often meaning nothing more framelike than "unity" or "coherence." *Plot structure* usually means *plot,* with little idea of beams and girders. Use it only for something you could diagram, like the ribs of a snake, and never use it as a verb. See *Jargon.*

POOR	IMPROVED
He structured the meeting.	He organized (planned, arranged) the meeting.

Sure. Too colloquial for writing: "It is *sure* a good plan." Use *certainly,* or otherwise rephrase.

That, which, who. *That* defines and restricts; *which* is explanatory and nonrestrictive; *who* stands for people, and may be restrictive or nonrestrictive. See *Restrictive, nonrestrictive;* see also *Who, which, that.*

The faucet *that* drips is in the basement.
The faucet, *which* drips badly, needs attention.
Of all the Democrats *who* supported him at first, none was more ardent than Jones.
Of all the Democrats, *who* supported him at first, none was more ardent than Jones.

There is, there are, it is. However natural and convenient—it is WORDY. Notice that *it* has here been referring to something specific, differing distinctly from the *it* in "It is easy to write badly." This indefinite subject, like *there is* and *there are,* gives the trouble. Of course, you will occasionally need an *it* or a *there* to assert existences:

There are ants in the cupboard.
There is only one Kenneth.
There are craters on the moon.
It is too bad.

But avoid *There is* and *It is,* and you will avoid some sludgy traps. They are part of the spoken language, like clearing the throat, and they frequently add just as little, especially when entailing a *that* or a *which:*

WORDY	IMPROVED
There are three men on duty.	Three men are on duty. [5 words for 6]
There is nothing wrong with this.	Nothing is wrong with this. [5 words for 6]
There are two things which are important here.	Two things are important here. [5 words for 8]
It is a habit which few can break.	Few can break this habit. [5 words for 8]
It is a shame that they had no lawyer.	Unfortunately, they had no lawyer. [5 words for 9]

These kind, these sort. Should be *this kind, this sort.*

They. A loose indefinite pronoun; tighten it:

POOR	IMPROVED
They are all against us, you know.	*Everyone* is against us, you know.
They launch our rockets at Cape Kennedy.	The *United States* launches its rockets from Cape Kennedy.

Do not use *they* with a singular antecedent.

WRONG	RIGHT
Everyone knows *they* should write correctly.	*Everyone* knows *he* should write correctly.
Every one of the students assumes *they* will pass.	*Every one* of the students assumes *he* will pass.

Till, until. Both are respectable. Note the spelling. Do not use *'til.*

Too. Awful as a conjunctive adverb: "Too, it was unjust." Also poor as an intensive: "They did not do too well" (note the difference in Shakespeare's "not wisely but too well"—he really means it). Use *very,* or (better) nothing: "They did not do well" (notice the nice understated irony).

Toward, towards.   *Toward* is the better, though both are acceptable.

Transition.   A word or phrase helping the reader to make the step from one paragraph to the next, or from one sentence to the next: *also, of course, but, to be sure,* and the like.   See pp. 41–43; 54; 100–103.

Transitive.   A verb that takes an object: "He *hit* him."

Transpose.   A direction to you, or to a printer, to exchange positions of letters, words, or phrases, marked thus:

n̲a̲d̲ he w̲e̲n̲t̲ ̸first.

so that it will read:

and he first went.

Trite.   From Latin *tritus:* "worn out."   Many words get temporarily worn out and unusable: *emasculated, viable, situation,* to name a few.   And many phrases are permanently frayed; see *Clichés.*

Try and.   Write *try to.   To try and do* means "to try and to do," which is probably not what you mean.   *Come and, go and, be sure and,* and so forth, should all likewise take *to.*

Type.   Banish it, abolish it.   If you must use it, insert *of:* not *that type person* but *that type OF person,* though even this is really jargon for *that kind of person, a person like that.*   The newspapers have succumbed, and we hear of *commando-type forces* for *commando forces,* of *a Castro-type dictator* for *another Castro,* of *the force of a Hiroshima-type bomb* for *the force of the Hiroshima bomb.*   The most accurate translations of *-type* are *-like, -ish, -esque,* and *-ate,* depending on sense and euphony: *Castrolike, Castro-ish, Russianesque, Italianate.*   English has many ways of saying it:

WRONG	RIGHT
essay-type question	essay question
Mondrian's checkerboard-type painting	Mondrian's checkerboard of a painting.
	Mondrian's checkerboardish painting
	Mondrian's checkerboardlike painting

WRONG	RIGHT
French-type dressing	French dressing
Italian-type spaghetti	Italian spaghetti [Be bold!— we neither know nor care whether it's imported.]
atomic-type submarine	atomic submarine
She was a Chris Evert-type girl.	She was like Chris Evert.
	She was a Chris Evert.
	She was a Chris Evert kind of girl.
	She was a Chris Evert type.
an apprentice-type situation	apprenticeship
a Puck-type person	a Puckish person, a Puck-like person

Unique.   Something *unique* has nothing in the world like it.

WRONG	RIGHT
The more unique the organization	The more nearly unique . . . .
the most unique man I know	the most unusual man I know
a very unique personality	a unique personality

U.S.   Acceptable abbreviation for "United States" as an adjective, with *the,* in phrases like *the U.S. Senate.*   But write *United States* out fully when it is a noun: "They migrated to the *United States*" (not "*to the U.S.*").   Nevertheless, *U.S.* as a noun (and even *US*) is gaining in some journals, and may eventually win general acceptance.

Use, use of.   A dangerously wordy word.   "Through [the use of] personification, he asserts a theme."   "In this sense, [the use of] physical detail is significant."

POOR	IMPROVED
He uses personification	He personifies . . . .
He uses inductive reasoning	He reasons inductively . . . .

Use to.   A mistake for *used to.*

Utilize, utilization. Wordy. *Utilize* means *use* (verb). *Utilization* means *the use* (noun). And the whole idea of "using"—a basic, universal concept—is frequently contained in the other words of your sentence.

POOR	IMPROVED
He *utilizes* frequent dialogue to enliven his stories.	Frequent dialogue enlivens his stories.
The *utilization* of a scapegoat eases their guilt.	A scapegoat eases their guilt.

Very. Spare the *very* and the *quite, rather, pretty*, and *little*. I would hate to admit (and don't care to know) how many of these qualifiers I have cut from this text. You can do without them entirely, but they do ease a phrase now and then.

Virgule. Avoid it, except to mark lines of poetry (see p. 445). Replace it with a hyphen if you must use such lumps as "work/play problem," "science/religion controversy"—but rephrasing to avoid the jargon is better: "the choice of work or play."

Viz. Pronounced "vi-DEL-uh-sit," after *videlicet*, the Latin word it abbreviates. It means "that is" or "namely." Put commas before and after it; do not italicize. See *Abbreviations.*

Wake, waken (awake, awaken). *Wake, woke, waked (awake, awoke, awaked)* are standard. *Waken, wakened, wakened (awaken, awakened, awakened)* are slightly different verbs meaning "to wake up" (intransitive) or "to cause to wake up" (transitive).

He *wakes* up early. He *woke* him up yesterday. He *has waked* them up every morning at seven.

Awake, awoke, awaked is usually intransitive:

She *awakes* easily. They *awoke* with a start. The birds *have* already *awaked.*

Waken and *awaken* are most frequently used transitively: "He *wakened (awakened)* his roommate." And they are more frequent in the passive voice. "He *was awakened* by loud knocking." Figurative usages prefer *awake* and *awaken: He was awake to the risk; his fears were awakened.*

Ways. Avoid it. Means *way:* "He went a short *way* into the woods."

Weather, whether. *Weather,* which means storms or breezes, rain or shine, is sometimes mistakenly written for *whether.* Whether the reader will smile or wince is problematical.

Well. See *Good.*

Whereas. Now a useful subordinating conjunction, preceded by a comma: "Hamlet is partly responsible for the tragedy, *whereas* Ophelia is wholly an innocent victim."

Whether. See *If,* and *Weather.*

Which. See *Who, that, which.*

While. Reserve for time only, as in "*While* I was talking, she smoked constantly."

WRONG	RIGHT
While I like her, I don't admire her.	*Although* I like her, I don't admire her.
The side roads were impassable, *while* the highways were clear.	The side roads were impassable, *but* the highways were clear.
The seniors eat in clubs, *while* the freshmen eat in their dormitories.	The seniors eat in clubs, *and* the freshmen eat in their dormitories.

Who, which, that. Relative pronouns, *relating* an additional and subordinate clause to some preceding noun or pronoun:

She *who falls* **falls far.**
The fall *that hurts least* **is the last.**
The fall, *which was severe,* **was not serious.**

Who may be either restrictive or nonrestrictive (see *Restrictive*): "The ones *who win* are lucky"; "The players, *who are all outstanding,* win often." *Who* refers only to persons:

FAULTY	REPAIRED
The girl *that* so chooses may enter dentistry.	The girl *who* so chooses may enter dentistry.
Some of the characters *that* wander around the stage	Some of the characters *who* wander . . . .

Use *that* for all other restrictives; *which* for all other nonrestrictives. See further discussion on pp. 419–420, "the *of*-and-*which* disease" (pp. 170–171), and pp. 143–144.

Avoid *which* in loose references to the whole idea preceding, rather than to a specific word, since you may be unclear:

FAULTY	IMPROVED
He never wore the hat, which his wife hated.	His wife hated his going bareheaded.
	He never wore the hat his wife hated.

Whom, whomever. The objective forms, after verbs and prepositions; but each is often wrongly put as the subject of a clause.

WRONG	RIGHT
Give the ticket to *whomever* wants it.	Give the ticket to *whoever wants it.* [The whole clause is the object of *to; whoever* is the subject of *wants.*]
The president, *whom* he said would be late	The president, *who* he said *would be late* . . . . [Commas around *he said* would clear the confusion.]
Whom shall I say called?	*Who* shall I say called?

BUT:
They did not know *whom* to elect. [The infinitive takes the objective case.]

Who's, whose. Sometimes confused in writing. *Who's* means "who is?" in conversational questions: *"Who's* going?" Never use it in writing (except in dialogue), and you can't miss. *Whose* is the regular possessive of *who:* "The committee, *whose* work was finished, adjourned."

Will. See *Shall.*

-wise. Avoid all confections like *marketwise, customerwise, price-wise, gradewise, confectionwise* — except for humor.

Would. For habitual acts, the simple past is more economical:

POOR	IMPROVED
The parliament *would meet* only when called by the king.	The parliament *met* only when called by the king.
Every hour, the watchman *would make* his round.	Every hour, the watchman *made* his round.

Would sometimes seeps into the premise of a supposition. Rule: Don't use *would* in an *if* clause.

WRONG	RIGHT
If he *would have* gone, he would have succeeded.	If he *had* gone, he would have succeeded.
	Had he gone, he would have succeeded [more economical].
I wish I *would have* learned it.	I wish I *had* learned it.

Would of. See *Could of, would of.*

EXERCISES

Refer to the Glossary as needed to clear up the following passages.

1. The US is presently leading the debate in the UN, *viz.* that concerning the energy crisis problem, accept for atomic research. They hope to reach an accomodation that will not effect the general economy or endanger the enviorment. Every country has their own point of view, of course, answers are not easily forthcoming and many smaller powers are disallusioned by the dilemna, since

delay may be disasterous, due to the fact that all countries face inflation. Some countries could care less. Some enthuse over prospects of high level profits from their principle exports, proceding to further fan the flames of arguement and resistence. An explosion is immanent.

2. Some students are prejudice unconsciously, and would never apollogize, no matter what occured. They are frequently not as considerate as those that appreciate the minoritys' point of view. They would have acted more maturely, if they would have been more socially aware, as of the 20th century. But everyday less students make these errors. Some courses in the regular curicula are a definate must for social awareness, since they cause the ballance of the students to discover their hidden prejudice, in may cases. These kind of courses center around the concept of how prejudice is acquired, and cause the student to understand his attitudes in connection with society.

3. Originality is a rare-type phenomena. Each creation may seem discreet to its creator, however, it usually resembles many others of it's type, even works of reknowned authors. These kind of works are actually enjoyable because we see the resemblances together with the differences. None of the performances of the same symphony are the same for each rewards anew. We persue novelty without realizing that we want similiarity too. The particular performance disolves into our general memory of the familiar work. The reason why we can listen to the same symphony, or see the same play, or even the same film again and again is because each experience is seperate and new. In the field of aesthetics, the performance gives us satisfaction if it has fit our general memory of the work. A memory that also changes slightly with each performance, resulting in a more perfect idea of the work, untill our idea takes on a kind of permanent existance.

4. Swimming is healthy, a never to be forgotten experience, it is believed by some authorities that it is the most generally healthy exercise transpiring. Many just lay on the beach and soak in the sun but it is sheer hypocracy as well as being lazy. In fact, many students like to infer that they have gone to Florida while they only have been sunning under a lamp in his/her room. Some sunning is alright, of course but too much will result in a burn and a poor quality tan. People using caution rarely ever get burned, especially with the use of an unchallangable lotion.

Section E
Rhetorical Devices: The Classical Heritage

The general strategies of rhetoric I have described in this book—even such familiar devices as parallelism—have all evolved through classical oratory, as it tested in its noisy forums the essentials of how one may persuade one's audience, how one may arrange one's phrases attractively, forcefully, and memorably. Both the structure and the devices are still with us, since, as Solzhenitsyn once remarked, human nature seems to change only about as fast as the geological surface of the earth. Consequently, we can strengthen our ideas of structure and phrasing by seeing how these devices have persisted, through differing ages and languages, in the essential dynamics of communication.

STRUCTURE: CLASSICAL AND MODERN

I had, with my classes, worked through the structural essentials —the inevitable beginning-middle-end, the internal principles of the argumentative edge, of ascending interest, of dialectical order, and of

516

comparison—before I realized how thoroughly they were already reflected in classical rhetoric. The classical form is still visible not only in the modern essay, but even in the modern scientific paper, which reproduces in most of its details the ancient Greek oratorical form that the Roman lawyer Cicero (first century B.C.) polished in his orations and outlined in his *De Oratore*.

You can detect this classic oratorical form almost anywhere you look in the literature and exposition of the Middle Ages and the Renaissance. Sir Philip Sidney turned to it automatically when he wrote *An Apologie for Poetrie*, as did John Milton for his famous *Areopagitica*. The great formal essayists, like John Henry Newman, followed it in more recent times. And today, as I have said, it appears universally behind the structure of the essay and the scientific report.

The form was adjustable; parts were sometimes omitted, and subdivisions added. But the usual form, as set forth by Cicero, Quintilian, and their followers, with the first three items matching our "beginning," and the last one our "end," was more or less like this, under the traditional Latin headings:

1. *Exordium* (or *Proem*). The introduction.

2. *Narratio*. General description of subject and background.

3. *Propositio*. The thesis, the statement of what is to be demonstrated or proved.

4. *Partitio*. Statement of how the thesis is to be divided and handled.

5. *Confirmatio* (or *Argumentatio*, or *Explicatio*). The chief evidence in support of the thesis; the body, the longest part, of the oration. Roughly, our "middle."

6. *Reprehensio*. The knocking-out of the opposition. Although the ancients, with somewhat more leisure than we, saved their merriment until after their own case was firmly established, the *reprehensio* contained exactly the refutations that must always accompany an enumeration of the opposition's claims. The structure of the *reprehensio* was exactly that recommended in our discussion of *pro*'s and *con*'s: setting up the opposition only to knock it flat.

7. *Digressio.* The name speaks for itself. The "digression" was intended to lighten the load. It could come anywhere between *exordium* and *peroratio,* with matters related, but not essential, to the subject.

8. *Peroratio.* The conclusion, summarizing the discussion and urging the thesis with greater eagerness and enthusiasm.

Shorter orations sometimes dropped the *reprehensio,* if no opposition had to be refuted, and absorbed the *propositio* and *partitio,* the statements of thesis and method, into the *narratio,* coming very near to what we have described as our "beginning." *Digressio,* which is largely decoration or relief anyway, was also frequently dropped, or inserted at some different place. Since these parts were movable, we have in the ancient form the larger framework of beginning-middle-end, of assertion and refutation, that we have already outlined for the modern essay in general. Here is how the modern scientific paper, or lab report, reflects the form of classical oration:

CLASSICAL	SCIENTIFIC
Exordium ⎫ *Narratio* ⎭	Introduction
Propositio	Purpose (thesis)
Partitio	Materials and methods
Confirmatio	Results
Peroratio	⎰ Discussion ⎱ Summary

The modern essayist has simply streamlined the classical form a little further than has the systematic scientist. The classical orator stated his case, faced the opposition, then stated his case again—and at some length—in his summative peroration. The essayist's only real alteration is in putting the *reprehensio,* the managing of the opposition, before his own argument rather than after it, for simple economy. By hitting the opposition first, he need state his own case but once, repeating only a little in his conclusion, which immediately follows.

CLASSICAL ORATION	MODERN ESSAY
Exordium ⎫ *Narratio* ⎬ *Propositio* ⎭	Beginning (with thesis)
Confirmatio ⎫ *Reprehensio* ⎭	Middle (*reprehensio* followed by *confirmatio*)
Peroratio	End

Here is a short essay of three paragraphs (Beginning, Middle, End), in which you may detect, by way of structural exercise, something of the old classical divisions. You will notice that the writer has stated the opposition (*reprehensio*) to introduce his thesis itself, an excellent beginning for a brief essay. In a longer essay, he would have begun more neutrally ("Chance plays a large role in our lives. We bump into an old friend in Paris. We lose our keys, or find a good restaurant."). And he would have put the world's disasters — the *con*-side, the *reprehensio* — in the second paragraph.

Happy Accidents

Every morning the newspaper brings us the world's most recent disasters. An earthquake in Turkey vies for horror with a landslide in Peru or a burning liner at sea. Planes crash, mines cave in, and wreckage strews the expressway. Among the usual robberies and murders are always a few bizarre accidents: deaths from stray bullets, falling hammers, or slipping ladders. Yet accidents can be happy. *Exordium*

Reprehensio

Propositio

The blessing in disguise has indeed become proverbial. The Grayton *Globe* recently ran an article about a woman who had been paralyzed from the waist down by a fall in her kitchen. She realized for the first time that cripples needed to feel useful, and frequently had skills for which they could find no employment. She organized a small company employing only cripples, taking contracts from larger companies for work that handicapped people could do, frequently in their homes, like assembling small parts for radio and television manufacturers. Seated in her wheelchair at her telephone, she discovered work for many handicapped people, depending on their capacities. *Narratio*

Confirmatio

Her accident had changed her life into something valuable both for herself and for others.

Peroratio
So accidents are not always bad. A personal tragedy may make us aware of human suffering, and transform our lives. We may understand people better, and may become kinder to each other. Or we might even dedicate ourselves entirely to alleviating human suffering. The loss of some physical ability may add to one's inner strength. The disaster that had seemed to crush us may prove the blessing in disguise — the accident that fulfilled our lives and made us truly happy.

RHETORICAL DEVICES

The Greeks had words for them, and the Romans improved the supply. We still run into the words from time to time; we still fall into the rhetorical patterns even when unaware of the terms. Sooner or later, the natural dynamics of expression will get you to many of the rhetorical devices the Greeks long ago discovered and named. But the terms, commonplace during ancient times, are today difficult to find listed in one place; and the devices, still more common than one might think, are such pleasant exercisers of the verbal torso, such excellent invigorators of the linguistic circulation, that it seems good to have them grouped and handy. I have had great pleasure in seeing the rhetorical modes as active in modern English as in ancient Greek and Latin, and in trying them out in my own idiom. Here they are, arranged for your convenience within functional categories (by no means mutually exclusive), and with pronunciations suggested for those your desk dictionary may not include. You can indeed increase your power by making these venerable devices your own, by having them ready, by learning through them the fair and beautiful play of language.

Alluding to the Familiar

anamnesis (AN-am-NEE-sis). "A remembering." You remind your reader of former success or catastrophe to emphasize your point.

This is the very day on which we lost last year. Again we meet a stronger team in our own stadium. Again injuries have wiped out our strongest hope. Again the weather looks hopeless.

parachresis (para-KREE-sis). You bring another's words into your own context, with new emphasis or effect.

As Ovid says of the sun: Ann sees all things.
Bill constantly follows John around, like Plato's shadow of a shadow.
When Thoreau said that the mass of men lead lives of quiet desperation he must have had Butch in mind.

paradiorthosis (para-die-or-THO-sis). You quote famous words with your own twist and without identifying them: a witty, subtle, and learned game much played by the Greek poets and T. S. Eliot.

The boredom, the horror, and the glory of life [Eliot's allusive twisting of "the kingdom, the power, and the glory"].

paroemia (pa-REE-mi-a). You apply proverbs to a new situation.

Even the rose has thorns [when a plan has drawbacks, or a girl a temper].
Every dog has its day. [Your opponent has just won the election.]
Man shall not live by bread alone. [He has just ordered steak.]
Never look a gift-horse in the mouth. [Someone has criticized the doorway of a new building given the university.]

Building to Climax

asyndeton (a-SIN-de-ton). "Without joining." You rush a series of clauses together without conjunctions, as if tumbled together by emotional haste (see pp. 414–415).

They tried, they fought, they did their best.

climax. You repeat the same word or sound in each succeeding phrase or clause — an intensified form of *anadiplosis* (see p. 528).

> Knowing that tribulation works patience, and patience experience, and experience hope. (Rom. v.3–4)

incrementum (in-kre-MENT-um). You arrange items from lowest to highest.

> The law will be kept in the shacks of the farms, in the tenements of the slums, in the bungalows and homes of the suburbs, and in the mansions of the countryside.

synonymy (si-NON-i-me). You repeat, by synonyms, for emphasis.

> A miserable, wretched, depressed neighborhood.

Intensifying

anacoenosis (ana-see-NO-sis). You heighten your style as if in urgent consultation with your audience, and with frequent rhetorical questions. You gain an urgent mixture of intimacy and elegance.

> If I be a father, where is mine honor? If I be a master, where is my fear? (Mal. i.6)
> Would we really want freedom? Would we really want liberty of all kinds? Would we really want anarchy more than peace of mind? We would, I think you will agree, gladly accept a restricted peace for some measure of quiet.

apodioxis (apo-die-OX-is). You reject an idea emphatically.

> Absurd! Now really! Well, after all!
> Can anything be less practical?

aposiopesis (apo-sigh-o-PE-sis). "A silence." You stop suddenly in midsentence, as if words fail, or as if a word to your wise reader has been completely sufficient.

But the cat . . . .
Do you believe that he can cope . . . ?
And in the name of common sense—!

apostrophe (a-POS-tro-fee). "A turning away." You "turn away" from your audience to address someone new—God, the angels, heaven, the dead, or anyone not present.

Hear, O heavens.
Death, where is thy sting?
Blush, America, for this stupidity.

ecphonesis (ek-fo-NEE-sis). Also called *exclamatio*. You cry out against something—usually in an apostrophe.

O most wicked speed, to post/With such dexterity to incestuous sheets.

erotesis (cro-TEE-sis). This is what we know as the rhetorical question.

Is this the best course? Will this pave the streets?

Irony

antonomasia (antono-MAY-zhia). You substitute an epithet, a label, for a person's real name, usually with ironic emphasis.

The Philosopher. The Blowhard. A Solomon. A Castro. A Mickey Mouse. The Swede.

apophasis (a-POF-a-sis). Also called *paralepsis* or *preteritio*. "A passing over." You pretend not to mention something in the very act of mentioning it. The effect is strongly, and sometimes hilariously, ironic. It was a favorite of Cicero's.

I shall not mention the time he failed to come home at all, or his somewhat wobbly condition at breakfast.
I shall not go into all his broken promises, his campaign speeches, or his scandalous treatment of his aged mother.
I pass over . . . .

We had perhaps better forget . . . .
I shall not mention . . . .

aporia (a-POR-i-a). "Doubting." You hesitate ironically between alternatives.

Whether he is more stupid than negligent, I hesitate to guess.
One hardly knows what to call it, folly or forgetfulness, ignorance or ignominy.

epitrope (e-PIT-ro-pe). You ironically grant permission.

Let her go, let her go, God bless her!
All right, go on, have a good time, kill yourself.

euphemism (YOU-fe-mizm). You substitute less pungent words for harsh ones, with excellent ironic effect.

The schoolmaster corrected the slightest fault with his birch reminder.
After a gallon of whiskey, he was slightly indisposed.

ironia (eye-RO-ni-a). Also called *antiphrasis* (an-TIF-ra-sis). You say the contrary of what you mean, in what is usually designated "verbal irony" (see *Irony*, p. 485, and Exercise 13, p. 199.)

He was a beauty.
She is so kind to her friends.
How thoughtful!

litotes (LIE-toh-teez). "Simplifying." You assert something by denying its opposite.

Not bad.
This is no small matter.
My house is not large.
She was not supremely happy.
He is not the wisest man in the world.

oxymoron (OX-i-MOR-on). "Pointed stupidity." You emphasize your point by the irony of an apparent contradiction or inconsistency.

A wise fool, a fearful joy, a sweet sadness, a quiet orgy.
Their silence is eloquent.
This somebody is nobody.

paralepsis (or **preteritio**). See *apophasis,* p. 523.

zeugma (ZYEWG-ma). "Yoking." You yoke two words so that one
is accurate and the other an ironic misfit (a favorite irony of
Edward Gibbon's in *The Decline and Fall of the Roman Empire*).

Waging *war* and *peace.*
Laws the wily tyrant *dictated* and *obeyed.*
Pacified by *gifts* and *threats.*
A blessing they *enjoyed* and *feared.*

Overstating, Understating

auxesis (awk-SEE-sis). You ironically use an overly weighty or
exaggerated term for the accurate one.

She is an angel.
He is a devil.
That pig ate all the olives.

hyperbole (high-PER-bo-lee). You exaggerate for emphasis, humorous or serious.

She cried like a banshee.

hypothesis. You illustrate with an impossible supposition.

If salt lose its savor, wherewith shall it be salted?
Even if he had a million dollars, he would be unhappy.
I'll come to thee by moonlight, though Hell should bar the way.

meiosis (my-o-sis). You make big things seem trifles, or substitute a
lighter word for ironic effect. The opposite of *auxesis* (see above).

He had three sandwiches and a quart of milk for his *snack.*
It was *nothing; a pinprick.*
He had a mansion in the country and another *little place* in town.

Posing Contrasts

antithesis.   You strongly and closely contrast your ideas.

> From rags to riches, from beans to beef, from water to wine.
> Man proposes, God disposes.
> A world in a grain of sand, a heaven in a wild flower.
> The world will *little note nor long remember* **what** *we say* **here,** but
> it can *never forget* **what** *they did* **here.**
> It was the best of times; it was the worst of times.

chiasmus (ky-AZ-mus).   "A crossing" — from the Greek letter *chi,* χ,
a cross. (Also called *antimitabole.*)   You "cross" the terms of
one clause by reversing their order in the next.

> Ask not what your country can do for you: ask what you can do
> for your country.
> What you write may mark your place in society — or place your
> mark on it.

comparison.   In an extended and balanced comparison, you match
your clauses almost syllable for syllable.

> My years are not so many, but that one death may conclude
> them, nor my faults so many, but that one death may satisfy
> them.
> He who loves pleasure shall be a poor man; he who loves wine
> and oil shall not be rich.

dilemma.   You catch the argument both ways, in a pair of opposing
suppositions.

> If you're so smart, why aren't you rich? If you're rich, why act
> so smart?
> If he is right, why disparage him? If he is wrong, why pay
> attention to him at all?

dissimile.   You emphasize the condition of something by saying
how dissimilar it is from the usual run of things.

> The foxes have holes, and the fowls of the air their nests, but
> the son of man has nowhere to lay his head. (Luke ix.58)
> One generation passeth away, and another generation cometh;
> but the earth abideth forever.

enantiosis (en-AN-ti-o-sis). Also called *contentio*. You emphasize contraries, often with *chiasmus*.

> One wouldn't hurt her; the other couldn't help her.
> Could not go on, would not go back.
> Serious in silly things, and silly in serious.

Refining, Elaborating

epanorthosis (EP-an-or-THO-sis). "A correction." You seem to "correct" yourself to reinforce your idea.

> Written not in tables of stone but in the fleshy tables of the
> heart. (II Cor. iii.3.)
> He asks, or rather demands, an answer.
> A gift-horse — no, a white elephant.

exegesis (ck-suh-JEE-sis). Also called *explicatio*. You clarify a thought in the same sentence.

> Time is both short and long, short when you are happy, long
> when in pain.

exergasia (eks-er-GAY-zhia). "A polishing." You put the same thing several ways.

> A beauty, a dream, a vision, a phantom of delight.

hirmos (HEAR-mos). "A series." You heap appositives together.

> All people, rich, poor, tall, short, young, old, love it.

horismos (ho-RIZ-mos). You elaborate a concept by defining it.

> Beauty is transitory, a snare for the unwary, an invitation to disaster.

Repeating

alliteration.   You repeat the initial letter or sound in two or more nearby words.

> The morning air was *c*ool and *c*risp.
> They have *b*ribed us with promises, *b*lackmailed us with threats, *b*ludgeoned us with prohibitions, and *b*led us with taxes.
> *Sp*eak the *sp*eech, I *p*ray you, as I *p*ronounc'd it to you, *t*rippingly on the *t*ongue . . . .

anadiplosis (ana-di-PLO-sis).   You repeat early in a clause a significant word from the end of the preceding clause.

> They rode in on a *wave* of fear, but the *wave* took them up the beach.
> Learn as though you would *live* forever; *live* as though you would die tomorrow.

anaphora (a-NAF-or-a).   "A bringing again."   You begin successive sentences or clauses with the same word or sound.

> The voice of the Lord is powerful.   The voice of the Lord is full of majestie.   The voice of the Lord breaks the cedars.   (Psa. xxix.4–5)
> The game is lost.   The game was finished before it began.   The game was a farce of sportsmanship.

antanaclasis (anta-NAK-la-sis).   You repeat the same word in a different sense, punning on it to drive home your point.

> Learn a *craft* so you may live without *craft*.
> *Care* in your youth so you may live without *care*.

epanalepsis (EP-ana-LEP-sis).   You end your second clause with the same word or sound that began your first clause.

A fool with his friends, with his wife a fool.
In sorrow was I born, and will die in sorrow.

epistrophe (e-PIS-tro-fee).   You end several sentences alike for emphasis.

They loved football.   They ate football.   They slept football.

epizeuxis (EP-i-ZYEWK-sis).   You double the same word for emphasis.

Romeo, Romeo, wherefore art thou Romeo?
Oh, John, John.
It is not, believe me, it is not.
War, war after war.

homeoteleuton (homeo-TEL-yu-ton).   You end successive clauses or phrases with the same sound.

In activity commendable, in commonwealth formidable, in war terrible.
He spoke wittily, praised the principal mightily, and ended happily.

paregmenon (pa-REG-meh-non).   You play upon derivatives of a word.

A discrete discretion.
A marvel of the marvelous.
The humble are proud of humility.

paronomasia (parono-MAY-zhia).   You pun by changing a letter or syllable.

His *sword* is better than his *word.*
Errors cause *terrors.*
Bolder in the *buttery* than in the *battery.*
Friends turned *fiends.*
Repining but not *repenting.*

ploce (PLO-see).   You repeat a word emphatically to bring out its literal meaning.

A *man's* a man, for a' that.
A *player* who is really a *player*.
In that battle *Caesar* was *Caesar*.

Substituting

hendiadys (hen-DIE-a-dis).   "One through two."   You divide what would be an adjective-and-noun into two nouns connected by *and*.

We drank from cups and gold [golden cups].
He looked with eyes and anger [angry eyes].

metaphor.   "A carrying across."   You describe something as if it were something else (see pp. 185–188).

All flesh is grass.
She was a horse.
She preened her feathers.

metonymy (meh-TON-i-me).   A kind of metaphor, in which you substitute an associated item for the thing itself.

The *White House* declares [for "the *President* declares"].
The *crown* decides [for "the *king* decides"].
The *hot rod* is here [for "the young man who drives a car in which the piston rods run at high temperatures is here" — *hot rod* is already a *synecdoche* for *car*].

parabola (pa-RAB-o-la).   You illustrate with a slight narrative touch, or "parable."   This is a *hypothesis* (see p. 525) somewhat nearer the possible.

It is as if a man were to hit the bull's eye without aiming, or indeed without even seeing the target.
But this is to count your chickens before they hatch.

paradiastole (para-die-ass-to-lee). In a kind of euphemism, you substitute a term remotely similar to the real idea, as in calling a reckless driver "playful" to underline his recklessness ironically.

The *generous* Mr. Smith [actually improvident].
The general's tactics were *cautious* [downright timid or cowardly].
Bill played a *conservative* game [obviously stupid].
She is *considerate* of her appearance [does nothing but work on it].

prosopopoeia (pro-so-po-pe-ya). You personify an inanimate object. Originally, the idea was pretending that an inanimate thing, an imaginary being, or an absent person (especially the illustrious dead) was speaking; now, more broadly, it is the general endowing of inanimate objects with human attributes.

Thou still unravished bride of quietness.
The stadium settled back for a lonely week.
This car is a sweetheart in every line.

synecdoche (si-nek-do-kee). You put (a) the part for the whole, (b) the whole for the part, (c) the species for the genus, (d) the genus for the species, (e) the material for the object it constitutes.

(a) He is a good *hand.*
(b) Here comes *Michigan* [for only the football team of one university within the state].
(c) a *cutthroat* [for any kind of murderer].
(d) the *felines* [for lions].
(e) He handles his *woods* well [for golf clubs made of wood].

Miscellaneous

hyperbaton (high-per-ba-ton). You transpose the normal order of words for elegance.

That the lady will surely enjoy.
Him the crowd adores.

martyria (mar-TIR-i-a). "Witnessing." You confirm something from your own experience.

> I have seen thousands standing with their rice bowls.
> Many times I have found the stadium only half filled.

metabasis (meh-TAB-a-sis). "Transition." Briefly reminding the reader where you and he are, where you have been, and where you are going.

> We have just seen some of radiation's immediate effects; now let us consider the long-term effects.
> I have already mentioned property taxes; now I shall consider those that hit everybody.

mimesis (mi-MEE-sis). "Imitation." You imitate the language of others.

> The cracker-barrel politician is just about *done gone* from the Southern scene.
> Try *to never split* your infinitives, if you wish *to further improve* your diction and *to really understand* good writing.

synchoresis (SIN-ko-REE-sis). You concede something, usually ironically, in order to retort with greater force.

> I admit that we have no business in their affairs, except the business of helping them, at their request, toward freedom and justice.
> They are surly, unmanageable, ungrateful. I admit it. But I deny that society can afford not to help them.

Section F
The Uses of the Library

A library's plenteous resources may, at your first entrance, seem more to bewilder than serve. You need guidance to profit by its riches. First, find the card catalog. It catalogs all the library's holdings—books, magazines, newspapers, atlases, books on books, guides to guides. It also will catalog all holdings in any of its satellites around the campus—the law library, the medical library, the forestry library, the transportation library, and whatever else has spun off recently, including storage libraries, which the growing pressures of our collections have forced into remote orbit. Then find the Reference Room, which holds the encyclopedias and other indexes.

Start with encyclopedias.

After you have picked your subject and made your tentative thesis, find the *Encyclopaedia Britannica,* and you are well on your way. The *Britannica* will survey your subject (for latest news, see latest editions, and the annual supplementary "year books"). Each article will refer you, at the end, to several authorities. If someone's initials appear at the end, look them up in the contributors' list (at the front of each volume), or in the index (the last volume of the set). The author is an authority himself; you should mention him in your paper, and look him up later in the card catalog to find what books he has written on the subject. Furthermore, the contributors' list will name several of these works, which will swell your bibliography and aid your research. The index will also refer you to data scattered through all the volumes. Under "Medicine," for instance, it directs you to such topics as "Academies," "Hypnotism," "Licensing," "Mythology," and so on. Since the *Britannica* now revises progressively, subject by subject, note the date on the copyright page to see how much you may need to bring your subject up to date. The *Encyclopedia Americana, Collier's Encyclopedia,* and the *Columbia Encyclopedia,* though less celebrated, will challenge *Britannica's* reign.

Here are some encyclopedias on special subjects:

AGRICULTURE
   Agricultural Index. 1916–. [Monthly]
   Yearbook of Agriculture. 1894–. [U.S. Department of Agriculture]

THE ARTS
Blom, Eric, ed. *Grove's Dictionary of Music and Musicians.* 10 vols. 1961.
Encyclopedia of Painting. 1955.
Encyclopedia of World Art. 1959–1968.
The New Oxford History of Music. 8 vols. 1954–.
Thompson, O. *International Cyclopedia of Music and Muscians.* 9th ed., 1964.

EDUCATION
   Harris, Chester W., ed. *Encyclopedia of Educational Research.* 1960.
   International Yearbook of Education. 1948–.
   Monroe, Paul, ed. *Cyclopedia of Education.* 5 vols. 1911–1913, repr. 1926–1928.

HISTORY

Adams, J. T., ed. *Dictionary of American History.* 6 vols. 1940–1963.
Encyclopedia of World History. 1972.
Worldmark Encyclopedia of the Nations. 1976.

RELIGION

Catholic Encyclopedia. 17 vols. 1907–1922. Revised 1936–, with looseleaf supplements.
Hastings, James, ed. *Dictionary of the Bible.* 5 vols. 1898–1904. Revised 1963.
———. *Encyclopedia of Religion and Ethics.* 13 vols. 1911–1912.
The Interpreter's Dictionary of the Bible. 4 vols. 1962.
Jewish Encyclopedia. 12 vols. 1925.
New Schaff-Herzog Encyclopedia of Religious Knowledge. 13 vols. 1949–1950.
Twentieth-Century Encyclopedia of Religious Knowledge. 2 vols. 1955.
Universal Jewish Encyclopedia. 10 vols. 1939–1943.

SCIENCE

McGraw-Hill Encyclopedia of Science and Technology. 15 vols. 1966.
Van Nostrand's Scientific Encyclopedia. 1968.

SOCIAL SCIENCE

Baldwin, J. M., ed. *Dictionary of Philosophy and Psychology.* 1940–1949.
Encyclopedia of the Social Sciences. 15 vols. 1930–1935.
Munn, Glenn G. *Encyclopedia of Banking and Finance.* 6th ed., 1962.

BIOGRAPHICAL ENCYCLOPEDIAS

Current Biography. 1940–.
Dictionary of American Biography. 22 vols., index. 1928–58, plus current supplements. [Abbreviated as "DAB" in footnotes.]
Dictionary of National Biography [British]. 22 vols. 1908–1909, indexes, plus current supplements. [Abbreviated as "DNB."]
International Who's Who. 1935–.
Kunitz, S. J., and Howard Haycraft. *American Authors, 1600–1900.* 1938.
———. *British Authors of the Nineteenth Century.* 1936.
———. *Twentieth Century Authors.* 1942. Supplement, 1955.
———. *British Authors Before 1800.* 1952.
Webster's Biographical Dictionary. 1971.
Who's Who [British]. 1848–. [Issued annually.]
Who's Who in America. 1899–. [Issued biennially.]

EXERCISE

1 To get a sense of how research changes knowledge in quantity and esteem, and of how encyclopedias differ in personality, compare two articles on the same subject in two different encyclopedias. The 1911 edition of the *Britannica* and the most recent one, published and continually updated by the University of Chicago, make interesting contrasts on such subjects as *Egoism, Poetry, Public Health,* or almost anything. Or you may contrast an article in one of the specialized encyclopedias, such as the *Catholic Encyclopedia,* the *Encyclopedia of World Art,* or the *Cyclopedia of American Government,* with an article on the same subject in one of the general encyclopedias like the *Britannica* or *Collier's.* Write an analysis that compares and evaluates the differing treatments.

Investigate the almanacs.

Benjamin Franklin compiled a collection of pithy sayings to see us through the year—*Poor Richard's Almanac.* But more useful to research will be the modern almanacs of facts, statistics, and events, year by year. If you want to know what the population of Nevada was in 1940, what the wheat crop was in 1950, what the rainfall was in 1960, or who your senator was in 1970—these are the books for you. Suppose you are writing about Eugene O'Neill's *Mourning Becomes Electra.* You could say many different kinds of things about that play: what each character represents in the play's diagram of forces, how the play relates to O'Neill's other plays, or to the Greek drama, which its title invokes. But if you want a glimpse of the play's career on Broadway, go to an almanac. Here you will find what other plays were running, how long O'Neill's play ran, who played the leading roles, when and where the actors were born, whether O'Neill won a Pulitzer Prize (he did) and for which play (not this one). This is not all on one page, of course; but the index will lead you. For almost any subject, you can find interesting facts and figures in the almanacs. Here are the most useful ones:

American Year Book. 1910–.
Americana Annual. 1923–.
Annual Register of World Events [British]. 1758–.
Britannica Book of the Year. 1938–.
Economic Almanac. 1940–.
Information Please Almanac, Atlas, and Yearbook, 1947–.
Statesman's Year-Book. 1864–.
Statistical Abstract of the United States. 1878–.
The World Almanac and Book of Facts. 1868–.
Yearbook of World Affairs. 1947–.

EXERCISES

2 Consult the current *World Almanac and Book of Facts* or some other from among those listed above for the date of some memorable event; the sinking of the *Titanic* or the *Lusitania,* Lindbergh's flight over the Atlantic, the United States' entry into war, the founding of the United Nations, the great stock-market crash, or the like. Now go to one of the other almanacs for the year of your event, and write an essay entitled, let us say, "1929" — a synopsis of the monumental and the quaint for that year, as lively and interesting as you can make it.

3 Go to the *World Almanac* and see what you can find out about the items listed below. Remember that if you want details about 1975, you must go to the *World Almanac* for 1976. Each succeeding year's *Almanac* will repeat many of the same facts, of course, but it will also drop many, such as last year's postal rates and former presidents of small countries: you must go back to the pertinent year for these.

  1. To whom were the first five Pulitzer Prizes in American Poetry awarded?
  2. What was the best selling nonfiction book in 1968?
  3. What was the best selling book of fiction in 1968?
  4. Who is the head of state, and with what title, of: Afghanistan? Algeria? Canada? Kenya? Mali?
  5. Who is the premier or prime minister of: Canada? China? Japan? North Vietnam? Yugoslavia?

6. Find the following facts about Canada: the capital, the population in 1968, the largest group by ethnic origin, the second largest, the smallest.

7. Write a paragraph on the history of Canada, being particularly cautious not to plagiarize.

Next go to the card catalog.

The catalog's 3×5 cards list all the library's holdings — books, magazines, newspapers, atlases — and alphabetize (1) authors, (2) publications, and (3) general subjects, from *A* to *Z*. You will find *John Adams* and *The Anatomy of Melancholy* and *Atomic Energy,* in that order, in the *a* drawers. The next page illustrates the three kinds of cards (filed alphabetically) on which the card catalog will list the same book — by author, by subject, and by title.

The Library of Congress and a few commercial firms prepare and sell author cards as a service for all libraries; from these, the libraries make their title and subject cards, and select their call numbers. On the cards in the illustration, notice the call number, the same on all cards for that book, typed by the library according to its system of classification. This number locates the book on the shelves, leads you to it (in open stacks), and identifies it on your call slip, if you wish to "call" for it. Notice that the subject card is made simply by adding the subject at the top of an extra author card. Title cards are made in the same way. The librarian usually follows the Library of Congress's recommendations for identifying the subject. The author card is filed under W (for Wiener), the subject card under C (cybernetics), and the title card under H (Human).

You will notice the two systems of call numbers printed at the bottom of the card: the Library of Congress and the Dewey Decimal. The Library of Congress's method has by no means supplanted the older system devised by Melvin Dewey in 1876. The Dewey system, with its ten divisions of knowledge, easily subdivided by decimals, brought order out of confusion. It became virtually standard throughout the United States, and made considerable headway in England. As our illustrative cards suggest, Dewey Decimal is still widely used. But Library of Congress is gaining ground. Big

Author Card:
the "Main Entry"

call number:

Dewey class

author's initial

author's name and dates

title

place, publisher,
and date of publication

number of pages

size of book

subject heading

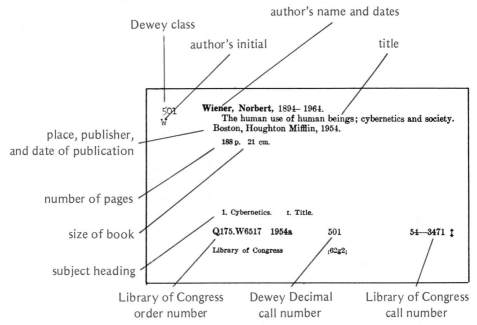

501
W

Wiener, Norbert, 1894– 1964.
    The human use of human beings; cybernetics and society.
Boston, Houghton Mifflin, 1954.

    188 p. 21 cm.

    1. Cybernetics.   I. Title.

    Q175.W6517 1954a   501   54—3471 ‡

    Library of Congress   [62g2]

Library of Congress   Dewey Decimal   Library of Congress
order number   call number   call number

Subject Card

subject heading

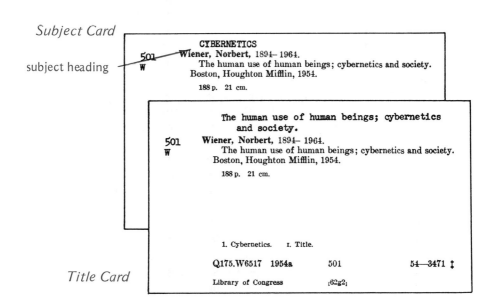

501
W

CYBERNETICS
Wiener, Norbert, 1894– 1964.
    The human use of human beings; cybernetics and society.
Boston, Houghton Mifflin, 1954.

    188 p. 21 cm.

501
W

The human use of human beings; cybernetics
    and society.
Wiener, Norbert, 1894– 1964.
    The human use of human beings; cybernetics and society.
Boston, Houghton Mifflin, 1954.

    188 p. 21 cm.

    1. Cybernetics.   I. Title.

    Q175.W6517 1954a   501   54—3471 ‡

    Library of Congress   [62g2]

Title Card

libraries need more and more subdivisions, to place a book among hundreds of a class. The Library of Congress, using letters for its general headings, offers twenty categories for Dewey's ten, and additional possibilities by combining letters with numbers.

The Dewey Decimal System

000 General Works	500 Natural Sciences
100 Philosophy	600 Useful Arts
200 Religion	700 Fine Arts
300 Social Sciences, Government, Customs	800 Literature
400 Philology	900 History, Travel, Biography

The Library of Congress System

A General Works	M Music
B Philosophy, Religion	N Fine Arts
C History	P Language and Literature
D Foreign History	Q Science
E,F American History	R Medicine
G Geography, Anthropology	S Agriculture
H Social Sciences	T Technology
J Political Science	U Military Science
K Law	V Naval Science
L Education	Z Library Science, Bibliography

Letters present some difficulties, of course. *I* and *O* have been skipped to avoid their confusion with numerals, and only three letters stand as initials for their categories. But in the older and the newer systems, you can see some interesting changes in the shape of human knowledge. "Religion" has lost some distinction, now sharing a category with "Philosophy"; "Philology" has become "Language" and has moved in with "Literature"; "History" has proliferated; "Politics" has become a science, with a category of its own. The newer system is far from perfect: "American History" has two letters, for instance, but "Anthropology" shares one with "Geography," which no longer seems its nearest relative. Knowledge, and the categories of knowledge, will change; the stock of books, and microfilms, will fluctuate in proportion; and our librarians will adjust their systems, endlessly and faithfully keeping their cards up to date.

Learn the catalog's inner arrangements.

If you have ever tried to find your library's file of the *New Yorker,* or the *New York Times,* your heart probably sank before the drawers and drawers in the N-section labeled "New York." The alphabet seems to have collapsed under the dominance of our city of cities. You discover that you need to know a little more than the alphabet to find your way. Here are some finer details of arrangement in the card catalog:

1. Not only men, but organizations and institutions, can be "authors" if they publish books or magazines, as do the following:

Parke, Davis & Company, Detroit
The University of Michigan
U.S. Department of State

2. Initial *A, An, The,* and their foreign equivalents (*Ein, El, Der, Une,* and so forth) are ignored in alphabetizing a title. *A Long Day in a Short Life* is alphabetized under *L.* But French surnames are treated as if they were one word: De la Mare as if *Delamare,* La Rochefoucauld as if *Larochefoucauld.*

3. Cards are usually alphabetized *word by word: Stock Market* comes before *Stockard* and *Stockbroker.* "Short before long" is another way of putting it, meaning that *Stock* and all its combinations with other separate words precede the longer words beginning with *Stock-.* Whether a compound word is one or two makes the apparent disorder. Hyphenations are treated as two words. The sequence would run thus:

Stock
Stock-Exchange Rulings
Stock Market
Stockard

4. Cards on one subject are arranged alphabetically by author. Under *Anatomy,* for instance, you will run from "Abernathy, John" to "Yutzy, Simon Menno," and then suddenly run into a title—*An Anatomy of Conformity*—which happens to be the next large alphabetical item after the subject *Anatomy.*

5. Identical names are arranged in the order (a) person, (b) titles and places, as they fall alphabetically.

Washington, Booker T.
Washington, George
Washington (State)
Washington, University of
Washington, D.C.
Washington Square **[by Henry James]**

"Washington," the state, precedes the other "Washingtons" because "State" (which appears on the card only in parentheses) is not treated as part of its name. The University of Washington precedes "Washington, D.C." because no words or letters actually follow the "Washington" of its title.

6. Since *Mc, M,* and *Mac* are all filed as if they were *Mac,* go by the letter following them: *M'Coy, McDermott, Machinery, MacKenzie.*

7. Other abbreviations are also filed as if spelled out: *Dr. Zhivago* would be filed as if beginning with *Doctor; St.* as if *Saint; Mrs. Miniver* as if *Mistress*—except that many libraries now alphabetize *Mr.* and *Mrs.* as spelled, and Ms. has found its place in the alphabet.

8. Saints, popes, kings, and people are filed, in that order, by name and not by appellation (do not look under *Saint* for St. Paul, nor under *King* for King Henry VIII). The order would be:

Paul, Saint
Paul VI, Pope
Paul I, Emperor of Russia
Paul, Jean

9. An author's books are filed first by collected works, then by individual titles. Different editions of the same title follow chronologically. Books *about* an author follow the books *by* him.

That is the system. Now you can thumb through the cards filed under your subject — "Cancer," or "Television," or "Hawthorne" — to see what books your library has on it, and you can look up any authorities your encyclopedia has mentioned. Two or three of the most recent books will probably give you all you want, because each of these will refer you, by footnote and bibliography, to important previous works.

Locate the books you need.

The card catalog may tell you: "Undergrad Library," "Graduate Reading Room," "Rare Book Room," "Engineering Library," "Storage." You will learn your own library's system, of course, from the staff and from your fellow students: which stacks are open, which closed, where the several rooms and libraries are, how to make out call slips, how to get at the books and get them out. But the card catalog tells you the primary fact of whether the library has the book at all. No card, no book. All the library's holdings are cataloged: newspapers, magazines, encyclopedias, dictionaries, indexes, atlases, microfilms. Your library can also help you to locate the book in another library, or to get information about it. For graduate research, if the book is not too rare, the library can arrange to borrow it for you from another library, or to supply you with microfilms or photostats of the parts you want.

Several other guides can help you find where in the world a book may be:

1. A *Union Card Catalog.* A few large libraries keep one of these: a catalog of cards in other libraries. Find out if your library has one, and browse it. It may prove useful someday.

2. The *Library of Congress Catalog of Printed Cards* and the *Library of Congress National Union Catalog.* These are big alphabetized volumes in which the cards, or their contents, are reproduced, eight or ten to the page. Cards for new acquisitions are reproduced in supplements issued quarterly.

3. The British Museum's *General Catalogue of Printed Books.* Similar to the Library of Congress's catalog, it lists the holdings in England's national library.

4. The *United States Catalog* and its supplements, the *Cumulative Book Index,* are volumes listing books printed in English. These identify publisher and date of publication but not location in a library.

EXERCISES

4 Go to the card catalog and pick a card at random. Write down everything you can learn from it about the author and the book. Is it classified according to Dewey Decimal or the Library of Congress? Whichever way, what would its number be in the other system? What general category is it in—Philosophy, Agriculture? What can you surmise from the other numbers and letters of the call number? What other cards have probably been made for it? Record everything you can learn or guess from the single card. Now, find the book itself, and report everything else you learn about it from the title page and the back of the title page.

5 Select some well-known literary work: *Walden, David Copperfield, Huckleberry Finn, Alice in Wonderland, The Wind in the Willows, A Farewell to Arms.* Describe how thoroughly it is cataloged by your library. Check cards for author, title, and subject. How many editions does the library have? Is the work contained within any *Works?* How many cards treat it as a subject? Does your library own a first edition? This last may require that you find the date of the first edition by looking up your author in an encyclopedia, checking available books about him, and perhaps checking in the British Museum's *General Catalogue of Printed Books,* or, for a twentieth-century book, *United States Catalog of Printed Books* or *Cumulative Book Index* to discover the earliest cataloging.

Find the indexes to periodicals and newspapers.

Indexes to periodicals do for articles what the card catalog does for books. Some index by subjects only, others by subjects and authors. They, too, will probably be in your reference room.

The card catalog or list of magazine holdings will tell you whether your library has a particular magazine, and where the bound volumes of it are shelved. Issues for the current year will be available, unbound, in some kind of periodical section, or room. But to find what is in the popular magazines, bound or unbound, you start with the *Reader's Guide to Periodical Literature*.

This is a long file of fat volumes, beginning in 1900, and kept current with supplements, now issued twice monthly, running only a few weeks behind the flood of articles in the magazines they index. They list these magazines inside the front cover; check this list first if, for instance, you are trying to find an article you once read at the barber-shop in some magazine called *Thrill*. You will discover that *Thrill* is not indexed, which is probably just as well, and you can shift your search to another sector. Also inside the front cover is a list of the abbreviations used in describing the articles. Studying them will enable you to read an entry such as this:

GAMBLING
   It's bye! bye! blackjack. D. E. Scherman.
   il Sports Illus 20:18-20+ Ja 13 '64

—and to translate it into this:

   Scherman, D. E., "It's Bye! Bye! Blackjack," *Sports Illustrated,*
     January 13, 1964, pp. 18-20. . . .

You learn that the article is illustrated ("il") and in volume 20, which you may need for finding it. You also learn that the article continues on back pages: "18–20+—which you would complete after you had found the article and read it through, as: "pp. 18–20, 43, 46–47." You will do well to write out as full a translation as you can on your own bibliographical card, or you may not understand the abbreviations when going to find the magazine or writing your bibliography. Other important general indexes are:

Book Review Digest. 1905–.
The New York Times Index. 1913–. [A wonderful guide to the news.
   Get the date, and you can read about the incident in most other
   newspapers for the same day, if your library lacks the *Times.*]
Nineteenth Century Readers' Guide . . . . 1890–1899, with supplementary
   indexing, 1900–1922.

Poole's Index to Periodical Literature. 1802–1906. [By subject only, but admirably supplemented by Marion V. Bell and Jean C. Bacon, *Poole's Index, Date and Volume Key* (Chicago, 1957). If you want to know what the reviewers thought of Webster's first *Dictionary,* or Hawthorne's *Scarlet Letter,* dip into *Poole's.*]

Social Sciences and Humanities Index. 1965–. [Formerly *International Index to Periodicals,* 1913–1964, this does for scholarly journals what the *Reader's Guide* does for popular ones.]

The Subject Index to Periodicals. 1915–1951. [Covers more than 450 periodicals in all fields, American and British. In 1961, it split into two, limited to Britain: *British Humanities Index* and *British Technology Index.*]

Here are some special indexes:

Annual Magazine Subject-Index. 1908–1949. [Particularly for history.]

Art Index. 1929–.

Bibliographic Index. 1937–.

Biography Index. 1946–.

Biological and Agricultural Index [formerly *Agricultural Index,* 1916–].

Catholic Periodical Index. 1930–.

Dramatic Index. 1909–1950.

Education Index. 1929–.

Engineering Index. 1884–.

Essay and General Literature Index. 1900–. [Very useful for locating particular subjects within books of essays.]

Index Medicus. 1879–1926; *Quarterly Cumulative Index Medicus.* 1927–.

Industrial Arts Index. 1913–1957. Succeeded by *Applied Science and Technology Index.* 1958–; and by *Business Periodicals Index.* 1958–.

International Catalogue of Scientific Literature. 1902–1921.

Music Index. 1949–.

Psychological Index. 1894–1936.

Public Affairs Information Service. Oct. 15, 1914–.

Technical Book Review Index. 1917–1929; 1935–.

Thompson, Stith. *Motif-Index of Folk-Literature.* 6 vols. 1932–1936.

And check your particular field for "abstracts"—indexes that publish brief summaries of articles—such as, *Biological Abstracts,* 1926–; *Chemical Abstracts,* 1907–; *Geological Abstracts,* 1953–; *Psychological Abstracts,* 1927–. These lists should prove more than adequate for your beginnings in any subject. You may expand your knowledge of such aids to research by examining Constance M. Winchell's *Guide to Reference Books* (eighth edition, with current supplements).

EXERCISES

6 Look up "Ecology" in the *Reader's Guide,* March 1961–February 1962, and translate the entries into complete statements by writing out the abbreviations. This will help you to use the table of abbreviations in the front of the book, and accustom you to getting the complete information before you go to the card catalog and stacks to find the articles themselves. Then, below each written-out translation, write a full bibliographical entry, as it would appear in your finished bibliography, looking up the article itself to complete the details.

7 Choose some subject like "Dog Racing," "Saudi Arabia," "Bowling," "Mushrooms," —anything that interests you—and write a short statistical report on the listings under this subject in the *Reader's Guide to Periodical Literature* over the past ten years. Does your subject have unusually fat or lean years? What kinds of magazines treat the subject? Can you infer anything from your data about fashions in magazines, or happenings in the world? Go to one article in the most prolific year to discover the reason for your subject's popularity.

8 Look up some event of the recent past (after 1913) in the *New York Times Index.* Write a paper on how the event is reported in the *Times* and in the other newspapers available in your library.

9 Learn to use the valuable *Essay and General Literature Index* by taking the following steps:

1. What essays on "Skepticism" appeared in books published between 1941 and 1947? Give the author, the essay's title, the book's title, and the pages.

2. Now, go to the card catalog and record the call numbers and full bibliographical data on three of these.

3. Look up an essay entitled "Pornography, Art, and Censorship" that appeared in a book of essays published sometime after 1969. Record the entry given in the *Essay and General Literature Index,* then give below it the call number of the book, together with the book's editor, title, place of publication, publisher, and date, all from the card catalog.

4. Find an essay on the moon by Harold Urey, published in a collection sometime after 1968. Again, record the entry in the *Essay and General Literature Index,* and full information from the card catalog.

5. Look up three essays published in anthologies between 1965 and 1969 on Gerard Manley Hopkins, recording each entry in the *Essay and General Literature Index,* and then following it by full data on the book, with call number, from the card catalog.

Browse the literary bibliographies.

In no field are books and articles so thoroughly and variously listed as in literary studies — by period, by field, by literary genre, by author, and so on. *Selective Bibliography for the Study of English and American Literature* (New York, 1971), by Richard D. Altick and Andrew Wright, admirably outlines the field. Begin here. It is the best, for amateur and professional alike, an indispensable guide to the guides. It will lead you to what others have said about the novels and stories and poems and authors you are studying. Here are some important landmarks:

I. ENGLISH LITERATURE: GENERAL

The Cambridge Bibliography of English Literature, 4 vols. Cambridge, 1941. Supplement (Vol. V), Cambridge, 1957.

The Concise Cambridge Bibliography of English Literature. Cambridge, 1958. [Handy and inexpensive.]

II. AMERICAN LITERATURE: GENERAL

Spiller, Robert E., et al., *Literary History of the United States.* Bibliography. *Supplement,* 1962, 1963.

Leary, Lewis, *Articles on American Literature, 1900–1950.* Durham, 1954.

Blanck, Jacob, *Bibliography of American Literature.* New Haven, 1955–. [Appearing in volumes, author by author, this promises to be the definitive bibliography for some time to come.]

Gohdes, Clarence L. F., *Bibliographical Guide to the Study of the Literature of the U.S.A.* Durham, 1959.

III. CURRENT LITERARY BIBLIOGRAPHY: GENERAL

"Annual Bibliography," *PMLA* (Publications of the Modern Language Association of America). 1922–. [April issue of this quarterly magazine. Since 1957, its international coverage has made it the supreme bibliography.]

Modern Humanities Research Association, *Bibliography of English Language and Literature.* 1920–. [Annual.]

English Association, *The Year's Work in English Studies.* 1921–. [Annual.]

IV. ENGLISH LITERATURE: CURRENT

"Bibliography of American Periodical Literature," *Speculum.* 1926–. [Quarterly. Scholarly essays on medieval subjects in American journals.]

"Literature of the Renaissance," *Studies in Philology.* 1917–. [Annual, April issue.]

"Shakespeare: An Annotated Bibliography," *Shakespeare Quarterly.* 1950–. [Annual, Spring issue.]

"English Literature, 1660–1800," *Philological Quarterly.* 1926–. [Annual, April issue, 1926–1948; July issue, 1949–.]

"The Romantic Movement: A Selective and Critical Bibliography," *English Literary History.* 1937–1949. Transferred to *Philological Quarterly.* 1950–. [Annual, April issue.]

"Current Bibliography," *Keats-Shelley Journal.* 1952–. [Annual, Winter issue.]

"Victorian Bibliography," *Modern Philology.* 1933–1957. [Annual, May issue.] Transferred to *Victorian Studies.* 1957–. [Annual, May issue.]

"Current Bibliography," *Twentieth-Century Literature.* 1955–. [Quarterly.]

V. AMERICAN LITERATURE: CURRENT

"Articles on American Literature Appearing in Current Periodicals," *American Literature.* 1929–. [Quarterly.]

"Articles in American Studies," *American Quarterly.* 1955–. [Annual, Summer issue.]

EXERCISE

10 Go to the card catalog and find *PMLA: Publications of the Modern Language Association of America.* (This is the world's most comprehensive literary bibliography, listing the annual international crop of scholarly articles and books on literary subjects.) Then, from the shelf, pick volume 84 (1969), which contains the "1968 MLA International Bibliography." Now, give the full bibliographical form of the first four entries concerning Emily Dickinson. Again you will have to consult the list of abbreviations at the front of the magazine. Finally, do the same for any British author of your own choosing.

Index

CHECKLIST

1. Thesis stated in one sentence? (pp. 8–10)

2. Thesis at end of first paragraph? (pp. 51–52)

3. Thesis clearly evident throughout paper? (pp. 11–13)

4. Each paragraph begun with topic sentence? (pp. 54–56)

5. Each with transitional tag? (pp. 99–103)

6. Most paragraphs four or five sentences long? (pp. 49–50)

7. Your best point last? (pp. 36–38)

8. Conclusion an inverted funnel? (pp. 59–61)

9. Generalizations, and thesis, free from fallacies? (pp. 209–219; 227)

10. Sentences show some variety? (pp. 159–162)

11. Long sentences exhibit parallel construction? (pp. 151–157)

12. No passive, no *There is* . . . , no *It is* . . . ? (pp. 165–169)

13. Colons and semicolons properly used? (pp. 424-428)

14. Commas before every *and* and *but* that needs them? (pp. 409–415)

15. A comma before every *which*? (p. 420)

16. Every *which* without comma changed to *that*? (pp. 170–171; 420)

17. Every excess *of, which, that,* and *the use of* dropped? (pp. 170–172)

18. Every noun-on-noun and *tion-of* revised? (pp. 171–175)

19. All excess wordage cut? (pp. 163–175; 193–195)

20. No sentence that could be misread?

21. Have you said it as briefly and clearly as possible?

SET ANY OF THESE POINTS ASIDE—
IF YOU HAVE AN IRRESISTIBLE RHETORICAL REASON.